Women,
Money,
and the
Law

WOMEN MONEY and the LAW

NINETEENTH-CENTURY FICTION, GENDER, AND THE COURTS

Joyce W. Warren

UNIVERSITY OF IOWA PRESS

IOWA CITY

University of Iowa Press, Iowa City 52242
http://www.uiowa.edu/uiowapress
Copyright © 2005 by Joyce W. Warren
All rights reserved
Printed in the United States of America
Design by Omega Clay

The University of Iowa Press is a member of Green Press Initiative and is committed to preserving natural resources.

Printed on acid-free paper

Library of Congress Cataloging-in-Publication Data
Warren, Joyce W.
Women, money, and the law: nineteenth-century fiction, gender, and the courts / by Joyce W. Warren.
p.   cm.
Includes bibliographical references and index.
ISBN 0-87745-953-3 (cloth)
1. American fiction—19th century—History and criticism. 2. Money in literature. 3. Women and literature—United States—History—19th century. 4. American fiction—Women authors—History and criticism. 5. Law and literature—History—19th century. 6. Economics in literature. 7. Courts in literature. 8. Law in literature. I. Title.
PS374.M54W37 2005
813'.3093553—dc22   2005045704

05 06 07 08 09 C 5 4 3 2 1

contents

acknowledgments

Particularly important to the writing of this book were the many libraries I worked in and the librarians with whom I worked. Among the libraries whose collections were essential to my research were the Sophia Smith Collection at Smith College, the Houghton Library at Harvard University, the Rutgers University Library, and the Missouri Historical Society. The New York Supreme Court records that were so significant a part of my work are housed in the Special Collections division of the Hofstra University Library, and special thanks go to then-director, Barbara Kelly, and to librarian Vicky Aspinwall for their unstinting assistance. Thank you also to Joseph Van Nostrand of the New York County Clerk's Office of the Records of the New York Supreme Court; the librarians at the Queens College Rosenthal Library; and the staff of the Bryant Library in Roslyn, New York, particularly the interloan librarian, Mary Carol Moore. I owe a special debt of gratitude to Leo Hershkowitz, professor of history at Queens College, who had the foresight and perseverance to salvage and preserve the seventy-five years of New York Supreme Court records that had been discarded by the City of New York. But for him, these women's stories would be in the dust bin instead of in this book.

I am grateful to the people at the University of Iowa Press, particularly my acquiring editor, Prasenjit Gupta, for believing in this book, and Mary Russell Curran for her careful and intelligent copyediting. I am also grateful to the University Seminars of Columbia University for assistance in preparing the book for publication. Material drawn from this work was presented to the University Seminar on Women and Society. An earlier draft of the introduction was printed in *Nineteenth-Century American Women Writers: A Critical Reader* edited by Karen L. Kilcup (Blackwell Publishers, 1998). Quotations from the Thomas Amlie Papers in the Wisconsin Historical Society Archives are printed with permission from the Society.

I want to thank the many scholars with whom I have exchanged ideas, particularly the members of the Nineteenth-Century American Women Writers Group, the Society for the Study of American Women Writers, and the Women and Society Seminar at Columbia University. Thank you also to my colleagues in the English Department and the Women's Studies program at Queens College and to the students in my classes, whose enthusiasm for nineteenth-century women writers confirmed my own interest and provided a further stimulus for my work. I owe special thanks to those colleagues in the field who read earlier versions of the text and whose substantive and thoughtful suggestions helped to make it a better book: Elizabeth Freeman at the University of California–Davis; Lori Merish at Georgetown University; and Denise Knight at Cortland College. Thank you also to my research assistants Wilfred Correa, Raquel Welch, and especially Taniamarie Nyland.

Finally, I want to thank the members of my family. My husband, Frank, not only took time out from his own work to proofread the final manuscript, but throughout the researching and writing of this book was always willing to discuss the most trivial question from within his field of expertise. Added to his supportive presence was that of my four children: Victoria, whose broad knowledge of literature and insightful reading of literary works provided me with an invaluable source of inspiration and information; Catherine, who was the first person to read the manuscript in its entirety and generously shared her knowledge of the law in commenting on what was then a much longer version of this book; Charlotte, whose fine critical judgment and delightful sense of humor brought pleasure and fellowship to the writing of this book; and my son Frank, who in sharing his knowledge of popular culture helped to provide the balance that makes the difference between esoteric and living scholarship. Altogether, these five people, more than any other resource, have helped me to understand and appreciate the lived experiences of nineteenth-century women.

WOMEN,
MONEY,
AND THE
LAW

---·◦◦◦·---

FRACTURING
GENDER

In Charlotte Perkins Gilman's short story "If I Were a Man" (1914), the female protagonist is magically turned into her husband. As she walks to work, she puts her hands in her pockets and feels money. Gilman writes: "All at once, with a deep rushing sense of power and pride, she felt what she had never felt before in all her life—the possession of money, of her own earned money—hers to give or withhold, not to beg for, tease for, wheedle for—hers."[1] In this sudden realization by her character of the "power and pride" that comes with the possession of one's own money, Gilman articulates the key to her analysis of the situation of women. As she wrote in her autobiography, "The basic need of economic independence seemed to me of far more importance than the ballot."[2]

In thus asserting the necessity of economic independence for women, Gilman broke with the cultural assumptions that had dominated the nineteenth-century attitude toward women, an attitude that cut across the lines of class and race. Most women, even those who were themselves the sole breadwinners for their families, did not speak out in favor of economic independence for women. Nineteenth-century culture defined upper- and middle-class white women as inherently domestic and assumed their exclusion from the market economy, while working-class families and the free black bourgeoisie expected their women to remain in the home if they could afford to do so.[3] The concept of woman's economic *de*pendence was an established "truth" of the dominant discourse in American society, and any counterdiscourse was effectively silenced, excluded, or marginalized.[4]

However, it is a mistake to assume that the narrative that emerged from the dominant discourse is the whole story. Although nineteenth-century society defined women as primarily domestic and situated them outside the marketplace except as exploited workers, and although many twentieth-century scholars accepted the earlier century's view of men's and women's "separate spheres" (which confined women to the private sphere while the public sphere was reserved for men), other scholars have questioned the accuracy of the concept. As Lora Romero points out in *Home Fronts* (1997), it is fallacious to accept as "true" the nineteenth century's "own dubious narrative about itself" or to fall into the trap of binarism and thus fail to recognize the complexity of perspectives within what has been characterized as a monolithic ideology of domesticity.[5] The social construction of separate spheres in nineteenth-century America was never more than a prescriptive model defining acceptable behavior for women by and within their contemporary society. For twentieth- and twenty-first-century historians, the ideology of separate spheres has provided a way of understanding what the expectations were for nineteenth-century women, but it should never be taken as the reality. As my reading of nineteenth-century women writers like Fanny Fern made clear to me some time ago, what women were supposed to do and what they did were often two different things. Moreover, the gendered spheres model is limited not only because it applies primarily to upper- and middle-class white women but also, and even more importantly, because it does not allow for intersections of race, class, and sexuality, which, as this study shows, were important considerations in determining gender identities.

Critics who have questioned the concept of gendered spheres have noted numerous ways in which nineteenth-century women transgressed the socially constructed boundaries.[6] Arguing that despite the nineteenth-century binary which assigned men to the public sphere and confined women to the private domestic sphere, some scholars have maintained that not only did many women—middle-class reformers, abolitionists, writers, and working-class laborers and labor organizers—function in the public sphere,[7] but female domesticity was implicated in and complicitous with the capitalist economy. Even when confined to the home as "nonproducers," women contributed to the capitalist economy by providing sanctuary from the marketplace and by symbolically representing the moral life that economic individualism denied. As Gillian Brown argues in *Domestic Individualism* (1990), domestic work in the home served to prop up and authenticate capitalism: "The domestic cult of true womanhood facilitated the transition to a life increasingly subject to the caprices of the market."[8]

Although Brown and others have pointed to women's complicity in the capitalist economy as consumers or to middle-class women's actions as writers or as unpaid public women, and most scholars have noted the wage-earning work of working-class women, few commentators have recognized the extent to which middle-class women were themselves engaged in economic pursuits.[9] In this study, however, I examine evidence which indicates that, in spite of cultural prescriptions and legal infirmities, women from every class were involved in overtly economic (that is, market- and money-based) activities. The pursuit of money itself was a much more important part of nineteenth-century women's lives than scholars have thought. The focus of this study is the extent to which women—working-, middle-, and upper-class women—were players in a money economy, not simply as consumers, behind-the-scenes domestic supporters of capitalism, or unpaid activists but as money earners, women who, like the fantasy woman in Gilman's story, sought to put their own money in their pockets.

I first gained an awareness of the extent of women's participation in American economic life from my reading of nineteenth-century American women writers, particularly those writers who, although well known in their day, were less well known in the twentieth and twenty-first centuries, if they were known at all. The more I read, the more I began to suspect that the fiction of female financial purity was just that—a fiction. Although the majority of nineteenth-century American writers —women as well as men—seemed to accept the official narrative, many women writers focused on economics in their works, and some women writers and reformers took what was a revolutionary position—asserting the need for economic independence as a lifelong goal for women. Instead of reifying contemporary definitions of gender, these writers displaced the notions of female dependency that supported male hegemony and substituted a new and radical gender identity.[10] Often recognizing the intersecting identities of class, race, ethnicity, and/or sexuality, they advocated behavior at variance with the behavior that their culture had defined as natural to them as women, thus fracturing the concept of gender. Demonstrating that gender identity is constituted by discursive forces, they introduced a new and politically charged discourse that defined women as economically independent. This assertion of a new identity for women is apparent in their works and/or in their lives.

Most women writers, however, even when they focused on economics in their works, did not advocate woman's economic independence—at least not publicly. Nevertheless, there were some writers who, either implicitly or explicitly, argued for women's economic autonomy. In the years following the economic crisis of 1837, for example, some women writers published fiction criticizing speculation and the accumulation of debt. Pointing out the impact that male economic failure had on the family, they called attention to the need for women to educate themselves economically—to pay attention to and, in some cases, even to take charge of the family's financial affairs.[11] Although these writers focused on economics as a family problem, other writers asserted a woman's right to economic independence as an individual. The first comprehensive assertion of women's rights written by an American woman was Sarah Grimké's *Letters on the Equality of the Sexes and the Condition of Women* (1838), which contained her 1837 letter on "The Legal Disabilities of Women." Expressing outrage at the legal system that allowed a man to dissipate all of his wife's property and made her a "cipher in the nation," Grimké called for a change in the "unjust and unequal laws" that denied women their rights.[12] One of the earliest writers who was a proponent of women's full financial independence was Lydia Maria Child, who in 1843 called for an end to the separation in the "characters, duties, and pursuits of men and women."[13] Margaret Fuller, in *Woman in the Nineteenth Century* (1845), the expanded version of her 1843 *Dial* article, was more specific, pointing out the hypocrisy of those who piously insisted that women's sphere was in the home but did not seem to worry about exploited seamstresses or black women in the fields.[14] Urging that women be trained to be "self-reliant" so that they could be independent of men, Fuller insisted that every path must be "laid open to woman as freely as to man" (260, 262, 346). And in order to emphasize the all-inclusiveness of women's potential occupations, she declared (in a phrase that shocked her contemporaries), "Let them be sea-captains, if you will" (345). Six years later Elizabeth Oakes Smith, in *Woman and Her Needs* (1851), addressed the same question, focusing even more explicitly on the economic aspects of women's equality. Every woman, she said, had the right to "pecuniary independence": "Let the avenues of wealth and distinction be open to her as freely as to the other sex."[15] Finally, women's need for economic independence was a major theme in Fanny Fern's revolutionary novel, *Ruth Hall* (1855), and in her newspaper columns, from her 1852 article "A Practical Blue Stocking," which describes a man's conversion from hostility to praise for a woman whose practical money-earning power had saved her family from ruin, to her 1870 article "Pay for Women," which argues outspokenly for women's right to earn their own money: "Why shouldn't women work *for pay*? Does anybody object when women *marry for pay*? . . . How much more to be honored is she who, hewing out her own path, through prejudice and narrowness and even insult, earns honorably and honestly her own independence."[16]

In the second half of the nineteenth century a handful of women writers produced what might be called "how-to books" for women, addressing the question of women's work. One of the first such books was Virginia Penny's *The Employments of Women: A Cyclopaedia of Woman's Work* (1863). Penny noted that although books had been written on many subjects relating to women—woman's sphere, woman's moral and religious influence, woman's domestic life—she had not found one book giving practical advice regarding how "women can earn a respectable livelihood."[17] After nine years of teaching school in Ohio, Illinois, and Missouri, Penny had given up her teaching position to spend three years doing research for the book. The result was a practical and useful encyclopedia of over five hundred occupations for women, including business and professional work as well as wage labor. Listed alphabetically within categories, the occupations included such varied jobs as reporter, merchant, fire arms maker, physician, root gatherer, photographer, baker, toy manufacturer, and astronomer. Penny described each occupation, providing such useful information as the money earned, the qualifications necessary for the job, the effect on health, a comparison between male and female wages, the length of time required to learn the business, whether women were paid while learning, the prospect of future employment, and whether or not the work was seasonal. Urging an end to prejudices that confined women to only a few traditional employments, Penny asserted that every woman should have the practical knowledge and opportunity to "enjoy the independence of a competency," not only poor women but women of leisure who might thus be saved from an "aimless and profitless life"; women, she insisted, are "as capable of acquiring a knowledge of any vocation as men."[18]

Penny had difficulty finding a publisher for the book, but a small Massachusetts firm agreed to publish it if she would pay for the typesetting and binding. The publisher printed a limited number of copies, and she was not able to sell enough to make a profit. Having used up all her savings, she was forced to sell her possessions—including the printing plates of the book. The Philadelphia printer who bought the plates published it in 1870 under a new title, *How Women Can Make Money, Married or Single*, and the book was an instant success.[19]

Another how-to book for women was published later in the century: Martha Louise Rayne's *What Can a Woman Do?* (1893). Rayne also supported economic autonomy for both single and married women, maintaining that every woman should have her "own private purse."[20] Emphasizing that a woman who works for a living should "feel no shame or embarrassment," she noted that the world was "full of women who must work or starve," or women who "prefer a life of single independence to taking up with one lame offer," or women who "are already married, but have no taste or strength for domestic work."[21] Rayne's book is not as inclusive as Penny's, however, focusing only on business and professional work, and the second half of the book is a collection of poetry and prose by literary women. The descriptions of the occupations provide some practical information, but they rely mostly on exhortations to women to be proactive in pursuing a profession, and each includes the stories of contemporary women who have succeeded in the field, which stories apparently are intended to provide an inspiration and example.

In addition to these and other writers who spoke out individually, the most vocal women who as a group advocated women's economic independence were the women's rights activists, who made a woman's right to economic autonomy a cornerstone of their platform.

In 1836 Ernestine Rose traveled and lectured throughout New York State in support of a bill that had been introduced into the New York Assembly to give married women some control of their property. That public opinion at the time was not hospitable to the idea is apparent in the fact that the bill failed; even more significant is the fact that Rose was able to obtain only five signatures on the petition in addition to her own. Both men and women refused to sign.[22] The next decade, however, saw the beginning of a shift in public opinion with respect to married women's property, particularly among women's rights activists. Contained in the resolutions passed unanimously at the Seneca Falls convention in 1848 were the assertions that "woman is man's equal" and that "all laws which prevent woman from occupying such a station in society as her conscience shall dictate" are unjust and invalid.[23] At the 1850 convention in Worcester, Massachusetts, the resolutions were more explicit, demanding that all "avenues of civil and professional employments . . . [be] thrown open" to women and declaring "that the laws of property, as affecting married parties, demand a thorough revisal, so that all rights may be equal between them; that the wife may have, during life, an equal control over the property gained by their mutual toil and sacrifices, be heir to her husband precisely to the same extent that he is heir to her, and entitled at her death to dispose by will of the same share of the joint property as he is."[24] Four years later in 1854 Elizabeth Cady Stanton appealed to the New York Legislature, urging passage of a married women's property bill that would enable all women to "control the wages they earn—to own the land they buy—the houses they build."[25]

Another group of women who argued publicly for women's economic rights consisted of women labor organizers. The women's strikes, or "turn-outs," at the Lowell cotton mills in Massachusetts in the 1830s, for example, were specifically about money. In 1834 the women textile workers—who earned only one-half of what men earned—went on strike protesting a wage reduction, and in 1836 they called a second strike because of an increase in their board without a corresponding increase in wages.[26] As Thomas Dublin notes in his study of work in nineteenth-century Lowell, the women went on strike for principally two reasons: to assert their rights and to maintain their economic independence.[27] The *Boston Evening Transcript* reported on February 17, 1834, that one of the leaders of the strike "mounted a pump and made a flaming Mary Woolstonecroft [*sic*] speech on the rights of women and the iniquities of the '*monied* aristocracy.' "[28] Invoking the spirit of 1776 in their defiance of their "tyrannical" employers, they signed a petition stating, "We remain in possession of our unquestionable rights"; comparing themselves to the founding fathers, they vowed to resist the "oppressing hand of avarice [that] would enslave us."[29] At the same time, women in other Eastern cities—straw sewers, seamstresses, and shoe binders—went out on strike, similarly maintaining their right to organize for better pay.[30] The New York Tailoresses, although not as militant as the Lowell millworkers, went on strike in 1831 to regulate prices, asserting that they needed to organize themselves in order to protect themselves: "Who is to stand between us and oppression? If we do not come to our own defence, what will become of us?"[31]

During the economic crises of the nineteenth century—the panics of 1837 and 1857 and the depression of 1873—mills were shut down, operatives were laid off, and wages were cut; the labor movement suffered setbacks each time, and women's labor organizations were particularly hard-hit.[32] Throughout the nineteenth century, however, women continued the struggle when they could, in spite of cultural views of "woman's place" and the hostility of male workers. One of the female labor organizers of the late nineteenth century, Mary Kenney, a Chicago wage earner who attempted to organize working women in the 1880s, spoke out forcefully in favor of women's economic independence. Kenney provides an important comment on the problems inherent in society's definition of women; she found that not only did men view women as dependent, but women themselves accepted this definition. Recognizing the need to redefine gender, she wrote in 1893: "If our mothers would teach us self-reliance and independence, that it is our duty to wholly depend upon ourselves, we would then feel the necessity of organization. . . . [But] the only protection [women] expect is the protection given them by men, not realizing that it is their duty to protect themselves."[33]

The voices of these women articulated the counternarrative—countering the conventional thinking of the dominant discourse in nineteenth-century United States. Most women writers and speakers presented their point of view in civil debate, but others were less civil; like the Lowell millworkers, they shattered the Habermasian image of civility with their oppositional point of view. Fanny Fern, for example, thrust herself into the public arena without apology, parodically portraying and ridiculing cultural definitions of feminine behavior, and, in diverging from the script constructed by her culture, committing "incivilities." Her language, the taboo subjects she wrote on, her satirical tone—and the mere fact that it was a woman who thus spoke out—introduced transgressive elements into what Habermas defined as the "public sphere of rational-critical debate" among bourgeois (white) men.[34]

A study of writers and activists, however, even in conjunction with other, more conventional writers, would not be sufficient to tell us about the role of economics in the lives of nineteenth-century American women in general. As published authors or reformers, they were public women. But what of the ordinary woman—the woman who did not write for publication or speak in public, the woman who was unknown except to her friends and relatives? How do we find out about her? Many women wrote letters and kept diaries, and wherever possible I have used this material to help determine the economic facts of their lives. However, although many women wrote to family and friends and kept journals, most of these writings have not survived.[35] Moreover, many other women did not write letters or write in diaries, particularly working-class women, some of whom were illiterate and most of whom did not have the leisure to write. Finally, letters and even diaries do not always tell the whole story; often the writer portrays a persona, selecting material about herself that is socially acceptable, material that leaves out behavior and thoughts that her culture would regard as aberrant. Where then can one find the stories of nineteenth-century women, the record of what they actually did or did not do with respect to money?

One source is the law courts. Exploring the narratives of women who were plaintiffs or defendants in court cases involving financial matters, I was able to learn about women who would otherwise be unknown. In doing the research for this book, I have had access to an untapped archive of material, a vast collection of legal records from the New York Supreme Court that have been expunged from the official record. In New York the Supreme Court is not the highest court; it is the trial court where initial suits are pled. In the 1970s this collection was to be discarded by New York City because of lack of space. The Supreme Court retained the decisions but discarded the testimony and all of the records that went to make up the cases—in other words, the "stories" behind the decisions. The records were salvaged by Queens College professor of history Leo Hershkowitz, who donated the collection to Hofstra University in 1994.[36] This collection has been invaluable for my study because it provides information about women whose stories exist nowhere else, women whose stories were in fact erased from history. I have looked at more than twenty-five hundred court cases in these records of the New York Supreme Court from 1845 to 1875, approximately 15 percent of which involve a woman litigant.[37] All but a handful of these cases focus on a monetary dispute. The stories that emerge from the cases make clear that, however emphatically the official narrative declared that women were economically dependent, functioned outside the marketplace, and were by definition excluded from direct economic involvement, the reality was different; not only were many women involved in the pursuit of money, but a large proportion of those women functioned independently. Their stories have never been published, but they are recorded in the testimony in court, in the complaints and depositions women submitted, and in the testimony of witnesses and the arguments of lawyers. For the most part, the women involved in these cases were too obscure to be written about in the major newspapers, and almost none of their cases became a *cause célèbre*.

New York is a good source of information about the legal system in nineteenth-century United States because other states relied heavily on New York law.[38] The New York Supreme Court is particularly useful for this study because its cases provide an unusually heterogeneous mix of women. As a center of immigration, New York City represented the most complete ethnic and religious mix in the country at the time. Some of the women were new immigrants; others belonged to established American families. They came from varied ethnic and religious backgrounds: the women were Protestant, Catholic, and Jewish, and their ethnicities included English, Italian, Russian, Irish, French, German, and African. Moreover, because the Supreme Court is the lowest state court, the trial court, its cases included working-class and middle-class women as well as wealthy women; the cases were not limited to high-profile cases or cases involving people with the money and power to appeal their cases to a higher court. In addition, since the court was the

"Court of the City and County of New York," the people involved in these cases came from both urban and rural areas. By considering cases in which women were plaintiffs as well as defendants, I have been able to look at a large group of women who were heterogeneous by personality as well. Some of these women were passive participants—women who were brought into the cases reluctantly, often against their wills; some of them were used or abused by male relatives for their own gain. On the other hand, other women were assertive—women who initiated the action, women who sought justice, women who acted independently, and women who used the law and the conventions of society to obtain justice and money for themselves.

A history of women and economics would be incomplete without looking at the lives of both public and nonpublic women. In order to determine if and how women dealt with economic questions, when and how money entered their lives, and what their relationship was to money, I examine the court cases from the New York Supreme Court and the stories that they tell, in relation to the lives and works of women writers who wrote about and/or questioned or challenged the economic restrictions of the dominant culture. The lives of women writers provide us with the stories of public women who earned money of their own, while their fiction chronicles the many ways that nineteenth-century women of different backgrounds were impacted by and dealt with legal and conventional restrictions on a woman's money-earning power. The court cases tell the compelling stories of individual nonpublic women, some of whom were defeated by and others of whom struggled against and triumphed over overwhelming legal obstacles and social pressures. Their actions ran counter to the official narrative, which scripted women as economically dependent and financially uninvolved, and seen in conjunction with the words and actions of women writers, they provide an illuminating counternarrative that significantly questions twentieth- and twenty-first-century assumptions about the lives of nineteenth-century women.

In spite of legal and social restrictions that discursively confined women to financial ignorance, then, a significant proportion of nineteenth-century women earned their own money or were otherwise directly involved in monetary pursuits. For the factory operative as well as for the lady, economics were a significant part of many women's lives. It is true that financial matters were not expected to form an important part of women's conversation, however. Just as nineteenth-century women were not supposed to talk about sex, neither were they supposed to talk about money; both were considered improper topics of conversation for "respectable" women. As a nineteenth-century woman told her daughter when the girl asked questions about sex, "nice girls don't talk about such things."[39] But just because women were not supposed to *talk* about sex or money does not mean that "such things" were not important aspects of women's lives. Although the woman described in the above anecdote, my grandmother, learned her lesson well and was careful to keep sex and money out of polite conversation, she was clearly an active participant in both: she was the mother of twelve children and for years the proprietor of a successful retail business that she founded when her coal-miner husband was out of work. In this study I have sought to go beneath the polite conversation and deconstruct the fiction of women's purity in financial matters. In order to do so, I have turned to the law courts, where people talked about matters that were not permitted into polite conversation.

This, then, is the principal reason why I have turned to the law courts to help illuminate women's economic activity: court cases provide us with a record of events and utterances that are less likely to appear in published works, in which authors and their publishers were under pressure to conform to conventional nineteenth-century ideas of a woman's role. But there are other reasons why the law courts are a natural resource for insight into women's economic lives. One important reason is that there is an underlying relationship between the law and nineteenth-century economic developments. As cultural legal studies scholars have pointed out, laws are not made in a vacuum. They are influenced by what is going on in a particular place and at a particular time in history. In his now-classic work, *The Transformation of American Law* (1977), Morton Horwitz breaks with earlier historians of the law who, as he says, did not ask questions about the effect that legal activity had on "the distribution of wealth." Maintaining that the legal system in nineteenth-century America was used to shape American economic growth, Horwitz contends that the laws were made to benefit commercial and entrepreneurial class interests at the expense of "farmers, workers, consumers, and other less powerful groups."[40] Although Horwitz's discussion does not concern itself with women as a group, his conclusion is relevant to this study. Women were among the "less powerful groups" in nineteenth-century American society, and as their status in the law courts reveals, the laws were not made to benefit them. David Gold, in *The Shaping of Nineteenth-Century Law* (1990), modifies and broadens Horwitz's conclusions. The law, he says, is not simply a "servant" of class interests, but legal thought is grounded in "broader cultural values": the law reflects the "worldview common to most Americans at the time," which in the nineteenth century, in Gold's analysis, was "individualism."[41] Since nineteenth-century individualism was inherently male (women were encouraged to be selfless and dependent while men were encouraged to be assertive and self-reliant), it is not surprising that a legal system shaped by such a worldview would discount women's economic role.[42]

Feminist legal scholars have extended these analyses, making women the focus of their studies and showing how cultural beliefs influenced and determined a pattern of misogyny in American law that kept women out of the developing market economy in the eighteenth and nineteenth centuries. It was not until the emergence of the critical legal studies movement in the last decades of the twentieth century that legal scholars took note of the gendered character of American law. As Joan Hoff points out in *Law, Gender, and Injustice* (1991), women are not mentioned at all in the U.S. Constitution; moreover, the Constitution does not even grant head-of-household status to single women, which they had had in England since feudal times.[43] During the Jacksonian era, says Hoff, the codification of law "concretized" these inequalities, public and private became increasingly separate, and "economic independence became inextricable with political independence."[44] The result was to exclude women's participation in the marketplace except as exploited workers. Particularly important is the fact that the law itself was an obstacle to women's participation in the market economy. As indicated in chapter 2, legal constraints prevented married women from owning property, making contracts, or appearing as independent litigants in court. Moreover, legal restrictions on a widow's inheritance, combined with the cultural predisposition of fathers to leave their money to sons rather than to daughters, gave widowed and single women little or no capital. As Debra Rosen points out in *Courts and Commerce* (1997), the law was the key factor in preventing women from participating in the market economy, not only in the nineteenth century but in the eighteenth century as well. In a much-needed corrective to historians who have maintained that women had greater economic power in the colonial period, she points out that because of women's legal constraints and men's power in the household, women never did have economic autonomy even in colonial America, when economic life was centered in the home.[45]

Not only is the legal system bound up with the cultural and economic development of the nation, but court cases are themselves important as indicators of cultural trends. Like the fictional stories we will be considering in this study, the record of litigation is also the construction of narrative. As scholars in the burgeoning field of law and literature have noted, both law and literature "attempt to shape reality through language."[46] Moreover, as scholars in the past few decades have increasingly recognized—in fields ranging from the new historicism to anthropology to feminist theory to queer theory—all narrative is somebody's story.[47] Interpreters of narrative need to ask such questions as, Who is telling the story? From what perspective? To whom? In what context? Whether or not the story is perceived as "true" is not dependent solely on external evidence but on how comfortably it fits into other stories already within the listener's frame of reference. As Michael Riffaterre points out in *Text Production* (1983), a "text's effects are in no need of verification."[48] Nineteenth-century lawyers, like lawyers today, with or without the collaboration of their clients employed the rhetorical devices and conventions best calculated to win a case, framing the case within a recognizable story, a narrative that the audience (judge, jury, and public at large) would be familiar with. In Riffaterre's definition, verisimilitude depends on references to the sociolect—the "myths, traditions, ideological and esthetic stereotypes, commonplaces, and themes harbored by a society, a class, or a social group."[49] Consequently, as Robert Ferguson notes in his analysis of the 1859 trial of John Brown, trials are "cultural barometers": they tell us a great deal about the ideas, prevailing genre, and cultural expectations of a particular time and place.[50] As such, legal narratives are an important gauge of women's economic activities and the cultural attitudes surrounding them.

The other feature of narrative that is important for this study is its particularity. Looking at court cases not simply as abstract legal arguments but as stories of individual women enables us to understand their human significance. Like works of fiction, the legal narratives focus on individual stories. It is not enough simply to know what the law was with respect to women's economic status; looking at women's stories enables us to see how individual women were affected by and functioned within the economic and legal realities of the time. As Paul Gewirtz comments in his introduction to *Law's Stories: Narrative and Rhetoric in the Law* (1996), treating law as narrative "encourages awareness of the particular human lives that are the subjects or objects of the law."[51] Comparisons between traditional concepts of justice and specific narratives of human experience underscore the importance of looking at individual stories. Wai Chee Dimock, in her study of the history of justice, *Residues of Justice* (1996), notes that whereas law and philosophy tend to regard justice as absolute or negotiable, literature presents us with an alternative language, one that reveals the "porousness" of the language of justice, "a porousness especially noticeable and especially worrisome when seen against the stubborn densities of human experience."[52] Moreover, legal narrative is particularly useful in looking at the trials of marginalized groups. As legal scholars in law and literature have noted, storytelling in court has a "particular power for outsider groups, particularly racial and religious minorities and women."[53] A principal focus of this study, then, is women's stories themselves, both the stories contained in the narratives of the court cases and the stories told in women's fiction. And, although I have theorized the implications of those stories, it is the stories themselves that are of primary importance. For, as Gewirtz points out, stories are "particularized," whereas theories are "more general," and the particularity of the stories is more revealing than the theory, for it "often consists of things left out of the simplifying character of general statements."[54]

I begin my study of the court cases in the 1840s, which was the decade in which some state legislatures began dealing with the issue of married women and the law. The first chapter tells the story of *Trust v. Trust*, a court case involving Mary and Joseph Trust, which lasted from 1856 to 1870. I have chosen to devote the opening chapter to this one case because it provides a good introduction to the issues and will help to familiarize the reader with the domestic and economic situation of nineteenth-century women. Moreover, this case will provide a useful reference point in subsequent discussions of economic and legal issues in the book. Chapter 2 is a discussion of the dominant discourse in the nineteenth-century United States, a discourse that penetrated into all aspects of American culture—political, social, religious, legal, economic, medical, and sexual—forming a definition of gender identity that essentialized women as economically, emotionally, and intellectually dependent. Important for an understanding of the situations portrayed in both the fiction and the legal narratives, and necessary for an interrogation of the extent to which women questioned or challenged the dominant discourse, this chapter provides an overview of the cultural context determining expectations for nineteenth-century women and includes a description of contemporary legal developments, particularly with respect to married women's property laws.

The succeeding chapters alternate between the court cases and discussions of the works by women writers. I have chosen this method of organization rather than isolating the court cases and the fiction writers into separate sections of the book because I believe that reading about the fiction writers and their characters in alternation with the stories of the real women in the court cases will help to clarify and highlight the relationships between the two more than would a method that segregated them into separate sections. At the same time, however, I have chosen not to attempt to discuss the cases and the fictional works within the same chapter, except for cross-referencing where relevant, because such a method would not effectively maintain the resonance and particularity of either. Chapter 3, "Economics and the American Renaissance Woman," looks at the works of five mid-nineteenth-century women writers, interrogating the differences between the thematic concerns of the women writers and those of the five male writers that F. O. Matthiessen focused on in *The American Renaissance*, the 1941 book that helped to establish an exclusionary tradition in American literature, a tradition that dominated literary criticism until near the end of the twentieth century.

Chapter 4 examines court cases brought by women plaintiffs and analyzes the hitherto-unrecognized extent to which nineteenth-century
women were involved in financial matters—as claimants seeking money
or property they claimed in their own right, as executors or heirs in inheritance cases, or as litigants seeking to obtain reparations for injury.
Chapter 5, "The Economics of Race," returns to women writers, looking
at four African American women writers and the intersections of class
and gender identity with respect to economics. This chapter explores
differences and similarities among them and in relation to the positions
of other writers, both white and black.

Chapter 6 moves from the plaintiffs to the defendants in court cases,
demonstrating the ways in which women were brought into money matters, sometimes as pawns of more money-savvy men and at other times
as astute litigants. Chapter 7, "Economics and the Law in Fiction," deals
with fictional portrayals of legal questions that impacted women
whether they were aware of legal or economic issues or not and provides
a significant counterpoint to the stories of actual women in the court
cases. Chapter 8, "The Economics of Divorce," chronicles the many and
varied court cases in which women either brought suit for or were sued
for divorce. This chapter explores the ways in which divorce functioned
as a leveler, on the one hand catapulting thitherto-sheltered middle- and
upper-class nineteenth-century women into a realization of the importance of financial matters in their lives, and on the other, forcing working-class women with no other resources but a wage-earning husband to
struggle for survival. Chapter 9, "Woman's Economic Independence,"
concludes the discussion of women writers with a look at three writers
who, in varying ways, made a strong case for woman's economic independence at a time when society insisted upon economic dependence as
the proper role for women. This chapter analyzes the work of mid- to
late-nineteenth-century women writers, noting differences among their
positions on economic issues and between their ideas and those of other
writers. The Epilogue concludes the book with an examination of significant developments with respect to economic realities and cultural attitudes extending into the twentieth and twenty-first centuries.

This study, then, explores the specifics of a multiplicity of court cases
and looks at numerous works by a varied group of writers, examining the

stories of individual women within the context of American culture, assessing how legal and cultural traditions affected women's lives, particularly with reference to class and racial differences, and analyzing the ways in which women were involved in economic matters. Any interpreter of cultural events or literary texts is writing from the perspective of a particular time and place and within the context of a particular set of circumstances or attitudes. My claim is not that I am a more neutral or impartial observer than other critics but rather that by looking at the literary works in juxtaposition with the court cases of actual nineteenth-century women, and by situating the multiplicity of their combined stories within the context of nineteenth-century culture, I provide a more nuanced understanding of the relationship between nineteenth-century women and the money economy than has hitherto been possible. It is only by looking at the specifics of many cases and many works and at the similarities and differences among the individual women involved in these cases and portrayed in these works—their actions and reactions—that one can begin to understand the economic situation of nineteenth-century American women.

chapter one

MARRIAGE
AND MONEY

TRUST V. TRUST

On November 24, 1856, Mary F. (Grew) Trust left her husband's house at
14 Greene Street in New York City after seventeen years of marriage and
six children.[1] One week after she left, on December 1, 1856, her husband,
Joseph W. Trust, a wealthy New York businessman, brought suit for divorce on the grounds of adultery, which she denied and countered with
her own suit. Thus began a long and embittered litigation that would last
for fourteen years. In this chapter, I explore this case in detail, first, because it tells a compelling story about one woman's struggle for justice,
and second, because the story that it tells reflects the issues involved in
hundreds of other stories that have emerged from the court cases I researched. Moreover, *Trust v. Trust* provides an important measure of the
economic and legal realities for nineteenth-century American women, illuminating the problematics of essentialist cultural definitions.

During the long period of litigation, Mary Trust proved to be a model
of perseverance, strength, and wit. In spite of cultural definitions of femininity that condemned her, in spite of poverty and hardship, in spite of
numerous setbacks, and in spite of her husband's lawyers' cleverest ma-
nipulations designed to harass her and delay the proceedings in order to
compel her to abandon her suit, she tenaciously pursued her rights while
time passed and her children grew up. Ultimately she forced her husband to concede all points and to give her a generous monetary settlement. Through the years her lawyers changed (one died, one left the
state), but her tactics remained the same: she followed her own guidance, seeking what she believed to be just recompense for the seventeen
years that she was married to Joseph Trust.

She used a very modern argument, claiming that her husband's business was prosperous *because* of the assistance that she had given him during their seventeen years of marriage; thus, she maintained, she was entitled to reap the benefits of his wealth. Her husband scoffed at her claims, and the judges never commented on her argument that she had assisted in her husband's success. But in the end the judges ruled in her favor, giving her a generous settlement, and then giving her an increase.

What is particularly interesting about Mary Trust's triumph is that at first she seems to have all the earmarks of a "victim": she was a scorned wife who had given the "best years of her life" and borne six children to a man who harassed her, tormented her, verbally abused her, and drove her out of his house, took her children away from her, and then used every argument he could to avoid paying her any money. Moreover, her actions when she left in 1856 suggest that she was as vulnerable and ignorant as one might expect a sheltered nineteenth-century middle-class woman to be. When she left her husband's house in 1856, she took with her her oldest child, Constance, then sixteen, and went to the Tremont House, where she had arranged to meet a friend, Dr. Samuel Lyons. She had with her eleven hundred dollars, which she had managed to save over the years by taking in boarders and by scrimping on what little money her husband gave her for household expenses. She gave the money to Dr. Lyons to buy tickets for them to California. Dr. Lyons left with the money and did not return.

This action suggests that Mary Trust was a naïf, as trusting as her name implies, sadly unable to recognize Dr. Lyons for the charlatan that he obviously was. But when we read more of her story, we can only conclude that if this was an act of naïveté, it was also an act of desperation. What we also learn, however, is that, far from being an ignorant, passive, domestic, and acquiescent model of "true womanhood," Mary Trust was everything that we have come to believe a middle-class nineteenth-century American woman was not: independent, assertive, money savvy, and legally astute. She refused to *be* a victim.

Interestingly, Mary Grew had been an independent businesswoman before she married Joseph Trust. She testified that she had had a successful business as a vendor of straw products, with a store at 67 Walker Street in New York City. After she married Joseph Trust on October 9,

1839, she gave up her business, and he took over her store for his own business. For the first year of their marriage, and before the children were born, she traveled as her husband's sales agent to major cities in the United States, successfully building up his business and expanding the distribution of his products. She testified in 1860, when she renewed her petition for alimony:

> Previous to the marriage of this petitioner [Mary] with the defendant [Joseph], this petitioner was engaged in and was carrying on a thriving and lucrative business as vendor of straw goods in her own name and for her own benefit at No. 67 Walker Street. Immediately after the said marriage the defendant induced the petitioner to discontinue her business and sent her off to Philadelphia, Washington, Baltimore and other large cities of the South and West to sell for him his "Dr. Gouraud's Italian Medicated Compound Soap" and other wonderful cosmetics and appropriated her store to the use of his said business. That since that time and for the last twenty years the defendant has been and is now engaged in the manufacture and sale of soaps, perfumeries, hair dyes, and other cosmetics having his principal depot at said 67 Walker Street.

In September 1840 Mary's first child was born, and thereafter she was active in New York, working in her husband's store and consulting on the manufacture and production of goods. In the next nine years Mary bore six children, all of whom were given imaginative names:

Constance Cornelia Trust, born September 7, 1840
Andreas Hopes Trust, born September 5, 1842
Hypatia Trust, born July 11, 1844
Felix Gouraud Trust, born September 15, 1845
Percy Bysshe Shelley Trust, born July 20, 1847
Volney Voltaire Trust, born November 19, 1849

Two of these children (Hypatia and Felix) died in infancy; the other four lived into adulthood. Whether the names were devised by Mary Trust or by her husband is unknown, but given her independent spirit and her creative and intelligent pursuit of the legal case, one suspects that she named them, seeking perhaps to expand her domestic horizons by naming her children after famous writers, philosophers, and historical figures, all of whom were known as free thinkers. *Cornelia* is the name of a Senecan-style tragedy translated by Thomas Kyd in 1594. *Andreas* is the title of a poem in Old English written between 750 and 950. *Hypatia* was a fourth-century woman philosopher in Hellenic Egypt who was killed for her beliefs; it is the title of a book about her, written by Charles Kingsley in 1853. *Felix Gouraud* was the name that Joseph Trust sold his products under and may be a misspelling of the last name of the Napoleonic general, Gaspard Gourgaud (1783–1852). *Percy Bysshe Shelley* was a nineteenth-century British Romantic poet and social rebel. *Constantin Volney* (1757–1820) was a French author known for his just and liberal spirit. And *Voltaire* (1694–1778) was the French satirist and philosopher, author of *Candide* (1759). The names suggest not only an awareness of and interest in history and literature but a sympathy with the assertive and rebellious individual.

In saying that Mary Trust's trust in Dr. Lyons to purchase tickets to California was an act of desperation, I am guided by an awareness of what her life was like as Mrs. Joseph Trust. Her husband was abusive and controlling; in today's lingo he might be called a "control freak." The difference, of course, is that whereas his expectation of absolute control would be unacceptable today, it was not inconsistent with the nineteenth-century definition of a husband. Although we do not know whether or not he physically abused his wife, he had a violent temper and attempted to control all aspects of her life. For example, he did his best to prevent her from having friends of her own. He bodily put out of the house women friends who came to call on her; he cursed at her in front of friends, causing them to leave in embarrassment; and on one occasion he physically attacked a male boarder with whom she was conversing. Joseph also sought to control Mary's behavior in her relationship with her children and resented any attempts on her part to participate in their training and education. He expressed his frustration in his application for the divorce in 1856, complaining of his wife: "She exercised an authority, control and vicious influence over said children, beyond the power of complainant to change." This was a legitimate complaint in the 1850s, since the law at the time gave a man sole control of the education of his children. When Pierce Butler, the Georgia plantation owner, divorced his English wife, Fanny Kemble, in 1849, his major complaint was that she interfered with the education of their children; one important difference between them was her opposition to slavery.

In an affidavit in 1860 the Trusts' daughter Constance revealed the kind of behavior that her mother had endured. I quote her statement in full because it is so specific in describing the ways in which Joseph Trust sought to control his wife:

> For many years previous to the separation of the plaintiff [Mary] and the defendant [Joseph], the conduct of the defendant towards the plaintiff was universally unkind, harsh, and cruel; it was at times very violent and passionate, and he would indulge in language towards the plaintiff in the presence of their children very profane and obscene. For several months just previous to their separation the violence of his conduct was uninterrupted. He seldom met the plaintiff so as to converse with her but that he called her by most loathsome and obscene epithets coupled with adjectives opprobrious and profane. He frequently called her, "You stinking bitch," "stinking prostitute," "damned whore," "cat of hell," and others of this nature equally obscene. These expressions he very frequently made use of towards the plaintiff; deponent [Constance] thinks it was every time he saw the plaintiff to converse with her. At such times the plaintiff generally removed herself to another room. Sometimes with this deponent [Constance] accompanying her she would lock herself in her own room to escape from the defendant. He would sometimes follow her there, and upon one of such occasions went into an adjoining closet separated from the plaintiff's room by a thin partition and there in a violent and loud tone of voice continued his language as before. Visitors who came to the house to see the plaintiff were obliged to leave the house by him; some he turned directly away, and some he caused to leave by his violent language to the plaintiff in their presence. At times he denied the plaintiff and her children sufficient food. He did on more than one occasion lock the outer door of the house while the plaintiff was absent, and oblige her with this deponent to walk the street many hours at a time.
>
> He frequently threatened to bring an officer to put the plaintiff out of the house, and an officer did come to the house and take the plaintiff off. She left his house in consequence of such treatment in 1856. Since that time I do not know that the defendant has provided the plaintiff with any food, clothing, or lodging or any means of procuring them. He has frequently prohibited the deponent from seeing or corresponding with her under penalty of

sending the deponent to Ohio to a school where he said the discipline was very rigid and the pupils were taught to do housework.

Added to Constance's testimony is the 1860 testimony of Catharine Rooney, who was a servant in the Trust household:

> I have often seen him put his fist in her face to hit her. He would then scold and curse and swear at her. He would often say that he would put her out of the house and have an officer to take her out. During the time that I lived with them I never knew of a gentleman coming to see the plaintiff. She always acted like a perfect lady and when he scolded and swore at her appeared very willing to do anything he wanted her to do.

When Joseph Trust could not control his wife's behavior by verbally abusing and threatening her and by putting her friends out of the house, he resorted to petty and cruel tactics. As both Constance and Catharine Rooney indicated, Joseph threatened to call the police on his own wife. However, this was not only a threat. The record indicates that on four occasions he did in fact call the police and have his wife taken to the police station on trumped-up charges that he later dropped—charges of "breach of the peace," "assault and battery," and "larceny." His motivation in doing this, as he himself testified, was to compel his wife to obey his wishes. In his testimony against her February 1860 petition for alimony, he said in March of that year:

> The reason the deponent [Joseph] abandoned the several suits and prosecutions against the plaintiff [Mary] referred to in her affidavit is that the plaintiff having promised to amend and reform her conduct and to cease annoying and molesting him, he considered it most advisable to stop the said proceedings. He was compelled to resort to said measures to induce her to desist from the assaults upon and brutal conduct toward the deponent and having produced that effect as well by the advice of the magistrate by whom she was committed to prison as by others, he adopted the course he did [i.e., dropped the charges].

In other words, Joseph Trust used the law to force his wife to comply with his standards of wifely behavior—which included obedience to her husband. Since his standards were the standards of the day, he could be certain that the "magistrate" and "others" would advise her to behave in the way that he desired. Legally he could not have her arrested for disobeying him or talking back to him, but by having her arrested on other charges, although he could not prove them and ultimately dropped them, he hoped that he could scare her into compliance and knew that he could count on the law to take his side.

Joseph Trust was also very tightfisted, which must have been difficult for Mary to deal with after having been economically independent before her marriage. Once she married him, legally all of her money became his.[2] Although his business was profitable, he found it difficult to part with money. The testimony of Dr. Alexander Gunn is particularly revealing. Joseph Trust called in Dr. Gunn when Mary was about to deliver her third or fourth child, both of whom died. Gunn testified that Joseph Trust was reluctant to pay him his fee even though his wife was dangerously ill. He was brought into the case by Mary Trust, the plaintiff, to testify to the question of their marriage, but his testimony is important also because of the insight it gives us into her husband's almost pathological refusal to part with his money—even when his wife's or his child's life was in danger. Gunn testified:

> Sometime in the year 1844 or 1845, while practicing as a physician in the city of New York, he [Gunn, the deponent] was called upon by the defendant in this action, Joseph W. Trust, who asked deponent if he was in the practice of attending ladies in confinement. Deponent replied that he was. He then asked what deponent's charges were for such service; deponent answered, from ten to twenty-five dollars. The defendant replied, that ten dollars was too much, that he could obtain plenty of physicians to perform the same service for two dollars and a half or three dollars. After a good deal of parley in which the deponent told defendant that he had already as much practice as he could well attend to, and did not desire his patronage, and without determining upon any price, the defendant requested him to attend his *wife* who was shortly after confined at his house in Sixth Avenue, New York, as deponent believes, near Twelfth Street. Deponent is certain that the defendant used the word *wife*, to designate the person whom he requested deponent to visit. Deponent went to the house described to him by the defendant as the place where the patient was to be found, and there found the plaintiff in this action in severe labor and dangerously ill. Deponent remembers seeing only one person present, besides himself. There was a great want of necessary attendance, waiters, and the means with which to treat the case judiciously, and in consequence thereof he determined never again to encounter

the responsibility where there was so manifest a want of interest and means. And consequently when he was sent for to attend the plaintiff on a subsequent occasion he declined to attend. The plaintiff was in a great deal of danger and during the whole time that deponent visited her, deponent does not remember that the defendant was once present. The defendant afterwards sent deponent five dollars for his services, which deponent returned to him, and he then sent deponent ten dollars.

The picture of Joseph Trust that emerges from the doctor's testimony is not a pretty one. Haggling about price while his wife was in the throes of a dangerous labor and refusing to spend the money to provide the "necessities" to make her delivery safer, he did not even manifest enough interest to be present himself. Although he was a wealthy man, he was a selfish one.

How did Mary Trust deal with her husband's stinginess? When he refused her money, she took in boarders in order to provide herself with money. This caused him great aggravation, and according to testimony, he cursed at and harassed her boarders in an attempt to get rid of them. On several occasions also, when he had refused her money, she helped herself to small amounts of the proceeds at the store, which she considered hers as well as his. The testimony of Margaret Dorsey, a clerk in Joseph Trust's store, gives us an idea of Mary's resistance. Called in as a sympathetic witness for Joseph Trust, her employer, Dorsey condemned Mary's behavior:

> On the 6th of June 1853, during the absence of defendant [Joseph], the plaintiff [Mary] entered his store and after violently abusing deponent [Dorsey], took by force and against her [Dorsey's] will from the money drawer the sum of six dollars; on the 9th of the same month, when deponent was alone, plaintiff again entered the store, used abusive language to deponent, among which was, "How dare you tell me that you were ordered not to let me take the money. If you attempt to interfere with me I will put you out of the store."

On other occasions, testified Margaret Dorsey, Mary Trust came into the store, taking money or arguing with her husband. On one occasion, she argued with him about the children, insisting, "I will be mistress of my own house." On another occasion, Dorsey said, in response to his ordering her to behave like a proper wife, "she said that she, plaintiff, would go on just as usual, treat the defendant just the same—as 'a damned jackass and a fool.'" Clearly, Mary Trust had a sharp tongue. The problem for Joseph Trust was that she was not the passive, acquiescent wife that nineteenth-century culture demanded. Joseph complained in 1864 that his wife was "a woman of imperious and dominating temper and disposition." She was, he said, "without the restraints and proprieties that belong to a woman in wedded life." All the guidebooks for wives instructed women to obey and revere their husbands.[3] But prescriptive behavior does not guarantee actual behavior, and cultural definitions are not universal. Mary Trust had a mind of her own; she resisted her husband's control and defended herself against his tightfistedness. Ultimately, she resisted her husband in other ways as well. According to his testimony, in 1852, four years before she left his house, she left his bed, refusing to have sexual intercourse with him.

It was after her husband had called the police for the fourth time and had her taken to the infamous Tombs prison, where she was incarcerated for thirty-six hours until he dropped the charges, that Mary Trust left home. Apparently desperate for a means of escape, she took all the money she had been able to find and asked Dr. Lyons to arrange for her and her daughter to go to California, which plan evaporated when Lyons absconded with her money.

After she left home, Joseph Trust brought suit for an absolute divorce on grounds of adultery, requesting that the marriage be dissolved "and the plaintiff be discharged from the obligations thereof and that the said Mary F. Trust be prohibited from contracting marriage during the life time of complainant and that the said Mary F. Trust be prohibited from having the care, custody, or control of complainant's children." All of these demands were within the law: in divorce settlements where one partner was found guilty of adultery, the guilty party could be denied the right to remarry, although the other partner was free to do so. Also, when a married couple separated in nineteenth-century America, the father legally retained custody of the children in preference to the mother.[4]

In early 1857 Joseph Trust was granted a divorce, but not on grounds of adultery. The divorce was a limited divorce or legal separation, in which

neither party could remarry. Consequently he was ordered to pay his
wife six dollars a week alimony. On hearing the outcome, he abandoned
the suit. She claimed that he abandoned the suit because he did not want
to pay alimony. He gave another reason that we will explore later, but his
other reason was clearly a way of getting out of paying Mary any money.
As Mary asserted in her subsequent suit, "as soon as the defendant
[Joseph] found that alimony had been awarded against him he discontinued the said action."

Meanwhile, Mary Trust, receiving no support from her husband (the
alimony was rescinded once the divorce suit was abandoned), lived with
her daughter at a cheap boardinghouse on the corner of Broome and
Elm Streets. Wanting to have her other children with her, on January 12,
1857, Mary went to Joseph's store when he was absent and took away with
her their son Andreas, then fourteen. Joseph claimed that the boy had
been living "happy and contented" with him and that his mother took
him "by force," but it is difficult to imagine a woman carrying off a four-
teen-year-old boy against his will. Five days later, on January 17, Joseph
obtained a writ of *habeas corpus* to recover both of the children (it is interesting that he did this only after the boy had been taken). He went with
the agent to his wife's boardinghouse, where the landlady, Mrs. Morris,
refused to surrender the children. Joseph then obtained another writ of
habeas corpus, this time against Mrs. Morris. The landlady, he said in his
petition, "confederated" with Mary as the children's mother, "claiming
[that the mother had] the right to have the care of said children irrespec-
tive of the authority and power of your petitioner in the matter." He was
successful in exercising his "authority and power," and the children were
taken away from their mother. He then sent Constance to boarding
school, forbidding her to correspond with or see her mother and threatening to send her to an Ohio school for domestic servants if she dis-
obeyed him. He also sent her costly gifts to try to bribe her to testify on
his behalf, and while she was dependent on him, she said very little.
However, after she had become independent and was able to support
herself as a teacher, her testimony, quoted above, was damning.

Joseph maintained control over Andreas by threatening to withhold
money for his education if he had any contact with his mother, and when
Mary contacted Andreas three years later for help in drafting a legal pa-

per for which she said she could not afford to pay the attorney's fees, Andreas told her that he would like to help her but that he was wholly dependent upon his father for his support and education and that his father would withdraw his help if he assisted her. Joseph sent the two younger boys, Percy and Volney, to school in Connecticut. In 1858 the resourceful Mary traveled to Connecticut to take one of the boys from his school and bring him back to her new boardinghouse, where Joseph could not find them. Joseph let her know through friends that he wanted the boy back at any cost and promised to give her twenty dollars if she would return the boy to him. He threatened to make trouble for her, and at last she sent a friend, Elizabeth Taylor, to tell him that she was destitute and that if he would give her twenty dollars, she would return the child—but not until he gave Taylor the money. She told Taylor she did not trust him. Taylor was afraid of Joseph, but Mary said he was violent only with her (Mary) and would not hurt her. Taylor obtained the twenty dollars, and Mary returned their son to his father.

On April 8, 1859, Mary Trust brought suit against her husband for a separation "from bed and board forever" on the grounds of "cruel and inhuman treatment, and abandonment." (In New York an absolute divorce was obtainable only on grounds of adultery, but one could obtain a limited divorce or separation on other grounds.) The law allowed that a husband could be ordered to provide for the support and legal expenses of an impecunious wife during the pendency of the suit. In June 1859 Mary made application for temporary alimony and expenses so that she could prosecute the suit, citing her husband's many holdings. But in his answer Joseph argued that he should not have to pay her anything. First, he said, he did not have the real estate and personal property or bonds in the amount that she claimed. Second, he said that business was bad and he didn't have enough money to pay his own debts.

At the same time, Joseph's attorney immediately moved for an order of reference—a legal practice of the time which required that a qualified jurist be appointed referee to hold hearings, collect the evidence, and ultimately deliver a report to the court. Mary's attorney objected, saying that she needed to have money first in order to continue with the case. Her request for alimony and fees was denied, but she was given leave to reapply after the referee's report was in. Joseph and his attorney swore that if the order of reference were granted, they would bring the case to a close in a few days. This was only the first of many delaying tactics, which seem to have been designed to free Joseph from the obligation of paying his wife any money. Although he had promised to bring the case to a speedy close, Joseph and his attorney delayed matters to such an extent that eight months after the order of reference was issued, only two witnesses had been heard, and of the twenty-three hearing dates, only two had been kept.

Mary testified before the referee from October 4, 1859, to February 2, 1860. Her testimony must have been very damaging to Joseph's case, because when she had finished, Joseph's attorney moved to have all of her testimony struck out on a technicality—that "she was an incompetent witness being the wife of the defendant," i.e., a wife could not testify against her husband. Her attorney objected, and the referee was reluctant to strike it out, but Joseph's attorney cited the law (the 64th, 66th, and 89th rules of the Supreme Court), and on March 6, 1860, the referee granted the motion to strike out all of her testimony. As her attorney noted, during all of the time that she was testifying, her testimony was "not then objected to by the defendant." It must have been devastating for Mary to have her testimony discounted, but she and her attorney countered with a motion to send a commission to Charlotte, North Carolina, to question Mary's daughter Constance, who had taken a teaching position there the previous year. Joseph opposed the motion and attempted to block the commission, but he was overruled, and on August 1, 1860, the commission examined Constance Trust, with the result that is quoted above—which was probably more damaging to Joseph's case than Mary's own testimony would have been since it came from a third party.

Meanwhile, Mary had not been awarded any money to allow her to continue the suit. Her motion for alimony and counsel fees had been denied on June 30, 1859, pending the completion of the referee's hearings. But the hearings continued much longer than had been anticipated because of delays caused by Joseph's attorney. On February 28, 1860, Mary reapplied for alimony and counsel fees, saying that she was "wholly destitute" of the means to continue the action. Her attorney stated: "The defense is conducted with unusual zeal and with the purpose as deponent believes of compelling the plaintiff to abandon the action without a final adjudication." In other words, if Joseph could delay long enough, he supposed Mary would have to give up the suit for lack of money and he would never have to pay her any support. Mary said that her attorney had not been paid and she did not have the fifty cents legal fee to pay her witnesses to come to the referee's hearings. Moreover, she could not afford carfare, she said, and had to walk one and a half miles each way to get to the hearings. Repeatedly she had come there, but her husband had not shown up and the hearings were canceled. She said she herself missed only two days, once because she was ill from having walked to the hearing the day before in snow and bitter cold and another time because she had been turned out of her boardinghouse the day before for nonpayment of rent and she needed to find a place to live. She brought in witnesses who corroborated her testimony that she was destitute and that she had been turned out of her boardinghouse because she could not pay her rent. She testified that although she was reluctant to "state all the mortifying particulars of her immediate distress," the fact was that she did not have enough to eat, a bed of her own, or sufficient clothing.

In contrast, she cited her husband's assets: He had "real estate and personal property to a large amount, and amply sufficient to enable him to give her sums as may be necessary for her support and counsel fees." She listed his holdings, being very specific: two lots on 90th and 100th Streets, worth $2,000 each; two other lots and leases for five years on two houses on Walker Street, valued at $2,000 per annum; a lease on the house on Greene Street and on a large three-story brick building for manufacturing valued at $10,000; and personal property, bonds, mortgages, etc., valued at $10,000. In addition, she said, for twenty years he had been in the manufacture of hair dyes, perfumes, and other cosmetics, the net proceeds of which were $6,000 per annum. As before, Joseph denied all of her allegations regarding his money, maintaining that he did not have any money and once again arguing that "business was bad."

On March 12, 1860, Mary's appeal for alimony and counsel fees was denied, but she appealed to the General Court, and on September 27, 1860, the judge granted Mary's motion for counsel fees and directed Joseph to pay her attorney $100. Once again, her motion for alimony was denied, but she was given leave to renew her application after the referee's evidence was in. Joseph refused to pay the $100 and attempted an appeal. But the judge said that the issue was not appealable and on October 23 issued an order for Joseph's arrest for contempt of court for refusal to comply with the court order; his bail was set at $250. Joseph eluded the sheriff, who reported that he could not be found. The judge ordered that Joseph be brought "before one of the justices of our Supreme Court on the 26th day of October at 10 o'clock in the forenoon." Again on October 26 the sheriff reported that Joseph could not be found. Rather than go to jail, however, Joseph ultimately paid Mary's attorney $100 along with the $250 bail.

Joseph's two arguments — that he did not have enough money and that business was bad — were the same arguments that he used over and over, and Mary and her lawyer were able to refute them with evidence of his assets. This was more difficult to do than it is today. Annual tax filings to the IRS had not yet been established; consequently there were no government tax records to access.[5] (Of course, even today tax records do not tell the whole story.)

Meanwhile, Mary had to await the referee's report. It was completed on December 12, 1860, a year and a half after the order was given. However, she did not have the $237 to bring out the report, and Joseph refused to pay it. On January 25, 1861, Mary returned to court. She pointed out that since the beginning of the suit in April 1859 she had not received any money from the defendant for her support. She was in "absolute want," she said, and was unable to raise the money for the referee's fee. Last week, she said, Joseph had asserted that she would "never receive from him the value of one cent," and she believed that it was "the determined purpose of the defendant [Joseph] to neglect to take up the report of the referee, well knowing that it is not within the power of the plaintiff [Mary] to take it up, and thereby virtually to defeat the proper determination of this action and to prevent the plaintiff from receiving any benefit therefrom."

Moreover, after she was awarded the counsel fees that Joseph had been forced to pay, he had been so angry about having to pay any money for her benefit that he had begun spitefully to harass her. She stated in her affidavit that he had "repeatedly sent to the keepers of the boarding houses where deponent has been staying printed pamphlets of his complaint against her in the Superior Court wherein he had alleged serious charges of adultery against her, which he can never prove, for the purpose of causing her expulsion from such boarding houses, and she has been expelled in consequence thereof." He had also been so "public" with his allegations, she said, that it was almost impossible for her to get any credit for food and lodging.

On February 14, 1861, the court ordered Joseph to pay the $237 for the referee's report plus ten dollars costs to the plaintiff for the motion, and Joseph was cited for default because neither he nor his attorney appeared in court. Eight days later Joseph's attorney reported that the money had been paid, but in order to protect his client from further claims upon him, he stated that the $237 had been paid by "a friend" since Joseph could not afford to pay it. His attorney contested the default ruling, citing the deaths of two of his [the attorney's] children as the reason why he was not in court. On March 23, 1861, the matter was turned over to a new referee, and ultimately the default was lifted. The December 1860 referee's report concluded that Joseph's charges of adultery against his wife were false. It also concluded, however, that her charges of cruel and inhuman treatment and abandonment against him were false. Consequently, neither party had grounds for divorce or separation, and Mary—if she continued to live apart from her husband—could receive no support from him. She could not prove "abandonment," which would have been grounds for obtaining a separation, because it was she who had left her husband. Joseph—whether deliberately or by his nature—had driven her out of the house by his abusive behavior. The testimony of his daughter and other witnesses certainly corroborated Mary's complaint against him. Today such behavior would be considered "cruel and inhuman treatment." However, by 1860 standards such behavior by a husband might have been vulgar and ungentlemanly, but it was not sufficiently "cruel and inhuman" to warrant a separation in New York—which gives us an idea of what a wife was expected to put up with.

This, however, was not the end of the litigation. By February 1864, Mary had discovered that Joseph was living with a woman named Martha Tompkins, by whom he had two children. He was living under the name Dr. Felix Gouraud, which was the name on the label of his products. Mary filed for divorce on grounds of adultery, alleging that the adultery had been in effect for seven years, which would mean that Joseph's relationship with Martha Tompkins began a year after Mary left his house. Mary demanded that "the marriage be dissolved absolutely, and that her said husband may be adjudged to make a suitable allowance for her and their children; and that during the pendency of this action temporary alimony may be awarded to her; and that this court will also direct the defendant to make her a suitable counsel fee to carry on and conduct this action." She asked for sixty dollars a week in alimony and five hundred dollars in counsel fees.

On March 12 Joseph denied the adultery charge and maintained that he could not afford to pay her anything. Again he insisted that he did not have as much money as she said he did, that he had debts and a mortgage. He said that he had paid for the education of the children and that "for these reasons he considered himself absolved of all legal and other obligations to support the plaintiff." However, in spite of his arguments, on April 4, 1864, the court awarded Mary $500 in counsel fees and $100 a month for every month that the action continued, retroactive to February 15, 1864. The order also said that the plaintiff [Mary] would be at liberty to apply at any time for an increase in alimony and counsel fees. This decision was a terrible blow for Joseph Trust, who had vowed that he would not pay Mary one cent and who had dropped his original suit because he did not want to pay her only six dollars a week. He appealed, and on September 28 the order on his appeal reduced the amount of the attorney's fee from $500 to $200 but required him to pay the $100-a-month alimony as per the order of April 4.

Enraged by this loss, Joseph refused to pay anything. He fired his lawyer and determined to act as his own attorney henceforth. Mary's attorney asked the court to issue an attachment for the arrest of the defendant for contempt of court for refusing to comply with the order, and once again, Joseph complied rather than go to jail: he paid the $200 counsel fee to Mary's attorney and began paying her $100 a month, starting with February 15, 1864.

Although Joseph had been required to pay Mary alimony for her support while the case continued, the case was still not settled a year later. Then, on January 5, 1865, the court ordered Mary's suit for divorce referred to a referee to frame the issues to be submitted to a jury that would try the case. The trial took place during May 1865 and resulted in favor of the plaintiff. Joseph, acting as his own attorney, appealed the decision to the Court of Appeals. His appeal was denied, however, and on April 5, 1866, the judge issued a final decree: Mary obtained her divorce. Ten years after she had left her husband, the marriage between the Trusts was dissolved on the grounds of Joseph's adultery. The order gave the plaintiff the right to remarry if she chose, and the defendant was required to pay his former wife fifty dollars a month until she died.

However, this was still not the end of the case. On May 6, 1868, Mary Trust's new attorney moved to increase the alimony to the $100 a month the referee had recommended in 1865. Mary claimed that her previous attorney, now deceased, did not consult or inform her of the terms and did not give her "an opportunity to show to the court what were the circumstances of the said defendant or how this deponent was situated." She gave a detailed account of Joseph's assets. He had a prosperous business, she said, which was even larger and more profitable than it was two years before when she was awarded alimony of $600 a year ($50 a month); his sales had increased to between $20,000 and $30,000 a year. In addition, she said, he received profits in rent money for the whole commercial building between Broadway and Mercer Street. And he lived in an expensive house with Martha Tompkins, a house which, according to his landlord, he leased for $1,500 a year. On the other hand, she said, she lived in a small frame house for which she paid $300 a year in rent. She lived with three of her children, two of whom, she said—her daughter and one son—were in delicate health and could not support themselves. She concluded her testimony by saying that if she had known of the arrangements that her lawyer was making with the defendant, she could have proven to the court that the amount of $50 a month was not sufficient for her needs and was not as much as the defendant should be able to pay.

Joseph Trust, no longer acting on his own but with a new lawyer, replied that his former attorney had made a legitimate arrangement with the plaintiff's attorney in 1866. Her lawyer, he said, had told him that the arrangement was made with her full knowledge and authority: "It being the intention of deponent [Joseph] to litigate said action further, it was agreed between the said plaintiff's attorney, this deponent, and the counsel of this deponent, that if deponent would let the matter rest as it was and not litigate the matter any further and pay her attorney his costs, he would accept as the amount of alimony to be paid the said plaintiff the sum of six hundred dollars per year." Clearly her attorney wanted to put an end to the litigation, knowing Joseph's track record in delaying litigation by contesting every suggestion that he pay support to his wife. And on Joseph's part, after being frightened by the judge's order of temporary alimony of one hundred dollars a month and the jury's recommendation that that sum be made permanent, he was willing to agree to drop the matter if her attorney agreed to take half that amount in alimony.

Joseph reiterated his previous arguments: he denied that he did business in the amount that she said—"not by half," he said—(which would still make him a rich man by nineteenth-century standards), and he maintained that business was bad. On June 17, 1868, the court ordered the case referred to a referee to inquire into the facts as to whether the alimony should be increased and if so, what would be the proper amount. The referee's report did not come in until the end of 1869. Meanwhile, Joseph stopped paying alimony altogether. Mary's attorney moved that an attachment be issued for Joseph's arrest for contempt and that his property be sequestered and a receiver appointed for the payment of alimony. On October 23, 1869, Mary obtained an attachment against him: if he did not comply with the order in three days he would go to jail. He complied: he paid the back alimony, the sheriff's fee, and costs of the motion.

The referee's report was issued in December 1869 and recommended that Mary's alimony be doubled, i.e., returned to the $100-a-month figure that the jury had awarded before her lawyer made the agreement with Joseph. However, Judge Ingraham, who heard the case, was reluctant to raise the alimony to such an extent and issued a statement of his opinion explaining that, since her children were grown (her youngest son was now twenty), she did not need more money, and since there had been an agreement made between the two attorneys, it might not be proper to break it. He wrote the following: "There is no reason to give alimony to the wife for the support of the daughter and but little for the son who should support himself. I am not satisfied with the propriety of increasing to the amount recommended, and after the agreement of the plaintiff's former counsel, I have some doubt as to the propriety of any increase." However, on December 17, 1869, he issued an order increasing the alimony by $200 a year, retroactive to May 17, 1868. Joseph was also ordered to pay the referee's fee of $200, Mary's attorney's fee of $150, and $10 in costs.

Even this increase was a severe blow to Joseph Trust. He refused to pay the increase or the referee's and attorney's fees but continued to pay the $50 a month he had been ordered to pay in 1866. In February 1870 Mary's attorney asked that a precept be issued for Joseph's arrest for contempt for noncompliance with the order. Joseph argued the case, requesting that the order of December 1869 be vacated and that the question of alimony be reheard. In April his motion was denied and an order was issued for his arrest, commanding the sheriff to "take the body of the said defendant and commit him to the prison of the city and county of New York, and keep and detain him there under custody until he shall pay" the full amount: $533.33 in back alimony, $160 to Mary's attorney, sheriff's fees, and $10 in costs. Once again enraged by his loss, Joseph fired his lawyer and substituted himself as attorney. However, rather than go to jail, he paid all of the money he owed, and he continued to pay the required alimony. There was no more litigation.

But there is more to this story. In his attempts to avoid paying his wife any money, Joseph Trust used two other rather singular arguments in addition to his oft-repeated assertions that he didn't have much money and that business was bad. First of all, he claimed that his wife had a profitable business as a female physician and earned plenty of money herself so that she didn't need any money from him. Mary denied and successfully refuted this claim. She herself swore that she had never earned any money in that way, and she called in a neighbor to testify that she was not a physician, that she was in fact destitute. The justices and the jury apparently believed her. After all, she was a middle-class woman, the mother of four living children, and a businessman's wife. She presented herself as destitute, as a woman who deserved the pity and compassion of the court. Moreover, the justices and the jury probably did not know (m)any female physicians. To them, her husband's accusation must have seemed absurd.

However, Joseph's argument that Mary earned money as a physician is a curious accusation. One wonders where he got the idea. One also wonders what she lived on during all of the time that the suit was in progress. Where did she get the money to travel to Connecticut, for example? It was not until ten years after she left her husband's house that the court finally awarded her alimony. During the later years her grown children may have helped to support her, and it is known that in 1864 she ran a boardinghouse at 374 Fourth Street. But what was she living on when she first left her husband in 1856? We know that she gave $1,100 to Lyons. It is difficult to believe that she had much more than that amount of money in reserve. It is not improbable, therefore, that she did in fact earn money as her husband said.

Joseph first made this accusation on June 28, 1859, in response to his wife's initial application for temporary alimony and legal expenses during the suit: "For several months past [she] has been engaged in business in this city as a female physician or Doctress and in the manufacture of pills under the name of Mrs. Damphier [*sic*], and that from said business the said plaintiff is realizing a very large and considerable profit, amounting to some ten dollars per week." In response to Mary's second application for alimony in February 1860 (the first having been denied), Joseph testified on March 9, 1860, maintaining that she was not destitute, that whenever he saw her—except in court—she was well dressed. He reiterated his assertion that she was supporting herself in medical practice, but this time he did not use the word physician: "She gets money either by practicing medicine or prescribing and vending medicine and medicinal pills and she is well able to support and maintain herself and has the same means for such purpose at the present time as she has had since the month of November 1856 when she voluntarily abandoned deponent."

We know that Mary Trust did take the name "Mrs. Dampier" after she left her husband. Elizabeth Taylor, the friend who had collected the twenty dollars from her husband for her, testified that when she first met Mary in 1857 or 1858, she knew her by that name: "She introduced herself to this deponent as Mrs. Dampier and presented to this deponent a card on which was engraved the name of Mrs. Dampier." It is not surprising that Mary Trust would change her name, since she was attempting to hide her child from her husband, but one wonders why she had an engraved card? Taylor does not tell us if it was a business card or a visiting card. The justices and jury did not question the assertion that she had a card; probably their wives and mothers had visiting cards. But, given Mary's reduced status, it seems unlikely that she would have had a visiting card; and if she had one left over from her life as Mrs. Trust, it would have borne that name. I suspect that the card was a business card and that the business that Mary Trust was engaged in was either the business her husband specified or some other related business. She had, after all, been in business for herself before she was married, and she had learned her husband's trade by helping him in his business. It is not far-fetched to believe that she used this knowledge to develop her own business after she left him.

Mary Trust was an enterprising woman—self-reliant before she married, independent during her marriage, and persevering in her efforts to force her husband to pay her alimony. She was not the kind of woman who would do nothing at all to support herself. I suspect that she did in fact support herself during the years that she pursued her suit. If she was not a physician as her husband said, she supported herself in some other way. In his anger at being asked to pay her alimony, Joseph Trust suggested that her boardinghouse was a house of "ill fame" patronized by prostitutes—which was apparently not what he believed but a way of prejudicing the court against his wife. It was also particularly insensitive to his children, since his daughter and two of his sons lived there. Moreover, it would not explain how she earned her money before she acquired the boardinghouse in 1864. Although she presented herself to the court as destitute, it seems clear that she was comfortably economically independent. As Joseph said in frustration in March 1864, "she has maintained and supported herself by some means not fully known to deponent for all that time, and in a manner shewing that she has the command of money and means, living in good houses, well furnished, and appearing in good and fashionable attire." Her son Percy testified in 1868 that his mother had three thousand dollars in Central Pacific Railroad bonds.

However, it was probably not difficult for her to persuade the justices and the all-male jury that she was a helpless woman who was destitute without her husband's support. They did not have access to government tax records, and if she was a female physician, pharmacist, or midwife (or had some other independent business), her clients were probably poor women whom the justices did not know and who could not be found unless she identified them. But most important, the justices and the jury were middle- and upper-class white men, and their expectations for a middle-class white woman were that she would be dependent upon her husband's support. She used the conventions of the day to construct a narrative that the male justices would find believable; her husband's accusation, although it probably was the truth, did not fit into their frame of reference.

The evidence suggests that Mary Trust used the cultural definition of womanhood for her own purposes. By presenting herself as the dependent female who fulfilled the male justices' image of women, she was able to force her husband to pay her a large settlement, which enabled her to obtain justice by permitting her to share in the profits of his business, which she claimed she had helped to develop. This was her principal motivation in pursuing the suit. As she pointed out when she sought an increase in 1868, she would never have agreed with the compromise worked out by her attorney; she wanted the opportunity to show the court not only her own situation but also her husband's *ability to pay*. In 1870 she pointed again to her part in his success: "He has a well established business, in a great measure produced by the aid and assistance of this deponent [Mary] during their marriage." What irritated her most was that he had all that money which she felt she had enabled him to earn; she felt that she would only obtain justice when she was able to acquire a good portion of it. There is ironic significance in the name that she took when she left her husband; Dampier was the name of a famous late-seventeenth- to early-eighteenth-century British buccaneer and navigator. Mary Trust was exploring new waters in leaving her abusive husband to pursue her own career; and in compelling him to hand over his money, she enacted the part of a bold and dauntless pirate. There is no way of knowing whether Mary Trust had this association in mind when she took the name Dampier, but given the imaginative names she gave her children, it is not unlikely. Certainly it is noteworthy that she did not simply revert to her maiden name of Grew, or call herself by a common name like Jones or Smith if she was seeking anonymity.

Mary Trust's second motivation was revenge against the man who had taken away her business, her children, and her friends and had inflicted so much pain and humiliation upon her. She knew that forcing him to pay her a large amount of money would constitute a powerful revenge—particularly on a man who was as close with his money as was Joseph Trust. I suspect also that she derived a wry pleasure from being able to have him arrested and put in jail for contempt after the way that he had had her arrested in his attempts to curb her independence.

Revenge was an important factor in her perseverance in the suit for another reason as well, a reason having to do with the other bizarre argument that Joseph used to avoid paying her any support. It was an argument so cruel that many women would have crumbled under the onslaught. He first used the argument to extricate himself from the need to pay alimony in his 1856 suit. When he initially sued for divorce and was ordered to pay his wife six dollars a week in alimony, he abandoned the suit, claiming that they had never been married. His attorney argued that there was no proof that there had been a lawful marriage between the Trusts and that therefore there could be no divorce; since there could be no divorce, Joseph should not have to pay her anything. In answer to Mary's request that she be paid an allowance and counsel fees during the pendency of the suit, Joseph's attorney pointed out in 1860 that the law books did not state that a man should pay support and counsel fees for a woman not his wife. Hence, she had to prove that she was his wife before she could receive money to pursue her suit. But in order to pursue the suit, she needed money. One of the things the referee was charged with in 1860 was to make a determination as to whether or not the Trusts' marriage was valid. Consequently, Mary could not apply for alimony until the referee's report was in. Meanwhile Joseph and his attorney delayed the referee's hearings for a year and a half, hoping to force Mary to abandon the suit.

In order to prove his allegation, Joseph produced a copy of an entry in the record book in Saint James Parish in London, which recorded his marriage to one Eliza Southwell on March 19, 1827. Since he was already married, he said, he could not be married to Mary. Mary attempted to prove that she was in fact lawfully married to Joseph. She pointed to his own statement under oath in his original complaint in 1856, in which he said that he had married Mary Grew on October 9, 1839. She brought in witnesses who swore that they had heard him refer to her as his wife. But she had no certificate or record to point to. When she left home in 1856, she did not take any papers with her, and the magistrate who married them had since died.

Today we don't know whether Joseph's argument was true or whether it was concocted in order to save him money. It is true that Joseph was selective in his claims about his marriage to Mary. In 1860, for example, he had had her testimony before the referee struck out on the grounds that a *wife* could not testify against her husband. And the language used by his attorney was ambiguous: he stated in 1860 that Mary had been refused alimony because "the marriage is denied by the defendant and is not established by proof" by the plaintiff. However, after hearing all of the evidence, the referee in 1860 and the jury and the referee in 1865 concluded that the Trusts were legally married. Joseph appealed unsuccessfully, and in April 1866, the judge ruled that the marriage was valid, granted Mary a divorce, and awarded her alimony.

Joseph's argument proved him to be either a bigamist or an adulterer —and in either case a scoundrel. His and Mary's children all had assumed that their parents were legally married, and Joseph's news was disturbing; if it was true, it would make the children bastards. Three of the children left their father's house as soon as they were of age and went to live with their mother. The fourth child, Percy, was sadly conflicted. He lived with his father and was wholly dependent on him for support in 1868, but he was attached to both parents, he said, and he "deprecated further litigation between them." Joseph's frustration with and hostility toward his wife, and his determination that he would not pay her any money regardless of cost, led him to inflict immeasurable pain on his children as well as on her. The publicity of the announcement that he had never married their mother would have caused his children (as well as Mary) a great deal of embarrassment, and his references to his children were cruel. In 1864, he said he refused to "contribute to the support of the plaintiff and of the several persons named in the said complaint called therein children of the said parties and of the said alleged marriage." The "several persons" must have been aggrieved to be referred to in this way by their father. In the same year Joseph complained that Mary had "instilled into the minds of the children her sentiments of disrespect and ill will towards" him. He did not need Mary to do so; he did it himself by the cruel way that he treated their mother and by publicly declaring them bastards. He did this to his children in order to avoid paying any money to their mother.

What are we to make of this story? Certainly the picture of Mary Trust that emerges from this case does not fit easily into cultural definitions of nineteenth-century womanhood. Although nineteenth-century women were defined as outside the marketplace, Mary Trust's experience was primarily economic. And as will become clear from the other court cases that we will examine here, she was not alone. Her story provides a measure of the many ways in which women—even "domestic" women—were involved in economic issues. First, she was economically independent before her marriage and after she was separated from her husband. Second, she assisted in her husband's business throughout her marriage as a not-so-silent partner. Third, during her seventeen years of married life she was constantly involved in a struggle to obtain money for her own and her children's needs. And fourth, in her life, as in the lives of other women, money was a measure of power: during the marriage and throughout the litigation, her husband used the withholding of money as leverage to assert control over her, and she used the acquisition of money as a means of asserting her own power.

Finally, then as now, litigation required money: if Mary Trust had not been self-supporting, if she had not had the money to pursue the suit, she would have had to abandon the case, as her husband hoped and expected she would. But it was her economic independence—whatever its source—that enabled her to pursue the litigation for fourteen years, ultimately to achieve what she regarded as justice.

———— ·❦· ————

chapter two

THE DOMINANT DISCOURSE

COMPULSORY DEPENDENCY

The case of *Trust v. Trust*, then, provides an illustration of how one belea-guered woman reacted to the circumstances of American society in the middle of the nineteenth century. The succeeding chapters examine fiction by women writers and the records of women involved in other court cases, women who, in their actions and/or in their words, in vary-ing degrees questioned the dominant discourse of American culture with respect to women's role in economic life. Before examining these counternarratives, however, we need to look at the factors that made up the official narrative. What were the discursive forces that defined gen-der in nineteenth-century American society? The most commonly cited in terms of gender restrictions, of course, is political discourse: women in the United States were unable to vote or hold political office through-out the nineteenth century; they did not receive the vote until the passage of the nineteenth amendment in 1920; and they are still dispro-portionately represented in government. This is the most well-known aspect of gender-limiting discourse. But there were many others; in fact, all aspects of nineteenth-century culture defined women as dependent. For purposes of analysis, I have identified six principal categories, other than the political, that helped to define women as economically depend-ent. This chapter begins with a discussion of legal discourse, outlining the origins of the laws themselves, and the changes in the laws that affected nineteenth-century women. The remainder of the chapter ex-plores the inscription of domesticity, followed by a consideration of reli-gious, medical, economic, and sexual discourse. The following discussion is not intended to be all-inclusive but to give a summary of the principal attitudes and strictures emanating from many areas of American culture. There was, of course, overlap among all of these categories, but by separating them we can better understand the multiple forces that constructed compulsory dependency, particularly economic dependency, as an essential characteristic of womanhood. The extent to which women challenged, questioned, or refused to be bound by these restrictions is the subject of this book.

The discourse that most effectively restricted all women, regardless of race or class, was the law, not only the law of racial slavery but also the law with respect to free women. American legal traditions derived from English common law. Under common law, if a married woman had money or other personal property of her own (through inheritance or through her own labor), legally it belonged to her husband. He could use her money in any way he wished: he could use it to support the family, or he could spend it on alcohol and other women or lose it through unwise investments. The legal discourse defining women as economically dependent derived from the doctrine of marital coverture. A married woman was "covered" by her husband; legally she did not have a separate identity. Man and wife were one, and that one was the husband. As William Blackstone wrote in his classic *Commentaries on the Laws of England* in 1765, "By marriage, the husband and wife are one person in law: that is, the very being or legal existence of the woman is suspended during the marriage, or at least is incorporated and consolidated into that of the husband; under whose wing, protection, and *cover* she performs everything; and is therefore called in our law-French a *feme-covert*."[1] Under common law, a wife could not sue or be sued, own personal property separately from her husband, retain guardianship of her children, sign contracts, will her property, or keep any money that she earned or inherited. Although she retained possession of any real estate that she owned, her husband controlled the management of it and was entitled to all rents or profits from it. Moreover, she could not sell it without his permission. The law of coverture, of course, applied only to married women. A single woman, although she could not vote or serve on a jury, had the same property rights as a man; as a *feme sole*, she could buy, hold, and sell property, sign contracts, and independently sue or be sued in court. She gave up all of these rights when she married.[2]

If a married woman was involved in a lawsuit, her husband had to be party to the suit. If she was the defendant—for example, if she owed money to someone, even if it was a debt contracted prior to her marriage—her husband was named as codefendant and was liable for her debt. If she wanted to bring suit, she could not sue unless her husband agreed to sue along with her. If he did not want to or could not be included as a plaintiff (because he was declared ineligible for legal reasons, because he disagreed with the suit, or because he was himself the defendant, e.g., in a divorce case), the woman had to petition the court to appoint a man to be her "next friend." This was a man, in addition to her lawyer, who would represent her in court. He performed the same function as a guardian appointed by the court to represent a minor (which put a married woman in the same category as a child). Her court-appointed "next friend" could be a father, brother, friend, or acquaintance—as long as he was male.

Married women were limited not only in terms of their legal identity in court but also by the inheritance laws. Under common law, a married woman could not write a will unless she obtained her husband's consent.[3] In New York the 1828 Revised Statutes specifically stated that a married woman could not write a will. An 1845 court case ruled that if her property was in trust she could write a will, but only if the trust specifically gave her that power.[4] In most states, when a man died, his wife was legally entitled to only a life interest in the third part of his real estate and a third of the surplus of his personal property after all creditors had been paid. On the other hand, if the husband was the survivor, he was legally entitled to all of their real and personal property (even if she had contributed more to the estate than he had).[5] Thus, when a woman's husband died, she could not gain full rights to the property he owned—not even to the house in which she lived. She inherited only one-third of it, and her children inherited the remainder in equal parts. If one of her adult children wanted his inheritance immediately, he could—and in the cases I studied, he often did—force the sale of the property, dispossessing his mother and sometimes even minor children who were still at home.

This system contained two forms of protection for the wife. Under common law, the married woman's right of dower—her inheritance of a life interest in one-third of her husband's real estate—had been established for her protection. Her husband could not sell or mortgage his real estate without her written consent to relinquish her right of dower.[6] The wife's dower right, along with her claim to one third of his personal property after his death—after his debts had been paid[7]—was intended to prevent the impoverishment of widows. In reality, however, women's ignorance of the law and dependence on their husbands' judgment (after all, the culture conditioned a woman to believe that she could not understand money matters) enabled a man to sell or mortgage his real estate if he wished to, including the family home, so that when he died, his wife could be left homeless; and if he had amassed sufficient debts, there would be little or nothing of the one-third left for her after his creditors were paid.

A second protection for women was the availability of equity trusts. A wealthy family could partly circumvent the restrictions of the common law by providing an independent settlement for a married daughter through the establishment of a trust. Marriage settlements had long been used by wealthy families in England to establish a separate estate for a married daughter through the equity or chancery courts. But equity did not provide any protection for the daughter of a working- or middle-class family who might not have any property to bring to the marriage. Moreover, because some of the American states did not have equity courts (for example, the New England states) and because, where the courts did exist, the process was complicated and expensive, Americans did not avail themselves of equity to the extent that it was practiced in England.[8] In 1848 journalist Jane Swisshelm wrote sarcastically of the difficulty of establishing a married woman's trust: "There is no use getting less than six legal gentlemen, . . . and the next six who examine it will pronounce it all wrong, and one chance against fifty but you will have to begin just where you started."[9]

The extent to which a married woman's rights were subsumed by her husband's is particularly apparent in the legal acceptance of domestic abuse. The common law assumed that physical abuse by the husband would occur and placed the burden of deflecting it on the wife. A wife could obtain a legal separation from her husband only if his abuse was life-threatening; otherwise, as James Kent wrote in his *Commentaries on American Law*, "the wife must disarm [a violent] disposition in the husband by the weapons of kindness."[10] Under common law, a man had the right to use physical abuse to "correct" his wife's behavior: "For, as [the husband] is to answer for her misbehaviour, the law thought it reasonable to intrust him with this power of restraining her, by domestic chastisement, in the same moderation that a man is allowed to correct his apprentices or children."[11] Throughout most of the nineteenth century, in the United States a man legally had the right to physically abuse his wife—"to beat her with a stick, to pull her hair, choke her, spit in her face, or kick her about the floor."[12] Changes in the law were a long time in coming, and they were enacted piecemeal, state by state. Massachusetts and Alabama passed a law in 1871 declaring that the above behavior was no longer legal. But a law in Pennsylvania attempting to criminalize wife beating in 1886 failed to pass. And even when laws were passed, custom prevailed and the law recognized physical abuse as a husband's prerogative, as long as the wife sustained no "permanent injury." As an 1874 North Carolina law stated, "If no permanent injury has been inflicted, nor malice nor dangerous violence shown by the husband, it is better to draw the curtain, shut out the public gaze, and leave the parties to forget and forgive."[13]

In the late 1830s and 1840s, individual states began to pass statutes to protect a married woman's property. However, the changes in the law were made not to benefit women but to protect male property. None of the laws in the 1840s protected a married woman's own wages or earnings. For the most part, even when the laws declared that a woman's real estate was her own separate property, the husband retained control of it. Some states gave the woman the right to sell her property, but other states required her husband's consent. Two factors led to the passage of these early laws. Some legislators, particularly in the South, were responding to the events of the Panic of 1837, which had caused many wealthy families to lose their property, and they were looking for a way to safeguard the wife's property from the husband's creditors. Other legislators, particularly in New England, were attempting to fill the gap created by the absence of equity courts, which in England and in states following the English example provided a means of creating a separate estate for the daughter of a wealthy family so that a man's son-in-law could not squander her inheritance.[14]

In the Northeast, however, there was another factor leading to the passage of married women's property laws—the agitation for reform and the growing recognition of women's separate identity. Although few writers supported the idea that women should vote or hold office, and many expressed the concern that to give married women control of their property would drive a wedge between husband and wife, there was also a change in the public view of women. Disparate voices argued in favor of woman's legal, economic, or political independence, and individual women challenged, by their words and by their actions, restrictive laws and social mores. The voices of women in the women's rights movement were increasingly effective in bringing about legislation, particularly the 1860 New York statute.[15] New York has often been erroneously cited as the first state to pass a married women's property act, a mistake due in part to New York's reputation as a leader in jurisprudence and due also to the publicity given to the 1848 statute at the time, particularly by women's rights advocates.[16]

The first state to pass a significant law to give married women some control of their property was Mississippi in 1839. Ironically, in this first step toward women's civil rights, the "property" protected by the law was primarily a married woman's slaves; four of the five sections of the law dealt with slave ownership. Two other slave states passed similar laws (Maryland in 1843 and Arkansas in 1846). Some southern states (Louisiana, Texas, and Florida) followed the community property system of Spanish law, in which the wife held her property separately, but her husband had the management of it and the right to all of the profits.[17] In the 1840s all of the New England states and three of the northwestern states (Iowa, Indiana, and Ohio) passed laws entitling a married woman to own property separately from her husband. In New York the chancery courts were eliminated in 1847, and the 1848 Married Women's Property Act was passed to fill the place formerly provided by chancery, which had dealt with equity marriage settlements. The New York law was passed on April 16, 1848, and Pennsylvania enacted a similar law the same year. The laws specified that property that a woman brought with her into the marriage or property that she acquired by gift or bequest after the marriage was to be "her sole and separate property, as if she were a single female."[18]

The belief of many, however, was that if a woman had control of her property, there would be domestic discord. Thus a Pittsburgh newspaper wrote in 1847 in response to the bill pending in New York: "We are startled—there is no word more expressive of the feelings of the writer—by a bill just brought into the Legislature of New York, legalizing *separate estates*—and consequently, separate interests—which under evil circumstances, are very likely to become adverse and antagonistic interests—between *man and wife*."[19] In 1850 James Fenimore Cooper wrote the novel *The Ways of the Hour* in opposition to the 1848 married women's property law in New York. Cooper reflected the opinion of many of his contemporaries when he asserted that the laws of nature and of God intended woman to be dependent upon man. If she possessed any money of her own, Cooper wrote, she should "reverently pour it into her husband's lap."[20]

Even when state laws were changed to give married women control of their property, then, tradition and social pressure made women slow to take advantage of their rights. The laws varied from state to state, and the wording in some of the laws was vague. Moreover, in the ensuing years, many of the first married women's property acts were challenged in the courts and their usefulness negated by the restrictive interpretation of conservative judges. For example, in 1858, although Pennsylvania had passed a married women's property act ten years earlier, the Pennsylvania Supreme Court ruled that since a husband and wife were one person, it was impossible to separate a wife's property from her husband's. Judge Woodward declared that to do so would "degrade the divine institution [of marriage] to mere concubinage."[21] And the following year, the Pennsylvania court determined that the act was not intended to provide a separate estate for the wife but simply to prevent the wife's property from being taken by the husband's creditors; Judge William Strong ruled that it was a "radical mistake to suppose that the act intended to convert the wife into a *feme sole*, so far as relates to her property. That is impossible while she is to continue to discharge the duties of a wife."[22] Because of the conservative interpretation of the property acts by the judiciary, the laws did not change a great deal in the lives of most women. The common law tradition was so entrenched in the legal system and in the public mind that it retarded change. The principal change was that the privilege of equity was theoretically extended to all women.

Moreover, since the married women's property laws that were passed in the 1840s only covered property that a woman brought into marriage or received as a gift or bequest during marriage, all of the money that a married woman *earned* was legally her husband's. None of the laws applied to a married woman's own earnings—money she received as wages or from the sale of items or services. The married woman who worked for wages in a factory, or sewed at home or in a sweatshop, or sold butter and eggs on a farm, or ran a boardinghouse, or opened a store or business— was not legally entitled to keep any of her earnings.

Before the Civil War only four states passed laws protecting the money that a married woman earned. On May 5, 1855, the Massachusetts legislature passed a law giving a married woman the right to own real or personal property; sell, contract, or sue and be sued; make a will; and have full control over her earnings.[23] In 1860 a similar law was passed in New York: the New York Married Women's Property Act of 1848 was extended to benefit working-class as well as upper- and middle-class women. The new law decreed that the wages that a woman earned after marriage were also to be her separate property, and she was given the right to sue or be sued in her own name, to conduct a business or trade, and to sign contracts.[24] New York's 1860 law was the most comprehensive state law governing married women's property. By 1861 eighteen states had established laws giving married women "separate use" of their property; ten prevented the husband's creditors from taking a wife's property; but only four states (Connecticut, Massachusetts, Maine, and New York) gave a married woman the right to her own wages.[25] Three states (Virginia, South Carolina, and Delaware) provided no protection for married women until late in the nineteenth century.

During the Civil War the women's movement was dormant: lobbying of legislatures ceased, and no petitions were circulated demanding women's rights. Susan B. Anthony commented that feminists were asleep on the subject of women's rights, having become preoccupied with abolition and the Civil War.[26] After the war, however, an organized women's movement campaigned for laws to give a married woman more rights, particularly the right to have control over her earnings. Even after the movement split in 1869, although the two wings of the movement disagreed on other issues, they came together on the issue of a married woman's right to her earnings.[27] It was not until the 1870s and 1880s, however, that other states followed the lead of Massachusetts and New York, instituting laws that entitled a married woman to her earnings. By 1887 two-thirds of the states had enacted some version of this law.[28]

Meanwhile, the judiciary continued its conservative interpretation of the married women's property acts in a relentless assault on the laws, severely diminishing the laws' effectiveness. In decision after decision, in state after state, judges applied common law principles whenever terms in the new laws were not fully spelled out. The courts ruled that a wife's earnings were her own *only* when she was abandoned by her husband or he was proven to have misspent the family's earnings or to be unable to support the family (e.g., he was a drunkard or mentally incompetent). In other words, she could claim her money as her own only if she could prove that she needed control of her earnings for her own and her family's protection. As long as husband and wife lived together and worked for a common purpose, the courts interpreted her paid labor as "housework," i.e., work done to contribute to the household. Under common law, the wife's labor and the fruits of her labor were the property of the husband as head of the household. Moreover, any household goods that she bought with her earnings (such as furniture and kitchen utensils) and any money that she deposited in a joint savings account were his property. The earnings covered under these conservative interpretations of the law included money the wife earned as a boardinghouse keeper, farmer, seamstress, receiver of rents, and factory operative. If she wished to claim her money for her "separate use," the courts demanded that she have written consent, or "express approval," from her husband. In *Birkbeck v. Ackroyd* (New York, 1878) the judge declared: "The bare fact that she [the wife] performs labor for third persons, for which compensation is due, does not necessarily establish that she performed it under the act of 1860, upon her separate account."[29] Thus, even after many states had awarded women control of some of their property, legal discourse continued to regard the married woman as a dependent domestic woman.

That the conservative actions of the judiciary reflected much of public opinion at the time is clear from the debate over the Civil Rights Act of 1866. Opponents of the legislation, in an attempt to defeat the bill, pointed out that it would apply to wives, giving women the freedom to make contracts without their husbands and thus threatening the marriage relationship. Republican supporters of the bill were quick to issue disclaimers, asserting that the bill certainly did not apply to wives and emphasizing that the discrimination it spoke of was based only on race. Wives would remain subject to paternal authority. Senator Edgar Cowan denied any other interpretation of the bill: "What was the involuntary servitude mentioned there? . . . Was it the right the husband had to the service of his wife? Nobody can pretend that those things were within the purview of that amendment; nobody believes it."[30]

The common law principle that gave a man the right to his wife's money was the legal fiction that a man and wife were one, and that that one was the husband. This principle also gave him all legal rights to the children. He could make any decisions regarding a child's education without consulting the mother; he could bind a child out as an apprentice without the mother's consent; and he had the right to appoint a person other than the mother as the child's guardian after his death. In cases of divorce or separation, he had "title" to all minor children; the use of the word "title" suggests a child's status as the property of the father.[31] For the most part, little was changed in the nineteenth century with respect to a mother's guardianship of her children. Five states passed laws indicating that in case of divorce or separation, the wife was to be awarded custody of her children if the husband was proved guilty of adultery, cruelty, or desertion. But other states maintained the father as the natural guardian or left it up to the courts. In the first half of the century, however, two principles evolved in the courts that occasionally interfered with the presumption of paternal custody: the concept of judicial discretion and a consideration of the child's interests. Massachusetts was the first state to legislate a change in custody law. In an 1855 amendment to the divorce law, the legislature specified that custody should be decided on the basis of the "happiness and welfare" of the children.[32] The 1860 New York Married Women's Property Act, in addition to its provisions for a wife's property and earnings, made a wife joint guardian of her children, but this section was repealed two years later. The statute was amended to include instead a section preventing a husband from binding out a child as an apprentice or creating a guardian without the mother's written consent.[33] Throughout most of the nineteenth century, the father was the preferred guardian of the children. Cases were decided by the courts on an individual basis, with the opinion being that unless the father were proved guilty of "grossly immoral conduct" or was "wholly unable to provide for the safety and wants of the child," custody would go to the father.[34] By the early twentieth century, considerations of the child's welfare, particularly in the "tender years" (when the mother was nursing the child), led to an increasing tendency to award custody to the mother, but court opinions indicate that the father was still the preferred guardian in most states well into the first quarter of the century.[35]

Just as the law affected all women, the discourse of domesticity had a wide-ranging influence on women, and although it was constructed primarily to apply to middle- and upper-class white women, its effect was felt in varying degrees by all women, regardless of class or race.[36] Although many nineteenth-century women worked for wages, a woman's need to earn money was usually regarded as an unfortunate (and, it was hoped, temporary) necessity—by the society and by the women themselves. As Alice Kessler-Harris points out in *Women Have Always Worked* (1981), societal expectations throughout the nineteenth century (and for more than half of the twentieth century) projected a domestic career for women with an occasional period of outside employment, usually before marriage and only if absolutely necessary: "Up until 1900 less than 20 percent of all women over fourteen were in the paid labor force at any one time. . . . Up until the 1960s, though many women worked for wages at some point in their lives, especially as young adults, the normal expectation was for women to be unpaid housewives."[37]

In the nineteenth century, middle- and upper-class white women were expected to remain in the home, and this image of the proper role for women established the criteria for American Victorian womanhood: domestic, pure, pious, and dependent.[38] Although, as indicated in the Introduction, there are many reasons to question the character and extent, as well as the accuracy, of this construction of women, nevertheless, this was the expectation most commonly expressed in contemporary discourse.[39] It is addressed explicitly in the advice books for women. Samuel K. Jennings, for example, wrote in *The Married Lady's Companion* (1808) that women should follow the teachings of the gospel and submit to their husbands as to God, and William A. Alcott in *The Young Wife* (1837) declared that woman was created to be "man's assistant": "The very act of entering into the married state," he said, required complete "submission."[40] The general opinion was expressed by the *Albany Daily State Register* in 1854, in response to women who had urged the passage of a law giving women equal legal rights in New York:

> People are beginning to inquire how far public sentiment should sanction or tolerate these unsexed women, who make a scoff of religion, who repudiate the Bible and blaspheme God; who would step out from the true sphere of the mother, the wife, and the daughter, and taking upon themselves the duties and the business of men, stalk into the public gaze, and by engaging in the politics, . . . upheave existing institutions, and overturn all the social relations of life.[41]

The ubiquitous nature of the assumption that women should remain dependent and in the home is apparent in the advice that Ralph Waldo Emerson gave at a women's rights convention in Boston in 1855. Woman, he said, was the "Angel in the parlor"; her proper function was to "embellish trifles." Asserting that a true woman would not wish to act for herself, Emerson concluded that if a woman wanted to get anything done, her best recourse was to rely on a "good man": "Woman should find in man her guardian."[42] Aside from Emerson's effrontery in making such a speech to a women's rights convention, the reality, of course, was that some women (those who were single by choice) would not want to take Emerson's advice, and many other women could not take his advice even if they wanted to: they did not have a "good man" to rely on.

It was not only middle- and upper-class women who adopted the goal of "true womanhood." White working-class women also aspired to domesticity as the dominant cultural model for women. The lives of working-class women were less restricted than those of middle- and upper-class women, and, particularly during the antebellum period, such women were often more independent and assertive; nevertheless, the attitude of most working women and their families reflected society's expectations.[43] For example, the grandson of one of the mill girls in a Massachusetts mill town noted that his grandmother "worked fourteen hours a day for fourteen cents an hour for six years"; but, he said (*"proudly*," the interviewer reports), "my grandfather . . . saved [his] money so when he married my grandmother, *she didn't have to work in the mills anymore*" [my italics].[44] The expectation and hope was that after marriage the woman would not have to work anymore—outside the home, that is. And certainly when the alternative was a twelve- to fourteen-hour day and low pay, it is not surprising that women were willing—even eager—to comply with society's expectation if they could. On the other hand, for many working women, complicity with social pressures and distaste for harsh working conditions were complicated by feelings of pleasure at the experience of economic independence. As one factory worker wrote home to her sister in the 1840s, "I feel independent of everyone! The thought that I am living on no one is a happy one indeed to me."[45] The difference, however, reflects the changes observed by Thomas Dublin in his study of New England working women between the early to late nineteenth century, *Transforming Women's Work* (1994). In the 1840s and 1850s, the Yankee farm girls working in the Lowell mills left home and moved into mill-owned boarding houses where they enjoyed a new kind of independence. However, later in the century with the influx of immigrant labor, not only did the competition for jobs reduce the wages, but the women lived at home with their families, where, Dublin notes, their wages were used as part of the household wage: "During the nineteenth century the character of female wage labor underwent a major shift, and work that initially offered women a degree of social and economic independence became more fully integrated within an urban family wage economy."[46]

Many free middle-class black men adopted the white ideal of domesticity as well; an important measure of success for a black man, as for a white man, was the extent to which he could afford to keep his women in the home. Even liberal black leaders who advocated education and other rights for women adamantly insisted that a woman's place was in the home. Martin Delany, for example, asserted that women should work only if forced to by economic necessity; black women who worked for any other reason, he wrote in 1852, were contributing to "the deep degradation of our race."[47] As James Oliver Horton writes in his 1986 study of antebellum gender attitudes among nineteenth-century free blacks, "Black liberation was often defined in terms of the ability of black women and men to become full participants in American life. . . . [This] entailed an obligation to live out the gender ideals of American patriarchal society."[48] Consequently, African American middle-class men sought to privatize their women by adopting the values of the dominant culture.

Given the importance of self-esteem for African American men emerging from the emasculating effects of slavery, and given their desire to counteract nineteenth-century stereotypes of blacks, it is not surprising that many middle-class blacks adopted the dominant culture's concept of aggressive maleness and dependent femininity. Yet as Carla Peterson notes, the ideology of the black male elite was a response to internal colonization, and although it was complicitous with the dominant culture, it also sought to subvert that culture. With respect to women, however, the adoption of white ideology was restricting: black men dominated national institutions and the emigration movement, effectively excluding black women from participation in decisions, emphasizing woman's domestic role, and attempting to "gender blackness as male."[49]

The discourse of domesticity, then, meant an ideal of dependent womanhood, regardless of race or class, and nineteenth-century legal discourse similarly cast women as dependent. Working in tandem with these restricting discourses was the influence of religion. Tradition and the law took women's money away from them; religious opinion erected obstacles against their earning any money of their own. Christian ministers used the Bible to defend the dependent status of women, citing St. Paul: "Wives, submit yourselves unto your own husbands as unto the Lord."[50] Women themselves had no voice in religious authority. As Abby Price pointed out at the Woman's Rights Convention in Syracuse in September 1852, "woman is denied a representation in all Ecclesiastical Assemblies"; "under all forms of religion she has been degraded and oppressed."[51]

American marriage laws derived not only from English common law but also from the Christian religion, which emphasized that the husband

and wife were "one flesh" and that the wife was represented by her husband.[52] In spite of the American emphasis on the separation of church and state, religion was an important factor in law decisions affecting women's legal status throughout the nineteenth century. In an 1845 legal treatise, Edward Deering Mansfield wrote that woman's role in marriage was decreed according to scriptural truth: woman was created for man; husband and wife were one flesh; it was the wife's duty to obey her husband; and the husband had the right to restrain the liberty of his wife: "The *custody* of the wife belongs to the husband. . . . This principle is evidently derived from the Scripture rule."[53] In an 1873 Supreme Court decision, *Bradwell v. Illinois*, when Myra Bradwell was denied admission to the bar (despite the fact that she had already passed the Illinois bar examination), Justice Bradley used religious language to support his opinion that, as a married woman, Bradwell was confined to the domestic sphere by "divine ordinance" and could not practice law: "The paramount destiny and mission of women is to fulfill the noble and benign offices of wife and mother. This is the law of the Creator."[54] That these legal opinions had economic consequences (other than the obvious one that a woman was denied entrance to an economically enabling profession) is apparent from the use of religious language to defeat attempts to pass married women's property laws. At the New York constitutional convention in 1846, for example, New York lawyer Charles O'Conor, in response to reformers' attempts to liberalize the definition of woman's role in marriage, particularly with respect to property rights, declared that marriage was a "sacred ordinance . . . based upon the gospel precept that 'they twain shall be one flesh.'" Consequently, he said, a wife should have "no debasing pecuniary interest apart from the prosperity of her husband."[55]

Religion was also used to keep women from working as public lecturers. When Angelina and Sarah Grimké began giving antislavery lectures in Massachusetts in 1837, the clergy publicly condemned their activities, maintaining that it was immoral and indecent for a woman to speak in public. The ministers published a public rebuke in a pamphlet titled *A Pastoral Letter of the General Association of Congregational Ministers* in 1837, calling for every woman to remain in the home "as becomes the modesty of her sex"; deploring "the mistaken conduct of those who encourage females to bear an obtrusive and ostentatious part in measures of reform, and countenance any of that sex who so far forget themselves as to itinerate in the character of public lecturers and teachers," the ministers warned that such conduct opened the way "for degeneracy and ruin."[56]

Theologians such as Horace Bushnell and John Todd warned of the dangers of women's "unsexing" themselves by pursuing "masculine" activities.[57] In October 1848, in response to the Women's Rights Convention at Seneca Falls earlier that year, the Reverend John W. Nevin wrote in his essay, "Woman's Rights," that the only "right" of woman was "her natural subordination to the headship of man"; any other "freedom," he said, was "monstrous in its very nature."[58] The Reverend Jesse Peck expressed the general opinion of the age regarding women's employment when he declared in an 1853 article entitled "The True Woman" that woman's sphere was exclusively domestic. Women, he said, were not suited for the "rude antagonisms and fierce collisions" of public and professional life; they were "meant for kindlier labor," exercising "delicate sentiment, deep felt sympathy, devout affection, and subduing tenderness."[59]

American Jewish women were subject to the same cultural restrictions as Christian women. As Diane Lichtenstein points out, the ideal of the Jewish woman was that of "the Mother in Israel," whose principal obligation was to her family.[60] This meant a dedication to "home and hearth" and the middle-class ideal of domesticity. Jewish women were "affected by the same social and economic currents that determined the status of the gentile American woman, for the German Jewish community in America, while retaining its Judaism, with seeming ease assimilated the mores, attitudes, and ideological patterns of the rising American middle class."[61] Both Christian and Jewish working-class women had to work for wages, but the middle-class ideal dominated the rhetoric of both religions.

Added to the proscriptions of religious rhetoric were the tenets of medical discourse. On many issues in history, the fields of religion and medicine have found themselves on opposite sides of a question; however, with respect to woman's role, medical opinion in the nineteenth century only confirmed religion's insistence on woman's domestic nature and dependence on man. Part of the reason for this was the opinion of many physicians that a woman's sexual organs were the source of all her ailments. The uterus, wrote Dr. William Dewees in 1843, exercised a "paramount power" over women's physical and moral systems and caused women to be subjected to twice the number of illnesses as men.[62] In the first half of the century, medical procedures tended to be invasive, with leeches, chemicals, and "cauterization" used on the female sexual organs to "cure" all manner of ailments, from, as Ann Douglas Wood wrote, "cancer to cantankerousness."[63] Although both men and women were subjected to harsh treatments, women were particularly vulnerable because of the assumption that their sexual organs were the source of so many physical and mental problems. Later in the century, Dr. George Austin, in *Perils of American Women* (1883), criticized the "mental agony and physical torture" that "thousands of women" had been forced to undergo, but he still held women's sexual organs responsible for numerous ailments; "indigestion, spinal irritation, many forms of neuralgia, headaches, mental irritability, and insanity," he said, were "all largely attributable to some disease of the ovaries."[64] Many doctors also believed that women's ills were the result of "unfeminine" activity. William Byford, for example, wrote in his 1864 treatise on the uterus that neuralgia was caused by the reading of "lascivious books" and too frequent "indulgence" in sexual intercourse.[65]

Particularly threatening to women who sought to engage in what society regarded as "masculine" activities were the dire warnings of respected members of the medical profession later in the century. Medical books claimed that woman's mental and physical structure was too delicate for independent pursuits. Dr. Edward A. Clarke wrote in *Sex in Education* in 1873 that mental effort damaged a woman's reproductive organs and consequently endangered the human species. Among the ills caused by education, he said, were neuralgia, insanity, sterility, and the inability to nurse one's child.[66] Clarke used religion as well as science to make his point that it was dangerous to give women the same education as men: "Identical education of the two sexes," he said, "is a crime before God."[67] Dr. Thomas Emmet, in *Principles and Practices of Gynaecology* (1879), warned that intellectual effort or other "exciting influences" during the onset of puberty impaired women's reproductive capabilities. A young girl, he said, "should be kept a child as long as possible, and made to associate with children. . . . Her mind should be occupied by a very moderate amount of study, with frequent intervals of a few moments each, passed when possible in the recumbent position."[68]

Not only would a woman's mental activity cause a host of ills to the woman herself, prevent conception, and jeopardize the continuation of the species, but a woman's involvement in anything other than domestic activity threatened the health of her children. S. Weir Mitchell designed his famous rest cure for women to enable them to be better mothers. As Mitchell wrote in *Wear and Tear; Or, Hints for the Overworked* (1887), brain work or schooling of more than three or four hours a day made women "sickly and weak," and, he claimed, "the sad inheritance falls upon their offspring." Particularly important were the years between fourteen and eighteen when a girl's sexual organs were developing; mental activity during the "sexual epoch," Mitchell asserted, would injure a girl for life and unfit her "for her duties as a woman."[69] The cure for women's "nervous disorders," he believed, was "absolute rest of the intellect" and "total inactivity"; the woman had to be made to subordinate her will to the doctor, whose will was "enlightened and superior to her own."[70] Such a prescription certainly would enforce the cultural emphasis on women's dependency.

It would be nice to think that the majority of people simply dismissed such medical information as "quack" advice. However, although there were criticisms of Mitchell's rest cure—the most well known of which is Charlotte Perkins Gilman's short story "The Yellow Wallpaper" (1892)— not only was Mitchell famous and highly respected, but his methods persisted into the twentieth century; in fact, the "rest cure" based on Mitchell's methods was practiced on Virginia Woolf from 1904 until her death in 1941.[71] Similarly, although there were protests against such dire warnings as Clarke's, his use of current scientific knowledge gave his book much credence. After the publication of Clarke's *Sex in Education*, women who had previously sought a college education in order to prepare themselves for a professional career found it difficult to persevere in the face of "scientific" evidence that warned them of the disastrous consequences of mental work. As one former student reported many years later, "We did not know when we began whether women's health could stand the strain of education. We were haunted in those days by the clanging chains of that gloomy specter, Dr. Edward Clarke's *Sex in Education*.[72] Clarke's claims were taken very seriously. When his book was first published, two hundred copies were sold in one day at the University of Chicago, and at the University of Wisconsin, which had admitted women students over a decade earlier, the trustees issued a disclaimer in 1877: "Every physiologist is well aware that at stated times, nature makes a great demand upon the energies of early womanhood. . . . It is better that the future matrons of the state should be without university training than that it should be produced at the fearful expense of ruined health."[73]

The message of all this medical advice, of course, was a clear warning to women to stay home. Medical opinion emphasized woman's role as wife and mother and warned against educational pursuits that would prepare a woman for a career alternative to marriage. Interestingly, Clarke's warning in *Sex in Education* did not apply to women factory workers or domestic servants. Their reproductive organs were not damaged in the same way that female students' were, he said, because they did not use their minds.[74] What this meant was that women could safely take jobs in which they were exploited, but they could not train for professional jobs that would make them competitors in the marketplace. Moreover, the enforced confinement to the home implicit in Mitchell's rest cure constitutes an extreme example of domesticity, which can be understood paradigmatically as agoraphobia—fear of the marketplace.[75] Medical science was thus used to enforce cultural strictures against woman's active participation in economic activities outside the home— except in the role of exploited worker.

Like the discourses of true womanhood, the law, religion, and medicine, economic discourse (the discourse of the marketplace itself) defined woman as dependent, whether from the perspective of business or labor. In the marketplace the most offensive infringement upon the rules of female dependency was woman's entrance into the world of business and investment. Women were assumed to be totally lacking in business ability, and any woman who dared to try her hand at finance was subjected to virulent criticism. Part of the reason for this is that the talents required for success in business were traditionally "masculine": aggressiveness and self-assertion. Moreover, it was regarded as vulgar for wom-

en to handle money, and in business and finance, money was in the fore-
front. In other professions a woman could pretend a disinterest in money
or delicately remain uninvolved with the money aspects of her career; a
woman's husband could do the negotiating for her, as, for example,
Calvin Stowe did for Harriet Beecher Stowe.[76] Or her father could accept
the check on her behalf, as Avis's father did for Avis in Elizabeth Stuart
Phelps's *The Story of Avis* (1877). However, there was no way to hide the
fact that the businesswoman or financier was involved in making money.
Of course, the final reason why such a career was particularly offensive
to the patriarchal culture was that it put a woman in a position superior
to men. Woman-as-wage-earner confirmed the gender hierarchy, but
woman-as-employer or money-manager threatened male hegemony.

In 1887 Henry Clews's *Twenty-Eight Years in Wall Street* expressed the
common opinion of women's investment ability: "As speculators, women
have been 'utter failures' "; they have no "real financial capacity" and can
only succeed by "extraordinary luck" or with the help of a man.[77] A
woman who succeeded in the world of finance was not praised in the way
that a successful man would have been. Hetty Green, for example, was a
late-nineteenth-century investor who amassed a fortune through her astute investments; when she died in 1916 she was said to be "the world's
richest woman."[78] Although Green's financial acumen was acknowledged
(she was worth $100 million, or $1.6 billion in 2005), she was criticized
for her "unfeminine" behavior. Known as "the witch of Wall Street," she
was variously called greedy, selfish, calculating, an unnatural woman, and
a "dollar worshiper."[79] Although Green's unconventional behavior certainly contributed to the negative opinion of her (her clothes, her living
arrangements, her prenuptial agreement, her divorce), it was her financial ability that inspired the most severe criticism.

Society's attitude toward a woman who was a successful businesswoman is succinctly described by Fanny Fern. In an 1861 essay, she observed that, unlike a successful businessman, a successful businesswoman was not praised.

> There are few people who speak approbatively of a woman who has a smart
> business talent or capability. No matter how isolated or destitute her condi-
> tion, the majority would consider it more "feminine" would she unobtru-
> sively gather up her thimble, and, retiring into some out-of-the-way place,

gradually scoop out her coffin with it, than to develop that smart turn for business which would lift her at once out of her troubles; and which, in a man so situated, would be applauded as exceedingly praiseworthy.[80]

More complicated is the early-twentieth-century case of Madame C. J. Walker, an African American businesswoman and the first American woman to become a millionaire wholly through her own efforts.[81] Walker began in 1904 with, as she said, a dollar and fifty cents in her pocket. After inventing a substance to prevent hair loss in herself, she developed a line of hair-care products for black women, including the steel hot comb for straightening hair, which superseded more painful methods like the one that had caused her and other women to lose their hair. Walker built up an international hair-preparations empire with her own factories, thousands of sales agents, a thriving mail-order business, beauty schools, and a chain of beauty parlors throughout the United States, the Caribbean, and South America.

Unlike middle-class white businesswomen who were criticized for being unfeminine, Walker was admired for her business prowess. White society did not object if a black woman was "unfeminine," and, for the most part, other African Americans were proud of Walker's accomplishments and encouraged by her example. The difference between cultural attitudes toward Walker's success and the success of white businesswomen underscores the importance of the intersection of race and class with gender identities. As a working-class black woman, Walker was expected to work. Consequently, she herself would not have been inhibited by middle- and upper-class notions of dependent womanhood, and whites and middle-class blacks would not object to her involvement in the marketplace. Criticism of her came from two other sources. First, race-conscious or religious blacks objected to her products for straightening hair, maintaining that she should not attempt to make over the black woman in the image of the white woman or that she should not change what God had created. Second, black businessmen did not want to be eclipsed by a woman. In 1912, for example, Booker T. Washington and other men at the National Negro Business League attempted to prevent Walker from speaking. But she forced her way to the podium and spoke anyway; the following year she was on the program.[82] For the most part, Walker was a source of inspiration and pride in the black community, particularly among black women. She herself encouraged women to enter business: "The girls and women of our race must not be afraid to take hold of business endeavors. . . . [They can] abandon the washtub for a more pleasant and profitable occupation."[83] Clearly, Walker was speaking from the point of view of the woman worker, not the idealized dependent angel in the parlor.

An earlier example of the successful black woman entrepreneur, although on a smaller scale, was Eliza Potter, who in the mid-nineteenth century built up a thriving business as hairdresser to wealthy white women. Functioning as what today would be called an independent contractor, Potter, who was born free in New York around 1820, began as a ladies' maid and nursemaid for what she referred to in her 1859 Franklinesque autobiography, *A Hairdresser's Experience in High Life*, as "people of *ton*."[84] In the 1840s, while working as nursemaid for a judge's family in Cincinnati, she moved with them to Paris, where she learned French, and after a falling out with the cantankerous judge, she went to work for a French countess, taking lessons in the art of hairdressing from "one of the best hair-dressers in Paris" (27). After a short stay in England, she returned to the United States and contracted out as hairdresser, both to individual clients and by appointment at various fashionable watering places. Determining early that without money she would "soon be without friends" (30), she used her talent and business acumen to build up a successful business and, as she said, "got on in the world by a little energy and perseverance" (40).

Potter's career took her from her home base in Cincinnati to Paris, London, New York, New Orleans, Vicksburg, Natchez, Saratoga, and Newport. The tone of her book suggests that she thoroughly enjoyed the pursuit of her business—not only the art of hairdressing and the money she made from it but also the places she went and the people she met. Although she regarded many of her customers as friends, she made clear that her main motivation was economic; as she told one man, "I worked for my patrons for their money" (282). Her talent and reputation enabled her to be choosy about whom she worked for, and she was independent spirited, remarking contemptuously on the way in which some women made "toadies" of themselves. Although she was not an active abolitionist, she spoke out about the cruelties of slavery, ultimately refusing to "come another season to the South to earn money that was made so hard by others" (172). After about fifteen or sixteen years of travel, she settled in Cincinnati, where she taught hairdressing and was much sought-after, with women willing to pay double the price so that they could say they had had their hair done by "Iangy," Potter's professional name (281). Clearly Potter's white customers did not object to her pursuit of a business career. As a working-class black woman, she was not expected by mainstream white society to assume the role of the dependent lady.

Not every woman who needed to earn money could become a successful businesswoman, of course; most working women worked for wages. There were few opportunities for women workers, however, and the pay was considerably lower than it was for men. The seamstress, the millworker, the domestic worker, the orphan, the widow, the wife or daughter of a poor man or a man who either could not work or who dissipated his family's money—all of these women, black and white, and of every class, found themselves with few options. If a woman had sufficient education and the correct manners, she could find a post as a teacher, a governess, or a paid or unpaid companion. Otherwise, her choices included work at subsistence wages as a seamstress, shopgirl, domestic servant, or factory operative; humble dependency as an unpaid servant in the home of a relative; or a place outside society as a sexual worker.

If traditional American society provided little help for working women, working-class organizations were equally hostile. After a flurry of activity among organized working women in the 1830s, women were increasingly closed out of the labor movement. Organized labor worked primarily to protect the interests of working-class men. In 1835 the National Trades' Union voted to oppose women's labor, and in 1836 it asserted that women's manufacturing work was "highly injurious to the best interests of the working classes." The reason for this, the men claimed, was that when women worked, they undercut men's wages and took jobs away from men; women would be better off, they said, if men received a "family wage" so that they could keep their women at home "to perform the duties of the household."[85] This reasoning, like Emerson's in 1855, assumed that every woman would have a "good man" to take care of her. But men were not only worried about their jobs. Another

concern was sexual freedom and the threat of immorality posed by independent workingwomen. When women work in factories, the National
Trades' Union warned in 1836, "their morals frequently depart."[86] Other
reasons that have been suggested to explain the exclusion of women
from the labor movement include the unemployment following the economic downturns; the introduction into the labor movement of immigrant workers with Old World ideas of "woman's place"; traditional ideas
about women's limited capabilities; the adoption by working people of
middle-class ideals of "true womanhood"; and the perception that
women's employment was only "temporary."[87] Another reason, particularly important for this study, was the increasing recognition that legal
means could be sought to gain labor reforms; since women could not
vote or hold office, they were excluded from the process. In the 1840s
and 1850s, for example, when Massachusetts workers began to appeal to
legislators to institute the ten-hour day and workers gave their support
to political candidates who were sympathetic to the concept, women,
who had been active in the labor movement, were increasingly left out.
Whereas the Lowell strikes in the 1830s were planned and executed
primarily by women, in the 1850s the leaders of the Ten-Hour Movement
in Lowell were all men—even though seventy-five percent of the Lowell
millworkers were women.[88] When the otherwise inclusive Industrial
Congress was formed in 1850, it did not include any women.

According to Christine Stansell, "By 1860, the possibilities of women's
trade unionism, evident in the 1830s, had disappeared."[89] The short-lived
National Labor Union in 1868 and the Knights of Labor in 1878 came out
in favor of "equal pay for equal work,"[90] but the craft unions kept women
shut out. By 1873 there were more than thirty national unions, but wom-
en were members of just two—and those two admitted women only reluctantly and with various restricting caveats after unsuccessful attempts
to drive women out of the trades altogether.[91] In 1898 the leader of the
New York Working Women's Society pointed out that because of the
unions' refusal to admit women, there were 40,000 working women in
New York City whose wages were so low that in order to survive they
had to resort to charity "or worse."[92] In 1900 women petitioned the
American Federation of Labor, complaining that they were being kept
out of the trade unions, but the A. F. of L. leaders justified the exclusion

on the grounds that women did not enter the workforce "permanently."[93] Although A. F. of L. president Samuel Gompers appointed several women to leadership positions, the affiliate unions either refused to admit women members or made women feel unwelcome and obtained inferior wages for them. A. F. of L. leaders testified before Congress that women "were not qualified" to work outside the home, and Gompers himself asserted that women belonged in the home and should work only if absolutely necessary.[94] Even some female labor leaders accepted the spheres binary. Leonora Barry, who traveled throughout the country lecturing and organizing for the Knights of Labor in the 1880s, believed that woman's natural place was in the home and asserted that "man should be the breadwinner."[95] In the discourse of the marketplace, women were regarded as inherently dependent; their entrance into the labor force was not regarded as "permanent" because it was assumed that they would or should soon leave to be supported by a man.

As Meredith Tax points out in *The Rising of the Women* (1980), the principal allies of working-class women were not working-class men but other women: middle-class reformers, settlement house workers, feminists, and socialist housewives.[96] Mary Kenney, a Chicago wage earner who had determined early that women needed to organize to protect themselves, pursued an independent course attempting to organize women workers in the 1880s; her main support came from Jane Addams at Hull House.[97] In 1892 Gompers appointed Kenney as an organizer for the A. F. of L., but despite her many successes, she was fired after six months, the executive board having concluded that it did not want to spend the money on organizing women.[98]

Not only did organized labor discriminate against women, but American Marxists did not help the cause of women either. The Marxists adopted the same values as bourgeois society with respect to women, idealizing woman in her domestic role. As Mari Jo Buhle points out in *Women and American Socialism, 1870–1920* (1981), the Marxists used "scientific" principles to reaffirm woman's traditional role.[99] Commenting on the devastation of the proletarian family by the exploitation of labor, Marx and Engels in *The Communist Manifesto* (1848) stressed the importance of "family ties."[100] As Buhle notes, the German American Socialists, influenced by Marx and by their own romantic view of woman, did not support women's rights (women's right to labor or to vote) and saw it as their duty to "protect woman's domestic role."[101] American Socialist Adolf Douai wrote in 1878 that "one of the most beautiful aims of Socialism was the restoration of family unity," and European Socialist Ferdinand Lassalle praised the "coziness" and "poetry of domestic life."[102] Ironically, this socialist romanticization of domesticity is not unrelated to the conservative emphasis on "family values" in the late twentieth and early twenty-first centuries: the aim of both campaigns is to secure women in the home as a means of effecting a political agenda. The issue of women and Marxism in the United States came to a head in 1872 with the ouster of New York's Section 12 from the Socialist Party because of its focus on women's rights. Obtaining the go-ahead from Marx, American Socialist Friedrich Sorge ousted the offending group, he said, in order to "purge" the party of middle-class "reformers" who were concerned with "women's emancipation and the right to vote."[103]

Although organized labor and Marxist Socialists did not encourage women's economic independence, there were socialist and reformist movements that explicitly advocated it. Laurence Gronlund, an independent American socialist, wrote in his 1884 book *The Co-operative Commonwealth* that in a socialist society the wife should be "invested with the potentiality of economic independence of her husband." However, although theoretically he maintained that economic equality was necessary in marriage, he concluded that most women would not work outside the home unless they were single or divorced, and he carefully differentiated between what he considered to be masculine and feminine employment (women, he said, were different from men intellectually and physiologically and were not suited for "men's" jobs).[104]

More egalitarian was Edward Bellamy's utopian novel, *Looking Backward*, published in 1888. Bellamy portrayed a future society in which women were economically independent; as one character comments, "That any person should be dependent for the means of support upon another would be shocking." Bellamy's book was a best-seller and provided a catalyst for women activists who founded a collectivist movement based on the ideas of political and economic equality outlined by Bellamy.[105] Other cooperative movements that were led by women also advocated women's economic independence. Such groups included those of Melusina Pierce in the late 1860s; Mary Livermore and Helen Campbell in the 1880s; and Marie Howland, 1874–1885. However, the ideas of these reformers were often utopian and did not gain a large following. Also, some of them were made unpopular by their inclusion of free-love principles.[106]

The discourse regarding women's sexuality was in fact the most difficult issue for women to deal with. In common thought, the concept of woman's economic independence was associated with sexual promiscuity; the independent woman was thought to be an immoral woman. Even so liberal a man as Robert Bonner, the editor of the *New York Ledger*, who was sympathetic to women's issues, was unable to separate women's economic independence from ideas of sexual promiscuity and antimaternal feelings. "Transplant" woman from the home to the marketplace, he wrote in an editorial in 1859, and she becomes a "monster, a man-woman." "The so-called 'strong-minded women' of the day," said Bonner, are women "with their own 'independent' platform, self-condemned as infidels, as contemners [*sic*] of marriage and its obligations, as the advocates of the 'largest liberty' in the indulgence of the passions."[107]

This, then, was the problem for nineteenth-century women: their culture associated women's independence, particularly economic independence, with sexual promiscuity and immorality; at the same time, however, their culture insisted upon female purity. Even to get oneself talked about was dangerous for a woman. For this reason, it was risky for a woman to advocate women's economic independence. Just as the term *communist* was damning in the 1950s and the associations given to the word *liberal* in more recent presidential campaigns put liberals on the defensive, so negative associations with the concept of women's economic independence forced nineteenth-century women either to deny any interest in the idea or to defend themselves against its pejorative associations. For the most part, American women writers in the nineteenth century either agreed with or did not try to resist this discursive construction of gender. The price was too high. It was not only that they would be labeled unfeminine or unwomanly but also that they would be labeled immoral.

Many nineteenth-century American women writers began writing as a "respectable" means of earning an income, and many novels portrayed a heroine who, finding herself in straitened circumstances, was able to earn her own living. In most novels, however, the heroine's work was regarded as a stopgap measure, necessary only to fill the years between childhood and marriage. Once the heroine found a man, she gladly gave up her job, and with it her independence, for what most readers would have agreed was her proper profession, wifehood and motherhood. This is the story in some of the most popular mid-nineteenth-century novels by women, for example, in Susan Warner's *Queechy* (1852), Maria Cummins's *The Lamplighter* (1854), and Augusta Evans Wilson's *St. Elmo* (1866).

Ironically, most women writers did not advocate economic independence for women even when they themselves were economically independent. Although they had in their personal lives often adopted the role of principal breadwinner for their families, in their fiction they continued to portray domesticity as the only acceptable goal for women. Why? It is possible that they did not believe it themselves but were astute enough to know that if they wanted to get their books published, and if they wanted to sell their books, they could not risk seeming to advocate what the public regarded as immoral or improper for women. Not only would such writing jeopardize their reputations as respectable women, but it would jeopardize their sales. Moreover, the two were connected: publishers for the most part would not publish, and the public would not buy, books by a woman who was regarded as immoral.

In order to understand just how important it was for nineteenth-century women writers to conform to public standards of morality and feminine propriety, one only has to look at how those standards shaped women's literary output and in some cases affected their careers. Kate Chopin, for example, found a ready market for her short stories in national magazines as long as they did not transgress the code of convention. After the 1899 publication of her novel *The Awakening*, which contained the sympathetic portrayal of a woman whose search for personal autonomy led her to commit adultery and leave her husband and children, she published only a few stories, and none with the kind of theme that had caused many reviewers to attack her and her novel as "immoral." In an essay written in 1900 she was careful to present herself as a conventional matron who preferred "wholesome" writing to coarse works that made for "unpleasant reading."[108] Chopin never published in her lifetime an even more radical work like "The Storm," which legit-imized female adultery and sexual pleasure. Lydia Maria Child's career as a popular writer was similarly impacted by her publication of a work that was considered radical and improper for a woman to write. Child was the author of two successful novels and the founder of the first children's pe-riodical, the *Juvenile Miscellany*. In 1833, however, she published the pam-phlet *An Appeal in Favor of That Class of Americans Called Africans*, one of the first antislavery books in the United States. After the publication of this "radical" text, people would no longer buy her books or subscribe to her children's magazine.[109] That some women writers deliberately modified their writing to conform to social prescriptions of femininity is apparent in the career of Caroline Kirkland. After the criticism she re-ceived for her outspoken and unconventional satire in *A New Home, Who'll Follow?* (1839), Kirkland toned down her writing and even went out of her way to establish her propriety by criticizing other women writers whom she regarded as imprudent. When her husband died in 1846, she was able to support herself and her children by her writing and editing, but she deliberately suppressed her private voice and, as she said, always wrote within the "restraints" of a "lady."[110]

It is clear, then, that women writers who transgressed the conven-tional code of behavior for "respectable" women risked losing the ability to earn a living from their writing. In any case, whether out of fear or conviction (and my guess is that it was a little of both), most women writers reiterated the dominant discourse. If a writer did introduce the idea of woman's economic independence into an occasional work, the situation was usually particularized in that work. For example, Rose Terry Cooke's "How Celia Changed Her Mind" (1891) portrays an "old maid" who finds that the independence of "single blessedness" is prefer-able to marriage to a tightfisted man, and Constance Fenimore Wool-son's "Miss Grief" (1880) illustrates the contrast between a less talented but financially successful male writer and a woman writer who cannot make a living from her superior but unmarketable writing. For the most part, women writers did not take a sustained stand in defense of woman's economic autonomy. Even when they themselves were economically in-dependent, they did not publicly advocate such a role for women.

Nowhere is this paradox more evident than in the example of one of the most influential "career women" of the nineteenth century, Sarah Josepha Hale, the editor of *Godey's Lady's Book*. Left a widow with five children in 1822, Hale supported herself for the remainder of her life, but in her columns she glorified women's domestic role. Throughout her life she maintained that men and women were confined to divinely appointed separate spheres; women's moral and religious purity necessitated that they remain in the domestic sphere. In 1848 she wrote in *Godey's* that a woman's "work" was "in the family or the social circle," and in 1852, she told women to remain at home as "guardians of whatsoever is good, pure, and lovely."[111] Although Hale supported women's education and urged that more job opportunities be open to women, she opposed votes for women and regarded women's employment as an option only for women who did not have a husband to rely on. She emphasized that women should be educated not for their own improvement but in order to become better wives and mothers.[112]

Although most women writers reified conventional notions of gender, there were some women writers who had struggled to support themselves and who publicly asserted the need for economic independence for women. Their realization derived in part from a recognition of the plurality of gender identity. Fracturing gender revealed intersections with other identities as well as gender—identities of race, class, and sexuality, for example. Generalizations about gender became impossible when one considered the differences of class or race. Although middle-class men like Emerson might comfortably assert the ideal of male protection of women, women writers who themselves had to work recognized the fatuousness of ideas like Emerson's. The fact was that men could not be counted on to protect women, particularly women whom they regarded as their racial or social inferiors. In fact, such women were fair game for sexual and economic exploitation by men. By pointing out the different treatment that women receive when they do not have money and/or are racially vulnerable, women writers—for example, Fanny Fern in *Ruth Hall* (1855), E. D. E. N. Southworth in *The Hidden Hand* (1859), Harriet Wilson in *Our Nig* (1859), Harriet Jacobs in *Incidents in the Life of a Slave Girl* (1861), Rebecca Harding Davis in *Margret Howth* (1861), and Frances Harper in *Iola Leroy* (1892)—called attention to the fallacies inherent in the myth of male protection of women. Moreover,

by demonstrating that many women needed to work but that job opportunities were severely limited, they called attention to the gender and
race of American individualism: white male Americans could hope to
better themselves by self-reliance and seek the American Dream, but
women were left out of the equation.

The construction of women as financially dependent ensured the
maintenance of patriarchal capitalism, and the association of female independence with immorality was an insidious way of preventing women
from attempting to change the status quo. In fact, the woman who was
able to assert publicly the need for women's economic independence often already had a blighted reputation or for some reason was regarded by
her society as ineligible for inclusion in the ranks of "true womanhood."
Like Madame C. J. Walker, who was an African American working-class
woman, or Fanny Fern, whose husband had already smeared her name
with false accusations of adultery, or Charlotte Perkins Gilman, who had
been demonized in the Hearst papers for leaving her husband and giving
up her child, women who spoke out in favor of women's economic independence often were able to do so only because they already had nothing
to lose.

chapter three

ECONOMICS AND THE AMERICAN RENAISSANCE WOMAN

WARNER, SOUTHWORTH, STOWE, CUMMINS, AND FERN

Although the majority of women writers did not advocate woman's economic independence, economics was a major factor in almost all of their works. This chapter looks at some of the most well known novels of the nineteenth century. Like F. O. Matthiessen in his influential 1941 study of nineteenth-century American literature, I confine myself here to texts published between 1850 and 1855, the period that Matthiessen designated the "American Renaissance."[1] Like Matthiessen, I also focus on five writers whose works I believe express the spirit of America at the time. As in Matthiessen's work too, the writers that I discuss in this chapter are white and middle class, and they are all of the same gender. However, unlike Matthiessen, whose five writers were all men (Emerson, Thoreau, Whitman, Hawthorne, and Melville), I consider only women writers. That this difference in gender radically changes the discursive focus of the works is due, I believe, not to any inherent differences in gender but to the legal and economic inequalities of the period. Whereas most of the male writers during this period wrote "romances" or were concerned with self-exploration, women writers during the same period were primarily concerned with practical social issues. Of particular importance to women writers was the question of economics: money, finance, and survival. The works I discuss here include Susan Warner,

The Wide, Wide World (1850); E. D. E. N. Southworth, *The Deserted Wife* (1850); Harriet Beecher Stowe, *Uncle Tom's Cabin* (1852); Maria Cummins, *The Lamplighter* (1854); and Fanny Fern, *Ruth Hall* (1855). These texts were among the most well known and most influential works of the period, yet all of them were dismissed by Matthiessen in his twentieth-century portrait of an "American Renaissance."[2] And they remained invisible throughout most of the twentieth century as literary critics, following Matthiessen's lead, focused primarily on male writers and self-exploration.[3]

All of these nineteenth-century women writers fractured the nineteenth-century concept of gender by entering the marketplace and by portraying in their novels the importance of economics for women. Subverting the cultural definition of female identity, they asserted a new economic identity for women—in their personal achievement of monetary success and/or in their portrayal of female characters who were involved in economic concerns and who, in some cases, achieved their own economic independence.

The dominant theme in all of these books is economics. The realistic struggle for survival portrayed in the works by midcentury women writers makes the posturing of an Emerson, Thoreau, or Whitman look almost ludicrous and underscores a serious omission in the romances of Hawthorne and Melville. Emerson, from the sanctuary of his private study in his comfortable home (which he had purchased with his wife's money), and Thoreau, who lived all of his life in his parents' home, had the luxury and the leisure to ponder issues of self-exploration—a luxury and a leisure that one does not have when one is struggling to survive. Although some critics have correctly identified connections between economics and these male-authored works not ostensibly "about" economics, the difference is that the concerns referred to in the works of midcentury male writers are a question of representation, not starvation. In their works, the women writers were dealing with practical economic concerns, whereas if economics enters the works of the male writers, it is generally through metaphor or abstraction.[4] Women writers (and working-class men) or their characters who themselves experienced the hardship of not knowing where the money would come from to keep

a roof over their heads were not in a position to deride the "imprisonment" of home ownership or the "encumbrance" of having a steady job,
as Thoreau does when he calls upon all men to "live free and uncommit-
ted."[5] Nor were women who were mothers and culturally defined as chief
caretakers for ailing family members in a position to cavalierly dismiss
the demands that children and other relatives might make upon them, as
Emerson does in "Self Reliance."[6]

The principal difference between the women's texts I discuss in this
chapter and the works by the male writers in Matthiessen's *American Renaissance* is the down-to-earth realism of the women's texts. Like legal
narratives, where a lawyer's persuasiveness depends upon his/her ability
to situate a client's story within the context of a familiar frame of reference (one that the jury will find "believable"), the fictional texts'
verisimilitude depends upon the reader's familiarity with the rhetorical
structure used and the situations portrayed. As Michael Riffaterre
points out, the realism of a text depends on how comfortably it fits into
"ready-made narrative and descriptive models that reflect a group's idea
of or consensus about reality."[7] The descriptions in these novels chronicled recognizable events and actions, particularly for women readers.
Moreover, many of the midcentury writers used the language of sentiment to describe familiar scenes and emotions, thus placing the narrative within a familiar genre. As Lauren Berlant points out in her 1992
essay, "The Female Woman: Fanny Fern and the Form of Sentiment,"
sentimental discourse established a wide audience of women, regardless
of race or class, and even though, as she noted, such hierarchical differences need to be addressed, female sentimental discourse itself "served
as a structure of consent" in which women found a "collective identity."[8]
In this respect, the language of sentiment reflected in many novels by
women might be compared to a kind of national consciousness-raising
discourse which, whether it was to be used politically or privately, gave
utterance to common experiences that women in isolation could recognize as more than one woman's experience. Not only do the women's
texts discussed in this chapter situate their stories within a familiar
genre and provide a mimetic reflection of everyday actions and events
that would have been familiar to the authors' contemporaries, but they

also manifest psychological realism in their portrayal of the motivations and/or emotional tensions that would have been part of many women's experiences.

Jane Tompkins, in her discussion of *Uncle Tom's Cabin* and *The Wide, Wide World*, has identified Christian mythology as a universal frame in these texts, maintaining that sentimental novels fit into the "order of things" structured by spiritual narratives of redemption and conversion with which the readers were already familiar from such sources as evangelical religion, the American Tract Society, and the McGuffey Readers.[9] Her analysis may work for these two novels, but it is not applicable to all midcentury novels by women, certainly not to Southworth's *The Deserted Wife* or Fern's *Ruth Hall*. Although Christianity was a given in much of the fiction, and the female protagonist sometimes relied upon religious beliefs for guidance or found them a comfort in times of stress, the question of conversion was seldom at issue, and some of these writers used religion in ways that were counter to the conversion narrative.[10] More important were the common secular narratives that reflected the reality of a majority of nineteenth-century women's lives, regardless of class or race: everyday events like shopping; the preparation of food; the care of children; concerns about money; dealing with death, particularly the death of a young child; and most significantly, the overarching situation of gendered powerlessness. These are the "ready-made narratives" that would have been familiar to most women readers. In fact, as Nina Baym points out in her pioneering work, *Woman's Fiction* (1978), even the tears in novels like Susan Warner's *The Wide, Wide World* were an important aspect of that realism. Although the tears might seem excessive to modern readers, for powerless nineteenth-century women, says Baym, tears were a "safe expression" of emotions like "anger and frustration" that were considered "unfeminine" and consequently forbidden to women in their culturally prescribed role of passive acquiescence.[11] Although the degree of powerlessness varied depending on a woman's class or race, all women were subject to restrictive laws. Certainly there were variations of powerlessness; one cannot say that the midcentury upper-class white woman was powerless in the same way that her domestic servants or slaves were. However, no matter how tyrannical she might have been over her servants or how privileged she was, she did not have real power: the law gave her husband ownership of any money or property she might have and allowed her no voice in legal or governmental decisions.[12] The effect of this powerlessness on women can be compared to what Wendy Brown calls the "woundedness" of the liberal subject, which is the result of the contradiction between supposed equality and substantive equality and is "expressed as feelings of powerlessness."[13]

One of the most important aspects of midcentury women writers' realism was a focus on the question of money—the lack of money, how a person acquired money, how it was spent, and (when money was short) how much things cost. Such concerns would have resonated with mid-nineteenth-century women readers, particularly married women, who, regardless of class, were legally barred from having money of their own—with the exception of a few upper-class women whose fathers had set up an equity trust for them. It is significant that American realism as a genre began with economically powerless women in the midcentury and was only taken up by male writers later in the century when the economic powerlessness of working-class men became an issue. For example, it was not until after a series of well-publicized, massive, and often violent strikes had called the nation's attention to issues of class conflict and economic exploitation that male writers in any numbers began to write realistic fiction dealing with money issues.[14]

In contrast, money is hardly mentioned in most of the works by antebellum male writers. Money was important for Hawthorne and Melville, who had to work to support their families. In some of their works—*The House of the Seven Gables* or *Moby-Dick*, for example—money is an issue for some of the characters: Hepzibah opens a cent-shop, and the hardworking sailors in Melville's tale are awed by the gold doubloon that Ahab nails to the mast. But money is not central to the characters' struggles. Emerson was preoccupied with money early in life: his family was poor after his father's death, he had to work for a living, and—in a callous display of fortune-hunting avarice—he refused to marry his first wife, Ellen Tucker, until she agreed to have her father's will revoked to give her husband complete control of her considerable fortune. All of Emerson's money problems were over once he married the tubercular Ellen, who died eighteen months after the wedding. He inherited her money when she died, and her death enabled him to quit his job as a minister—a "compensation" that he later referred to with pleasure.[15] His own money problems thus solved, he could afford to ignore economics in his writings, where he dealt primarily with abstractions. Thoreau, too, did not have to worry about money. In *Walden* he gives an account of his expenses, but they are hardly realistic ones, considering that the land was loaned to him rent-free by Emerson and he could go home to his parents or to the Emersons' every day for dinner. Moreover, unlike many women writers, he was wholly "unencumbered" by the need to support a family and children.[16] Whitman did not have to support a family either, although he did have to support himself, and he worked, first as a schoolteacher and then as a journalist; however, he was a notorious freeloader, and as he wrote in *Leaves of Grass*, he liked to "loafe at my ease"—in which "occupation" he was enabled by his mother and sisters, who allowed him to live rent-free while they cooked for him.[17] In his writings, the common people that he praises never seem to be suffering from economic exploitation or want; he eulogizes them for their "local color" interest and romanticizes the panorama of people the way another poet would a varied landscape, listing the "woolly-pates" working in the sugar field, the "Yankee girl" working in the factory, the "drunkard," the "opium eater," and the "prostitute" with her "tipsy and pimpled neck." Without comment on or a recognition of the suffering of these "others," he appropriates their "color" for his own use and concludes optimistically (and arrogantly), "And of these one and all I weave the Song of Myself."[18]

In three of the works under discussion here, the woman author is writing from personal experience; the struggle for economic survival is her own struggle. The autobiographical basis for the novels increases the poignancy of the economic theme and helps to explain why money was so important for the authors. Susan Warner's *The Wide, Wide World* reflects Warner's own family's loss of money and the hardships that came with that loss. Southworth's *The Deserted Wife* reflects her own experience when her husband deserted her, leaving her and her children in poverty. And Fanny Fern's *Ruth Hall* is based on her own experiences after her husband died in debt and her family refused to help her and her two children. Harriet Beecher Stowe did not experience the impoverishment of these three authors, but her husband, Calvin Stowe, was not a practical man, and the births of seven children one after another left the family in constant need of the money she could earn from her writing. Of the five women authors discussed in this chapter, only Maria Cummins had no money worries; her father was a judge, and Cummins, who never married, lived at home with her family all of her life.[19]

Not only is economics a dominant theme in all of these novels by women, but economic matters are the moving force behind the action in the novel. In each case the catalyst for the action is the lack of money. The money is lost because of what I call the three *d*'s: death, desertion, or disaster. In *The Wide, Wide World* and in *Uncle Tom's Cabin*, the action of the novel results from economic disaster: Mr. Montgomery and Mr. Shelby have lost a great deal of money, and it is this loss of money that forces the ensuing events. In *The Deserted Wife* Hagar is deserted by her husband and left without money and with two children and a third on the way. In *The Lamplighter* the action ensues after the death of Gerty's mother in the home of slum-dweller Nan Grant, who drives the child out into the street. And in *Ruth Hall* the action follows the death of Harry Hall, whose death leaves Ruth impoverished with two children to support.

What is most important about the loss of money in these novels—as in many women's lives at the time—is that the loss of money takes place without the female protagonist's knowledge of how it happens *and* she has no power to prevent it. It happens to her; she doesn't make it happen. In *The Wide, Wide World*, when Ellen's father loses his money, Ellen questions her mother, but her mother is wholly ignorant of her husband's business affairs.[20] In *Uncle Tom's Cabin* Mrs. Shelby does not know anything about her husband's debts, so that when he tells her he has sold Tom and Eliza's son, she is shocked. Her husband has made unwise investments and is in danger of losing everything—including her home— yet Mrs. Shelby is "entirely ignorant" of his financial affairs.[21] Moreover, although she opposes the sale of the slaves, she is powerless to stop it. Similarly, Ruth Hall has no understanding of Harry's business problems until after he dies and his creditors take everything, and Hagar, in *The Deserted Wife*, believes that her husband is wealthy until he abandons her, and the house and all of its contents are sold to pay his creditors.

In all of these novels by women, even though the female characters do not control the economic framework, they feel its impact. Culturally constructed as powerless and dependent, with proscriptions against entering the marketplace, the female character finds herself in dire economic straits. An important theme in all of these novels is that, although her culture excludes her from economic realities, the woman is part of them anyway. Despite her cultural exclusion, she is *de facto* very much a part of the economic picture, whether she knows anything about it or not. It is this fact that the women novelists assert. They differ in their solutions and attitudes to the problem, but they all call attention to the big lie that constructed women as outside the money economy yet made them equally vulnerable to economic shifts of fortune.

Scholars who have discussed women's "complicity" with capitalism have focused on middle- and upper-class women's comfortable domesticity and have tended to overlook the frequency with which that domesticity was disrupted by economic disaster or the price that many women had to pay for it. Such realities are underscored in the court cases I researched, many of which reveal the economic and legal vulnerability of women. In each of the novels under study in this chapter, economic developments have a life-changing impact upon the characters. In *The Wide, Wide World* Ellen and her mother are separated, Ellen is sent to live with her aunt, and her mother dies. In *The Deserted Wife* Hagar Churchill must learn to support herself and her three children or starve. In *Uncle Tom's Cabin* Mrs. Shelby experiences a dramatic realization about the wrongs of slavery, Tom and Harry are sold, and Tom is separated from his family and ultimately killed by Simon Legree. In *The Lamplighter* Gerty is an abused child for five years until she is taken in by the old lamplighter. And in *Ruth Hall* Ruth is thrust into poverty, shunned by her former friends, separated from one of her children, and struggles to support herself. This chapter looks at each of these novels, exploring the economic discourse in the texts and the authors' varying conclusions regarding the question of woman's economic involvement.

In 1850, the year that saw the publication of Hawthorne's *The Scarlet Letter* and Emerson's *Representative Men*, Susan Warner's first novel was published. The sales for *The Wide, Wide World* were "unprecedented"; except for *Uncle Tom's Cabin*, it was the "most famous and popular book of the day."[22] Warner's novel is particularly important for its realism; Henry

James compared her use of realistic detail to that of French realist Gustave Flaubert.[23] Warner meticulously portrays the details of common everyday events: shopping, eating, preparing food. And an important part of those details is the focus on money. From the beginning of the novel, money is established as a central concern. The first sentence of the novel raises the specter of economic disaster: "Mamma," the child Ellen asks her mother, "what was that I heard papa saying to you this morning about his lawsuit?" (1:9). Two pages later, Ellen's mother, Mrs. Montgomery, tells Ellen that her father has lost the lawsuit and hints at what it will mean: "This lawsuit, Ellen, has brought upon us more trouble than I ever thought a lawsuit could" (1:11). For Ellen and her mother, the "trouble" means that Ellen and her beloved mother will be separated forever. The germ of the novel, then, focuses on the question of how women's lives were impacted by economic forces over which they had no control: the flux of the market, a man's business failure, and the vagaries of the law courts.[24]

Susan Warner (1819–1885) had experienced a similar shift in fortune in her own life, and a brief look at her experiences shows us how closely related are some of the true-life stories of women writers, their fiction, and the court cases in terms of the impact of economic reversals on women's lives. When Warner was in her teens, her father lost most of his money in a series of lawsuits following the Panic of 1837. The family had to give up their fashionable home in New York City and move to an isolated farmhouse on Constitution Island. This sudden loss of money and status diminished the Warner sisters' marriageability, thus closing off the principal career option open to women of their class. Several years later, when Henry Warner was unable to pay the mortgage on his remaining property, they had to sell all of their furniture at a public sale. Warner's sister Anna, in her 1852 novel *Dollars and Cents*, which chronicles the financial ruin of a family patterned after the Warners, describes how the family watched "like mice in a cage of rattlesnakes" while the appraiser priced their possessions to be auctioned off.[25]

Like the Warner sisters, who had no consciousness of money until their father lost his fortune, and like many of the women in the court cases who were brought into court after a husband or father died or became entangled in legal problems, Ellen's mother finds that economic ignorance is no protection from the consequences of economic disaster. Like other middle- and upper-class women of the time, who were conditioned to believe that a concern for money was vulgar, Mrs. Montgomery prides herself on the fact that she does not know anything about her husband's business affairs. As she says to Ellen, "I am not apt to concern myself overmuch about the gain or the loss of money. I believe my Heavenly Father will give me what is good for me" (1:11). She does not know what the lawsuit is about nor even what kind of business will take her husband to Europe. She describes the latter to Ellen in vague terms: "He has agreed to go soon on some government or military business to Europe" (1:11). Although Warner does not criticize Mrs. Montgomery's ignorance of money matters, and the novel's spiritual theme seems to endorse her transcendence of such concerns, the novel provides a graphic illustration of the manner in which money-ignorant women were nevertheless a part of the market economy.

Once the money has been lost, Mrs. Montgomery is thrust into an awareness of money matters, and the focus of the first few chapters is on how she and Ellen cope with that new awareness. Mrs. Montgomery wants to provide her daughter with a bible and other items before she has to leave her. When she tells Ellen that she wants to buy her a bible, Ellen's response reflects the new situation. "But Mamma," she says, "I thought you couldn't afford it." Mrs. Montgomery replies, "I will find ways and means" (1:29). Mr. Montgomery will give his wife only a small amount of money, however, just enough for clothing that is absolutely necessary. Moreover, he is not a man whose will can be challenged, and his wife knows "better than to ask for a further supply" of money (1:33–34). Instead, she sells her mother's ring and takes her daughter on a clandestine shopping expedition that is recorded in great detail. Mrs. Montgomery's lack of money of her own and her timidity about asking her husband for any reflect the reality of the average nineteenth-century woman's life, one that is described by many nineteenth-century women writers, who tell of the humiliation suffered by women as they are forced to plead for money for necessities from a husband who uses his control of money as a means of asserting his power. Thus, Fanny Fern writes in the *New York Ledger* in 1856 of how a husband will require his wife to provide the "household stores" but then inquire of her "how she spent the surplus shilling of yesterday's appropriation."[26] It is a mistake to assume that nineteenth-century women had an easy command of money, as is sometimes implied in studies of consumerism. Some did, but the average woman was dependent upon her husband's good will for any money that she had access to. In writing of consumerism, Lori Merish, in *Sentimental Materialism*, mistakenly assumes that mid-nineteenth-century women had access to their own money because of the passage of Married Women's Property Acts.[27] However, as I indicated in chapter 2, before the Civil War only four states had Earnings Acts (including New York in 1860) that gave a woman control of her own earnings. Property Acts passed earlier applied only to property that a woman inherited and thus only benefited some wealthy women. Moreover, for the most part, the acts were not retroactive (the retroactive section in New York's 1848 statute was ruled unconstitutional the following year) and thus did not apply to women who were already married.

The pages that describe Ellen's shopping trip with her mother represent another aspect of the book's focus on economic issues—not the traditional economics of market production but the economics of the individual consumer. The realism of these descriptions is contained in their reflection of what would have been a recognizable experience for many contemporary women: the difficulty of obtaining money of their own and the consequent necessity for careful decision-making. Instead of simply telling us what Mrs. Montgomery bought her daughter or showing the child happily opening her gifts, Warner walks the reader through the *process* of the selection itself. The author describes the characters' careful selection of each item, portraying the way in which they weigh and consider the many criteria—practical, aesthetic, emotional—that contribute to their decisions. The first stop, after Mrs. Montgomery has sold her ring, is a bookstore, where Ellen is to select a bible. The detailed description of Ellen's difficult decision as she considers the many bibles on display, along with her mother's practical advice, constitutes a lesson in the art of careful spending.

At the same time, however, the act of shopping is not portrayed as superficial or trivial, as in the modern image of a stereotypical trip to the shopping mall—an image that falsely divorces shopping from other aspects of a person's life. This is not carefree consumerism. Instead, the author weaves together the details of the shopping itself with a multiplicity of other facets of the characters' lives: the difficulty of obtaining the money, the relationship between Ellen and her mother, and a portrayal of the pain and conflicted feelings that affect them. For example, when Ellen realizes that Mrs. Montgomery has sold her mother's ring, she is distressed: "'Mamma,' said Ellen in a low voice, 'wasn't that grand-mamma's ring, which I thought you loved so much?'" Mrs. Montgomery replies, "I did love it Ellen, but I love you more." Although Mrs. Montgomery reassures Ellen that she can remember her mother without the ring, the author tells us how difficult it was for her to give it up: "There were tears, however, in Mrs. Montgomery's eyes, that showed the sacrifice had cost her something; and there were tears in Ellen's that told it was not thrown away upon her" (1:33). Similarly, when they are in the bookstore, Mrs. Montgomery watches Ellen as the latter excitedly ex-amines the bibles, and she is overwhelmed by sorrow at the thought that she must soon leave her child: "Mrs. Montgomery gazed with rising emotions of pleasure and pain that struggled for mastery, but pain at last got the better and rose very high. 'How can I give thee up!' was the one thought of her heart. Unable to command herself, she rose and went to a distant part of the counter, where she seemed to be examining books; but tears, some of the bitterest she had ever shed, were falling thick upon the dusty floor, and she felt her heart like to break" (1:35).

Thus, whereas modern clichés about shopping separate the act of shopping from other aspects of experience, Warner's realism integrates consumer spending into the complexities of a person's life: the person's emotions, her relationships with other people, indications of what else is going on in her life at the time, and the question of where and how she obtained the money to shop with. The psychological realism in the de-scription of Ellen's and her mother's motivations and emotions, particu-larly the description of Mrs. Montgomery's reaction to the knowledge that she will soon be parting from her daughter forever, fit easily into a frame of reference that would have been familiar to most nineteenth-century women readers, particularly readers who had lost a child, which was a more common experience than it is today. Moreover, the senti-mental language used to describe Mrs. Mongomery's emotions would have similarly been familiar to the readers, who would recognize (and perhaps identify with) both the experience of losing a child and the way of describing the emotions evoked by such an experience.

After Ellen has selected her bible and her mother has paid for it, they go to a "large fancy store." The reader discovers that shopping is not a common occupation for Ellen; it is clear that she and her mother are not regular consumers: "It was the first time she had ever seen the inside of such a store; and the articles displayed on every side completely bewitched her" (1:37). Mrs. Montgomery buys her a portable writing desk and all of the necessary supplies; the primary reason for this purchase, of course, is so that Ellen can write to her mother while they are separated. The description of the purchases required to outfit the desk provides a valuable cultural artifact for today's reader as the characters discuss the advisability and necessity of each purchase. The list of necessary items— no "merely showy matters"—includes letter paper, large and small; envelopes of both sizes; notepaper; ink in an inkstand that "shuts with a spring" so that the ink will not spill during Ellen's travels to her aunt's; ink powder to make more ink; "little wax matches, that burn just long enough to seal one or two letters"; quills and steel points to make pens; a "plain ivory" pen handle; a knife "to make the pens"—one with two blades, "a large as well as a small one . . . to mend a pencil sometimes"; red, blue, yellow, and green sticks of wax to seal letters with; a seal "with Ellen's own name on it." Finally, with the addition of several other items, their purchases are complete. As in the selection of the bible, the selection of each item requires discussion and the weighing of various criteria. Once again, also, Warner integrates other aspects of the characters' lives into the description of the act of shopping, referring, for example, to Mrs. Montgomery's poor health, Ellen's conflicted emotions (joy at obtaining the gifts and sorrow that the reason for them is that she must leave her mother), and again, Mrs. Montgomery's knowledge that she will probably never see her daughter again. Thus we are told that as Mrs. Montgomery "placed in the desk one thing after another, the thought crossed her mind that Ellen would make drawings with those very pencils, on those very sheets of paper, which her eyes would never see!" (1:41–42).

The next shopping expedition is undertaken by Ellen alone, and this section provides a good example of how the novel's practical realism is combined with fantasy. First we see a realistic description of how Ellen and her mother solve a problem that many of Warner's readers would have been able to relate to: how to obtain necessary goods when a mother is ill, and how a novice manages to cope with uncaring service personnel. Ellen's mother wants to buy some fabric so that she can make a dress and a coat for Ellen before Ellen's journey to her aunt's, but Mrs. Montgomery is too unwell to venture outside in the bad weather. After several days have passed and the weather is too cold and her mother no better, Ellen hits upon the idea of going by herself. At first her mother is dubious, but Ellen presents her with a practical plan: "You tell me exactly what coloured merino you want, and give me a little piece to show me how fine it should be, and tell me what price you wish to give, and then I'll go to the store and ask them to show me different pieces, you know, and if I see any I think you would like, I'll ask them to give me a little bit of it to show you; and then I'll bring it home, and if you like it, you can give me the money, and tell me how many yards you want, and I can go back to the store and get it" (1:57).

In her description of this shopping venture, Warner reveals not only the complex relationship between personal and economic issues, but also provides a lesson in "buyer beware" training. In the store Ellen is confronted by Mr. Saunders, a sales clerk whose insolence and impatience are combined with dishonest tactics, and she is only saved from catastrophe by an "old gentleman," a kind stranger who apparently has the know-how and the money to cow the clerk into helping her honestly. When Ellen asked to look at the merinos, Mr. Saunders told her the prices were higher than they really were and refused to cut off a small sample for her to take home to her mother. Instead, he bullied her and attempted to pressure her into buying a coarser cloth. The old gentleman, who had witnessed the interchange, is disgusted at the clerk's behavior and threatens to have him discharged. He demands that the clerk cut off a sample of the merinos that Ellen had selected and calls him on the price: "I know it was only twelve—I know your tricks, sir" (1:59). This kind man then accompanies Ellen back to her home, where he waits while her mother chooses between the two samples, and then he accompanies Ellen back to the store where (like a fairy godfather) he not only assists her in the purchase of the material for the coat and dress, but with his own money he buys her fabric for a second dress and on the way home takes her into a millinery shop to buy her a bonnet for the cold weather. As if this is not enough, he buys delicacies for her and her mother and later sends more food to their home (1:55–59). Thus, Ellen's introduction to shopping becomes not only a way of obtaining consumer items but also a way of gaining knowledge of the ways of the world and of the importance of money. The reader sees that, although a shopper must be wary of dishonest clerks, a person with money and influence has the power to control any situation.

The problem for the modern reader (in addition to the concern that the stranger could be a pedophile) is that the old gentleman seems a mirage more than a real person and somehow does not fit into this otherwise realistic portrayal of practical money matters. In fact, he never appears again in the novel, and we do not even learn his name. He seems to exist solely for the purpose of solving Ellen's problem in dealing with the dishonest, bullying salesclerk. Warner's use of the old gentleman as a *deus ex machina* to come to Ellen's rescue in the store provides a paradigm for the way in which Warner deals with the economic questions that her novel poses. Whereas some of the other authors we look at in this chapter urged that women take control of their own economic destinies, Warner advocated acquiescence and solved economic problems with fantasy. Mrs. Montgomery tells her daughter at the beginning of the novel, "Though we *must* sorrow, we must not rebel" (1:13), and Warner's novel preaches self-control for women. Ellen must learn to control her anger and rebellion and accept her fate as the result of God's will. Although Jane Tompkins makes a strong case for the empowering effect of this spiritual acquiescence, it is no more than a means of bearing what one believes one cannot control.[28] Other authors that we look at in this chapter provide more practical solutions. In *The Wide, Wide World* Ellen's problem is resolved happily for her at the end of the novel when she marries: her husband tells her that he will keep a drawer full of money for her to use as she pleases; she will never want again. He shows her a concealed drawer in the antique desk he has given her. The drawer is "lined with gold and silver pieces and bank bills." "Here," he says, "you will always find what you want in this kind. I shall never ask you how you spend it."[29] The drawer of money is like the bag of gold that Jack steals from the giant after he climbs the beanstalk: no matter how much gold one takes out of it, the bag will never be empty. But "Jack and the Beanstalk" is a fairy tale. Warner's solution to economic problems for women is a fantasy solution (and one that Warner herself never realized in her own life). The unanswered question, of course, is, What will happen if Ellen's husband loses his money as her father did?

E. D. E. N. Southworth (1819–1899) in *The Deserted Wife* (1850) provides a different solution to the question of woman's economic role. Unlike Ellen, Hagar Churchill cannot rely on her husband for financial security. In fact, by the end of the novel it is he who relies on her. Moreover, she does not practice passive acceptance, trusting in God and her husband. The principal conflict in the novel is her refusal to submit to her fate or to her husband. And although the author apparently believes that she is wise ultimately to control her wild spirits, she (Southworth) shows how Hagar is able to channel them into a professional career rather than subdue her spirits in blind obedience to a husband whose judgment is inferior to hers.

First published serially between 1848 and 1849, before Melville began writing *Moby-Dick*, *The Deserted Wife* tells the story of Hagar, whose biblical name suggests the Egyptian mother of Ishmael.[30] As an outcast and wanderer in the desert with her son, the biblical Hagar experienced the alienation and destitution that is reflected in Southworth's protagonist, who stands alone, destitute and outside of society, until she finds the "hidden spring" of talent that proves her salvation. Southworth gives her the temperament of an adventurer, and the similarity in names between her and Melville's character underscores the difference in gender. Whereas Melville's Ishmael is free to ship out to sea, Hagar's mobility is curtailed by her responsibility for her three young children. As a child growing up in the wild surroundings of Heath Hall, Hagar is "fearless" with a "spirit of adventure and inquiry,"[31] but as a woman, she becomes legally and economically subject to a tyrannical husband. She was noted for her "independence; her free, strong, glorious spirit!" (208–209), but after her marriage to Raymond Withers, her spirit "withers" under his torturous disapproval and determination to "clip her eagle wings" and "crush" her will (306–307). As her husband, he is the legal owner of all of her personal property (257), and in an attempt to subdue her and display his power over her, he sells her beloved horse, Starlight, and her two dogs, Romulus and Remus. Helpless before his economic power, she temporarily submits, saying, "I wish you joy of your automaton" (306–307).

After Raymond moves Hagar to his home in New York State, he demands that she dress and behave "harmoniously," by which he means in quiet submission to his will. Suffocating under her husband's oppressive rule and removed from her friends and family, Hagar feels "her dependence upon him" (318–319, 326). Southworth graphically portrays the way in which a nineteenth-century woman, without legal or economic power, could be robbed of her individuality. Hagar's story reflects the stories that emerge from many of the law cases discussed in the chapter on divorce, where a woman seeks legal redress after what often are years of abuse, sometimes physical but at other times verbal and emotional, like the abuse that almost destroys Hagar. In the nineteenth-century courtroom, from the point of view of male judges and juries, this "story" did not carry any weight. As legal historian Mary Frances Berry points out in *The Pig Farmer's Daughter and Other Tales of American Justice* (2000), "Whose story counts in legal decisions rests heavily on who controls political and economic power."[32] In *Trust v. Trust*, for example, Mary Trust's story of her husband's abuse does not move judge or jury; it does not even move the magistrate who sent her to the Tombs, where her husband had her locked up on blatantly fraudulent charges in order to force her submission to him. For them, the "true" story was that of a disobedient wife. The difference here is that in Southworth's novel we have the wife's story; Southworth details the accumulation of abuse from the wife's point of view. Although Hagar's story would not have held up in court, it apparently gained a sympathetic hearing from a "jury of her peers"—the women who read Southworth's novels and helped to propel her to fame and fortune as a novelist.

Raymond also attempts to control his wife through her children after their twin babies are born. This was a common theme in the court cases. Since legally a husband had custody of the children and the right to determine their education, he could force his will on his wife by threats regarding the children, and she had no legal recourse. Raymond's approach is more subtle. Telling her that the babies have made her ugly and that they disrupt the "harmony" of his household, he demands that Hagar put them out to nurse (347–348). When she refuses to part with her children, he withdraws all affection and says he wants nothing from her "until you give me your *will*" (352–353). After weeks of this torture, she breaks down and weeps (and unlike Warner's Ellen, she is someone who never cries), but Raymond coldly insists that there can be no reconciliation without her "unconditional surrender" (356). Instead of yielding, Hagar turns to her music. She finds release in the "grand harmonies" that she plays and feels "power" in her music (375). Raymond, however, is attracted by the "soft melodies" of Hagar's cousin, Rosalia, and accepts a post overseas, abandoning his wife and children to run off with Rosalia and leaving Hagar nothing but his debts. Like the women in so many court cases who were impoverished by their husband's indebtedness, Hagar is left penniless. The house and all of its contents are sold to pay his creditors, and Hagar returns to the crumbling Heath Hall with her two baby girls and pregnant with a third child.

Here Southworth introduces an important theme that runs throughout her fiction: the importance of economic independence. Hagar feels new life pouring into her at the realization that she is in her own home: "She was *at home*, under her OWN roof; what if the house were half a ruin—it was HER OWN. . . . There was a sense of independence in that, and of pride in the thought that for this house she was not indebted to Mr. Withers" (463). The house still belongs to her because, as I indicated in chapter 2, under common law, a wife retained possession of any real estate that she owned, although her personal property and any income that she might realize from the real estate legally belonged to her husband. With a house to live in but with no money, however, Hagar needs to find a means of support. She considers and rejects the traditional occupations for "genteel" women: needle work? (she can't sew); teaching? (she is not well enough educated); private music teacher? (her pride shrinks from what she regards as a humiliating occupation). Southworth's listing of the meager supply of occupations open to women looks forward to her 1859 novel, *The Hidden Hand*, in which the girl Capitola, living on the streets of New York, can find no work until she disguises herself as a boy.

Ultimately Hagar determines to use her musical talents and enters into a career as a professional singer. Her greatest motive, Southworth tells us, is "to achieve . . . an independence" (505–506). But she is also pleased that one of the advantages of this career is an "opportunity of seeing the world," and after a season of "splendid successes" in New Orleans, she embarks on a yearlong European concert tour accompanied by her children (501). It is important to note that one of her considerations in choosing this career was that professional singers not only could make money but were "respectable"—an important consideration for a woman of the 1820s (501). Hagar amasses a huge fortune and uses some of her money to renovate Heath Hall.[33]

The novel ends with a reconciliation between Hagar and Raymond, but on very different terms. He is bankrupt, and although she loves him, she no longer "worships" him. He will never again exert power over her. In fact, she is the one with the money and power. For example, when she tells him that she has imported foreign workmen to repair Heath Hall because she feels indebted to Europe since that was where she made her money, he accepts her decision without so much as a raised eyebrow. Formerly, he would have sneered or somehow indicated his disapproval of what he might have called her "rash" or "whimsical" behavior, but she is decisive and tells him she knows she is right. All he can do is murmur his assent.[34]

One might say that Raymond is a humbled Rochester. The difference is that in *Jane Eyre* (1847) it is Rochester who has changed: he has become weak and needy because of his blindness. In *The Deserted Wife* the one who has changed is Hagar: she has become stronger and more confident of her power. In this sense, Southworth's novel is a rewriting of Charlotte Brontë's novel, empowering the woman in her own right without making the empowerment dependent upon a weakening of the man. Moreover, although Jane finds her fortune through the traditional route of marriage, Hagar makes her fortune herself. And finally, in *The Deserted Wife* there is no "madwoman in the attic"; instead there are mad*men*—a lunatic uncle and his unstable son, Raymond. In fact, the novel suggests that the pathetic condition of Reverend Withers's former wife, who commits suicide, is due to her mad husband's treatment of her. "Do not marry him!" she warns Hagar's aunt, Sophie, before she dies, or you too will suffer "a blighted life!" (97). This woman is not insane, Sophie concludes: "She spoke sense, truth, sad, sorrowful truth" (106).

The Deserted Wife is a rewriting of another Brontë novel as well, Emily Brontë's *Wuthering Heights* (1847). But Hagar of Heath Hall, the dark and passionate girl who gallops over the moors in a wild frenzy, does not need a Heathcliff to realize her selfhood. She *is* Heathcliff. That the recently published *Wuthering Heights* was on Southworth's mind when she wrote this wild tale of the Maryland heaths and cliffs is suggested by her use of other concepts from Brontë's novel. Rosalia's lawyer is named Mr. Linton, and Grove Cottage represents a conventional contrast to Heath Hall just as Thrushcross Grange does to Wuthering Heights. Both novels tell the story of a passionate but unhappy love affair, and both novels are characterized by their portrayal of shocking physical and emotional violence. But most reminiscent of *Wuthering Heights* are the parallels between Hagar and Heathcliff. Both characters are dark and wild, outsiders who in childhood were assigned H-names that suggest their character (Hagar's birth name is Agatha; Heathcliff's is unknown). And most of all, both characters are ill-treated, abused in their youth. Heathcliff, a starving urchin when he comes to Wuthering Heights, is at first well treated by Mr. Earnshaw. But after Earnshaw's death, Hindley treats him like a servant. Hagar is abused by her mad step-uncle, Rev. Withers, who sometimes smiles upon her and sometimes thrusts her from him as though she were a "viper" (148). In a fit of violence, he even throws her out of the open window. The result of this erratic mistreatment is to make both Hagar and Heathcliff become hard and self-reliant, unable to trust anyone. As Hagar says of herself: "At first I consoled myself for the want of affection, and, afterwards, I grew really independent of it!" (221). Not only have they become hard, but they can barely contain their raging passion. Thus Hagar says that she knows she is not "soft and weak like other women!": "I am *hard*—my muscles are like tempered *steel*—they imprison a strong grief that rages, burns, and rends, finding no escape, no vent, no expression!" (282). This is certainly a good description of Heathcliff as well. Other parallels between Heathcliff and Hagar include the fact that both are poor, too poor to be viable marriage candidates: Heathcliff overhears Catherine telling Ellen Dean that she cannot marry him because he is too poor, and Emily Buncombe tells Gusty May that he must not think of marrying Hagar because she is too poor. But most important of all is the fact that Heathcliff and Hagar both leave home for an extended period of time to earn their fortunes, returning to Wuthering Heights and to Heath Hall, respectively, when they are very rich.

What is the significance of these parallels with the two Brontë novels? The significance lies in the fact that the parallels are parallels with a difference: Southworth takes the two most famous heroines of the mid-nineteenth century and rewrites the script, giving them the attributes of a man. She does not "masculinize" her heroine, however. What she does is give her heroine the economic independence and worldly success that give a man his power.[35]

This is particularly apparent in the attraction that Hagar gains after her ascent to power. Raymond's liaison with Rosalia had not been consummated before she fled from him, and when Rosalia returns to Heath Hall, she declares to Hagar that she does not love any man; she loves Hagar: "I love *you*, wish to love you *only*, to worship, to serve you" (573). Although there is a suggestion of lesbianism in this declaration, Southworth does not follow up on the suggestion. Rosalia's declaration is primarily Southworth's way of indicating the sexual attraction and virility that come with economic and worldly success and power. Not only does Hagar's power attract Rosalia, but it attracts Raymond also. After Hagar's astounding success, Raymond realizes that he is magnetically drawn to her, and Rosalia seems "flat and uninteresting" by comparison (493).

Economic independence, then, becomes a principal theme of this novel; it is not only the focus of the main plot but is reinforced in the subplots as well. Sophie Churchill is gratified when she discovers she can earn her living by teaching. Emily Buncombe urges her son Gusty to save his money and buy land: "I wish you to accumulate property Gusty—that is to say only *this*—spend as little of your limited income as possible, lay by the balance until you get enough to purchase a piece of land and build a home" (428). When he marries Rosalia, he is able to do just that: "Rosalia's fortune, left to accumulate at compound interest as it had been, now amounted to the snug little sum of twenty-five thousand dollars; no plum, certainly, but still enough, taken with his income, to give

Gusty a fair start in the world, at least to purchase that small estate, and build, ornament, and furnish that beautiful little home" (579).

Hagar does not continue her career after her reconciliation with Raymond, but neither does she give it up to become dependent upon him. She has already earned a fortune and does not need to work any more than Heathcliff does when he returns to Wuthering Heights. It is presumed that her money is invested wisely to provide a comfortable income. In this novel, Southworth was writing the story of her own abandonment by her husband and her subsequent rise to fame and wealth as a popular writer. There was no reconciliation with Frederick Southworth in real life, however; as Southworth said of one of her other novels, the happy ending was not "warranted by the facts."[36] The reader wonders why Southworth would bother to reunite her heroine with a man who had treated her so cruelly. Southworth's portrait of Raymond as an emotional abuser is so realistically portrayed that one suspects that she drew from her own experience with her husband. In later years she would not speak of his treatment of her, except to say in a letter to her daughter, "I do forgive, but I cannot forget."[37] She never reconciled with him. But the fictional alternatives—that Hagar live the rest of her life in "single blessedness" with her children as Southworth did, or that she form a "Boston marriage" with Rosalia, or that she divorce Raymond and marry Gusty May—would not have been popular among Southworth's readers. And in the novel it is clear that the fairy-tale reconciliation is not what interests Southworth. She is much more interested in the economics of Hagar's story.

Rather than focusing on the economic situation of a protagonist, Harriet Beecher Stowe (1819–1899) in *Uncle Tom's Cabin* makes economics an overarching feature of the book. Critiquing slavery within the context of capitalism, she shows the evils that result when financial concerns are the principal criteria and human beings are defined as saleable property. Stowe does not advocate a radical change in the socioeconomic system; rather, she urges broad-based moral reform, warning that Americans must become more humane—that is, more concerned with their fellow human beings than with individual gain. In the 1850s, most abolitionists

saw capitalism as a positive alternative to slavery: "free labor" as opposed
to slave labor.[38] Some critics have identified Stowe as a critic of capitalism itself and have linked such a critique to the model of gendered
spheres. According to this school of criticism, Stowe associated capitalism with maleness and urged America's salvation from commercialism
through the "maternal care" of woman's sphere.[39] However, although
Stowe deplores capitalism's excesses, her concern in *Uncle Tom's Cabin* is
not to subvert the system but to show how it has lent itself to traffic in
human beings. The cure, she believed, was not a takeover by women but
the establishment of a society governed by what Stowe defined as the
principles of Christian love, which in her view were within the province
of both men and women. In the novel, opposition to slavery does not divide neatly along gender lines. Moreover, Christianity's condemnation of
slavery (as opposed to the pandering of weak ministers) is reiterated
throughout the novel, most notably in the powerful concluding sentence,[40] and the titular hero of the novel is a Christ figure whose turn-
the-other-cheek philosophy and ability to stand up to Simon Legree
when no one else will win him the respect of all of the characters in the
novel (even, in a warped way, of Legree himself). Although Stowe's portrayal of a black man as a Christ figure was a revolutionary act at the
time, it led in the twentieth century to charges of racism against her
for portraying a black man as "unmanly." Although a case can be made
against Stowe's inability to envision a wholly assimilated society in the
United States, criticism of her as a racist for a "feminized" portrayal of
Tom is more of a comment on American standards of masculinity than
an identification of racism, particularly in an author for whom Christ
represented an ideal type of man.[41]

The year that *Uncle Tom's Cabin* began appearing in serial form, 1851,
was the year that Melville's *Moby-Dick* was published. Melville's Ishmael
tells us that whenever he feels depressed, he goes to sea. "It is a way I
have of driving off the spleen," he says.[42] However, Stowe's slave characters do not have that luxury; even more than a white mother, they are denied the freedom of movement that Melville's character takes for
granted. Appalled by the passage of the Fugitive Slave Act of 1850, a law
that made it a crime to give aid or succor to an escaping slave, Stowe had
set out to write a work that, as her sister-in-law said, would make the

"whole nation feel what an accursed thing slavery is."[43] The antislavery message of her book has an economic basis: she shows how slavery results from American individualism and a prioritizing of the profit motive.[44] Economics are at the center of her book.

First of all, she focuses on slavery as a business. Governed by the same laissez-faire rules that drove other nineteenth-century American business ventures, the business of buying and selling human beings required no moral or humane considerations; the only motive was the profit motive. This aspect of slavery is highlighted throughout Stowe's novel. In his first real speech, the slave trader, Dan Haley, brags of how he got a slave cheap and made a big profit on him (12). Similarly, when he sees Eliza, he thinks only in terms of her monetary value: he says to Shelby, "You might make your fortune on that ar gal in Orleans" (15). Later Shelby describes Haley as "a man alive to nothing but trade and profit" who would "sell his own mother at a good percentage" (46). Not only did the sale of slaves bring a profit, but the earnings of slaves provided a profit for the slaves' owners as well. George Harris's master holds the patent to George's invention and "makes money out of it" (121). In an extreme example of the profit-driven man, Stowe introduces Simon Legree, a man who uses everything "as an implement for money-making" (369). When Cassy wants Legree to stop mistreating Tom, she does not appeal to his humanity (he has none); instead, she uses the only argument he understands, the argument of money and profit. She reminds him how foolish it is "to pay twelve hundred for a fellow, and use him right up in the press of the season," and she points out that Legree will lose his wager with the neighboring plantation owners regarding who will have the biggest crop that season (404).

Stowe consistently uses the discourse of business to describe the buying and selling of slaves. When Haley hires the slave catchers Loker and Marks to find Eliza and Harry for him, for example, the language is that of a business deal: they discuss the terms, Haley offering "ten per cent on the profits," but Marks and Loker insisting on fifty dollars down as a "retaining fee" (81). Similarly, Topsy has been raised by a "speculator" who buys babies cheap and sells them later at a profit in the same way that a speculator in the stock market would buy and sell stock or a cattle dealer would buy and sell cattle. We are told that "speculators buys 'em up cheap when they's little, and gets 'em raised for market" (262). And when one of Haley's slaves commits suicide after he sells her baby, Haley puts her down in his "account-book" under "losses" (147).

The most incriminating business term that Stowe uses is the term "property." By applying this term to human beings, along with other objectifying nouns, while at the same time highlighting the humanity of her slave characters, Stowe underscores the horrors of slavery. The original subtitle of the novel was "The Man Who Was a Thing," emphasizing the fact that Tom, whom the reader comes to know as a human being, is, under slavery, only a "thing." But, as Stowe tells us regarding George Harris, although he is a "thing" in the eyes of the law, his "flashing eye" and "troubled brow" show "too plainly that the man could not become a thing" (22–23). The chapter in which Eliza and Tom find out that Harry and Tom have been sold is entitled "Showing the Feelings of Living Property on Changing Owners" (42). When Shelby promises Haley that he will help in the "recovery of your property," the reader recoils at the realization that the "property" is Eliza's beloved child, Harry (53). To emphasize that this reduction of a human being to an object is not an isolated instance, Stowe shows us in the chapter "The Slave Warehouse" an "abundance of husbands, wives, brothers, sisters, fathers, mothers, and young children" whom she describes as "human property" (350). By listing the slaves in their relationships to other family members, she draws attention to the humanness of the "property" while at the same time excoriating the impact that slavery has on families.

Stowe's object, of course, was to elicit a recognition of the humanity of people whom the law had reduced to saleable objects. In order to accomplish this, she not only called attention to the horror of treating human beings like property but also sought to force the white reader to identify with the slave. This is particularly apparent in her use of parallel names for black and white characters, for example, George Harris (Eliza's husband) and George Shelby (the Shelbys' son); Harry (Eliza's son) and Henry (the Birds' dead child); and Emmeline (the slave girl who is bought by Legree for sexual purposes) and Evangeline (Eva, the daughter of the St. Clares). Throughout the novel Stowe portrays slaves in situations that white readers could identify with, particularly the then-common situation of a mother who has lost her child, an almost universal experience for parents during those days of high infant and child mortality—and an experience that Stowe herself shared. Not only would her readers have been able to relate to the heartbreak of such separations, but they also would have responded to Stowe's oblique parallels with well-known literary situations. For example, most of her readers would have been familiar with Warner's *The Wide, Wide World*. Stowe's description of the slave mother Susan's advice to her young daughter Emmeline before the slave auction parallels Warner's description of Mrs. Montgomery's parting message to Ellen. Emmeline's mother says, "Take your Bible with you, and your hymn-book; and if you're faithful to the Lord, he'll be faithful to you" (354). Yet, Stowe notes, Emmeline's mother knows "that tomorrow any man, however vile and brutal, however godless and merciless, if he only has money to pay for her, may become owner of her daughter, body and soul" (354). The "wide, wide world" that Emmeline is thrust into when she is parted from her mother is a more dangerous one than Ellen faced, and if Ellen was vulnerable, the slave girl is wholly without protection. Fifteen-year-old Emmeline is bought by Simon Legree, who forces her to become his concubine. If, as Stowe surely intended, the reader remembers Mrs. Montgomery's concern for Ellen—her purchase of a bible for her beloved daughter and her earnest advice to trust in God—the reader cannot help but associate the two situations, and this association drives home the chilling horror of Stowe's picture, where an innocent young girl can be bought by any man who "has the money to pay for her."

Not only does Stowe use business language to describe the dealings of slavery, but she shows how slavery functions as part of the American myth of individualism and the American Dream: it provides a welcome opportunity for an enterprising man to rise in the world. At the beginning of the novel, Dan Haley, the slave trader, is described as "a low man who is trying to elbow his way upward in the world" (11). Later Haley himself says he is just trying to do a "good business": "All I want is a livin' . . . ," he says; "that's all any on us wants" (68). He doesn't philosophize about his business any more than Silas Lapham does about selling paint in Howells's *The Rise of Silas Lapham* (1885). Like Lapham, Haley is proud of his product: he uses "good management," he says, and does not abuse his slaves the way some traders do; that way he does not bring damaged goods to the market and can get the highest prices for them (16–17).

But it is not only the "vulgar" who profit from slavery. As other critics have noted, Stowe finds the gentleman just as guilty as the trader.[45] The novel opens with contrasting portraits of Haley and Mr. Shelby, yet they are both engaged in the same business. As Haley says to young George Shelby when George tells him he should "be ashamed" of himself for selling slaves, " 't an't any meaner sellin' on 'em, than 't is buyin'!" (116). Stowe comments that although the reader may be disgusted at the callousness of the trader, it is important to remember that the trader cannot function without "gentlemen" to support his business and buy his wares: "Who, sir, makes the trader? Who is most to blame? The enlightened, cultivated, intelligent man, who supports the system of which the trader is the inevitable result, or the poor trader himself? . . . In what are you better than he?" Stowe asks the reader (148). In addition to condemning the buyers and sellers of slaves, Stowe condemns anyone who stands by and lets slavery happen. Believing that he can be a "neutral spectator" in a system that he deplores, St. Clare is surprised to find that the bible condemns those who do no positive good as well as those who actively do evil. His cousin Ophelia tells him, "Perhaps it is impossible for a person who does no good not to do harm" (336). Thus Stowe lists the "respectable" people who defend slavery: "Planters, who have money to make by it,—clergymen, who have planters to please,—politicians, who want to rule by it" (241). Even the North is not exempt from blame, Stowe notes, because many people in the North do not hesitate to profit from slavery. For example, when Emmeline and her mother are sold along with other slaves, it is "a member of a Christian church in New York, who will receive the money, and go thereafter to the sacrament of his Lord and theirs, and think no more of it" (353). This Northern businessman does not like slavery in theory, but, Stowe says sarcastically, "there were thirty thousand dollars in the case, and that was rather too much money to be lost for a principle" (353).

In Stowe's view, then, slavery was based on economics. The defenders of slavery, she insisted, were only defending their pocketbooks. If the economic picture shifted, she said, slavery's defenders would change their tune. As St. Clare points out, even the clergy would shift their posi-

tion: "If something should bring down the price of cotton once and forever, and make the whole slave property a drug in the market, don't you
think we should soon have another version of the Scripture doctrine?"
(202). Stowe portrays slavery as very much a part of the capitalist economy; profit and gain are the chief motivating factors. The role of the
planters is, like that of the capitalists, "appropriating one set of human
beings to the use and improvement of another, without any regard to
their own" (250).

Where do women fit into this economy? The slave women, of course,
are "property" to be bought and sold. Middle- and upper-class women,
however, are expected to be outside the economy. The attitude among
the men is that women "don't understand business," by which they mean
the buying and selling of slaves. Haley comments to Shelby when the latter tells him that his wife will not want to sell Eliza's child, "[Women]
han't no sort of calculation" (15). As noted earlier, Mrs. Shelby is "entirely
ignorant" of her husband's business affairs (21). When she finds out that
he is in debt, she asks him to tell her something of his finances so that
she can help, but he dismissively exclaims, "You don't know anything
about business" (274). Yet, comments Stowe, "The fact was, that though
her husband had stated she was a woman, she had a clear, energetic, practical mind, and a force of character every way superior to that of her husband" (275).[46] Mr. Shelby not only refuses to allow his wife to have any
knowledge of his business affairs, but he will not allow her to earn any
money of her own. When she says that she can earn money to redeem
Tom by giving music lessons, her husband exclaims: "You wouldn't degrade yourself that way, Emily? I never would consent to it" (275).
Whereas working-class women worked for wages, the middle- or upper-
class woman was not supposed to know anything about money. Mrs.
Shelby is doubly powerless: she is kept ignorant of her husband's
finances, and she cannot earn any money of her own. If she had possessed money before her marriage, it would have become her husband's
property after their marriage. Thus, although she herself does not want
to sell Tom or Harry, she is powerless to prevent it. Whereas class restrictions prevent Mrs. Shelby from working for money, Chloe, Tom's wife,
takes a job with a confectioner and resolves to save her wages to redeem
her husband. Later we see how proud Chloe is of her ability to earn

money. She insists on saving the very bills with which she had been paid in order to show Tom "her capability" (465). Stowe's portrayal of this contrast between Mrs. Shelby's compulsory helplessness and Chloe's pride in her earning power provides an ironic comment on the differing economic situation for women across the classes. It foreshadows the contrast still in existence half a century later in Edith Wharton's *The House of Mirth* (1905), in which upper-class Lily Bart, who is raised to be an "ornament," finds it impossible to support herself, although working-class women like Nettie Struther do it every day.[47]

Not only are women in the slave-owning classes economically power-less and, like northern women, at the mercy of the vicissitudes of their husbands' or fathers' finances and health, but, according to Stowe, they are impacted by the economics of slavery in other ways. Stowe portrays Marie St. Clare as an example of the negative effects slavery can have on women of the slave-owning classes. Selfish and indolent, Marie contrasts sharply with St. Clare's industrious and energetic New England cousin, Ophelia, suggesting that Marie's spoiled selfishness is the result of her pampered condition under slavery (185–194, 224). Moreover, when, as the widow of St. Clare, she possesses the power to make economic decisions, she acts selfishly, ordering all of the slaves to be sold, including Tom, even though she knows that her husband had promised Eva to set him free.

Stowe's emphasis on the importance of money in American society is underscored by the experience of Cassy and Emmeline when they es-cape from Simon Legree. Before leaving Legree's house, Cassy helps her-self to the money in his desk. When Emmeline tells her that it is stealing, she replies bitterly that the money has been "stolen from poor, starving, sweating creatures"—the slaves. It is necessary to take the money, she says, because "Money will do anything" (433). Stowe confirms the po-tency of money later when she says that no one is suspicious of Cassy and Emmeline in town. Cassy's "evident command of money," she says, pre-vented suspicion: "People never inquire too closely into those who are fair on the main point, of paying well" (452).

In Stowe's view, then, economics is the key to slavery and to American society. In *Uncle Tom's Cabin* Stowe critiques slavery as an institution that thrives within a society which discounts human concerns and focuses on profit and gain. Like Dickens, who also criticized aspects of nineteenth-century society, Stowe does not demand a radical change in the economic system. More radical thinkers have since criticized both authors for not advocating such a change. However, as George Orwell wrote in his liberal defense of Dickens, although Dickens did not demand a radical change in the economic system, he called attention to injustice and provided a much-needed moral judgment that resonated throughout his society. Moreover, said Orwell, "it is not at all certain that a merely moral criticism of society may not be just as 'revolutionary' as . . . the politico-economic criticism."[48] Similarly, Stowe's book was the most influential American book of its time, calling attention to the injustices of slavery in a dramatic and unanswerable way. If she did not advocate economic change, she clearly advocated an end to slavery, and most critics will agree that it was the publication of her book, more than any other single factor, that brought Americans to the war that ended slavery. As Abraham Lincoln is said to have commented when he met her in 1862, "So you're the little woman who wrote the book that started this great war!"[49] And it was her novel, translated and published all over the world, that gained such sympathy for the abolitionist cause that England and France, although their governments stood to gain economically from a Southern victory, did not enter the Civil War on the side of the South because, due in large measure to the influence of Stowe's novel, public opinion in those two countries would not have tolerated it.[50]

The mammoth best-seller *The Lamplighter*, by Maria Cummins (1827–1866), appeared in 1854, the year that Thoreau's significantly less popular *Walden* was published. Although *The Lamplighter* did not influence international politics in the way that Stowe's novel did, it did gain international recognition. The "most talked about novel of its time," it was translated into French, German, and Czech and was listed in the Tauchnitz library of authors—"a sure sign of Cummins's international popularity."[51] The novel sold so well that its wide sales—forty thousand copies in the first two months—caused Nathaniel Hawthorne to write in envious pique to his publisher excoriating all women writers and damning Cummins's novel in particular. On January 19, 1855, he wrote to his publisher:

"America is now wholly given over to a damned mob of scribbling women, and I should have no chance of success while the public is occupied with their trash. What is the mystery of these innumerable editions of the Lamplighter, and other books neither better nor worse?—worse they could not be, and better they need not be when they sell by the 100,000."[52]

Why was Hawthorne so harsh on Cummins? The book itself is not offensive or controversial. Rather, it is its very conventionality that irritated Hawthorne. In his next letter, and after reading Fern's *Ruth Hall*, which he praised, he qualified his comments, saying that the "only condition under which a woman ever writes anything worth reading" is when she defies convention.[53] Why were people buying a book about a slum girl who went from rags to riches, learning to love God and gaining the education that enabled her to earn her own living as a teacher, until at the end, she marries a rich man whom she loves? Why indeed? The book contains all of the stuff of nineteenth-century American mythology: virtue *is* rewarded; America *is* the land of opportunity; hard work and perseverance *do* pay off; and for women, piety and selfless devotion to God and her conscience *are* the best route to happiness. And in case anyone missed any of these truisms, the book is heavily sprinkled with moralizing comments, which give the reader the sense that she/he is having an intimate conversation with a wise friend who has had to struggle in the world. Moreover, *The Lamplighter* did not infringe on any of the established feminine proprieties: the heroine cannot be accused of being wild and defiant like Hagar or vulgarly self-assertive like Ruth Hall. Although Gerty becomes economically independent, the author makes clear that she is only doing God's will, not her own. And at the end of the novel, she gives up her economic independence to assume the traditional feminine role at the hearth of her husband. She will rule through moral suasion, not through economic power. Maria Cummins was much more circumspect than Southworth or Fern in her portrayal of economic struggle, relying upon the traditional happy ending. Whereas Hagar gains and maintains the upper hand through her acquisition of great wealth herself, Gerty, after she proves that she is capable of earning her own living, gives up her teaching to live with the Grahams and later marries a man who has acquired money of his own.

Basing her novel on the image that begins Warner's *The Wide, Wide World*—the image of a child watching the lamplighter light the street lamps—Cummins capitalizes on the popularity of Warner's novel but extends and revises the image, making it her own. Whereas in Warner's novel the lamplighter is a nameless figure whom the lonely Ellen watches out of the window of her fashionable home, where she lives with her loving mother and distant father, in Cummins's novel, the lamplighter becomes a person of great importance to Gerty, who is destitute, alone, and friendless. When she was only three, her mother had died and she was left in the care of slum-dweller, Nan Grant, who abuses her and after five years drives her out into the street. The kindly old lamplighter, significantly named Trueman Flint, takes her in and raises her as his own child. Cummins's novel is an odd mix of social realism and fantasy. The reader knows that although there may be people like "True," there are also people who would not only *not* help the helpless child but would be eager to use her for their own purposes. As Capitola Black in Southworth's *The Hidden Hand* says when she explains why she disguised herself as a boy on the streets of New York, she needed not only to find a job but also to protect herself: "Being always exposed, sleeping out-doors, I was often in danger from bad boys and bad men."[54] Gerty's rescue by Uncle True, if not impossible, is, like many events in *The Lamplighter*, improbable, and in this respect the book lacks the realism of some of the other novels by women writers.

However, the focus on economic issues grounds the novel in a way that is not found in romance. *The Lamplighter* begins with an underscoring of the importance of money: the protagonist has none, and unlike Ellen, who at least has an aunt to go to, or Ruth Hall or Hagar, who are adults when they are impoverished, Gerty is only eight years old and alone when she is driven out into the street. The early scenes portray the brutalizing effects of poverty, and Gerty's life with True is hard. Still, it is important to note that *The Lamplighter* is not a social protest novel; it is an American success story. In "Class and the Strategies of Sympathy," Amy Schrager Lang, noting that public discourse in mid-nineteenth-century America avoided the question of class conflict, maintains that Cummins's novel is emblematic of what she defines as a tendency to focus instead on "images of harmony," which, says Lang, were associated with the stability of constructed gender distinctions and the "idealized middle-class home."[55]

Without analyzing the implications of the scenes of poverty, then, Cummins focuses on her protagonist's progress from untutored slum child to idealized middle-class womanhood. Gerty finds a mentor in wealthy but blind Emily Graham and goes to live with Emily and her father in their country home. Emily educates her and teaches her about God, and like Ellen Montgomery, Gerty learns self-control and acquiescence. Just as Ellen's mother had said, "Though we *must* sorrow, we must not rebel" (1:13), Emily tells Gerty that people can be happy only if they "have learned submission" and are able to see in the "severest affliction . . . the hand of a loving Father, and, obedient to his will, kiss the chastening rod."[56] However, an important difference between the two novels is that, unlike *The Wide, Wide World*, *The Lamplighter* differentiates between obedience to God and to man.[57] Gerty (now Gertrude) knows that acquiescence does not mean going against her conscience. When she refuses to go on the southern tour with the Grahams because she wants to stay and help the poor Sullivan family, Mr. Graham is offended and angry. But Emily Graham tells Gertrude she is "brave" and "good." "You are in the path of duty, Gertrude," says Emily, "and will be rewarded by the approbation of your own conscience" (156). The author makes clear that Gertrude is right, referring to Graham as a "tyrant" and a "dictator" (165, 167). He is a "*selfish* man," Cummins says, who, because he had "supported and educated Gertrude . . . either *could* not or *would* not see that her duty lay in any other direction" (165).

For Gerty, economic independence is not a necessity to keep the wolf from the door as it is for Hagar and Ruth Hall; in fact, Mr. Graham wants her to continue to live with his family. But economic independence is a necessity if she is going to follow her conscience. As long as she is dependent upon Mr. Graham, she must submit to his will. In an attempt to use his economic leverage to force her to his will, Graham tells her that if she goes against him and leaves his house, he will withdraw all assistance from her. And he suggests that she is counting on the help of Willie Sullivan, now in India, and who, Graham sneers, has probably forgotten all about her. It is then that Gertrude issues her manifesto: "I assure you I neither look to him or any one else for support; I intend to earn a maintenance for myself" (169). As she says later to her other mentor, Dr. Jeremy, she had felt it was her duty to submit to Graham until "higher duty" forced her to do otherwise (182).

When Gertrude leaves the Grahams to care for the ailing Mrs. Sullivan and her old father in Boston, she must support herself. In fact, before she made her declaration of independence to Graham, she had already been offered a position as a teacher. Once established in Boston, she works hard, doing double duty as teacher and nurse. Cummins describes her struggle: "Her trials and cares are multiplying. A great grief stares her in the face, and a great responsibility; but she shrinks not from either. No! on the contrary, she thanks God that she is here; that she had the resolution to forsake pleasure and ease, and, in spite of her own weakness and man's wrath, to place herself in the front of life's battle, and bravely wait its issues" (189). It is easy to see how women readers in the 1850s would respond to Gertrude's travails. Many women probably saw their own problems reflected in her situation and found comfort and uplift in her brave struggle. For example, since women were the principal caretakers for the sick and the elderly, they would have identified with Gertrude's struggle to care for the Sullivans. But even more important is Gertrude's defiance of Mr. Graham. Her problem with Graham represented a common situation for women of all classes: dependent upon a father or husband for monetary support, and without legal rights, women lacked the autonomy to take a stand on issues with which their male protector disagreed. Hagar cannot keep a horse and dogs if her husband disapproves, and Mrs. Shelby cannot prevent the sale of Tom and Harry. After the Seneca Falls Women's Rights Convention of 1848, many women who had signed the Declaration of Sentiments at the convention later requested that their names be deleted because of opposition from a husband, father, or brother when they returned home.[58] The man with the money had power over women's decisions, large and small. The woman reader who felt oppressed would have found vicarious pleasure in reading of Gertrude's defiance of her male protector, especially since Cummins renders the defiance socially acceptable by making it a matter of religious conscience. But the result—that Gertrude becomes economically independent and thus independent of the "tyrant"—would represent a sweet reward.

That economic independence is an important theme in the novel is underscored by Cummins's portrayal of Patty Pace, an unmarried woman who, although she says she would have liked to marry, has been happy and successful in her career as an upholsterer (138). Her importance in the novel becomes clear when we find that she is responsible for Willie Sullivan's acquisition of a fortune (247–248), for Willie is the man that Gertrude will marry. After Mrs. Sullivan and her father die, Gertrude holds on to her independence. Friends urge her to live with them, but as she tells Dr. Jeremy, she wants to be independent—partly, she says, to show Graham, who had predicted that she would fail (202–203). Later, when Graham asks her to accompany his family on a tour of Europe to act as blind Emily's companion and she gives up her job to follow her "duty," Dr. Jeremy recognizes how great her sacrifice is: "It's the greatest sacrifice that ever I heard of! It is not merely giving up three hundred and fifty dollars a year of her own earning, and as pleasant a home as there is in Boston; it is relinquishing all the independence that she has been striving after, and which she was so anxious to maintain" (213).

Gertrude does not have to give up her independence yet, however. She returns to her position as a teacher, and she and Emily live independently together at a boardinghouse in Boston. Cummins tells us that in her later life, Gertrude often thought of this period as "the time when she and Emily lived in a beautiful world of their own" (293–294). This homosocial relationship is short-lived, however. In spite of her strong endorsement of Gertrude's independence, Cummins concludes the novel on a traditional note. Having rejected the marriage proposal of the wealthy Ben Bruce—who is shocked that a "penniless girl" would "forego such an opportunity to establish herself" (238)—Gertrude will marry Willie Sullivan. Although Gertrude rejects Bruce's "business proposition," Cummins makes clear that she will "establish herself" even better as Willie's wife. Moreover, in the end, Gertrude's superior class affiliation is established when she finds out that she is the daughter of Philip Amory, the stepbrother of Emily Graham, who marries Emily at the end of the novel. But the reader knows that although Gertrude will not want, due to Willie's fortune, she also will no longer be independent. Thus, although Cummins flirts with the idea of woman's economic independence, her conventional ending and emphasis on submission to God's will throughout the novel keep Gertrude's story squarely within the comfortable and safe frame of the sentimental novel.

Fanny Fern's *Ruth Hall*, on the other hand, portrays a heroine whose goal is economic independence. Of these five writers, Fern was the only one who spoke out strongly and publicly and unequivocally for economic independence as a lifelong goal for women. We look at her work in more detail in chapter 9, which deals specifically with that question. This chapter examines Fern's novel *Ruth Hall* in terms of its unusual portrayal of financial matters with respect to women. Published in 1855, the same year as Whitman's *Leaves of Grass*, *Ruth Hall* focuses on day-to-day money matters. Unlike Whitman's poem, Fern's novel does not romanticize labor, nor does it ignore questions of money. In fact, money is at the heart of the novel.[59]

This concern with money derives from Fern's own experiences, not only as a middle-class woman without money but, after her husband died in debt, as a working woman. Whereas the other writers discussed in this chapter were middle-class women who wrote, Fern worked at working-class jobs and lived in working-class neighborhoods. Working as a seamstress, living in cheap boardinghouses, fraternizing with their residents, shopping for a meager supply of food at local shops, Fern effectively crossed into the working class until she metamorphosed into Fanny Fern.[60] Like anyone who moves from one class to another, she was influenced by her former predilections, but she was able to identify with working-class women, to put herself into their shoes, so to speak, because she had been there herself. Thus she wrote often from the perspective of working-class women, not only calling attention to and deploring the exploitation and ill-usage that they experienced but also dramatically illustrating the humanity of women who had to work for a living, including shopgirls, seamstresses, domestic servants, and prostitutes. Consequently, of the five writers discussed in this chapter, Fern was the one most able to transcend a middle-class perspective. In essay after essay, Fern either puts herself in the place of the working woman or asks the employer to do so. In an 1868 essay, for example, she writes that her sympathies are "on the side of the servants" and says to the mistress, "I would like to see you do better in their place."[61] In an 1862 essay entitled "Whose Fault Is It?" she addresses the mistress of the house regarding her domestic servant: "As to the girl's 'bettering herself,' let her take the chances, if she chooses, as you have." Fern concludes with the story of a servant who, when asked for her references, replied, "and where are *yours*, ma'am?" Fern comments: "There was more justice" than "impertinence" in this reply.[62] Fern made her position explicit regarding all classes of people, writing in the *Ledger* in 1861, "How foolish we are to decry any class of persons . . . if only they have truth and honesty."[63]

Ruth Hall turns on the question of how the protagonist is going to support her family, and the novel chronicles her income and expenses. For example, when Ruth's book is first published, she looks through its pages and thinks of the struggle for survival that it represents: "She could recall the circumstances under which each separate article was written. Little shoeless feet were covered with the proceeds of this; a little medicine, or a warmer shawl was bought with that."[64]

In the course of Ruth's struggle, the reader learns of each specific economic problem that she faces. When her husband dies, we see her father and father-in-law arguing about who should support her and her children, each maintaining that the other should (66, 70–71). We learn of her attempt to gain work sewing and hear the factory owner telling his wife that he had to refuse her employment because she did not have anyone to leave her children with, and he has a no-children company rule for his forty employees. When he asks his wife if she knows of anyone who might be able to give her some sewing work to do at home, his wife says the only woman she knows who puts out work never employs "any of those persons who 'had seen better days' [because] she couldn't drive as good a bargain with them as she could with a common person, who was ignorant of the value of their labor" (80–81). Money is not only a factor in terms of employment, however. We see Ruth's hard-hearted cousins, the Millets, discussing the high rents in their fashionable neighborhood and the forty dollars their daughter needs for a new jacket while they refuse to help Ruth except to let her use their kitchen to do her washing, "provided she finds her own soap" (86). We see Ruth's former friends refuse to call on her when they see the poor neighborhood she lives in, while they speak of the fifty-dollar collar one of them has just purchased

(81–82). We see little Katy's return from her grandfather, who has grudgingly given her a dollar for her mother, and her meeting with a compassionate friend of her deceased father, who gives the child money. When Ruth opens the package and Katy realizes it is money, she is overjoyed: "'Money!' exclaimed Katy. 'Money!' clapping her hands. 'Oh! I'm so glad. He didn't say it was money.'" (91). That the child is aware of the importance of money to the family is an indication of how significant money is in this novel.

Fern shows us how Ruth attempts to earn money. For one thing, she sews late at night while her children sleep. However, the reader learns that she does not earn much money sewing, and we see how hard she must work: "Only fifty-cents for all this ruffling and hemming," Ruth thinks with discouragement; "only fifty cents! And I have labored diligently too, every spare moment, for a fortnight" (96). Next, Ruth tries to find a position as a teacher, but when she asks her cousins for a letter of recommendation, none is forthcoming. Instead, the author shows us her cousins' consumption of money in contrast to Ruth's want. Mrs. Millet says that she must get more lace for her daughter Leila's dress, commenting that "ten dollars will not make much difference" (97). And Leila offers to "help" Ruth by buying her coral pin, which, says Leila, will go well with her new dress. When Ruth objects that the pin was a gift from her husband, Leila sneers, "I thought you'd be very glad to part with it for *money*," and pays her only a dollar and a quarter for it although it is worth much more.

Money, then, is the focus of this novel—both money that must be worked hard for and money that is spent thoughtlessly, money as a means of bare survival and money as a source of power. In calling attention to money as a very real aspect of women's lives, Fern gave voice to an important fact of life that middle-class women had been conditioned to ignore, or at least to feign ignorance of. As Lauren Berlant notes, Fern throughout her writings provides a model in herself, testifying to women's silencing and showing that women can speak out, that they do not have to accept the formula for femininity with which they have been inscribed by their culture.[65] As Fern wrote to Harriet Beecher Stowe in 1868, she and Stowe understood about "speaking up in meetin'"—a phrase Fern often used to describe the phenomenon of a woman speaking her mind in a man's world.[66] And since nothing speaks louder than the acquisition of money by the formerly powerless, the importance of money in the novel is underscored by the graphic but (by nineteenth-century standards) very "unfeminine" image at the end of the novel—the only picture in the book: a picture of the stock certificate worth ten thousand dollars that Ruth has earned by her writing. With this picture, Fern figuratively thumbs her nose, not only at the people who had injured her personally but at all those who would circumscribe women generally.

The emphasis on economics evident in these five works by women writers during the period that Matthiessen designated the "American Renaissance" is certainly in vivid contrast to the absence of economic concerns in the works that Matthiessen sees as reflecting the spirit of American democracy. By obliterating the American Renaissance woman from the literary landscape, twentieth-century critics, following Matthiessen's lead, evolved an idealistic portrait that might be attractive as a cultural icon but is certainly not a representative one. America at mid-century was not wholly given over to the contemplation of abstractions; it was interested in bread-and-butter issues. In fact, as economic historians have pointed out, the middle of the nineteenth century was a period of vast social change, with the market economy rapidly replacing the household as the center of production and commercialization overtaking all aspects of life. The average American was busy "getting and spending." The American Dream was—and still is—primarily a dream of economic success.

For the most part, mid-nineteenth-century women were excluded from that dream, except insofar as they constituted part of the reward. Yet it was the woman writer who portrayed the economic basis of American society in her books. Stowe's *Uncle Tom's Cabin* explicitly explores the relationship between slavery and the market economy, and Southworth and Fern show how a woman must be able to attain her own economic independence in order to survive in a world in which economics is the key. In *The Deserted Wife* Hagar works hard at developing a successful career as a singer, and Fern's protagonist, Ruth Hall, becomes a successful writer. Both women become wealthy and powerful through their own efforts, and the authors applaud their energy and determination. The careers of the two protagonists reflect the life experiences of their authors, who raised themselves up from poverty through perseverance and the self-sustaining use of their talents. The other two women writers, although they focused on economics in their novels, did not embrace the concept of woman's economic independence. When Gertrude in *The Lamplighter* defies her guardian and refuses his help, Cummins is careful to make clear that it is not only so that she can maintain autonomy and gain economic independence but so that she can follow her conscience. And when Ellen goes out into the "wide, wide world," it is not to earn her fortune on her own.

American culture told women that they were not a part of their country's economy, but these women writers knew that economics were crucial for women. The American Renaissance woman's work reflects the spirit of America, where economics drove the economy and fueled ambition and progress. But in many of the women's portraits of America, economics also fueled injustice, cruelty, and inhumanity. If the male writers during the American Renaissance wrote on democracy, as Matthiessen claimed, many of the women writers during that period and in the following decades wrote on a failure in democracy. Perhaps this is one reason why their questioning has been obscured by the certainty of the male voice. It is not surprising that our culture has preferred to listen to Emerson's pontifications of self or Whitman's optimistic ode to the Republic rather than to the equally powerful questioning of a society in which economics are more important than equality, where differences of gender and race mean poverty and powerlessness, and where compassion takes a back seat to an emphasis on the self.

chapter four

THE WOMAN
PLAINTIFF

If the works of these five American Renaissance women writers provide
an indication of the nature of economic concerns among nineteenth-
century women writers, the court cases that I looked at make clear that
those concerns were not confined to public women. In spite of proscriptions against women's involvement in money matters, large numbers of
nineteenth-century women went to court to gain money or property
they claimed belonged to them. In more than half of the New York
Supreme Court cases that I looked at involving women, not counting divorce cases, a woman was the plaintiff. The suits were brought by women
of all classes and backgrounds—from the widow who sued her deceased
husband's debtors, to the woman who kept a boardinghouse or other
rental property, to the moneylender or mortgager, to the seamstress or
milliner or retailer who sued to obtain payment for goods or services, to
the white woman who sued to retain possession of slaves whom she
claimed as her "property," to the woman who sued to gain compensation
for an injury or to litigate an inheritance. This chapter looks at specific
cases, focusing on what the issues were for women plaintiffs and how individual women dealt with those issues.

A number of these cases involved independent businesswomen. One
such woman was Elizabeth Judah.[1] The widow of Benjamin Judah, she
lived at 126 Waverley Place with her son, Samuel B. H. Judah, whom she
named as her sole executor when she died on February 11, 1860.[2] Elizabeth Judah owned rental property, and in 1848 she brought suit against
William A. Riker, who, she claimed, had broken into her rental premises
and done damage amounting to hundreds of dollars. At the jury trial
which began on October 10, 1849, she claimed that he had not only
caused extensive damage but, by occupying the unit for ten days against

her will and refusing to leave, she said, he also cost her profits because she could have been renting the unit to someone else. Riker maintained that he was renting the premises and that his lease entitled him to "do repairs." However, her attorney pointed out that Riker had not paid any rent (which Riker conceded) and reported that when he (the lawyer) had inspected the premises he found that they were not improved, that damage had been done, and that items, including the fire grates, were missing. The jury verdict found for the plaintiff, and Riker was ordered to pay Judah $83, damages, and costs. Riker's lawyer made a motion for a stay of execution and obtained permission to prepare for a new trial. In December 1850, however, the defendant's motion was denied, and Elizabeth Judah was awarded her money.

This was the first in a series of court actions by the Judah women, members of a family that became prominent in New York real estate in the 1850s and 1860s. Elizabeth's son, Samuel Judah, was a member of the law firm Judah and Dickinson, which represented her at the 1849 trial. Her family connections may or may not have helped her win her case, but they apparently did help her and later Judah women to become particularly savvy about their legal and economic rights. Elizabeth Judah did not only own rental property; she also acquired and foreclosed mortgages. When she died in 1860, for example, her son Samuel Judah, as executor of her will, substituted for her in a lawsuit in which she had foreclosed a mortgage on Elisha and Frances Bloomer, a mortgage that Elizabeth Judah had acquired from the previous owner of the mortgage.

Another Judah woman who was a widow and an independent businesswoman was Henrietta B. Judah. In 1854 she foreclosed a mortgage on Joseph Churchill and sold the property (two brick buildings at 143 and 188 Spring Street in New York City). Realizing a substantial profit from the sale, she forced the eviction of the current residents and businesses. In the 1860s Henrietta Judah foreclosed other mortgages that she had acquired, one on Gilbert and Eleanor Jerrett in 1862. After the property was sold and Judah had taken the amount due her, Eleanor Jerrett claimed the surplus moneys, $6,121.51, asserting that she had owned the premises, not her husband.

Among the court cases in this study were many that involved women who, like the Judah women, made money by acquiring mortgages. Women acquired mortgages in order to receive a regular income from the interest payments, and when the party was unable to pay the mortgage, the mortgage-holding woman foreclosed. Another way that a woman could make money from mortgages, in addition to receiving income from the interest payments or foreclosing when the party defaulted, was by selling the mortgage. Widows and single businesswomen were more often owners of mortgages than were married women, although after April 1860 the plaintiff's marital status was not apparent. Before 1860 a married woman who owned property separately from her husband had to obtain a "next friend" to represent her in court before she could sue to foreclose on a mortgage. In such cases her husband could not act for her, but he had to approve her decision. Thus Caroline Fitch, a married woman who owned a mortgage "in her own right," in 1854 asked the court to appoint as her "next friend" John Bailey of Brooklyn to foreclose on a mortgage of six hundred dollars on the property of William and Louisa Vermilyea in Richmond County. Her husband, Ackley Fitch, signed a statement acknowledging that he was present when she signed the petition asking for a next friend and indicating that he gave his consent. Another married woman, Mary Milliken, who in 1854 acquired "in her own right" the mortgage on four houses and lots on Seventh Avenue, foreclosed on the property ten years later. In an earlier case in 1856 she had needed a "next friend" in order to bring suit in a different case regarding "her individual and separate property," but by 1864 the Married Women's Property Act of 1860 enabled her to sue in her own name. The owner of the Seventh Avenue property, George Clark, had sold the property to various parties, none of whom was told of the outstanding mortgage to Milliken. She brought suit and obtained a court order for police assistance to enable her to take over the property. She then sued Clark along with the other owners, demanding her money. Interestingly, one of the owners was another businesswoman, Eliza Jumel, who owned two of the houses; she rented them out, employing an agent to collect her rents.

Women plaintiffs did not seem to be any more concerned about foreclosing mortgages on family homes, even of widows with children, than were male mortgage holders. The following are just a few of the many foreclosures by women. In March 1860 Phebe Bazen foreclosed a mortgage of thirty-five hundred dollars on the property of Alexander Davis and his wife. In 1863 Nancy Bacon foreclosed on the house of James and Amelia Gilmore. Elizabeth Kelly, who held several mortgages, foreclosed on the house of Edward and Sarah Porter in 1856, and three years later she foreclosed on the house of a widow, Mary Grant, forcing the sale of the house and the eviction of Grant and her three children, two of whom were minors. In 1864 Mary Ann Flinn foreclosed on the house of Bridget Devereux, a widow with three dependent children. In each of these cases, there was nothing left for the family who owned the house.

The mortgages ranged from mortgages on modest family homes to mortgages on extensive holdings of residential or commercial property; they also varied in the amount of money invested, extending from a few hundred dollars to large mortgages of hundreds of thousands of dollars. We can get an idea of how much these amounts of money meant to the women who foreclosed on the mortgages and to the home owners who lost their homes by looking at the annual incomes of working- and middle-class families. The average income of a steadily employed working man at midcentury ranged from three to six hundred dollars a year; a working woman earned one-third to one-half that amount. Clearly, at a time when a seamstress earned as little as fifty cents a week, a woman in a shoe factory earned a dollar fifty a week, and a female operative in a textile mill earned three dollars a week, a woman did well to earn even a few hundred dollars on one mortgage.[3]

All of the above mortgages were under $5,000, which, although it was a substantial sum at the time and obviously beyond the means of the families who lost their homes, does not represent big-time investment. But women also were involved in big-money real estate. In 1855 an independent businesswoman, Ann Baehr, foreclosed on a mortgage to Augustus Brown on three hundred acres of subdivided land in Seneca, New York, in Ontario County. The land was sold at auction for $11,400, and she received the amount owed her, $6,269.70 plus interest and costs. The surplus money went to the owner of a second mortgage. Baehr's business dealings included the acquisition of several mortgages of varying amounts. When she died in 1868, for example, her executor took over a foreclosure on which she had received a judgment against Charles Latham and Nathan Stockwell with interest due from September 27, 1859. In 1868 the judgment was still unsatisfied by $1,292 and Latham had moved to South America, but the court ordered a levy against the defendants' personal and real property to be paid to Baehr's estate.

An important example of a big-money investor is Ann Elizabeth Yates, who in 1856 brought suit against Archibald Watt to foreclose a mortgage on a vast tract of land in Harlem between Ninth and Fifth Avenues and several thousand city lots in downtown New York City, the total value of which was $300,000. The property included the sixty-two-acre family homestead in addition to 4,800 city lots, some of which were sold to Central Park. Watt's daughter, Mary Pinckney, pleaded with Yates not to sell the homestead in Harlem; it had long been the family home, she said. In an effort to save the homestead, she insisted that she was now the owner, not Watt, and claimed that Watt had transferred it to her in 1843. However, as in the other cases, money trumped sentiment. After all of the property was sold and Yates and others had obtained their money, there was a surplus of only $289.53, which was paid to Pinckney.

Some women, then, were important players in the money game, even to the extent of giving the lie to the stereotypical image of the despised forecloser of mortgages. Henrietta and Elizabeth Judah, Elizabeth Kelly, Mary Ann Flinn, Ann Elizabeth Yates, and other women mortgage holders were as ruthless in foreclosing mortgages as any mustache-twisting male villain in a nineteenth-century melodrama. They were also entrepreneurial businesswomen. The mortgages that they held were sometimes mortgages that they had inherited, but more often they were mortgages that they had acquired on speculation with the intention of earning a profit from the interest payments or from selling the mortgage, or, if the owner defaulted, from the forced sale of the property. The number of foreclosures indicates that there were many other women who owned mortgages from which they obtained regular income, buying and selling as their finances permitted. Almost one-sixth of the women plaintiffs brought suit to foreclose mortgages held in their own names— mortgages on both residential and commercial property, mortgages against women as well as men, mortgages against male business owners as well as against widows with dependent children. Such evidence provides a cautionary note against the tendency to romanticize nineteenth-century women. Given the opportunity, women could be as callous and financially ruthless as men.

However, lest we go too far in the other direction and romanticize all women plaintiffs as aggressive, independent businesswomen, it is important to note that sometimes women involved in court cases were paper litigants who were used by others. One such paper litigant was Lucy Bates. In March 1853 a suit was brought against Abraham Valentine in the name of Lucy Bates, claiming that he owed her three thousand dollars for a loan that she had made to him the previous year. Valentine's grocery business had failed and he had left the state, and the judge ordered the contents of Valentine's store sold at auction in order to repay Lucy Bates for her loan. However, in April 1853, before the money could be paid, two other creditors brought suit against Valentine: Theodore Van Brunt and Charles Watson demanded that the money from the profits of the sale of Valentine's goods, which amounted to twenty-eight hundred dollars, be paid to them rather than to Lucy Bates. They claimed that the alleged loan to Bates was fraudulent, that it had been devised by Valentine in order to cheat his creditors. Bates, they said, "was a woman without money or means and it is a mere pretence of her lending or advancing the amount specified." The judge ordered that payment be suspended and ordered that Lucy Bates appear in court. However, when she was presented with a subpoena, she refused to attend "to be examined as a witness." John Odell testified that he served her with a subpoena four times. On the first occasion, he said, when he asked her if Valentine "had absconded to cheat and defraud his creditors, she was very much confused and made no reply." When he asked her if she had lent any money to Valentine, she "did not appear to know any thing about it, and gave very evasive answers." When he returned to present her with a subpoena another time, he was told that she was "sick in bed." The next day he returned with the deputy sheriff, and they had to chase her around the house before they were able to present her with the subpoena. The scene he describes is a sad one. Lucy Bates, he said, "after much difficulty and endeavoring to evade the sheriff by going from one room to the other closing doors to shut him off, the said deputy sheriff succeeded in subpoenaing her." A former employee of Valentine's testified that he had never heard of Valentine's borrowing any money from a Lucy Bates, nor had he seen her name on the books or ever heard Valentine mention her name.

Lucy Bates never appeared in court. However, her husband, Alfred Bates, testified on June 10, 1853, that he had loaned Valentine three thousand dollars. He had made the loan in his wife's name, he said, in order that she might hold the note "as her own property," but she "had no personal knowledge" of the loan. He denied that there was any "fraudulent intent." He had loaned the money in October 1852, he said, but in March 1853, after learning that Valentine was insolvent, he had instructed his attorney to issue an execution to collect the amount of the loan. At the end of June, Valentine returned from the West Indies, where, he claimed, he had gone for his health and not to escape his creditors. He denied that the loan was fraudulent and showed a bank statement which indicated that he had deposited three thousand dollars in the bank in October 1852. His brother and his former partner also testified in his favor. Ultimately, the judge denied Van Brunt's and Watson's motion to stop payment to Bates. Was the loan fraudulent? If Alfred Bates did loan Valentine the money, why had he done so in his wife's name without even telling her about it? Did he use her name to conceal his participation in the deal? Had any money actually changed hands? Or were Van Brunt and Watson correct to assume that Valentine and Alfred Bates had concocted the plan in order to prevent Valentine's creditors from getting his money? We cannot know for certain the answers to these questions. However, what is clear is that Lucy Bates was a paper litigant—a woman who was used by her husband and/or the defendant for their own purposes, which were probably fraudulent.

There are other cases, however, in which the women plaintiffs were clearly the initiators of the suits. One such woman was Ann Moore, a businesswoman in New York City. On June 4, 1847, Ann Moore brought suit against Albert L. Comstock, her former business partner. She claimed he owed her money and presented as evidence a signed agreement. The case involved the examination of "several hundred items of account between the parties as co-partners and extending back for a period of from six to ten years." After hearing evidence on both sides, the judge concluded on March 24, 1848, that the defendant owed the plaintiff a total of $4379.59, including interest. The defendant attempted to have the judgment set aside, and in a series of motions calculated to delay the case, he sought a retrial. But on July 3, 1848, his claim was thrown out and Ann Moore was awarded the full amount of money owed to her.

Another businesswoman who sued her partner was Cornelia Ferry. On February 1, 1866, she had signed an agreement with James T. Wilson to form a partnership to carry on the business of soap manufacture at 356 Pearl Street, selling soap—"fancy, plain, and domestic"—to retail dealers. She paid two thousand dollars into the partnership, and Wilson agreed to provide the "goods and fixtures" from his previous business. One month later she brought suit against Wilson. Acting with her attorney, Thomas Dunphy, she accused Wilson of taking from the partnership twelve hundred dollars' worth of stock, which he had disposed of fraudulently, keeping the money for his own use. Also, she said, he was collecting money from customers and keeping the money for himself. She wanted the partnership dissolved and sought an injunction against Wilson, restraining him from doing any further business. She demanded an accounting of all of the dealings of the partnership and asked that a receiver be appointed by the court to collect the money due and pay any liabilities. Once the accounts had been checked, she said, Wilson must pay her everything that was due her. She brought in as a witness William Busteed, a retailer to whom Wilson had proposed a fraudulent deal. Busteed testified that Wilson had delivered soap to him from the partnership and had said that he would sign an invoice for payment although Busteed had not paid anything. Busteed said that Wilson told him that "he intended to convert the soap or the proceeds thereof to his own use." Cornelia Ferry's husband, George W. Ferry, testified that he had been present during the signing of the partnership agreement, and he confirmed her claims, accusing the defendant, Wilson, of "fraudulently removing" soap from customers like Busteed and of "applying it to the defendant's own use in fraud of the plaintiff." The court ruled in favor of Ferry.

It was not only businesswomen who went to court because of money problems. Women who were not actively involved in financial matters became involved in litigation over money. In 1866 Agatha Banks brought suit against her niece Charlotte Conover for over seven thousand dollars. When Charlotte was a small child, her parents had died, and her grandparents took her in. At the insistence of her aunt, Agatha Banks, she came to live with Banks in November 1853 when she was seven years old, and she remained in her aunt's home until 1862. In the latter year, a large amount of money "came to her unexpectedly by virtue of the last will and testament of a person in no way related to her." Like Pip in Dickens's *Great Expectations* (1860), she went from poor dependency to comparative wealth through the generosity of an acquaintance. After long litigation, in 1865 the case was settled, giving her "full possession of the property bequeathed to her." In the meantime, she had moved out of her aunt's house and married. Her unexpected inheritance soon became a nightmare for her as her relatives descended upon her like vultures. Her uncles demanded money from her, causing trouble between her and her husband and threatening to cut her off from all family relationships. Charlotte testified that they, along with her aunt, "influenced by malice and spite," were "carrying on against her a systematic persecution." Her aunt took her to court, demanding reimbursement for the "board, lodging, clothing, and care and attention" that she had provided for Charlotte from the time that Charlotte came to live with her as a child. Agatha submitted a bill and obtained an order of attachment against Charlotte's property. Charlotte's lawyer procured a stay of proceedings and an order invalidating Agatha's bill, maintaining that it was not specific: it did not give dates or prices of clothing, etc., nor did it state the nature of the "care and attention" provided.

Agatha's lawyer responded by saying that it was impossible for Agatha to be more specific in her bill since she had not kept receipts over the years, but he pointed out that the bill contained amounts of money that Charlotte had paid "on account," which, he said, "proved" that she had agreed to reimburse her aunt. During the nine years that she lived with her aunt, for example, Charlotte had done certain unpaid chores such as a child might do for her parents, and Agatha had included them on her "bill" as work done "on account." Thus for the year extending from November 1, 1855, to November 1, 1856, when Charlotte was nine and ten years old, Agatha entered the figure $26 for "running errands and attending door" at fifty cents a week and deducted that amount from the amount that she claimed Charlotte owed her. When Charlotte was older, she had "copied letters and assisted Mrs. Banks in her correspondence," for which Agatha entered the $52 at a dollar a week "on account." In her testimony, Charlotte protested that such duties were not done "on account" but simply to help out her aunt. Agatha's bill also included recent cash payments totaling $285 that Charlotte had given her. Agatha listed them as payments "on account," but Charlotte stated that they were simply gifts. Charlotte testified that during the time she lived with her aunt, Agatha had never indicated that she expected Charlotte to reimburse her. Nevertheless, Agatha's lawyer was able to have the stay and the order to invalidate Agatha's bill stricken from the record.

This case is a good example of the way in which legal narrative functioned to persuade the court with a story that the justices would find believable. In this lawsuit, the two sides put differing constructions on the case: Charlotte's attorney described the case of a poor orphan who was being persecuted by her mercenary relatives, while Agatha's attorney portrayed Agatha as a benevolent guardian who was being cheated by her now-wealthy niece. Today's reader is more apt to "buy" Charlotte's story, since her aunt's claims seem so clearly to be manufactured after the fact—that, as a child, Charlotte, in doing chores around the house, was paying "on account" for her aunt's care with an inheritance that at that time she did not even know she was going to receive. But in 1868, given the nineteenth-century's emphasis on the unquestioning respect due to adult authority by children and the cultural inscription of women as passive and gentle, the case for Charlotte was not so certain. The justices apparently had a difficult time accepting the narrative that portrayed an adult guardian and a woman as mercenary and calculating. Ultimately the parties settled out of court in February 1868, and there is no record of the terms of the settlement. I suspect that Charlotte agreed to give a sizeable amount of money to her aunt and to her two uncles, for which they signed a *quid pro quo* agreeing that they would not hound her for any more money.

Sometimes a male relative was eager to take advantage of a woman's ignorance of the law. Such a man was David Thorp, the brother-in-law of Sarah Thorp. In 1845 Sarah's husband, Gould Thorp, died, leaving her with five children. In his will he appointed her coexecutor with his partner, William Woodhull, and his brother, David Thorp. The three executors agreed to divide up the responsibilities: Woodhull would manage the stocks and bonds; David Thorp would manage the real estate, collecting the rents and paying the taxes; and Sarah Thorp would take charge of the children. David Thorp was to pay the bills for the children's support and education out of the real estate profits. Two years later Woodhull died, and Sarah took over the management of the stocks and bonds. The following year, however, her brother-in-law began neglecting to pay for the support and education of the children. When Sarah questioned him, he was vague, saying that the real estate was not profitable enough, but when she asked to see his accounts, he made excuses, claiming that he was too busy or that he hadn't recorded the information yet. Ultimately, Sarah was notified that he had not paid the real estate taxes, and she was in danger of losing the property. In 1852, she brought suit against David Thorp, maintaining that he had abused his role as executor and that he was using the money from her husband's estate for his own business (he was a stove merchant). By her calculations, she said, he owed her children $4,305.70. She demanded that he be removed from his appointment as executor and that she be made sole executor. She pointed out that she had managed the stocks and bonds after the death of Woodhull, investing the interest and making a profit of $2,000. Her brother-in-law claimed that he did not owe her anything, but the court ordered him immediately to pay the taxes out of the money in his hands and referred the case to a judicial referee. David Thorp's attorney made a motion to dismiss the case on the ground that it was illegal for one executor to sue another. However, the referee said that since it was the Thorp children that David Thorp was accused of depriving of their money, the case could continue if the children were made parties to the suit, which Sarah's lawyer immediately moved, and she won her case.

In another case a woman was similarly cheated by her brother-in-law. In 1859 Isabella Hasbronck's husband died, leaving her $10,000 in his will. His brother Julian Hasbronck was named sole executor to his will, and he proved to be untrustworthy. Three years later Isabella sued her brother-in-law, claiming that he had paid her only $580 in all that time. Her attorney asserted that she and her children—Henry, age two, and Maria, age 4, when their father died—had "no other means of livelihood" other than the money that Julian controlled. The court ordered Julian to pay Isabella $10,280. Her attorney noted that Julian was now "insolvent," having assigned his property to someone else. Since it seemed clear that he had assigned his property deliberately to avoid having to pay Isabella, she was able to obtain an execution against Julian's property voiding the assignment. Unfortunately for Isabella, Julian appealed, and the decision was ultimately reversed and the case ordered to be retried. However, there is no record of a new trial after 1862. Either Isabella gave up, or, what is more likely, the parties came to a settlement out of court.

It is impossible to draw any general conclusions about the participation or influence of men in women's legal actions other than the very human one: when it was in a man's interests (or at least not contrary to his interests) to help a woman litigant, he probably did if he could; when it was not, he probably did not. Consequently, some women were helped by male relatives or friends, some were victimized by them, and some were not affected one way or the other. For the most part, women were on their own to seek legal counsel and pursue their cases as best they could.

In most simple property disputes, the law of property prevailed in the courtroom. In a capitalist society, the litigant who could prove that he/she had been defrauded of property had the most "believable" legal argument. Sometimes, however, as in the case of *Banks v. Conover*, the issues were unclear and the justices had to choose which narrative to believe. In the case of Sarah Thorp, her narrative prevailed, whereas Isabella Hasbronck's did not, at least not on appeal, probably because her brother-in-law pled hardship, a plea that won sympathy for him and created a competing narrative that the justices found familiar and thus believable: the story of a hard-working businessman whose business was failing was, perhaps, easier to swallow than the story of a man who had deliberately defrauded his brother's widow and orphaned children of their inheritance.

A particularly interesting case in respect to the question of male influence is the 1848 case *Brock v. Pettet*, which provides an example of a situation in which a man's actions were useful to one woman in the case but not to the other. As in a number of cases in which women were the plaintiffs, this was a case of a widow who, acting as executor for her deceased husband's estate, brought suit to compel payment of an outstanding debt. It was atypical, however, in several respects. First of all, both the plaintiff and the defendant were women. John Brock died on January 10, 1848, and nine months later, his widow, Rebecca Brock, "sole executrix" of his estate, sued Mary Pettet for $4,000, which she claimed Pettet owed her husband.

Pettet said that it was true that she had owed that amount to John Brock, but she claimed that he had forgiven the debt. He had obtained a judgment against her in 1843, she said, but when the deputy sheriff came to her house on September 22, 1843, and stated that he had an execution against her property, Brock sent the sheriff away. She testified that she "called Mr. Brock who was in the house at the time and upon [her] telling him what had occurred he immediately told said deputy sheriff that he had never authorised the issuing of said execution and dismissed him from the house." Pettet claimed that John Brock had been the "intimate friend" of both herself and her deceased husband, that he visited her almost daily, and that he had declared in the presence of witnesses "that he would never claim anything whatever from her but that he forgave her all she owed him, that the judgment never should be enforced against her in any way." She also testified that he had given her financial advice. She said he had met with her and her lawyer in order to discuss the advisability of her selling her business (the Battery Hotel). She said Brock advised her to "invest the proceeds in some way so as to realize a certain income," and, she added, he promised that if there should not be a sufficient sum raised to "secure her an income of $8,500 per annum," he would make up the difference himself. Brock, she said, told her that he did not wish to see her "continue to work so hard as a business of that nature [hotel keeping] required." Pettet called in two witnesses who testified that they had heard Brock state that he had canceled the debt, and one declared that Brock had said not only that he had canceled the debt but also that he had "provided for her comfortably." In this case the defendant, Mary Pettet, succeeded in preventing Rebecca Brock from collecting the money owed her husband. One wonders why John Brock canceled Pettet's debt. The answer is that Mary Pettet was not an anonymous debtor of Mary Brock's husband; in fact, the evidence suggests that she was his mistress. He visited her daily and took an unusual interest in her affairs, canceling her debt, advising her financially, and setting up a fund for her support. It is clear that Mary Pettet was a very good friend of John Brock's, although she was obviously not a good friend of his wife's.

Apart from the question of the relationship between John Brock and Mary Pettet, this case is significant as an example of women's involvement in financial matters. One way in which a woman in the nineteenth century became involved with money was in her role as widow. The widowed Mary Pettet was herself an independent businesswoman. She ran a hotel, which she may or may not have inherited from her husband. On the advice of John Brock, she planned to sell the hotel and invest the profits in order to obtain a substantial annual income. Her relationship with John Brock clearly helped her win her case, even at the expense of Brock's wife. Whether their relationship was sexual or not, Pettet profited from her friendship with a financially savvy man. Yet, although Pettet profited from the help of John Brock, Rebecca Brock did not: she was out four thousand dollars plus the money her husband had invested to help Mary Pettet. John Brock's involvement with Mary Pettet did not help his wife, yet he did help his wife in another way—by making her executor of his estate. In this sense he helped Rebecca Brock more than Isabella Hasbronck's husband helped Isabella; Hasbronck appointed his brother executor, thus enabling his brother to cheat his wife out of ten thousand dollars. Sixteen percent of the women plaintiffs in this study were acting as executors, usually of their husbands' wills. I found only one case in which a woman was executor for another woman's will.[4] Some women were named sole executor (*executrix*, in nineteenth-century parlance), while others were named co-executor along with an adult child or children (always sons), a male friend of the husband, or a brother-in-law. As executor, a woman was drawn into financial decisions that she had not been involved in before, and she had economic power that she had not had as a married woman.

However, Rebecca Brock was not good at managing her deceased husband's money. After losing $4,000 to her husband's presumed mistress, Mary Pettet, Rebecca Brock almost lost the remainder of her inheritance by investing it naïvely. She made a loan of $12,000 to Charles Robinson, a brewer of ales who promised to pay her 7 percent interest, which she expected to be able to use as regular income to support herself. As she later testified, "Robinson represented himself as very wealthy." However, he defaulted on the loan, and when she brought suit against him in 1860, she won a judgment of $12,345.12. Unfortunately, she then discovered that he did not have the money to pay her; like Julian Hasbronck, he had transferred all of his assets out of his name, a move that she claimed was an attempt to defraud his creditors, of which she was one.

Robinson apparently had numerous creditors, and the previous year he had begun divesting himself of his assets. In 1859 he had signed over his $20,000 farm to Theodore Treadenburg, and when Treadenburg died, Robinson reassigned it to Mary McComb, a woman with whom he was living with their two children. Brock, through her lawyer, claimed that the "sales" were fraudulent, that neither Treadenburg nor McComb had paid anything for the farm. She also pointed out that his other divestments were fraudulent as well. Robinson had owned three houses in Brooklyn valued at $15,000, but he had assigned them to McComb, who again did not pay anything for them. He owned mortgages on land in Wisconsin worth $33,000, which he "sold" to McComb fraudulently for a promissory note. In addition, he owned a mortgage for $15,000 in Michigan and real estate in New York State, all of which he transferred to a trust for his wife, Elizabeth, in order to induce her to discontinue her suit for divorce. In the trust agreement, he directed that after Elizabeth's death the property in the trust was to go—once again—to Mary McComb. Brock also listed furniture, silver plate, jewels, and other personal property, which she said Robinson pretended he had transferred to his wife, and she pointed out that although he said he had sold his gold watch to McComb, he was still wearing it. (McComb claimed she let him wear it as a favor.) He was living with McComb on his own farm in Hudson, but she pretended to hire him for $50 a month. Brock said that she had discovered that Robinson planned to leave the state. She demanded that he be prevented from leaving, that all of the pretended sales be voided, and that he pay her the money he owed her plus interest and the cost of the suit. There is no record of the outcome of this case, which was apparently settled out of court.

Rebecca Brock's story provides an indication of the limitations on women's financial involvement. Whereas Sarah Thorp, when she took over the handling of her husband's estate, realized a profit by investing in a known stock and bond market, Brock was unwise to invest so large a sum of money—money that was necessary for her support—in an unknown venue, basing her financial decision on a man's representation of himself as wealthy. Ultimately, Rebecca Brock (or her lawyer) was astute enough to pursue the case, recognizing the fraudulence involved in Robinson's sudden divestment of his assets, but her initial investment was naïve. However, we cannot judge Brock's financial decisions by today's standards. In the 1850s it was not expected that a woman would invest in the stock market. Women did not work on Wall Street except as scrubwomen or prostitutes. Moreover, even Sarah Thorp was not an active trader; she simply invested the interest from her deceased husband's existing stock. It probably would not have occurred to Rebecca Brock to use her twelve thousand dollars to acquire a portfolio. As I pointed out in chapter 2 of this book, custom frowned on women who attempted to become involved in stock market dealings. In Edith Wharton's *The House of Mirth* (1905), when Lily Bart gets the unconventional idea that she might invest in the stock market, she has to find a man to do it for her in order to obscure her own "unladylike" involvement. And in the late nineteenth century, Hetty Green was called the "witch of Wall Street," not only because of her unusual lifestyle but primarily because of her anomalous position as a woman in a man's world.

Rebecca Brock's suit against Robinson was representative of a number of cases in which a woman sued to recover payment of a loan she had made. As was the case with Brock, in most instances the woman had made the loan as a way of earning income through the interest payments, and these cases, along with the foreclosure cases, provide evidence of ways in which women sought to earn a regular income in an age when women were barred from the most lucrative occupations. Six percent of the total number of women plaintiffs in this study and 22 percent of the women plaintiffs who brought suit to obtain money or personal property were women who sought repayment of loans they had made. As with the foreclosures, the cases that came to court were only the ones in which the person who obtained the loan had defaulted on his or her payments. But the fact that so many of these cases existed suggests that moneylending was not an uncommon means of earning a living for nineteenth-century women. Just as Jews in medieval Europe turned to moneylend-

ing when they were barred from owning land, nineteenth-century wom-
en of all backgrounds in New York, barred from most professions and by
custom kept out of the business and investment world, found in moneylending and mortgage holding attractive alternatives to the poorly paid
labor available to them.

Moneylending was not confined to one class or ethnic group of wom-
en. All it required was that the woman have on hand enough capital to
make the loan. Such capital could be a substantial amount of money belonging to an upper-class woman and could come from an inheritance, as
in the case of Rebecca Brock's $12,000, or it could be a smaller amount
of money that a middle- or working-class woman had earned or had obtained from the sale of personal property. The latter was the situation of
Catharine Elligott, who in 1864 sued Michael Burke for $1,000 plus in-
terest for two small loans that she had made to him in 1858 and 1859. Elligott was illiterate and signed her deposition with her mark. She complained that Burke had left town in order to defraud his creditors. She
had gone to his house, she said, and his eldest son had advised her to see
a lawyer and attach his father's property as soon as possible because
there were other creditors looking for him. Burke was a house agent and
had absconded with $659 in rents. She obtained an attachment against
Burke's property, which was sold to pay her and the other creditors.

In some cases women did not lend the money for profit but to help
out a friend or relative. In 1839 Pamelia Arents loaned $78 to Stephen Ar-
ents (her brother or brother-in-law), and he signed a promissory note
stating that he would repay the money with interest within five months.
Nine years later the money still had not been repaid, and Pamelia Arents
brought suit against him. He was ordered to pay her $131.06. This case
was unusual, however. In most cases in which a woman loaned money to
a relative, if the relative defaulted on the loan, the woman probably did
not bring the case to court, either settling privately or absorbing the loss
in the interest of family harmony.

Moneylending was a risky way of earning money, since the debtor
could default, transfer his assets, or leave the state, but if a woman was
able to pursue her case, she could usually regain at least some of her
money. And the problem loan was the exception. In most cases—the
ones that never came to court—the debtor gradually repaid the loan

with interest, and the woman lender obtained the interest as a way of supplementing her income. There is no way of knowing how many women made such loans, but as with mortgages, the fact that so many cases came to court indicates that the practice was not uncommon. However, most women who were involved in moneylending kept a low profile since, like investing in stocks or holding mortgages, it was not regarded as a properly "feminine" occupation. Cultural attitudes toward such activities are made clear in an 1870 story in *Godey's Lady's Book*, "My Wife and the Market Street Phantom." In the story the "lady capitalist" who loans money to the male narrator is compared to the "other woman" in a marriage, the author thus insidiously associating women's money-making activities with illicit sexual behavior. Describing the lender as "definitely a woman out of her sphere," the anonymous author decries her savvy business methods, which, as Fanny Fern wrote in 1861, in a man "would be applauded as exceedingly praiseworthy."[5] Clearly, entrepreneurial moneymaking was seen as a man's prerogative in nineteenth-century American culture; yet, as the court cases reveal just as clearly, many women transgressed the prescriptive barriers imposed on them.

Another way for nineteenth-century American women to earn money was through rental property—from the boardinghouse that a woman lived in herself and out of which she rented rooms to the larger venture through which she rented out commercial or residential space in other building[s] that she owned. Renting to boarders was a less transgressive way for women to earn money than was moneylending—partly because it was a "domestic" occupation (it took place in the woman's home) and partly because not much money was involved. However, larger ventures were entrepreneurial, and it is interesting to note that when nineteenth-century authors portrayed women renters, the renters were usually poor women who were struggling to support themselves by taking boarders into their home rather than women entrepreneurs who owned several business properties. Yet, judging from the lawsuits in this study, women were involved in both types of renting. Altogether, 3 percent of the women plaintiffs and 11 percent of those who brought suit to obtain money owed to them sued tenants for nonpayment of rent.

One example of the woman who took boarders into her home was Anna Andriot, who was abandoned by her husband and in 1857 rented a portion of her house at 507 Broadway to Alice Morgan for seventy-five dollars a month. Alexander Lawrence agreed to pay the rent if Morgan defaulted on payments. (The records do not give any indication of why Lawrence agreed to pay Morgan's rent; he could have been a relative who agreed to cosign for her, but since it was very uncommon for a "respectable" nineteenth-century single woman to live alone, it is possible that he was maintaining an establishment for his mistress.) When the rent was not paid in January or February of 1858, Andriot brought suit against Lawrence. He did not deny that the rent was owed, nor did he deny that he had agreed to pay it. Instead, he claimed that since Andriot was a married woman, she was incapable of making a contract and could not own property separately from her husband. The case took place after the 1848 Married Women's Property Act, which gave women the right to own property that they inherited, and the court ruled against Lawrence, awarding Andriot $579.92. Lawrence appealed to the General Court, however, and the order was reversed on the grounds that the law did not give a married woman the right to contract. Andriot amended her complaint and brought a new suit against him, which resulted in her favor. In what appears to have been a delaying tactic, Lawrence appealed twice, and each time the appeal was abandoned because he failed to appear or to file in time. In July 1865 Anna Andriot (who had resumed her maiden name of Prévot) urged that the defendant not be allowed to vacate the default judgment against him and appeal again. She pointed out that she had brought suit more than seven years ago for rent "justly due." The only reason the defendant refused to pay, she said, was because she was married. But, she insisted, due to the provisions of the Married Women's Property Act, this objection was "groundless." She had owned the premises separately from her husband, she said, and in any case, she was now divorced, and since her husband had left her, she was "greatly in need of money." She received no support from her husband, she said, and had to rely solely on herself for support. She pleaded with the court not to grant further delay to the defendant. If Lawrence's appeals were delaying tactics designed to tire out Andriot or use up her resources, his tactics backfired, because he delayed so long that the 1860 Married Women's Property Act was passed before the case was settled. Although the act was not retroactive and would not apply to an action that dated from

1858, it gave a married woman the right to sue in her own name, and since it extended the 1848 act to include a married woman's earnings, it reflected a more liberal climate of opinion regarding married women's property. This, combined with Andriot's appeal as an abandoned woman trying to support herself, made Lawrence's delays appear frivolous. The court found in her favor.

Margaret Bard was another married woman who sued for nonpayment of rent. However, Bard did not rent space in her house; she owned commercial and residential rental property and employed an agent to collect the rents for her. In February 1860, she brought suit against Almon Griswold. Her rental agent testified that Griswold owed a total of $1,722.78 in back rent. Griswold claimed that he had assigned the premises to A. H. Swift, but the agent pointed out that Griswold was Swift's partner in business and profited from the business done on the rental premises. In another case, Margaret Bard sued Eugene Lynch in 1863 for nonpayment of rent. He had signed as surety for Louis Fitzgerald, who owed one year's rent of $1,300. The defendant did not deny that the rent was owed. However, he said that he could not pay it because his "business had been broken up by the political troubles of the country" (the Civil War). He offered to pay with lots that he owned in Flushing, but Bard declined the lots, and the parties settled for a $1,000 cash payment.

Another woman who made money by renting space outside her home was Julia Battersby. In September 1860 she had rented a house at 50 West Sixteenth Street to Robert Shear and his wife. In April 1861 Battersby brought suit against Shear's brother Leroy Shear, who had signed as security. The Shears owed five months' rent, or $714.43. After she sued and received a judgment for that amount, the Shears made a motion to reopen the case, asking for damages of $500 and claiming that the premises were in disrepair—that the roof leaked and the gas, water, and range were out of order. Battersby asserted that their claim was false and only concocted by them in order to get out of paying the rent. She pointed out that they had inspected the premises thoroughly before renting, and she brought in as a witness Mary Tuers, who had lived in the house when they came to look at it. Tuers testified that Robert and his wife had gone "through the house and examined everything" before renting. She also noted that when Battersby rented the premises, the "gas and water were working." Battersby's attorney pointed out that the Shears had not said anything about a leak or defects in the fixtures until Julia Battersby took them to court. In July 1861 the court denied the defendant's motion to reopen the case and ordered Shear to pay Battersby the back rent of $714 plus ten dollars in costs. What is noteworthy about all of these lawsuits is the woman plaintiff's perseverance in pursuing her case; in doing so, these women revealed a businesslike tenacity that contrasts sharply with the idealized image of the passive, acquiescent nineteenth-century woman.

A particularly interesting case that involved unpaid rent was the 1867 case of *Hannam v. Reid*. What is most unusual about this case is that the participants were almost all women. The defendant and plaintiff were women, and thirty-two of the forty witnesses were women. In November 1866 Jane Reid, a dressmaker who owned her own business, leased a house and dressmaking establishment at 125 West Ninth Street to Caroline Hannam. The lease was for five years at five hundred dollars per month, with Hannam reserving the option to purchase the house, which Reid wanted to sell. Since Hannam was new to the dressmaking business, Reid agreed to help her learn the ropes. She volunteered to work with her at her establishment until January 1 and introduce her to clients. Hannam told Reid that she had sufficient money for the rent and to purchase the property; she said she owned an eight-thousand-dollar mortgage on unencumbered property in New York City. However, Reid, who was eager to sell her property, testified that she found out later that Hannam had "misrepresented her circumstances" and was not in a position to purchase the property. On March 25, 1867, she called on Hannam with her brother-in-law, Spencer Brown, and demanded that Hannam relinquish the lease and pay her more than one thousand dollars that she (Reid) claimed Hannam owed her for trimmings and other materials. According to Reid, Hannam was willing to relinquish the lease but refused to pay her the money. The next month Reid brought suit against Hannam for nonpayment of her March rent of five hundred dollars, and on May 15 Reid instituted proceedings to repossess the house. Five days later, Reid obtained a warrant for possession, and with the help of a city marshal, Reid was placed in possession of the property and Hannam was evicted.

Hannam countersued, claiming that Reid was not a resident of New York State and consequently could not bring suit in New York. In early May 1867 Hannam obtained an attachment on Reid's house, effectively halting Reid's repossession of it. Both women produced a long list of witnesses regarding the question of Reid's residency: sewing girls, dressmakers, a cartman, a washerwoman, and relatives. The witnesses for Hannam claimed that Reid had told them she lived with her brother and mother at 58 Essex Street in Jersey City. They testified that although Reid came to the house every day in November and December to help Hannam get established in the business, she left in the evening, returning to her brother's house in New Jersey. Reid's witnesses, on the other hand, all swore that Reid did not live in New Jersey but lived in New York. They said she had lived in the Ninth Street house along with Hannam until January 1, when she had moved in with her niece's family, Stephen and Marion Fogg, on 168 West Tenth Street. Reid's attorney made a motion to vacate Hannam's order of attachment, but the motion was denied on May 13, 1867. The judge gave Reid leave to renew her motion, which she did. However, her new motion was denied.

It is impossible to know who was telling the truth about the residency of Reid. One of the litigants was obviously lying, and one wonders if that litigant's witnesses were recompensed in some way for giving false testimony. It is significant that all of the working women who testified for Reid were no longer working for Hannam, while the women who testified for Hannam were still working for her. The court apparently did not believe Reid's claim that she had been living in New York. Moreover, one of the sewing girls testified that when she went to the Foggs' house to leave a message for Reid, Marion Fogg, Reid's niece, said that Reid had asked to board with her but that she was a "queer boarder" since she was rarely there. Hannam maintained that Reid had never claimed to live anywhere but in New Jersey until after she (Hannam) obtained an attachment to prevent Reid from suing on the ground that she was a nonresident. Reid had a strong motivation in proving a New York residency, which would give her the right to dispossess Hannam. Reid had leased the house to Hannam with the assumption that Hannam would buy it but had later discovered that Hannam was not as well off as she pretended. If Hannam had the income from an $8,000 mortgage, as she claimed, at 6 percent interest, this would give her only $480 a year, and her monthly rent was $500. Unless she had money from other sources, Reid was correct to conclude that she was not in a position to buy the house. Once Reid realized this, she probably attempted to force Hannam to surrender the five-year lease so that she could sell the house to someone else. It is possible that she already had a potential buyer. In her testimony, Reid said that she would not have leased the house to Hannam but for Hannam's "assurances" that she would purchase the house. In fact, Reid stated that when Hannam first came to see her she had told Hannam that she would not lease the house and would not even show her the house and furniture if she was "not prepared to buy."

In terms of class, the women involved in the case were primarily working women—sewing girls, dressmakers, a washerwoman, a nursemaid. Some were illiterate. The few men—except for the cartman—were of a higher social status: one of Hannam's attorneys testified for her, a brother and brother-in-law of the litigants were physicians, and Reid's niece's husband owned a business. The litigants were both from middle-class families, working women who had been widowed and were forced to support themselves. Both had some property: Reid owned the house in which she had her dressmaking business (she had either purchased her house with her earnings as a dressmaker or had inherited it), and Hannam had the income from an $8,000 mortgage.

The testimony in this case provides a graphic illustration of the drop in social status that a nineteenth-century middle-class woman suffered when she was widowed and had to support herself. It also provides a vivid picture of the lives of the working women involved in the case. Hannam, after her husband died, was forced to struggle to support herself in a business with which she was unfamiliar and for which she was ill-equipped, and Reid, who similarly had had a drop in fortune but had succeeded in building up a business, was eager to give up the business because it was wearing her out. Their employees—for example, the sewing girls Eliza Conway and Lavinia Springsteen and a dressmaker, Jennie Taylor—all worked at least a ten-and-a-half-hour day, coming to the house to work at 8 A.M. and leaving at 6:30 P.M. A dressmaker, Elizabeth Van Wie, boarded in the Ninth Street house, which on the one hand was convenient but which also meant that her workday extended into the evenings.

The forewoman, Caroline E. Brand, worked the longest hours—a thirteen- or fourteen-hour day—arriving at the house before eight o'clock in the morning and not leaving until nine or ten o'clock in the evening. Her time after 6:30 P.M., she said, "was generally occupied in the preparation of work for the girls next morning." According to Brand's testimony, Reid "always aided" her in this late work, and these long hours may help to explain why Reid wanted to sell the business. A seamstress, Mary McKay, and a dressmaker, Mary Jane Reese, said that they came to work at eight o'clock in the morning and "generally left from half past six to seven in the evening, but that on several occasions . . . when business was pressing," they did not leave until nine or ten in the evening. The owner of the business not only did dressmaking work late into the evening but also rented out the extra rooms in the house to boarders in order to supplement her income.

Thus the struggle to make a living, particularly for the experienced dressmakers, involved long hours and the kind of commitment that excluded the possibility of marriage or other interests. A major compensation, however—in addition to the fact that their work provided a livelihood—was the independence that they gained. A further compensation implicit in the testimony of the working women and perhaps peculiar to this type of small woman-run business was the apparent feeling of camaraderie that the women felt for each other. Working together in one house in a small business run by a woman, they were more like a matriarchal family than anonymous workers in a factory. They took their meals together and in some cases slept in the same bed (Van Wie testified that she slept with Reid in the Ninth Street house). I do not mean to romanticize the situation; obviously there were tensions, of which the lawsuit is the most obvious, and just as women mortgage holders could be ruthless, women business owners could be exploitative. But in this case the good feeling (about themselves and about their work) that is evident in the testimony of the working women contrasts with the despair reflected in nineteenth-century fictional portrayals of workers in factories. It is a feeling that comes only with autonomy and independence and differs sharply from the picture of the women workers described by Melville, for example, in "The Tartarus of Maids" (1835), by Elizabeth Stuart Phelps in "The Tenth of January" (1868), and by Rebecca Harding Davis in "Life in the Iron-Mills" (1861)—all of which works describe women workers in a large factory setting. In these cases, of course, the workers are described by middle-class writers who are projecting their feelings about the situation onto the workers. In the case of the women workers in *Hannam v. Reid*, we are reading the women's own testimony. It is important to note that these women do not see their lives in one-dimensional abstract terms: they do not categorize themselves as "working-class women" or "exploited workers"; they are people who live multifaceted lives like everyone else. Labels that might be useful for political reasons are limiting and condescending when one is attempting to understand the nuances of a person's life. It is no accident that middle-class critics who form abstract conclusions about people based on such labeling usually couple their use of the label with the word "they."

We can gain a better understanding of this common failing if we look at some of the cases of women plaintiffs who sued to obtain money owed for goods or services. Like the case of *Hannam v. Reid*, these cases also involved women who worked for a living. In 1855 Catharine Fleming sued Thomas O'Connell for a debt that he owed her of $159.81 for goods she had delivered to his grocery store. She obtained a judgment for that amount on December 10, but O'Connell refused to pay it. The court subpoenaed his father, Eugene O'Connell, who was in possession of the contents of Thomas's grocery store. The judge ordered an attachment against the property of both O'Connells and an order for their arrest for contempt in disobeying the order to pay. In 1859 Catharine Downey, a seamstress, brought suit against Elizabeth Brenknall for the sum of $72 for "work, labor, and services done and performed," for which Brenknall had never paid her. Downey assigned the case to Henry Rowe, who bought the case from her and instituted proceedings against Brenknall. In a similar case, Catharine Healy sued David Coope in 1866 for the $134.02 that he owed her for work she had done. When he didn't pay, she obtained an execution against him. In all of these cases, the woman had done work for or delivered goods to the defendant, and the defendant had defaulted on payment. The voices of the women in *Hannam v. Reid* and the initiative taken by litigants like Catharine Healy, Catharine Fleming, and Catharine Downey provide a reminder of the problematics involved in categorizing people by class, when in doing so, one loses sight of the individuality and shifting identities of the person. As Wai Chee Dimock points out in *Residues of Justice*, working women are both "workers" and "women"; they are not speaking out of a "singular body called the 'working class.'"[6]

A further indication of the way that women lived their lives is suggested by the cases of women who brought suit to regain possession of personal property other than money. Although money was not the immediate goal, what was at stake was the potential monetary value of the "property." Perhaps the most common type of case was the case of the woman whose household furnishings were in danger of being repossessed. Before she was married, Harriet Newell purchased furniture from Amasa and Walter Cate. In 1856 she married Daniel Hedges and borrowed $748.72 from the Cateses, using the furniture as collateral. Since then she had paid $370 on account. But in 1857 the Cateses brought suit to repossess the furniture. They claimed that she owed them $578, but she insisted that she only owed them $378, which she said she was willing to pay. She countered their suit with a suit of her own in which she obtained an injunction against them, restraining them from claiming the furniture. Since this suit was prior to the 1860 law, Harriet Newell Hedges had to sue in conjunction with her husband, Daniel Hedges.

A different type of personal "property" suit that women were involved in was the suit to free African slaves who were brought from a slave state into a free state. The case of *Lemmon v. The People of New York* began in 1852 when Louis Napoleon, described as a "colored citizen of this State," obtained a writ of *habeas corpus* to free eight slaves who were brought by their owner, Juliet Lemmon, from the state of Virginia, a slave state, into New York en route to Texas. The slaves—one man, two women, and five children—were named Emeline, Robert, Lewis, Amanda, Nancy, Ann, Lewis, and Edward. In this case, a woman, Juliet Lemmon, sought to recover her "property," and women were themselves part of the "property" in question. The New York judge decreed that, according to the laws of New York, the "colored Virginians" could not be detained against their will, and on November 13, 1852, he set them at liberty. A group of wealthy New Yorkers, including the trial judge, donated money to the Lemmons to compensate them for the loss of their slaves, and the freed slaves left New York for the greater safety of Canada.

This was not the end of the matter, however. Five years later the state of Virginia—hoping to use the incident as a test case that would establish the right of slaveowners to retain ownership of their slaves in free states—provided attorneys' fees so that the Lemmons could bring the case to the New York Supreme Court. In *Lemmon v. The People of New York*, Jonathan Lemmon maintained that the state of New York did not have the right to deprive his wife of her "property," but in December 1857 the New York Supreme Court affirmed the order of the previous judge. Lemmon appealed to the New York Court of Appeals, and in March 1860 the order was reaffirmed. The appeals judges cited the 1817 statute emancipating slaves in New York and the Revised Statute of 1830, which declared free any slave brought into New York: "No person held as a slave shall be imported, introduced, or brought into this State, on any pretence whatever. Every such person shall be free." Although the 1830 statute had contained a clause excepting slaves brought into the state in transit, the statute had been amended in 1841 to specifically exclude that clause. In answer to Lemmon's argument that the Constitution holds that no citizen shall be deprived of "life, liberty, or property without due process of law," the People argued that Lemmon had not been deprived of property since the colored Virginians "ceased to be property when he brought them into the state of New York." The Constitutional provision requiring states to return fugitives did not apply in this case, said the presiding judge, because the people in question were not fugitives; their owner had voluntarily brought them into a jurisdiction where "their servile condition was not recognized." After losing the case in the New York Court of Appeals, the state of Virginia planned to appeal to the U.S. Supreme Court, where, in light of the 1857 decision in the Dred Scott case, the Lemmons would have had a good chance of winning. But before the Lemmons had a chance to begin the case, Virginia seceded from the Union and the Civil War began.[7]

The Lemmon case is paradigmatic of the type of lawsuit in which women are both players and nonplayers. Juliet Lemmon "owned" the slaves, yet it was her husband who was the primary mover in the case, and it was the state of Virginia that, for political reasons, pursued the case even after the Lemmons had been compensated for the loss of their "property." Moreover, the case also provides an additional corrective to

the idealization of nineteenth-century women: like the mortgage holders who could be callous or the moneylenders whose business methods
could be calculating, the slave-holding woman could be hard. If Juliet
Lemmon disagreed with her husband's pursuit of the case, she never
publicly said so, although, of course, the laws being what they were, she
would not have had the power to countermand him if she had wanted to.
In any case, the result was the same: she was a party to the lawsuit that
claimed possession of eight slaves. Nineteenth-century women may
have been idealized as gentle and kind, but they were not always so when
money and property were involved. Frances Harper said as much in her
speech to the Woman's Rights Convention in New York in 1866, "We
Are All Bound Up Together": "I do not believe that giving the woman
the ballot is immediately going to cure all the ills of life. I do not believe
that white women are dew-drops just exhaled from the skies. I think
that like men they may be divided into three classes, the good, the bad,
and the indifferent."[8]

Women not only sued to regain personal property of various kinds
but also were involved in litigation to recover real property owned in
their own names. In 1859 Fanny Mills brought suit to regain possession
of her house. She had purchased the house on Twenty-Ninth Street in
New York City with her own money in 1852, but she was advised that as a
"married woman and using her own separate property to pay for the
same," she should "have the deed taken in the name of some third person
as trustee to hold and convey to her when called upon to do so, in whom
she could repose confidence." The 1848 law entitled her to the "separate
use" of any "real and personal property" that she brought into a marriage
or that she inherited after her marriage. However, the law did not give
her the right to the separate use of her personal property once she used it
to purchase real property. Nor could she be confident that the converted
property would not be liable for her husband's debts. Consequently,
Fanny Mills chose to "repose confidence" in her husband's brother,
William Mills, who bought the house in his name and gave her a written
statement saying that he held the deed for her as trustee. She paid
$8,500 for the property and picked up an $8,000 mortgage. Soon after
she bought the house, she made "extensive repairs." The house having
"increased very much in value," she requested William Mills to obtain a

$10,000 mortgage for her, which he did. In 1857, however, the partner of her other brother-in-law persuaded William to take out a $5,500 mortgage to help them in their business and assured William that Fanny would "know nothing about it." She did not know anything about it until early 1859, when George Thompson, who held the mortgage, brought suit to foreclose on the mortgage and sought to obtain an order to sell her property at auction.

Because of the mortgages she herself held on the property, Fanny Mills could not pay off Thompson's mortgage. Consequently she was in danger of losing her house. She brought suit to restrain Thompson from prosecuting the foreclosure and sale, claiming that the mortgage was "a fraud upon her, and [was] illegal and void." Thompson said that he did not even know that she had any claim to the premises until after he began the foreclosure. He had not even named her as a defendant in the suit! When she confronted William Mills regarding why he had mortgaged the property without her knowledge, he maintained that he "thought that her husband had approved of the mortgage." She was able to obtain a stay of proceedings on the sale until there could be a determination in the foreclosure suit. By 1863 the case was not yet settled, however. Early that year Thompson died, and Fanny Mills demanded that his administrators' names be substituted immediately so that she would not lose any more time in the case. This case is an example of the mess that a woman could become enmeshed in due to the law's and custom's refusal to grant a married woman economic and legal autonomy. Her brother-in-law had consulted her husband about the mortgage, he said, but had not asked her—even though the house was her own separate property. And her husband apparently had not bothered to discuss the question with her either. She, like many other women, was dependent upon the advice of others and made the mistake of assuming that her male relatives would advise her wisely and treat her fairly.

Women plaintiffs also became involved in economic matters in other ways than by seeking to gain control of personal or real property that they themselves claimed to own or had personally earned. Primary among these other cases were the lawsuits to obtain damages for injury. Some of the lawsuits to claim damages due to injuries were similar to cases one might see in the law courts today, but others were not. One type of case that we no longer see was the suit for breach of promise. Although today this type of suit might seem frivolous, in the nineteenth century, when women had few career options other than marriage, a man who backed out of a long-term courtship would be comparable to a business partner who absconded with the profits: the woman's livelihood and a significant investment were at stake.

When the woman was pregnant, the stakes were even higher and her investment greater than in a suit for breach of promise alone. The birth of an illegitimate child would greatly reduce, even nullify altogether, her chances of forming a "legitimate" partnership—marriage—with anyone else. In 1866 Jennie Pullman, who as a minor was represented in court by her brother, Henry (she was nineteen), sued James Byrne for breach of promise and asked for ten thousand dollars in damages. She lived with her widowed mother and brothers and sisters in Hudson, New York, and Byrne, who worked for the Internal Revenue Department on Cedar Street in New York City—which appointment he had through his father, who he said was "influential" in Washington—was introduced into her family in Hudson by one of her brothers. He began calling on her in May 1866, and, her mother testified, "he acted in all respects like a suitor" so that she "thought he was paying his honorable addresses to her daughter Jennie with the view of soliciting her hand in marriage." Jennie told the court that he "solemnly promised to make her his wife" and said that between June and November of 1866 he wrote her fifteen letters in which he said that he loved her and wanted to marry her. However, when she told him she was pregnant, she said, he urged her to have an abortion, and when she refused, he sent her some medicine that he told her would cause a miscarriage. Instead, it caused her to become sick. He insisted that she burn all his letters, which she did, including the one that gave her directions on how to take the medicine. Finally, on November 29, she told her mother that she was pregnant, and her mother contacted her oldest brother, Henry, in New York City. Her brother went to see Byrne at his office and demanded that Byrne marry his sister. Byrne refused but said that he would support her if she came to live in New York. Indignant at the slur contained in such a proposition, Henry and Jennie brought suit against Byrne, who was arrested and put in jail. At first, Byrne had not denied that he was the father of her unborn child, but later he denied it and claimed that she had had sexual intercourse with other men. Jennie's family produced testimony from character witnesses in Hudson, including her minister. All testified that she was "a pure and virtuous girl, modest and chaste in her appearance and conduct." Her character, they said, was "good and above reproach." However, Byrne's lawyer produced two men who said they had had "illicit intercourse" with Jennie and signed depositions to that effect. As was not uncommon in such cases, the men were probably paid to perjure themselves. But, on the basis of their testimony, Byrne's bail was reduced to one thousand dollars, and he was released. The case was later abandoned or settled out of court.

Under common law, the father of a seduced girl could sue her seducer for damages on the ground that he had lost his daughter's "services," the assumption being that her pregnancy and motherhood would reduce her ability to work in or outside of the household. By extension, the impairment of the daughter's marriageability also placed an economic burden on the parents, who would not be able to marry her off and, unless they ejected her from the house, would have to support her along with her illegitimate child. In the 1860s this economic argument was used by Barbara Hilke, a widow, in her suit against Jacob Debes. Hilke's daughter Margaretta had worked as a servant in the home of the Debes family and had become pregnant by Jacob Debes, the son of her employer. Margaretta testified that Jacob had promised to marry her, but he had abandoned her after she became pregnant, and his family had discharged her. The baby was born on March 31, 1863, and Barbara Hilke brought suit in May, claiming that Jacob's conduct had "contributed to injure and deprive me of my daughter's work." According to the law, she said, she was "entitled to the services and custody of her minor child." Not only had her daughter's pregnancy deprived her of her daughter's services, she said, but she also had to spend money nursing her and caring for her when she was pregnant. Barbara Hilke asked ten thousand dollars in damages. The Hilkes had emigrated from Germany four years earlier, and Barbara was illiterate; she signed her affidavit with an *X*. The Debes family, on the other hand, although they also were of German descent, were not recent arrivals and were of a higher social class than the Hilkes. Jacob's father owned a cigar store, they employed several servants, and

Jacob's mother could write her name. Jacob was arrested on May 28, 1863, and his parents sought to have him released. His mother signed an affidavit asking to let him go, and Jacob's lawyer brought in four men who—like the two men brought in by James Byrne's lawyer—were willing to swear that they had had sexual intercourse with his accuser. Margaretta, on her part, maintained that she had had sexual intercourse only with Jacob, and her lawyer asked the men what they had "been promised" for testifying. It is significant that at least two of the men worked for Jacob's father. On July 7, 1863, the judge denied Jacob's motion to vacate the order for his arrest. The case ended on March 12, 1866, when the judge found for the plaintiff, ordering Jacob to pay Hilke two thousand dollars, plus court costs of $127.38.

In these breach-of-promise cases, two competing stories were presented to the court. The narrative presented by the woman's lawyer follows the lines of the familiar seduction story: a virtuous woman has been "seduced and abandoned" by an often higher-class man. In this narrative the sympathy lies with the woman, who, although she may be faulted for her moral lapse, is seen as weak and consequently vulnerable to the more sophisticated machinations of the man. The woman is the victim of a scoundrel. Contemporary audiences would have recognized the story from numerous well-known novels, for example, Samuel Richardson's *Clarissa* (1747–1748), Susanna Rowson's *Charlotte Temple* (1791), and Elizabeth Gaskell's *Ruth* (1853). The same story would also be familiar to judge and jury from the well-worn object-lesson tales preached by the clergy and by concerned friends and relatives of susceptible young women. The other narrative that competed for believability with this narrative in the courtroom was the story presented by the lawyers for the defense of the man. In this story a manipulative, corrupt woman schemes to force an innocent man to marry her, presumably for his money and status. This is the story that the lawyers for James Byrne and Jacob Debes hoped to establish with the (apparently purchased) testimony of other men who swore that they had had sexual intercourse with the young women. Which story the judge and jury believed would depend on the evidence that each side could produce and the effectiveness of the lawyers in couching their stories within the familiar frame. The bought testimony tarnishing the sexual character of the young woman, even if it was not sufficient to entirely persuade the jury that the woman's accusation was false (particularly when combated by a parade of credible witnesses for the prosecution swearing to her virtuous character), was often enough to at least raise doubts in the minds of some of the members of the jury so that the jury was unable to find wholly in her favor.

Women also sued for damages because of slander. In 1868 Josephine Baëssa sued John Guédan for slander, claiming damages of ten thousand dollars. Unlike the plaintiff in an earlier suit, she did not mention refusal of credit as a reason for the damages she claimed but instead said that she "became sick and was in bad health" because of Guédan's lies. Witnesses testified that Guédan had told them that Baëssa was an immoral woman, that she had swindled an elderly woman out of her money and jewels, and that she had had a child with her brother-in-law, whose family she lived with. All of the stories were false, she said, but people had believed them. One of her witnesses, Victorine Gérard, testified that Guédan had told her the stories and that after she heard them she believed that Baëssa was a "vile and immoral creature" who was "unfit for [my] company." A wine merchant testified that Guédan told him he was leaving for Europe in a few days, and Guédan was arrested and put in jail with his bail set at seven hundred dollars. His lawyer made a motion to vacate the order of arrest, but it was denied. There is no further record of the case, which was either withdrawn or settled out of court.

Slander was—and is—a difficult thing to settle or "cure." Once something is said, it is said, and sometimes a would-be plaintiff might have found that the publicity surrounding a lawsuit, instead of clearing her name, only spread the slander further. For a nineteenth-century woman, slander was particularly dangerous. Since her principal career option was marriage, she had to be extremely careful to protect her reputation, because most men would not seek a marriage partner in a woman whom they regarded as "damaged goods" (unless they were like the practical Benjamin Franklin, who was glad to get his wife "cheap").[9] In E. D. E. N. Southworth's *The Hidden Hand* (1859), Capitola fights a duel because of a man's slander, and in Louisa May Alcott's "Behind a Mask" (1866), Jean Muir says of the slanderer: "He menaces that which is dearer than life—my good name. A look, a word can tarnish it; a scornful smile, a significant shrug can do me more harm than any blow."[10]

More serious even than breach of promise or slander was rape. Although nineteenth-century women—even more than women today—sought to hide rape because of the shame associated with it, some cases did come before the courts. In April 1860 Bertha Arnold, a fifteen-year-old who lived with her parents, Hirsch and Alice Arnold, on the third floor of 206 Sixth Street, brought suit against Levy Cohen, a middle-aged married man who lived in the same building on the first floor. She testified in a written deposition that on February 22, 1860, he came into her room and asked where her parents were. On finding that they were absent, he "took hold of this deponent and put his arms around her neck and endeavoured to make this deponent submit to his embraces, but that this deponent repulsed him, and endeavoured to make him desist and to free herself from his grasp, but that said Cohen kept hold of this deponent and threw her violently upon the floor, and seized her hands and held her down upon said floor, and endeavoured to violate her person, and beat and bruised this deponent causing her great terror and alarm, and great pain and personal injury and suffering and so continued to do so until deponent's parents returned and drove him away, having as deponent is informed and believes heard her cries from the street." Apparently her parents did not plan to prosecute until a week later after Cohen attacked her again, this time in the corridor on the first floor of the building. He "violently assaulted and struck this deponent and knocked her down and kicked her, inflicting great pain and bruising and injuring her to such an extent that she was unable to arise from the floor or to walk, and that the injuries thereby inflicted upon deponent by said defendant made her ill for a long time." Bertha, represented in court by her father as guardian, sued Cohen for five thousand dollars. A year later the case was settled out of court. It is important to note that the wording of Bertha's deposition avoids saying that the act was consummated on either occasion. If it was, the parents probably chose to portray the crime as attempted rape rather than rape in order to protect their daughter, whose marriage chances would have been diminished if she had in fact been "deflowered," even if the deflowering was the result of enforced rape and not a consensual act.

In an 1867 case, however, the word rape was used. Jane Bothwell sued George A. Barney, who, she said, "violently assaulted and committed a rape upon and ravished" her in November and again in December in his paint store at 40 Hudson Street. She had suffered injuries from the "force and violence" of his assaults, she said, and "was suffering severely from physical debility both in mind and body." She had become pregnant because of the rapes, and, she testified, "in consequence of the defendant's conduct she has been ill and is unable to attend to her business."

In these cases the victims were very young and unmarried. In another case, however, the plaintiff was a widow with five children, the oldest of which was fifteen. In January 1870 Mary Beale sued Moses Rosenberg for "prolonged rape," asking twenty thousand dollars in damages. Beale's husband had been a Confederate general, but she was in a "very reduced state of pecuniary circumstances and was forced to do business in New York in hosiery and fancy goods to support herself and her children." Rosenberg was a wholesale dealer from whom she had purchased goods. On April 18, 1869, she said, when making a delivery to her house, he raped her when she was alone. On April 24 he raped her again in the presence of her little girl. All summer, she said, even after she moved, he had forcibly entered her residence and raped her. Although the shame of rape kept her from reporting him for some time (she said that she "was afraid of the disgrace to herself and her five children"), after it was repeated many times she was made "sick bodily and with mental anguish" to such an extent that her business suffered. Due to her illness, she said, she could not work and had lost business. Her witnesses all testified to her character and confirmed that she had become sick over the past several months. Frederika Fischer said that recently she had "laboured under some great trouble." Another witness said that he had known her since she was a child but that recently she seemed to be suffering from "some secret cause of trouble and anxiety." Her doctor said that she was very ill and was "unable to provide for herself on account of her infirmities." Rosenberg was arrested, but he denied that he had raped her. He claimed that she had made up the story in order to get out of paying his bill of $209.35, and he began an action against her. There is no further record of the case. Considering the disgrace associated with rape, however, it seems unlikely that Beale would have made up the story simply to avoid paying a bill.

In all of the cases that I looked at, I found only four cases of rape. Obviously, that figure does not reflect the actual number of rapes that took place in New York between 1845 and 1875. What it does tell us, though, is that women were very reluctant to have the fact of rape made public. Even today, even after the publicity given such works as Susan Brownmiller's *Against Our Will* (1975), which called attention to the need to deal seriously with rape charges; and after the passage of rape-shield laws to prevent lawyers from questioning women about their past sexual experiences; and after the "sexual revolution," which changed the standards of female respectability; and in spite of journalists' agreement to honor the rape victim's anonymity, women are still reluctant to report instances of rape. The humiliation and shame associated with rape, and the woman's fear of publicity, the knowledge that she may be disbelieved, and her reluctance to relive the experience on the witness stand combine to make rape still the most underreported crime.[11] In the nineteenth century, when a woman's "purity" determined her marriage chances and her good name was her principal resource, and when there was no protection for rape victims—in the courts or in public opinion—women would not come forward unless they had to. Either their families dealt with the issue privately, or the woman (and her family) kept quiet about it and prayed that she would not become pregnant. Most women would not want the scandal of the publicity. And a working-class white woman—if she was raped by a man of a higher social class—or an African American woman would have little recourse in the courts since society considered such behavior acceptable; poor white women and African American women were considered wanton and consequently "available." In the cases I found, it was only after the experience was repeated and the situation became dangerous that the women went to court.

Rather than prosecuting a criminal case, all of these plaintiffs in the rape cases sought damages in a civil suit, a procedure that derived from the common-law tradition with respect to seduction, with the difference that instead of the father seeking reparations because of the loss of his daughter's services, the woman herself sought reparations for her economic disability. Thus, just as in a breach-of-promise suit, economics was a crucial factor in rape cases. All of the plaintiffs sought monetary compensation; Jane Bothwell and Mary Beale claimed that the physical injury and mental anguish caused by the sustained period of rape prevented them from conducting their businesses, and the father of Bertha Arnold presented the case as attempted rape in order to avoid destroying his daughter's marriage chances—which was, of course, an economic argument.

It is interesting that the men accused of rape in two of the four rape cases were Jewish. One might conclude that this was the result of prejudice or fear of the exotic, a possible frame-up, as in Bernard Malamud's 1966 novel, *The Fixer*, except that one of the victims was apparently also Jewish. Of course it is possible that one reason these two cases came to court was that the plaintiffs' attorneys may have believed that it would be easier to obtain a conviction against a man whose religion and culture were alien and consequently suspect.

Other cases in which a woman sued for damages included cases resembling lawsuits that are common in the courts today—cases involving injuries from accidents. In 1865, for example, Magdalena Enders, acting as guardian for her stepson, Charles, began a lawsuit against the Hudson River Railroad Company for twenty-five thousand dollars in damages. Charles, who was eleven at the time of the accident, was run over by a horse-driven railroad car in October 1864. One of his arms was severed above the elbow, four of his fingers and a part of his thumb on the other hand were cut off, and, according to the testimony of his doctor, he suffered brain damage. His attorney charged the railroad company with negligence and claimed that because of his injuries, Charles would have to "lead a life of pauperism" unless he was awarded damages. Witnesses testified that Charles was crossing at the crosswalk, but that the driver was not looking where he was going and made no attempt to stop. Bystanders had to run after him to get him to stop. They also testified that the flagman was not at his post. Charles said that he was going to the market for his mother, that he was carrying a market basket, and that the cars were not in sight when he stepped off the curb. Magdalena Enders, who signed her affidavit with an *X*, testified that Charles's father had died soon after the accident and that Charles did "not have the same mind" since his accident. His attorney said he was "wholly helpless" and did not have "a dollar in the world." All of these factors would suggest that Enders might win a sizeable settlement. However, in a surprise move at the trial, the railroad company produced evidence that the driver had been hired by an outside company owned by one Charles Platt, who had a contract with the railroad company. The latter's attorney maintained that Platt's company was responsible for the accident, not the railroad company. Today, under the law of agency, the outside agency would arguably be recognized as an agent of the railroad company, and the railroad company would be responsible. However, in 1865 the case was dismissed, and Enders was ordered to pay adjusted court costs of $209.45. The judge "expressed his regret at being compelled" to dismiss the case. Enders's lawyer sought a new trial on the basis that the railroad company had illegally withheld the information, introducing documents at the trial that he and his client had no knowledge of, but his motion was denied, and there is no record indicating that Enders sued Platt's company. The probability is that she did not have the money to pursue the case.

Other cases ended more happily for the plaintiff. For example, in an 1867 case, Mary Isaacs, a nurse and the mother of eight children, sued the Third Avenue Railroad, claiming that the conductor had pushed her off the car while the car was still in motion. The principal breadwinner in her family, her husband having been "badly wounded in action" during the Civil War, Isaacs was laid up for several months after the accident and since then had been unable to work regularly. She asked $10,000 in damages. The jury awarded her $3,500. In an 1870 case a child, Catherine Doran, was awarded $2,000 in damages when her hand was crushed in a ferry incident that caused her to lose the use of her right hand. And in another case the same year, Angelina Seabrook sued John Hecker, a baker, whose stacked ovens fell on her home, crushing the roof and destroying furniture as well as causing injury to the plaintiff. She was awarded $1,759.42.

All of the cases in which the woman plaintiff sought damages because of injuries due to rape or slander, accident or assault, occurred after 1860. The only cases I found in which a woman sought damages before the 1860s were breach-of-promise cases. This shift tells us something about the shifting position of women. The 1860 New York State law had enabled married women to bring suit in their own name, and taking a man to court to gain damages for injuries, whether physical or reputational, particularly the claim of economic impairment by the woman herself, reflects the growing assertion of independence by women evident in the women's movement, the movement for married women's property rights, and the struggle for the vote.

The evidence of all of these cases in which women plaintiffs sought financial satisfaction is overwhelming. In spite of law and custom, which kept women out of the public marketplace, the reality was that few women could escape involvement in money matters. Many women needed to earn money, and the court cases reveal some of the ways that they managed to do so—ways that would otherwise remain invisible to the historian. Given few opportunities in conventional society, they found other less conspicuous means: acquiring mortgages, lending money, renting rooms and commercial property, and providing goods and services. Married women supplemented their husband's incomes while unmarried women, widows, and abandoned wives earned what they could to support themselves and sometimes their children. Other women became embroiled in litigation not as active businesswomen or women claiming property of their own but as claimants who were thrust into the world of economics through inheritance or injury.

At some time in their lives, a large proportion of nineteenth-century women were involved in financial matters—whether they wanted to be or not. This involvement cut across not only class lines but racial lines as well. The next chapter looks at works in which women writers portray some of the ways in which economics played a role in the lives of African American women—both slave and free. Then in chapter 6 we turn to lawsuits in which the woman was the defendant. Even more women were drawn into financial matters in this way, sometimes as victims or unwilling partners but other times as aggressive businesswomen. The woman who sought to play the role of the idealized nineteenth-century woman, who, as defined by her culture, was ignorant of and uninterested in money matters, often found that such a role was an impossible fiction. The reality was that money was at the heart of American capitalism, and women, in spite of their prescribed role outside the marketplace, were very much a part of American culture.

chapter five

THE
ECONOMICS
OF RACE

HARPER, WILSON, CRAFTS, AND JACOBS

If African American slave women were "property," how were free African American women affected by economics? In certain respects, it was less problematic for free African American women to assert their financial independence in the nineteenth century than it was for white women because black women were outside of white society. White society *expected* black women to work.[1] In fact, as Hazel Carby points out, one of the problems for nineteenth-century African American women was to confront the dominant ideology of womanhood "which excluded them from the definition 'woman.'"[2] Since "woman" in the nineteenth century denoted dependent femininity, the black woman's exclusion from such a definition, although demeaning, had the result of freeing her from compulsory dependency. In addition, an alternative standard of womanhood already existed among African Americans. Nineteenth-century black women had access to a positive standard of independent womanhood that was not available to white women: the free black woman who worked for her own money was socially superior to the slave woman. Consequently, for black women the ability to earn one's own money had a positive association that did not exist for white women. For example, in Harriet Jacobs's *Incidents in the Life of a Slave Girl* (1861), Linda Brent has as a role model her grandmother, a free black woman who runs her own business and is highly regarded in the community. There were few such role models for white women. As chapter 4 indicates, there were many white women who were economically active, not only as wage earners but as businesswomen and/or as litigants in legal disputes; but society did not hold them up as role models, and much of their activity was invisible.

In spite of this alternative standard for African American women, however, and in spite of (but also because of) white society's definition of black woman as worker, free nineteenth-century African American women were often subjected to the same gender restrictions as white women. Middle-class black women (eager to dissociate themselves from the degradation of the enforced labor of slavery and the association of black-woman-as-worker) could find empowerment in the domestic role. As discussed in chapter 2, many nineteenth-century African American male leaders believed that the best way to gain equality with whites was to adopt the values of white society; this meant acceptance of the binary definition of woman as dependent and man as independent. The impetus behind the emphasis on binary roles among blacks in the nineteenth century and in the early twentieth century was the desire to reverse white America's view of black men as passive and black women as degraded workers. As Mary Helen Washington points out in *Invented Lives: Narratives of Black Women, 1860–1960*, the late nineteenth century to the early twentieth century was a period of intense race hatred. Black male leaders, in struggling against their own oppression, were often unwilling to accept black women as equals, and black women were defensive: "With a race to uplift and every poisonous slander against its women and men used to justify continued oppression, black women race leaders could hardly be expected to reject the ideals set up for 'true women' for what they were: a fanatical method of sexual repression prescribed by white men to oppress and control women."[3] In this chapter we look at four African American women authors, both slave and free, examining their constructions of black female subjectivity and comparing their varying perspectives on women and economics.

In her writings and lectures and in the way she lived her life, African American writer, lecturer, and activist, Frances Ellen Watkins Harper (1825–1911) articulated her belief that women should be self-sufficient. Her reconfiguring of gender and racial identity enabled her to envision a new role for women and particularly for black women. Although she believed in the importance of woman's domestic role, Harper expanded female identity to include both economic independence and public leadership. Her fracturing of gender and race helped her to eschew the definitions of identity promulgated by the dominant culture. Although Harper accepted many aspects of nineteenth-century white culture's definition of femininity (domesticity, motherhood, piety), she refused to buy in to the dominant culture's notion that the way to assert men's independence was to enforce the dependency of women.

Harper was the most successful nineteenth-century African American writer, and as Frances Smith Foster points out, "one of the most important women in United States history."[4] Despite her importance and her success during her lifetime, however, Harper was ignored during most of the twentieth century. Until the late twentieth century, her books were out of print, and when literary critics deigned to mention her works, they did so with condescension. Harper's political aesthetic was out of fashion during a period dominated by the New Criticism, and as Melba Joyce Boyd notes, the opinion of African American male critics was often clouded by what Boyd calls a "blackmale" bias and the need to maintain the patriarchy of the canon.[5]

Born in Baltimore in 1825, Harper was the only child of a free African American mother.[6] After her mother's death when she was three years old, she was raised by her aunt and attended the prestigious Baltimore Academy for Negro Youth, founded by her uncle, William Watkins. The school provided a rigorous education, stressing biblical studies, Greek and Latin, and elocution, in addition to mathematics, history, and geography. William Watkins was also interested in training political and social leaders, and the school graduated numerous orators and public servants. The academy was an excellent preparation for Harper's later career.[7] When she was thirteen, Harper took a position with the Armstrong family, where she was able to continue her education; the family owned a bookstore and encouraged Harper to read as much as she wanted during her free time. In 1850 Harper accepted a position as the first woman teacher at Union Seminary near Columbus, Ohio, a school founded by the African Methodist Episcopal Church. In 1853 Maryland passed a law establishing that any free black who entered the state would be enslaved, and Harper realized that if she returned to Maryland to visit friends or relatives in Baltimore, she would be made a slave. Soon after the law was passed, a black visitor to Maryland was enslaved and later died from his suffering. Harper later wrote to her friend William Still: "Upon that grave I pledged myself to the Anti-Slavery Cause."[8] In August 1854 she began her lecturing career with a lecture in New Bedford entitled "The Education and Elevation of the Colored Race." This was at a time when it was not considered appropriate for women to speak in public. In 1852 the Sons of Temperance had prevented Susan B. Anthony and other women from speaking at a temperance meeting in Albany, and most Americans would have agreed with educator Horace Mann, who said in 1852 that when a woman speaks in public "she unsexes herself."[9] In the face of this attitude, Harper delivered her first lecture; its success is indicated by the fact that soon afterward she was employed by the Maine Anti-Slavery Society, becoming the first African American woman to be employed by a lecture society (*Brighter*, 11, 40). From 1856 to 1859 Harper supported herself as a traveling lecturer in Pennsylvania, New Jersey, New York, Michigan, and Ohio, sending money from her earnings to William Still for use in the Underground Railroad.

On November 2, 1860, Frances Watkins married Fenton Harper in Cincinnati, Ohio. Using money that she had earned from her lectures and publications, she helped her husband buy a farm near Columbus. The couple had a daughter, Mary, and Harper spent the next four years as a farm wife. On May 23, 1864, however, her husband died in debt. The farm was sold, and Harper again found herself dependent on her own resources. She described the horror of this legal deprivation in "We Are All Bound Up Together," a speech delivered to the Eleventh National Woman's Rights Convention in New York in May 1866.

My husband died in debt; and before he had been in his grave three months, the Administrator had swept the very milk-crocks and wash tubs from my hands. I was a farmer's wife and made butter for the Columbus market; but what could I do, when they had swept all away? They left me one thing—and that was a looking-glass! Had I died instead of my husband, how different would have been the result! By this time he would have had another wife, it is likely; and no administrator would have gone into his house, broken up his home, and sold his bed, and taken away his means of support. (*Brighter*, 217)

It did not matter that it was primarily Harper's money that had purchased the farm; legally a wife's property belonged to her husband. Consequently, when her husband died, the farm was sold to pay his debts. Harper used this experience to illustrate the importance of legal equality for women: "Justice is not fulfilled," she said, "so long as woman is unequal before the law" (*Brighter*, 217).

Having lost her property and her livelihood, Harper began once more to earn her living from her lectures and her writing. When the Civil War ended, she traveled in the South, lecturing and meeting with small groups to discuss education and racial uplift. She published a number of books as well as essays and poems in periodicals. Her works include two editions of *Poems on Miscellaneous Subjects* (1854, 1857); *Moses: A Story of the Nile* (1869); *Sketches of Southern Life* (1872); three short novels serialized in the *Christian Recorder*: *Minnie's Sacrifice* (1869), *Sowing and Reaping* (1876–1877), and *Trial and Triumph* (1888–1889); a novel *Iola Leroy, or Shadows Uplifted* (1892); and four books of poetry written between 1894 and 1900. Most of Harper's books were reprinted many times, and by 1871 there were twenty editions of her first book, *Poems*. William Still wrote in 1872 that at least fifty thousand copies had been sold of the four books she had published up to that time (779).

The heroine of Harper's novel *Iola Leroy*, like the earlier heroine of her novella *Minnie's Sacrifice* and Janette in the 1859 short story "The Two Offers," dedicates herself to "a life of high and holy worth."[10] In *Minnie's Sacrifice* Harper writes that instead of writing of a quadroon woman who marries a white man and is lost to the race forever, she has chosen to write of such a woman who maintains her allegiance to her race and lives "a life of lofty self-sacrifice."[11] The same words can be used to describe Harper herself. Whether the topic of her lecture or of her writings was antislavery, racial uplift, education, antiblack violence, women's rights, or temperance, she said what she earnestly believed. The word *earnest* appropriately describes Harper and the heroines of her fiction.

At the same time, however, Harper was very practical. She supported herself all of her life, and she was an astute packager of her own product. She believed passionately in the ideas that she articulated, but she also demonstrated a good understanding of what was marketable. Harper was in tune with her audience, unlike Harriet Wilson, for example, whose attempt to earn a living from her writing was a failure because she did not write what any of her potential readers wanted to hear. Wilson's *Our Nig* alienated abolitionists and Northern whites and was a "downer" for black readers. Harper, on the other hand, was successful because what she said appealed to her audiences—black and white. For Harper, economics was the key—the key to activist success, the key to racial uplift, and the key to women's empowerment. She also believed that character was important and steadfastly insisted that economic advancement without character was worthless. But in her works she returns again and again to the importance of economic success—certainly a very American theme, at least with respect to white male achievement.

First of all, economics was an important part of Harper's activism. On the simplest level, she understood the need for material support for the causes she espoused. For example, she used her earnings to support fugitives on the Underground Railroad, constantly giving money to help the cause, even after she was cautioned by her friend William Still not to jeopardize her own future. Also, in the 1850s Harper espoused the cause of "Free Produce," urging an economic boycott of slave-produced goods. Her support of an economic boycott of slave-produced goods reveals a clear awareness of the importance of economics. "Could slavery exist long if it did not sit on a commercial throne?" she asked in a letter written from Maine on October 20, 1854 (*Brighter*, 45). The campaign did not succeed because not enough people supported it.[12] However, Harper's recognition of the significance of economic pressure was very modern. Carla Peterson notes that Harper was aware of the economic issues involved in slavery and points out that she also used an economic argument against colonization: that no nation could afford to part with four million of its laboring people.[13]

Harper also emphasized the importance of economics in the elevation of the black race. On the one hand, she stressed the building of character and spiritual values. In her 1859 essay "Our Greatest Want," for example, she argues that spiritual worth is more important than money or education: "It may be true that the richer we are the nearer we are to social and political equality; but . . . it does not seem to me that money, as little as we possess of it, is our greatest want. . . . We need more unselfishness, earnestness, and integrity. Our greatest need is not gold or silver, talent or genius, but true men and true women" (*Brighter*, 103). Harper never diverged from this belief that spiritual worth and character were the "greatest want." However, particularly in her later writings, after her experiences in the South had shown her the impotence and low self-esteem that come from ignorance, poverty, and prejudice, she was very practical in her emphasis on economic advancement as crucial to racial uplift. In a lecture in Mobile, Alabama, in 1871, Harper urged the former slaves to educate themselves and their children and to become economically independent by buying land of their own: "Get land, every one that can, and as fast as you can. A landless people must be dependent upon the landed people. A few acres to till for food and a roof, however humble, over your head, are the castle of your independence, and when you have it you are fortified to act and vote independently whenever your interests are at stake" (Still, 775–776). The protagonists in *Minnie's Sacrifice* similarly urge the newly freed slaves to acquire land, and they stress the importance of building factories and establishing industry (68, 74).

Harper supported the Fifteenth Amendment, but she did not think that by itself the vote would help. Traveling through the South during Reconstruction, Harper saw how vulnerable a poor man was; she saw men sell their votes for a sum of money or a bag of sugar. "While I am in favor of Universal Suffrage," she said, "yet I know that the colored man needs something more than a vote in his hand." What he needs, she said, is first of all to have a good home life, and second, to have financial security: he needs "character, wealth and influence . . . to build for himself more 'stately temples' of social condition. A man landless, ignorant and poor may use the vote against his interests; but with intelligence and land he holds in his hand the basis of power and elements of strength" (Still, 770). When referring to the progress of her people, Harper invariably referred to economic matters: "Colored people," she wrote from Georgia in 1870, ". . . are beginning to get homes for themselves and depositing money in the Bank" (Still, 770).

Twentieth-century male critics of Harper's 1892 novel *Iola Leroy* criticized her for not writing with the anger and urgency of the authors of other social protest novels in the 1890s. Robert Bone condescendingly attributes Harper's less belligerent tone to her advanced age and implicitly also to her gender; she is not an "angry young man."[14] Such criticism fails to see the anger beneath Harper's measured tones or the urgency and political significance of her perspective. Also, written from a male bias, it misses the radicalism of Harper's emphasis on woman's role as intellectual leader, particularly in the late nineteenth century, when many African American men did not regard women as their intellectual equals. The American Negro Academy, established in 1897, for example, refused to accept women as members, and as a letter in the *Colored American Magazine* states, many black men believed that women were "inferior in intellectual capacity to men."[15] Defying this conventional view and fracturing gender definitions that would relegate women to second-class status, Harper wrote and spoke as an intellectual leader and urged other women to join her in the cause of racial uplift. Her novel *Iola Leroy* presents a case for a black intellectual elite composed of women as well as men.[16] In the novel, Iola and Lucille are perceived as race leaders along with certain male characters, and educated black men and women come together for "conversaziones" to discuss the important issues of the day.

However radical Harper was in her aspirations for women, she, like Stowe, did not advocate a change in the economic system. Once slavery was abolished, her goal was to integrate blacks into American economic life. Harper wanted to see African Americans plug into American capitalism. In "Fancy Sketches" (1874) the characters discuss the need for blacks to become part of the economic system: "It would be an excellent plan if some of our colored men who possessed money could only unite upon some plan by which we could build up some thriving industries of our own" (*Brighter,* 229). Harper's ideas are consistent with the self-help ideas of American individualism and the American Dream.[17] The 1874 essay concludes with a plea for black self-reliance:

> The most important thing then for us to consider, is not simply what this party will do for us; or the other against us; but what are we going to do as for ourselves, to diversify our industry, build up our character, better our condition, and intensify our spiritual life. Congress may make its statute books black with laws for our defence, but all the help that comes from without is not like the help that comes from within. (*Brighter,* 230)

Although Harper wrote for both blacks and whites, much of her writing was intended to provide guidance for blacks. Her poems and stories were used as textbooks in the freedmen's schools in the South. The novel *Iola Leroy* ends with a note by the author, expressing the hope that her novel will have a twofold effect. On the one hand, she hopes it will awaken all Americans to "a stronger sense of justice and a more Christ-like humanity" toward black people. But the novel is also directed at African Americans themselves: she says that she hopes it will inspire them to "embrace every opportunity, develop every faculty, and use every power God has given them to rise in the scale of character and condition" (282). Character is important to Harper; but so is social condition. And social condition is dependent upon economics.

What was most radical about Harper's economic ideas was her extension of this emphasis on economics to her discussion of women. Harper's position on women and economics derives from her redefinition of gender and race. On the one hand, Harper asserts black women's right to white female identity, reversing society's construction of the black woman and appropriating for her race the dominant society's definition of woman. At the same time, however, as Hazel Carby notes, she "reconstructs womanhood" to produce an "alternative discourse of black womanhood."[18] In Harper's definition, woman was characterized by the qualities of true womanhood (piety, domesticity, and gentility), but she also had the potential to be independent, intellectual, self-sufficient, and a leader. The self-reliant protagonist Janette in Harper's 1859 story "The Two Offers" is both self-dependent and *engagée*, and the description of her gives us an idea of Harper's conception of a praiseworthy woman's life: "Too self reliant to depend on the charity of relatives, she endeavored to support herself by her own exertions, and she had succeeded. Her path for a while was marked with struggle and trial, but instead of useless repining she met them bravely, and her life became not a thing of ease and indulgence, but of conquest, victory, and accomplishments. . . . She had a high and holy mission on the battle-field of existence" (*Brighter*, 107, 114).

Harper insisted that women needed the opportunity to be able to support themselves. In "Fancy Sketches" (1874) she describes the unfortunate situation of an African American teacher who lost her job after the state outlawed segregated schools. Although the author agrees with the law in the long run, she sympathizes with the young woman. The problem, says Harper, is that there need to be more opportunities opened to women, particularly black women; there needs to be "some plan for opening the fields of occupation for us. If white women feel that they are limited by their sex, how must it be with us? . . . What they call limitation would be to us broad liberty" (*Brighter*, 230). Harper delineates the practical results of women's economic independence in an 1878 speech, "Coloured Women of America," noting that "women as a class are quite equal to the men in energy and executive ability." After mentioning several women who worked hard to help their husbands financially, she describes the situation of a number of entrepreneurial single women who "saved considerable money from year to year, and are living independently." Since the end of slavery, she said, many women have saved their earnings and have "homes of their own bought by their hard earnings" (*Brighter*, 271–273). In her poem "Learning to Read," the former slave, Aunt Chloe, tells how education helped her to gain financial independence:

> Then I got a little cabin—
> A place to call my own—
> And I felt as independent
> As a queen upon her throne. (*Brighter*, 206)

Aunt Linda in *Iola Leroy* starts a baking business during the Civil War, and after the war she has saved enough money to help her husband buy land on a plantation (154). As I indicated above, Harper herself had helped her husband buy a farm. Although she lost that investment due to the law regarding a married woman's property, she later bought her own house in Philadelphia.

The importance of woman's economic independence is underscored in *Iola Leroy*. As one of the characters states near the end of the novel, "We cannot begin too early to teach our boys to be manly and self-respecting, our girls to be useful and self-reliant" (253). After the Civil War, Iola comes north with her uncle and grandmother. However, she is not content to remain idle in her uncle's house even though, as he says, "there is no necessity for [her] to go out to work": "Uncle Robert," said Iola, after she had been North several weeks, "I have a theory that every woman ought to know how to earn her own living. I believe that a great amount of sin and misery springs from the weakness and inefficiency of women. . . . I am going to join the great ranks of bread-winners." (205)

Iola's assertion sounds very much like that of Christie Devon at the beginning of Louisa May Alcott's 1872 novel *Work*;[19] however, Iola's decision to work is complicated by problems of race. Although she is light-skinned, she refuses to "pass" for white, and on several occasions she loses her job when her race is detected. However, she perseveres, asserting, "Every woman should have some skill or art which would insure her at least a comfortable support. I believe there would be less unhappy marriages if labor were more honored among women" (210). Even when Iola marries Dr. Latimer, she does not wholly give up her work. Their union brings together two people who have a "high and holy mission" (268). After their marriage, Iola teaches Sunday school and works with the church to help the young and the old and the needy. Although she works as a volunteer rather than doing paid work, she, like Harper herself, is passionately dedicated to the education and elevation of her race.

The second heroine in *Iola Leroy*, Lucille Delany, also continues to do meaningful work after she marries, although in her case she does paid work. She and her husband, Harry, run a flourishing school, and she continues her work as a teacher: "Lucille gives her ripening experience to her chosen work, to which she was too devoted to resign" (280). Like Iola and Frank Latimer, and Louis and Minnie in *Minnie's Sacrifice*, Lucille and Harry are joined in the holy mission of racial uplift: "Through the school they are lifting up the homes of the people" (280).

Harper allows her secondary heroine to continue with paid work after marriage, but her principal protagonist, Iola, although she "works," takes on a more traditional role. Teaching Sunday school and doing church work do not conflict with nineteenth-century white definitions of gender. Janette in "The Two Offers" is closer to Harper herself, supporting herself throughout her life and dedicating her life to service. However, since Janette never marries, Harper is not faced with the need to decide whether or not Janette would continue with her work after marriage. Moreover, as Mary Helen Washington points out, "service" to others is perfectly compatible with the cult of true womanhood: the true woman works unselfishly for others.[20] Of Harper's heroines, then, Lucille Delany is the most radical: she refuses to give up her paid work after marriage. It is interesting that of the two heroines in *Iola Leroy*, Iola appears white while the novel emphasizes that Lucille has no white blood in her veins (199). It is possible that Harper found it easier (or at least knew that it would be more acceptable) to conform to popular thinking and have her "black" heroine take the unconventional route and continue working for pay after marriage, while her "white" heroine fulfilled the more traditional role defined by white society.

Although Harper accepted some of the feminine qualities that conventional society ascribed to womanhood, she fractured the concepts of gender and racial identity, deconstructing and expanding their definition. An African American woman was as chaste and ladylike as the "true woman" of white society, but a "woman" was also self-reliant, intellectually and politically active and assertive, and economically independent.

Whereas Harper was a free, Southern-born, middle-class woman, what of the free Northern-born, working-class black woman? In her autobiographical novel, *Our Nig* (1859), Harriet Wilson (1825–1900) tells the story of her life in antebellum New England.[21] While Harper was educated at a prestigious school in Baltimore, Wilson received only three years of education at a small country school in New Hampshire.[22] While Harper was part of the black intelligentsia, whose writing and lecturing brought her into contact with many intellectuals and reformers, Wilson was an indentured servant whose friends—at least for the first forty years of her life—were, like herself, of yeoman or working-class background. And, while Harper published numerous books and essays, and during most of her life received wide acclaim for her work, Wilson published only one book, which was unread and unreviewed in her lifetime, and the facts of her authorship remained unknown until one hundred and thirty years after the book's publication.[23] The only similarity between them in their personal lives is that for both authors one parent was white and the other was black. Even here, though, there are major differences. Whereas Harper's mother was black, Wilson's mother was white. Moreover, whereas Harper's father was not married to her mother (interracial marriage being illegal in the South at that time), Wilson's parents were apparently legally married.

In *Our Nig*, the protagonist Frado's struggle to survive physical abuse, deprivation, and neglect—which reflects Wilson's own struggle—contrasts sharply with the privileged position of the white male writers of the "American Renaissance" discussed in chapter 3. Wilson did not have a family to support her, as Thoreau had, or a wife's money to depend on, as in the case of Emerson. Moreover, doors were closed to her not only because of her race but also because of her gender and class. As John Ernest points out in *Resistance and Reformation in Nineteenth-Century African-American Literature*, not only is Wilson regarded as object because of her race; she is also "woman-as-object" and "worker-as-object."[24] Triply marginalized, Wilson portrays a protagonist whose chances are further compromised by a violent childhood in which she is subjected to brutal treatment by a pathologically prejudiced and hateful woman. Once Frado reaches adulthood, however, her principal concern is to earn her own living. Like the white women writers discussed in chapter 3, many of whose works reflect their own struggle for economic survival, Wilson focused on an issue that was paramount in her life—economics.[25] Wilson's motivation in writing the book was, as she says in her preface, to earn money to support herself and her child, and as Karla F. C. Holloway comments in "Economies of Space," Wilson's novel "constantly offers reminders of its economic motive" in the repeated use of "economic metaphors" and in its sparse narrative and rhetorical structure.[26] Contrasting Wilson's narrative technique and its relationship to her economic motivation with the way in which Harper's political and inspirational motivation is reflected in her expansive language and greater contextual complexity, Holloway concludes that, despite these differences, both works share the common metaphor of the slave market.[27]

The importance of economics in Wilson's text is apparent in three areas: the economics of poverty, the economics of greed, and the economics of independence. Wilson establishes the economic theme at the very beginning of her work in the preface. She needs to support herself and her child, she says, and she hopes that sales from the book will enable her to do so: "Deserted by kindred, disabled by failing health, I am forced to some experiment which shall aid me in maintaining myself and child without extinguishing this feeble life." She concludes her preface by making a plea to her "colored brethren" to buy her book: "I sincerely appeal to my colored brethren universally for patronage, hoping they will not condemn this attempt of their sister to be erudite, but rally around me a faithful band of supporters and defenders."[28] One suspects that Wilson also had other motives in writing *Our Nig*. She certainly must have derived some satisfaction from having the opportunity to tell her side of the story—to reveal the cruelty of Mrs. Bellmont, to critique the hypocrisy of some abolitionists, to reveal her mistreatment by her husband—and however modestly she apologized for her "defects" as an author, the fact that she wrote at all indicates that she took pleasure in demonstrating that one of her "humble position" had the ability to write—and publish—such a work.[29] Nevertheless, her overt assertion of economic necessity and her undisguised plea for patronage are indicative of the foregrounding of economic issues throughout her book.

The book begins with a forceful portrayal of the economics of poverty. In describing Frado's white, working-class mother, Mag Smith, Wilson emphasizes the importance of money in all of the major decisions in Mag's life. First of all, Mag is seduced by a man of a higher social class who lures her with promises of "ease and plenty her simple heart had never dreamed of" (6). Abandoned by her lover and shunned by the townspeople, Mag resolves to support herself: "She vowed to ask no favors of familiar faces; to die neglected and forgotten before she would be dependent on any" (8). After she has supported herself for two years, however, the influx of cheap immigrant labor into the town undercuts her ability to support herself (8). After several years of suffering and hardship, Mag accepts the marriage proposal of Jim, a "kind-hearted African," who promises to rescue her from poverty. Again, as Wilson makes clear, her decision is based on economics: the reader may philosophize upon the "impropriety of such unions," says Wilson, but "want is a more powerful philosopher" (13). Finally, after Jim's death, Mag's decision to give Frado to the Bellmonts is an economic decision. She and her common-law husband, Seth Shipley, are unable to find work, and after several years of hardship, they decide that they cannot afford to keep both children; they take six-year-old Frado to the Bellmonts and leave town to find work elsewhere (16–23).

Just as Wilson emphasizes economic necessity in the story of Frado's

mother, she also emphasizes economics in her portrayal of Mrs. Bellmont. In this case, however, rather than being a question of the economics of poverty, it is the economics of greed.[30] Mrs. Bellmont decides to
keep Frado because Frado will work for free as an indentured servant,
and unlike hired girls, she won't be able to leave, however harshly Mrs.
Bellmont treats her. Hence, Mag decides to leave Frado at the Bellmonts. Describing Mrs. Bellmont as a "she-devil," Mag says, "She can't
keep a girl in the house over a week; and Mr. Bellmont wants to hire a
boy to work for him, but he can't find one that will live in the house with
her" (18). Mrs. Bellmont is willing to keep Frado, as she says, "to make
her do my work" (26). The relationship is wholly based on economics.
She feels no responsibility for Frado's physical or spiritual health. When
Frado is sick, Mrs. B. beats her mercilessly because she is not doing her
work fast enough (82). And when Aunt Abby takes Frado to religious
meetings, Mrs. B. forbids Frado to read the bible, ordering her to "put up
the book, and go to work" (87). Wilson tells us that Mrs. B. takes no interest in her except for the work Frado will do for her, which "was all the
responsibility she acknowledged" (87). She refuses to allow Frado to go
to church because she does not want to lose her economic value. She
tells her husband: "Just think how much profit she was to us last summer. . . . She did the work of two girls" (90). Profit is her only concern.
"I'll beat the money out of her, if I can't get her worth any other way,"
Mrs. B. asserts when her husband objects to the beatings she inflicts on
Frado (90). And ultimately, when Frado rebels, she wards off Mrs. B.'s
blows by appealing to her mercenary nature: " 'Stop!' shouted Frado,
'strike me, and I'll never work a mite more for you' " (105). When Frado's
term of indenture is over, Mrs. B. is beside herself at the thought of losing her free servant; she attempts to persuade Frado to remain, telling
her she is "ungrateful" to leave a "home of such comfort." However,
Frado replies that she has "had enough of such comforts" (116). Even after Frado has left the house, Mrs. B.'s obsession with money is apparent
in her refusal to pay the doctor when Frado is brought back, ill, and in
her refusal to take her in a second time—even though Frado's ill health is
a direct result of Mrs. Bellmont's mistreatment of her (120, 122).

Not only is the economics of greed emphasized in Mrs. B.'s treatment
of Frado, but it is the motivating factor in her attitude toward other

characters as well. The principal reason for Mrs. B's hatred of Aunt Abby, Mr. B's sister, for example, is her resentment of the fact that through Abby's father's will, Abby is entitled to part of the homestead (45). The elder Bellmont apparently wrote the will to protect his widowed daughter from his daughter-in-law.[31] Mrs. B. is also motivated by money concerns in her attitude toward her own children. She attempts to coerce her daughter Jane into marrying for money even though Jane does not love—or even like—the man her mother insists that she marry. And she attempts to break up her son Jack's marriage because his wife is "not worth a copper"; she exclaims, "Hadn't she any property? What did you marry her for [?]" (111, 113–115).[32]

Thus Wilson chronicles the economics of poverty in relation to Mag Smith and the economics of greed in relation to Mrs. Bellmont. The third way in which economics is highlighted in the work is in relation to Frado herself, first of all, in the economics of independence. James, her principal defender in the Bellmont family, encourages her in "self-reliance," which he feels will be "of service to her in after years" (63). As the years pass, and the term of her servitude draws to an end, Frado, plagued by poor health, wonders if she can succeed in "providing for her own wants," but "she resolve[s] to try" (110). She works for a while, but then she falls ill. Even when she is bedridden and her body is in pain, however, Frado is strengthened by her resolve to support herself: "The hope that she might yet help herself, impelled her on" (123). Once she feels well enough to sew again, she determines to find a way to be independent. Wilson writes: "Then came the old resolution to take care of herself, to cast off the unpleasant charities of the public" (124). Frado leaves New Hampshire for Massachusetts, where she hopes to support herself by making straw bonnets. She finds a woman who teaches her the trade, and together they sew and read, Frado being concerned that "every leisure moment" be "carefully applied to self-improvement" (124). After her marriage, Frado enjoys a brief period of relief in "looking to another for comfortable support" (127). However, this period is short-lived, and she soon finds that her trust has been misplaced. Her husband leaves her for long periods during which she must support herself, and she once again feels the strength of "self-dependence" (127).

Increasingly, however, Frado's drive toward economic independence is interwoven with the economics of poverty. As with her mother, it becomes a question primarily of survival. Her husband abandons her, leaving her ill and pregnant, and "the horrors of her condition nearly prostrated her" (128). She is forced to go to the county poor home, where she delivers her baby, remaining in the poor home until her husband returns unexpectedly later that year. But he is not home long before he is gone again, once again leaving her to her own resources. After a series of such absences, during which time she struggles to "toil for herself and child" (128), she receives the news that her husband is dead. Placing her son in a foster home, she "procured an agency, hoping to recruit her health, and gain an easier livelihood for herself and child" (129). At the end of the book Frado is given a "valuable recipe" and begins manufacturing this "useful article for her maintenance" (129). In the appendix, Allida tells us that this "useful article" was a recipe for hair dye that a compassionate stranger had given to Wilson, and for a while it provided her with a livelihood (137). Unfortunately, however, her health began to fail again, and unable to peddle her product, she determined to support herself and her child by writing her autobiography—the book that became *Our Nig* (137).

Thus the writing of the book itself represents an economic statement. As I indicated earlier, Wilson in the preface urges her "colored brethren" to buy her book to assist her in supporting herself and her child. Three of the letters in the appendix reiterate Wilson's plea. Allida writes: "I trust she will find a ready sale for her interesting work; and let all the friends who purchase a volume, remember they are doing good to one of the most worthy" (137). And Margaretta Thorn writes: "I hope all those who call themselves friends of our dark-skinned brethren, will lend a helping hand and assist our sister, not in giving, but in buying a book" (140). Economics, then, are a paramount concern in this book, even overtly the *raison d'être* of the book itself.

In *Our Nig* Wilson seems to be obsessed with economics. Economic concerns are introduced into the discussion of almost every character and event. In addition to their role in the principal aspects of the novel discussed above—the poverty of Mag Smith, the greed of Mrs. Bellmont, and the career of Frado—they appear peripherally on almost every page. For example, when Frado is ill and must be taken in by a town resident at public expense, she is placed in the home of a Mrs. Hoggs, who, Wilson says, "was a lover of gold and silver, and she asked the favor of filling her coffers by caring for the sick" (122). After her mistreatment at the hands of the mercenary Mrs. Hoggs, Frado is taken in by kind Mrs. Moore, who, we are told, had known better days before "misfortune" (brought about by a branch of the Bellmont family) had deprived her of her wealth. Thus economics creeps into the discussion one way or another: either a person is mercenary (Mrs. Bellmont and Mrs. Hoggs) or a person is victimized by the mercenary (Mr. Moore and Frado herself). Moreover, the fact that Mrs. Moore's husband gave up and abandoned her and her children after his own economic defeat at the hands of the Bellmonts gives the lie to Emerson's advice to women—relying on a "good man" doesn't always work. Frado herself becomes a victim of this philosophy when her husband abandons her. Moreover, even before her husband leaves, Frado discovers that he himself is a fraud. One of those "professed fugitives from slavery," he earns money by lecturing—telling apocryphal stories of his experiences under the lash. Frado learns that "he had never seen the South, and that his illiterate harangues were humbugs for hungry abolitionists" (128). Money, it seems, is an all-too-common human motivator.

Cynthia Davis suggests that Wilson's emphasis on the "economic motivations that underwrite human relations" is indicative of the book's relationship to the slave narrative.[33] I would extend this suggestion to include its relationship to works written by people who had to struggle for economic survival, white or black. It is not only within slavery that human relations can be determined by economics. Wilson's working-class origins and her own financial difficulties after she leaves the Bellmonts contribute to her economic problems along with her race. Not only does the book chronicle Frado's attempts to earn money and the obstacles that stand in her way, but it provides us with a picture of the impact of economic realities on a working-class woman who, without a safety net to rely upon, must become economically independent or starve. In this respect, class represents the principal difference between her and some of the middle-class women—both white and black—whose assertions of independence we have discussed thus far. Harper's middle-class African American heroine, Iola Leroy, for example, tells her uncle that she wants to work because she *wants* to be independent, whereas he urges her to stay in the home, saying there is no necessity for her to work (205). Cummins's white heroine, Gertrude, in *The Lamplighter*, severs with Mr. Graham and strikes out on her own despite his urging her to remain in the family. But Wilson and her protagonist do not have a home and family to provide economic and emotional support.

Both Wilson and her fictional character are reduced to the same straits as their impoverished mothers: each must place her child in someone else's home because she cannot afford to care for the child herself. Fortunately for Wilson, the family who cared for her son was a kind family, who, without the racial prejudice or mercenary greed of Mrs. Bellmont, provided a good home for him until he died of "fever" at the age of seven. In the appendix Margaretta Thorn tells us that "he has a home where he is contented and happy, and where he is considered as good as those he is with" (139). Wilson was luckier than her mother in her choice of a foster home. But the cyclical significance of this ending outside the novel provides a tragic comment on the economic theme of Wilson's book: no matter how hard she struggled to "elevate" herself and to earn her living, she ended up with no alternative but the one taken by her impoverished and desperate mother. If she was dealt the race card early in life, it is only one card in her hand. When it is added to the poor health caused by years of beatings, her class, her unlucky choice of a husband, and her lack of a safety net, it is clear that the deck is stacked against her.

Frado's—and Wilson's—"progress" in this novel is cyclical. Exploring the economics of poverty, greed, independence, and then poverty again, the novel becomes an interrogation of the Emersonian principles that underlie the myth of American individualism and the American Dream. Self-reliant and determined, and free to shape her destiny, Frado ends up in the same situation that her mother was in a generation earlier.[34] What Emerson left out, Wilson seems to be saying, was a consideration of the realities of life outside the control of the individual: race, gender, health, childhood trauma, treatment by other people, and dependent children.

Significantly, however, Wilson's own life after the publication of *Our Nig* and the death of her son followed an upward trajectory. In fact, she was ultimately able to realize her earlier ambition of economic independence. Her health having improved, she apparently was able to build up a business selling hair products. Although she certainly did not become as successful as Madame C. J. Walker (discussed in chapter 2), she was able to support herself.[35] But even greater success came with her involvement in the Spiritualist movement. By 1867, she had become well known as a lecturer and medium, speaking to crowds of thousands throughout the Northeast, where, as one newspaper reported, her lectures "excited thrilling interest" and constituted an "eloquent plea for the recognition of her race."[36] She also functioned as a "clairvoyant physician," sometimes affixing "Dr." in front of her name, and in 1870 she married a white man eighteen years her junior. Both were listed as physicians in the Federal Census of that year. For the last thirty-five years of her life, she was financially and socially successful, speaking on platforms with such notables as Victoria Woodhull, lecturing on such topics as children's education and labor reform, and entertaining a wide circle of friends at her home. When she died in 1900 at the age of seventy-five, a "massive and impressive" granite tombstone was erected over her grave.[37] But it is important to note that Wilson's success came only after the deaths of her husband and son had left her free to pursue her own independent path, and, even more important, after she had found in the Spiritualist society the supportive "family" that she had never had.

Whereas Harper and Wilson (and Wilson's protagonist) were born free, Hannah Crafts's *The Bondwoman's Narrative* tells the story of a woman who was born in slavery. Written in the 1850s, the novel was unpublished until 2002, when it was edited by Henry Louis Gates, Jr., who had purchased and researched the manuscript.[38] Although we do not know if the name Crafts is the author's real name or a pseudonym, or to what extent the narrative is the story of the author's life, Gates presents sufficient evidence to authenticate the date of the manuscript and to verify Crafts's racial claims: we know that the manuscript was indeed written in the 1850s and that the author was probably an African American woman.[39] Moreover, internal evidence suggests that she was a former slave. She uses the real names of people, some of whom are traceable, as, for example, the Wheeler family, whom Crafts identifies as her last owners. Crafts reveals an intimate knowledge of the Wheelers such as might have been acquired by a woman who worked in the family as a "bond-woman," and what she tells us coincides with information gained from John Hill Wheeler's diary and other data. Moreover, as Gates points out, there would have been "no commercial advantage" for a white person to claim to be a slave.[40] In view of all of this evidence, I will treat Hannah Crafts's work as an autobiographical novel. There is no reason to believe that she is not what she claims to be on her title page: "A Fugitive Slave Recently Escaped from North Carolina." Since the writing of the novel predates the publication of Wilson's *Our Nig*, Crafts's work is probably, as Gates claims, the first novel by an African American woman.[41]

Within the institution of slavery, human relationships are based wholly on economics. Under capitalism, the employer-employee relationship is based on economics, but although economics may determine the employee's lifestyle and standard of living and circumscribe his/her choices, he/she is nevertheless free to establish an independent life off the job, so to speak. In the slave-owner relationship, however, since the slave is the property of the owner, the economic relationship is constant; it permeates all aspects of the slave's life and lasts until his/her death. Although many slaves managed to maintain a sense of community and culture, the slave could not have a life independent of the economic relationship with his/her owner except insofar as the owner willed it; even the slave's family was not his/her own. In this novel by a former slave writing about her experiences under slavery, then, it is not surprising that a major thematic concern in Crafts's work is economics. Even more intensely than white women writers of the same period or free black women writers like Harper and Wilson, Crafts focuses on money and class. Chapter 1 alone contains sixteen references to economics in as many pages. Crafts introduces a mention of money or financial matters into the initial description of almost every character, and economics provides the catalyst for all major events and the basis for almost every story within a story.

First of all, economic concerns enter into the introduction of each character. Beginning her emphasis on economics with her introduction of herself, Crafts describes her awareness of her status as a slave in economic terms, spelling out her exclusion by class and her lack of monetary recompense. In the second paragraph of the novel, she writes, I "soon learned that my African blood would forever exclude me from the higher walks of life. That toil unremitted unpaid toil must be my lot and portion without even the hope or expectation of any thing better" (6). In the next paragraph she introduces her master, and the two major pieces of information she gives us are economic. He supplies his slaves with food and clothing from "motives of policy," i.e., he is a practical man and wants to protect his investment as he would with his "horses or other domestic animals" (6). But it is "whispered" that he has lost his fortune (13). Next we meet Aunt Hetty, the white woman who teaches Hannah to read and write. Crafts tells us that she and her husband are "very poor" (7). Expanding on this economic introduction to the couple, Crafts explains that they had previously been wealthy: "Wealth had been theirs, with all the appliances of luxury, and they became poor through a series of misfortunes" (9). Next we meet Mrs. Bry, the white housekeeper. Again, the first thing we are told about her establishes her economic status. Like Aunt Hetty and her husband, Mrs. Bry has seen better days: "The loss of her husband's India ship and his consequent failure in business" have "reduced her to the extremity of accepting the situation of housekeeper" (19). The next two characters to be introduced are the master's bride and her presumed guardian, Mr. Trappe. They are both characterized initially in economic terms, with a mystery surrounding them that will prove to derive wholly from economic considerations. Hannah's new mistress is introduced as a representative of her class, and although this class identification becomes ironic later, initially we are introduced to a woman of aristocratic bearing, with "haughty eyes" and a "deferential and defiant" manner (27, 28). Similarly, Mr. Trappe is introduced in terms of his profession and monetary worth: he is said to be a "lawyer of wealth and position" (32). After meeting them, we meet Lizzy, the mistress's quadroon maid, and although she herself has no money, she introduces herself in relation to her class claims. She proudly boasts of her "good family" connections, asserting that "good blood was an inheritance" (33). Crafts says that when a slave of mixed blood heard mention of an "honorable gentleman" from whom he or she claimed descent or saw a "great lady . . . in jewels and satins the priveledge [*sic*] of thinking

[']he or she is a near relative of mine['] was a very great privelage [*sic*] indeed" (34).

This, then, is how Crafts introduces her characters in the early chapters, and she follows this pattern throughout the novel. A few characters, particularly minor characters, are not characterized in economic terms, and we are given other information about each of the characters in addition to his/her relationship to money. But the economic references—money and/or class—are a constant, appearing in almost every introduction in the novel.

Not only does Crafts use economic terms to introduce her characters, but she also uses economic *raisons d'être* for the major plots contained in the narrative—and this sentimental/gothic novel tells multiple stories. The first principal story centers on the mystery surrounding Mr. Trappe and Hannah's mistress, and the catalyst for this story is wholly economic. Trappe has discovered that Hannah's mistress, Mrs. Vincent, is descended from a slave woman. She is the only "property" that remains from her father's lost estate, and Trappe is determined to profit from his knowledge of her origins. Throughout the telling of this tale, Crafts consistently highlights the economic basis of the story. First of all, she tells us that Trappe was the executor for her mistress's father's will, and when Hannah asks Lizzy what kind of hold Trappe has over her mistress, Lizzy makes the cryptic comment that perhaps "he wished to sell her" (34)—this before Hannah or the reader knows of her slave antecedents. Crafts says that Trappe will use the secret to his own "profit and advantage" (36), and later Hannah overhears a conversation in which Trappe complains that Mrs. Vincent has not paid him the "monthly stipend" she had promised to keep him quiet (37). When Mrs. Vincent objects that "the bank which contained [her] property" has failed, he tells her that her husband's "property is mortgaged to its fullest extent, and that notwithstanding his position he is in fact a poor man" (39). She pleads with him to save her husband's honor, but he replies, "Pecuniary interests are to[o] valuable to be set aside" (40). It is Trappe's threat—to tell her husband in order to extort money from him or to sell her himself—that drives Mrs. Vincent to escape with Hannah and leads to all of their subsequent adventures.

"Pecuniary interests" are Trappe's guiding principle in all that he does, and as Crafts shows, other people share his credo. After Hannah and her mistress run away, they are found by some men whose motivation is wholly economic: their principal concern is the "large reward" offered for the women (71). And when the men bring them to jail for safekeeping, the jailer describes the situation in economic terms: "Couldn't afford to lose 'em—bring heaps of money" (77). Economic concerns are behind even what seems to be a kindness. The jailer tells Hannah that Trappe has hired a physician to care for the ailing Mrs. Vincent: "He fears that she will lose her beauty, and then . . . she would be much less valuable" (87). He wants her cured, says the jailer, or it will be "two thousand dollars out of his pocket" (87). When the two are brought before Trappe, he reveals that this is not the first time he has used his legal knowledge to obtain information about a woman who has been passing for white. In fact, he says, it is his "line of business"; "it brings gold—bright gold" (98). When Mrs. Vincent dies after being told that her purchaser will come to look at her the next morning, Crafts comments that a "deeper shadow" seemed to pass over Trappe's face. She wonders if it is due to his conscience or to "a vision of pecuniary loss" (100). The reader concludes that it is the latter when the next day Trappe comments coldly to the slave trader, after telling him that Mrs. Vincent is dead: "I reckon it a clear loss of two thousand" (104). The two then discuss the difficulties in dealing with "wenches," and the trader tells of how he had lost more than ten thousand dollars because women had died before he could sell them. One woman, he said, "jumped into the river when she found that her child was irretrievably gone" (104–105), and the reader is reminded of Lucy in *Uncle Tom's Cabin*. Another, he said, was torn by bloodhounds, and he had to sell her "for a song" (105). Trappe then sells Hannah for twelve hundred dollars, after haggling with the slave trader and showing off her finer points the way one would sell a horse (106). When Hannah leaves with the trader, Saddler, he tells her that Trappe "buys only for speculation" and "has no more feeling than a bit of iron" (113). Hannah later hears someone else say essentially the same thing about Trappe, adding, in words that echo those said about the slave trader Haley in *Uncle Tom's Cabin*: "He would not have hesitated a moment to sell his own mother into slavery" (232). Saddler defends his own trade using words that again are reminiscent of Stowe's novel: "Respectable people, honorable gentlemen, grave Senators, and even the Republican Presidents buy slaves; are they better than I am who sells them?" (115).

This is the end of the first major episode in Crafts's novel. It not only is based on economic concerns but is characterized by economics throughout. The next episode—Hannah's stay with the Henrys—is a kind of transitional oasis before the final episode, her life with the Wheelers. The Henrys are among the few characters in the novel who are not introduced in economic terms. However, economic matters soon become a part of this episode. When Mrs. Henry hears from the man who has inherited Hannah after Saddler's death, Hannah pleads with the kind Mrs. Henry to buy her: "All I ask is to feel, and know of a certainty that I have a home, that some one cares for me, and that I am beyond the gripe [grip] of these merciless slave-traders and speculators" (125). But Mrs. Henry says that she cannot buy her because her father had exacted a promise from her on his deathbed—that she would "never on any occasion . . . sell or buy a servant" (127). It turns out that her father had been a slave trader but had felt such remorse when he was dying that he required his daughter to make this promise. The irony, then, is that in this home where all is kindness and economics was not used to introduce the inhabitants, all of the property and money that belong to the family derive from this "trafficker in human flesh and blood" (126). Economics intrudes even where we least expect it. But we should not be surprised to find that economics is key even in the Henry household, since, from the first, we know that the Henrys are slave holders.

Hannah's life with the Wheelers is also characterized in economic terms. Mrs. Wheeler dictates a letter to the heir of Hannah's owner, lying about Hannah's qualifications in order to obtain a "bargain" (153), and after Mrs. Wheeler buys her, Hannah realizes that she is "hers body and soul" (155). In Washington, the principal action revolves around Mr. Wheeler's unsuccessful search for a new government position for which he hopes to be paid "about two thousand a year" (164)—significantly, the same amount that Trappe hoped to get for Mrs. Vincent. And the incident that sets in motion the events that will lead to Hannah's escape—Mrs. Wheeler's attempt to petition for an office for her husband while inadvertently in blackface—derives from this economic cause. Finally, Hannah's determination ultimately to run away is based on distinctions of class: she cannot bear the thought of living with the field hands and being "married" to one of them. This fate, she says, would be the "most horrible of all[,] doomed to association with the vile, foul, filthy inhabitants of the huts, and condemned to receive one of them for my husband" (205).

If questions of economics and class permeate the story proper, they are no less apparent in the stories within the story, of which there are principally three. Each of these centers around the economic basis of slavery, demonstrating the excesses and potential for human cruelty inherent in a system that diminishes people to the status of property. Sir Clifford de Vincent's torture of Rose, for example, is only possible in a system that gives one person absolute power over another (20–25). And the significantly named Mrs. Wright's attempt to help Ellen escape is "right," according to "the dictates of humanity," yet it is "wrong" in a system in which human relationships are wholly governed by economics (81–84). The third story carries to extremes what is referenced several times in the novel (more openly than in most slave narratives)—the sexual use of female slaves by their white owners.[42] Mr. Cosgrove's sexual use of his female slaves, his wife's crazed reaction to her discoveries, and the tragedy that ensues underscore the destruction wrought not only upon the slave victims and the children of these unequal unions but on white family relationships (172–194). Making economics the key to human relationships is never justified, Crafts seems to be telling us over and over again. Her use of gothic elements in her storytelling is more than a narrative device; it portrays the chilling excesses that are built into the system, thus providing a vivid dramatization of a truth that Americans did not want to see. As Mrs. Wright says, "I have learned what all who live in a land of slaver[y] must learn sooner or later; that is . . . to say that all is right, and good; and true when you know that nothing could be more wrong and unjust["] (84).

Just as Hannah Crafts focused on economics in her fictionalized slave narrative, so Harriet Jacobs (1813–1897) made economic concerns a principal feature of her memoir of slavery. In *Incidents in the Life of a Slave Girl* (1861), Jacobs tells the story of her life as a slave in Edenton, North Carolina, her seven-year concealment in her grandmother's garret, and ulti-mately her escape to the North. She uses fictional names for her charac-ters, calling herself Linda Brent, but thanks primarily to the research of Jean Fagan Yellin, we know that the principal facts of the narrative are an accurate rendition of Jacobs's own life.[43] Since slavery, as I indicated ear-lier, is based on economic human relations, it is not surprising to find that economics is a major part of Jacobs's work as well.

Particularly noticeable in *Incidents* is Jacobs's unusual and frequent use of actual numbers to denote monetary transactions and her focus on people as property. Page 1 of the narrative tells us that Linda Brent's slave father, a carpenter, was allowed to work at his trade and live rela-tively independently "on condition of paying his mistress two hundred dollars a year."[44] Also on page 1 Linda tells us that her father saved his "hard earnings" and tried unsuccessfully to purchase his children; that she was so shielded as a child that she didn't even know she was a "piece of merchandise"; and that her grandmother had been set free but had been captured and sold to a hotel keeper who took good care of what he realized was a "valuable piece of property" (5).

The next page is similarly filled with references to monetary transac-tions and people as "property." Jacobs tells us how her grandmother, even while a slave, began her own business selling her much-sought-after crackers. The "business proved profitable," Jacobs says, and her grand-mother saved her money, hoping to be able to buy her children. But the hotel keeper died, and although his wife kept the hotel as her dowry, the grandmother's children were divided among his heirs, and her youngest son, Benjamin, was sold for seven hundred and twenty dollars (6). Ben-jamin was sold so that each of the heirs would have an equal share "of dollars and cents" (6). On the same page Jacobs tells the story of her grandmother's lost three hundred dollars, a story that she returns to more than once later in the narrative. It seems that her grandmother had managed to save three hundred dollars toward the purchase of her chil-dren, and her mistress borrowed this money as a loan, promising that she would pay it back (6). But, notes the narrator, a promise to a slave is not legally binding since "a slave, *being* property, can *hold* no property" (6). We later learn that the loan was for a silver candelabra and that the money was never repaid (11). The next two pages—the last pages in the chapter—describe the death of Linda's mistress and the results of her will: instead of freeing twelve-year-old Linda, as Linda and her friends had hoped, the will "bequeathed me to her sister's daughter, a child of five years" (7–8).

As Linda tells us in the first sentence of chapter 2, she "was now the property of their [the Flints'] little daughter" (9). This chapter is as money oriented as chapter 1. Linda describes the death of her father and the Flints' refusal to let her go to him, Mrs. Flint putting her to work instead preparing for an evening party. Linda comments that her owners did not care that her father had died; to them "he was merely a piece of property" (10). This chapter also tells us the important story of how Linda's grandmother became emancipated. Her mistress had promised that she would set her free when she died, and "it was said that in her will she made good the promise" (11). However, Dr. Flint was executor, and he put the grandmother up for sale. The narrator quotes the advertisement, thus highlighting the reduction of people to property: "public sale of negroes, horses, etc." (11). But other townspeople knew of her mistress's intention to set her free, and when she came up for sale, everyone refused to bid on her until an elderly woman (her mistress's sister, later identified as "Miss Fanny") bid fifty dollars—and set her free (11–12). Also significant in this chapter with respect to Jacobs's focus on economics is the narrator's description of how Dr. Flint had impregnated his slave women and then sold them and their babies. The narrator comments that "the guilty man put their value into his pocket" (13).

All of these references to money transactions and people as property appear in the first two chapters—the first nine pages—of the narrative, and their dense accumulation as an introduction to the work is an indication of the importance of economics in Jacobs's story. How and why economic issues are so prominent in the work is apparent in the number and type of references to money. Jacobs's frequent use of exact figures when she tells of the sale or purchase of a slave dramatizes the horror of this reduction of people to things. And since the reader is reading the narrative from the point of view of the "other"—the slave or "piece of property" herself—and is getting to know Linda and her family and friends as people, the reader sees slavery not from the point of view of the slave owner or even of the distant Northerner but from the perspective of the slave herself. The reader gains what Jacobs said in her preface she hoped the reader would gain: a "realizing sense" of what the situation is for a slave, who can be bought and sold and, if she is a woman, can be used for sexual purposes. The effect of this identification with "property," combined with the accumulation of information about prices for people we have come to know intimately, is to conjure up an appalling "what if" question for the reader: What if another person had absolute control over me and my children, with impunity before the law?

I will mention only a few of the many other times when actual money amounts are discussed in the work. For example, we had been told that Linda's Uncle Benjamin was sold at the age of ten for seven hundred and twenty dollars. Later, Jacobs tells us that at twenty, Benjamin, who was mistreated by his master, was put in jail for six months for trying to escape, and at the end of that time his master sold him—but Benjamin's imprisonment had so weakened him and reduced his value that his master could get only three hundred dollars for him. Jacobs comments, "The master had been blind to his own interest" (23). Soon Benjamin escaped again, this time successfully. His mother offered to buy him, but he had escaped to New York, and he refused to let his mother use her "hard-earned dollars" for him when he was already far away from slavery (23–24). Instead, his mother bought her other son, Philip; Jacobs tells us that she paid eight hundred dollars for him (26). A particularly important reference to the purchase of an individual is contained in Linda's deliberate involvement with Mr. Sands, who she hopes will "buy" her from Dr. Flint: "I was sure my friend, Mr. Sands, would buy me . . . and I thought my freedom could be easily obtained from him" (55). She also is confident that he will similarly "buy" her children. Dr. Flint, however, spitefully refuses to sell her or her children, and the ensuing subterfuge whereby a trader buys the children for Sands, who gives them to Linda's grandmother, graphically underscores the significance of money. Again, a specific dollar amount is mentioned: the children and Linda's brother William are sold by Flint for a total of nineteen hundred dollars (105).[45] The last time a specific amount of money is mentioned is many years later, after Linda has been living in the North for some time. The Flints' daughter's husband comes to New York looking for her, and Linda's employer, Mrs. Bruce, pays him three hundred dollars to buy Linda and end her slavery (199). Although Linda is glad to have her freedom, she recoils at the idea that she has been "sold" like an "article of property": "A bill of sale is on record, and future generations will learn from it that women were articles of traffic in New York, late in the nineteenth century" (199–200).

The other salient economic theme in *Incidents*, in addition to the theme of human property, is the concept of woman's economic independence. Linda's goal is not only freedom but financial independence. She has a strong role model in her grandmother, who owns her own home and conducts a successful baking business. She also has the example of Miss Fanny, the relative of Dr. Flint who had freed her grandmother. Linda comments on the benefits of Miss Fanny's independence, noting that the Flints do not have power over her: "Fortunately she was not dependent on the bounty of the Flints. She had enough to be independent; and that is more than can ever be gained from charity, however lavish it may be" (89). Thus the Flints could not forbid her to buy and set free Linda's grandmother, nor can they prevent her from maintaining a friendship with her.

Jacobs also calls attention to the powerlessness of married women (Fanny is unmarried) because of the restrictions of property laws, which, as we saw earlier, gave all of a woman's property to her husband. In the South, this meant that if a woman owned slaves, they became the property of her husband after marriage—unless they, like any other property, were protected by a trust. Jacobs tells the poignant story of a woman who owned one slave woman and her children, all of whom she treated kindly, having educated the children and trained the daughters in religious virtue. When she married, however, her husband claimed the family as his property. The father of the children, who was a free man, came to plead with her to protect his children, but she answered: "I can do nothing for you now, Harry. I no longer have the power I had a week ago" (50). Her husband sold the boys and appropriated the girls for his sexual use, only to sell them later after they had borne his children (50–51). That a husband's appropriation of a woman's slaves was considered a significant problem is clear from the fact that, as I indicated in chapter 2, the first married woman's property law in the country was passed in Mississippi in 1839 primarily to protect a woman's slave "property."

With these examples of the power that comes with economic independence and the lack of power that comes with its absence, it is not surprising that Jacobs asserted her goal of economic independence. Although, as critics have noted, her narrative emphasizes community in a way that is lacking in the more individualistic male slave narrative,[46] Jacobs strives toward independence. When Linda arrives in New York and sees the conditions under which her daughter, Ellen, is living, she states her resolve: "I was impatient to go to work and earn money, that I might change the uncertain position of my children. . . . My greatest anxiety now was to obtain employment" (166–168). Once she obtains a position with the Bruces, she begins to save money to buy a home for herself and her children and to educate her children: "The money I had earned, I was desirous to devote to the education of my children, and to secure a home for them" (179, 187). Although Jacobs herself was not able to buy her own home, she managed to give her daughter, Louisa ("Ellen"), a good education. And as the narrator of her work writes at the end of the narrative, "my story ends with freedom; not in the usual way, with marriage" (201). Although, as some critics have maintained, there are aspects of the sentimental novel in Jacobs's work, this is not one of them.[47] Unlike Crafts, who tacks onto her fictionalized autobiography the typical happy ending of a sentimental novel—complete with mandatory husband, a "neat little Cottage," and the proximity of "rose-vines and honeysuckle" (237–239)—in a short wrap-up chapter that seems less "real" than even the gothic elements in the work, Jacobs ends her narrative with an assertion of independence and a tribute to some of the people who helped her in her struggle, particularly her grandmother.[48]

Race, then, is a significant factor in an economic analysis of women's writing, but as with any other variable, it must be factored in along with other aspects of an individual's situatedness. Class differences and the writer's closeness to slavery helped to determine the intensity and character of the writer's economic concerns. But in all instances, it is clear that nineteenth-century women of color, like white women, focused on economic issues with greater intensity and frequency than did white male writers of the same period.

———·—⟨∞⟩—···———

chapter six

THE WOMAN
DEFENDANT

In the court cases dealt with in chapter 4, the women litigants were plaintiffs. However, in the court cases involving women litigants, not counting divorce cases, 49 percent involved a woman as one of the defendants. In most cases when the defendant was female, the plaintiff was male, but occasionally both plaintiff and defendant were women. Sometimes the woman was a defendant along with others—her husband or children or other litigants involved in the same case; at other times she was the sole defendant. Women defendants were taken to court for primarily three reasons: for nonpayment of debt, in a mortgage foreclosure, and in inheritance litigation. In some instances women defendants were brought into court as pawns of male litigants. Of primary importance in this study are the particularities behind these facts and the significance behind those particularities.

One of the principal reasons why nineteenth-century women were taken to court was for an outstanding debt—a debt for which a woman and her husband were jointly responsible, a debt the woman owed on her own, or a debt her deceased husband had owed. As discussed in chapter 2, before the 1860 Married Women's Property Act in New York, a married woman's husband was responsible for his wife's debts, even debts contracted before she was married to him. Also, before 1860 all of a woman's earnings were the property of her husband and consequently subject to his debts. After the 1848 Married Women's Property Act in New York, however, personal or real property that a woman inherited was protected from her husband's creditors.

This chapter explores some of the ways in which the laws played out in specific cases involving women in debt, beginning with cases that predated the 1860 Married Women's Property Act. In 1852, for example,

Walter Barber sued Sarah and Franklin Case for payment of a promissory note that Sarah had signed.[1] Although the original debt was Sarah's, she and her husband were both named as defendants, and it was her husband who was expected to "satisfy" the debt. Moreover, as the case proceeded, particularly with the shenanigans of the plaintiff's lawyer, Sarah's name was lost sight of. The amount due was $238.26, including interest. On June 1, 1852, Barber won a judgment against the Cases, but to his knowledge they did not pay the debt. Two years later he accidentally met Franklin Case on the street and asked him when he was going to pay his wife's debt. Case informed him that he had paid it to Barber's lawyer, John Cook, soon after the original judgment two years before. When Barber confronted Cook, Cook claimed he had never received the money. However, Case went to see the clerk at the Kings County court and found a document dated July 2, 1852, stating that the debt had in fact been "satisfied." When told of the document, Cook declared that it must be a forgery. Barber then took Cook to court, calling in witnesses who swore to the collection of the debt. At this point, Cook changed his story: he denied that he had ever told Barber that the Cases had not paid. Instead he presented a "bill" for his services, claiming that he did not owe Barber any money, but that Barber owed him for all of the work he had done. On November 2, 1854, the judge found against Cook, ordering him to pay Barber $260 or show cause why he should not be arrested. Cook's attorney—his father or brother, George Cook—appeared for him and obtained a stay of proceedings, but in August 1855, Cook was ordered to pay the plaintiffs $260 with interest from August 24, 1852. It is interesting to note the way in which this case, which derived from a woman's debt, was conducted entirely by men. It is possible that Sarah Case contributed to the negotiations in the case; she may even have earned the money to repay the debt. But in the official court records, only the male players have a role.

Sarah Case was married to her husband when she signed the notes. However, husbands were also sued for a wife's indebtedness that predated the marriage. In 1858, for example, Robert and Thomas Emmet brought suit against Margaret Pierce and her husband, William Pierce, for a debt that Margaret (then Finnegan) had contracted before her marriage. The Emmets, acting as trustees, claimed that she owed their client

$990.67. Under the law, her husband was obligated to pay the full amount with interest.

In the above cases, the wife had contracted the debt on her own. In other cases, the couple had incurred the debt as co-partners. In 1854 John B. Murray sued Celestine and Charles J. Gaillard for nonpayment of rent. On April 30, 1853, the Gaillards, a French couple who came to New York from Philadelphia, had jointly signed a five-year lease for a house at 334 Broadway. They agreed to pay $8,400 a year at $700 a month and moved in on May 1. In August Charles's business failed and they disappeared, leaving four months' rent unpaid, a total of $2,800. Murray sued them for that amount, with interest, and since they could not be found—word was that they had left the state—he claimed their property, the furniture and clothing they had left behind. In this case, the man and woman acted together, but it is clear that Celestine Gaillard was dependent upon her husband, subject to his success or failure in the marketplace. He had initially left town without her, telling the plaintiff's lawyer to tell her that he had gone to Jersey City to escape his creditors. Seeing that she would be left to pay the piper, Celestine had quickly left town also, either to follow her husband or to strike out on her own. The narrative that emerges from the court proceedings does not reveal whether or not she knew where he had gone. It is possible that she did know and that her husband's reference to Jersey City was a red herring to throw his creditors off the scent. Alternatively, he may have given the attorney a fake place name in order to throw his wife off the scent also. In any case, as Murray stated in court, the possessions left behind in the house and which he claimed to cover their debt were mostly Celestine's, so that even if she reconnected with her husband in New Jersey or elsewhere, she had lost everything else.

In a similar type of case, but different in that the husband and wife were apparently in business together and did not disappear, Christian Born sued Noelle and James Speyers as "co-partners and joint debtors" for goods sold to them in 1855 and for which they owed $1,252.81 plus interest. In February 1856 a "judgment by default" was issued against James Speyers for a total of $2,664.84. Two years later he returned to court with his attorney, a "member of Congress," who claimed that his "official duties" had prevented him from following up the matter sooner. He had received no notice of the entry of judgment, he said, and made a motion to have the judgment declared void on the grounds that it was in James Speyers's name only whereas the original suit was against Noelle and James Speyers as co-partners. The judge ruled in January 1859 that the judgment against James be "set aside and vacated," and the case against Noelle and James Speyers was reopened. There is no record of the final outcome of the case, which was settled out of court.

In all of the above cases, the lawsuit was brought against husband and wife together. In other cases, however, an unmarried woman was the sole defendant. And after the 1860 Married Women's Property Act in New York, a married woman could be sued on her own as if she were a *feme sole*. In 1856 Charles Fetch sued Mary Purdy for "services performed" for her by Timothy Burger and for which she owed Burger $30. Purdy paid Burger the $30, and her attorney, James Beers, testified that the debt had been settled. Acting as Purdy's agent, Beers had arrived at a compromise with Burger, which Burger accepted to satisfy the claim. In contrast to this simple cut-and-dried case was the case of another single debtor, Mary McCarthy, who owed George Hussey $930.24. Hussey obtained a judgment against McCarthy in September 1865, but she never paid it. Instead she disappeared, and he spent over two years looking for her. In March 1868, Hussey returned to court. He had located McCarthy, he said, but he was afraid that if she were served with a show-cause notice, she would "move beyond the jurisdiction of this court" and disappear again. The judge ordered her arrest and set bail at $1,000.

Whereas Mary McCarthy had in fact gone into hiding to avoid paying her debt, William Elliott falsely claimed Jane Weeks's disappearance as a ploy in order to avoid having to pay her. In a jury trial in 1864 Weeks had won a judgment against him for $689.83 for "certain goods and chattel" that he had received from her. On December 5, 1864, Elliott signed a statement promising to pay the full amount of the judgment in $50 monthly installments, but after he had paid $200, he stopped paying. Meanwhile, he brought suit against Weeks, claiming that she had "converted certain goods to her own use" that he said belonged to him: "seven carpets, a walnut rocking-chair, and a sole leather trunk." However, he deliberately did not serve notice on Weeks, and she had no knowledge of his lawsuit against her. Pretending that he did not know where she was, he obtained a default judgment against her of $645. In December 1865, when Weeks's attorney attempted to claim the balance of the sum Elliott owed to Weeks, Elliott made a motion to let the two judgments cancel each other out. However, Weeks's attorney pointed out that the goods he claimed Weeks owed him for were the same goods for which Weeks had won a judgment against him. Moreover, argued her lawyer, it was false that Elliott did not know Weeks's whereabouts, and he moved that Elliott's judgment against her be vacated. Weeks testified that she had lived at the same address for ten years; Elliott, she said, knew very well where she lived. He had even seen her on the street several times during the time when his fraudulent lawsuit was pending. On March 8, 1866, the judge denied Elliott's motion to vacate Weeks's judgment against him, and Elliott was mandated to pay her the balance owed. Elliott's trumped-up lawsuit and false claims were not a very astute plan to avoid payment. One wonders if he believed he could get away with these shoddy deceptive tactics because Weeks was a woman. If so, he was mistaken.

A case in which a man clearly sought to take advantage of a woman's ignorance of the law was the 1865 case of *William Murphy v. Sarah Murphy*. Sarah had an independent dressmaking business at 176 East Ninth Street. Her husband, who was unemployed, suspected that she was going to sell the business, and in order to prevent her from selling out and keeping the money for herself, he took her to court. Claiming that he was a co-partner in the business, he obtained an injunction against her, preventing her from selling or from doing business. Sarah testified that the business was hers alone. She had had the business before she was married, she said, and had continued to run it independently. Her husband had worked as a butcher in Washington Market when they were first married, she said, but for two years he had been unemployed and had been "supported wholly by her." She pointed out that all of the goods in the store were purchased in her own name and "upon her own independent credit." Moreover, she said, the store and dwelling were leased in her name, the money in the bank was in her name, and she paid her twenty employees with her own money. Sarah's attorney brought in witnesses from some of the firms from whom she bought goods, and they testified that she had bought goods "upon her own individual credit for six years." William, on his part, insisted that he was a co-partner in the business and claimed that she had requested him to change the name on her bank account to "Murphy and Wife" but that the bank refused to do it unless she came in person. When questioned as to why he didn't tell her she had to go in person to change the names, he said lamely that he hadn't mentioned it to her because he "didn't want to bother her." Obviously, he had attempted to make the change without her knowledge, hoping to gain possession of her money.

Fortunately for Sarah Murphy, William's lawsuit came after the 1860 Married Women's Property Act in New York, which entitled a married woman to her own earnings, and after the banking law of 1850, which enabled a married woman to have a bank account in her own name.[2] Otherwise, her husband would have had full control over her money in the bank even without a name change and would have had the right to all of her earnings from her business. Before the change in the laws, of course, he would not have needed a lawsuit to attempt to prove that he was a co-partner; he would have had legal title to all of her money simply by virtue of being her husband. The court found for Sarah in this case, and the judge ordered that William's injunction against her business be vacated. He also gave Sarah leave to prosecute to recover damages sustained by her under the injunction when she had been unable to do business. This case is a graphic example of the practical effect of the 1860 Married Women's Property law in New York. It is important to remember, however, that in 1865, the date of the Murphy lawsuit, New York was one of only four states that had such a law protecting a woman's independent earnings.

Another type of case in which a woman was taken to court for debt was the case in which a woman was sued for her deceased husband's debts. This was the type of case that often left a woman in dire economic straits as her husband's creditors claimed whatever assets she had. And, as we saw in previous chapters, it was a common cause of the impoverishment of widows. Fanny Fern's husband was involved in a long lawsuit that left him heavily in debt, and after his death in 1846, his creditors descended upon her, leaving her and two small children in poverty.[3] And Frances Harper wrote in her 1866 speech "We Are All Bound Up Together" of how when her husband died in debt in 1864, their farm was sold to pay his creditors, and she was left with nothing but her mirror and her little daughter.[4] In 1858 Ellen Standley, the widow of William Standley, was sued by Bartlett Smith and Samuel Jacobs, both of whom had recovered judgments against William Standley during his lifetime, but the debts had never been paid. Smith claimed $168.91 and Jacobs $1,062, and according to common law, all of a man's debts had to be paid before any money could come to his widow. The 1860 law protected only money that the woman earned independently. Thus, when Charles Morrell, formerly an attorney in Orange County, sued Elizabeth Wallace and her son, John Wallace, in 1861, claiming that her deceased husband owed him money for his "services rendered as a lawyer," if he could prove that the money had not been paid, her husband's estate would be liable for the debt. She asked for a change of venue, which was denied, and the case was referred to a judicial referee. In a different case in 1862 the same Charles Morrell sued Clarissa Smith, widow of Joshua Smith, for $228.02, which he said she owed for his legal services in a "suit against Galloway." In an attempt to prove that the debt was hers and not her husband's, he insisted that the earlier case had been brought by her as a single woman. However, she pointed out that she was not single at the time, that she had been married in 1842 and was "not responsible herself for said money." Using the law to defend her interests, she pointed out that when she married "all her property was thereupon delivered to her husband." She asserted that she had never hired Morrell, that his bill was for $108.65 (not $228), and that her husband had paid it during his lifetime. She asked for a change of venue to Orange County, maintaining that she was "old and poor in health" (she was sixty-five) and a trip to New York City would be too difficult for her. Moreover, she said, all of the papers pertaining to the case and all of the witnesses necessary to prove her case were in Orange County. The judge granted the change of venue.

In the above cases, the plaintiff sought to recover money from the husband's personal estate for his outstanding debts, and his creditors would have to be paid before his widow could claim any of the money. However, a widow was not liable for money owed by a business firm with which her husband was associated. In *George Parrish v. Lythe Ferguson and Mary Wait* in 1858, Parrish sought to recover money owed by Mary Wait's husband's firm, a general store in Truxton, Cortland County. Bringing suit for goods delivered to the firm of Ferguson and Company, Parrish maintained that it was Mary Wait, not her deceased husband, Samuel Wait, who had been co-partner with Ferguson in the firm. This was the only way that he could make her liable for the debt. The plaintiffs had no proof that she was Ferguson's co-partner except that her husband apparently had on at least one occasion said that she was. In her deposition, however, Mary Wait denied that she was ever a partner in the firm. Her husband, she said, was Ferguson's partner until he (Wait) died in February 1858. She said that witnesses from Truxton, including the clerk in the store and people from the businesses with which his firm did business, would testify that Samuel Wait "had charge of the business with said Ferguson and transacted business and signed the firm name as partner and was known as such in the business and with customers of the firm." The lawyers for the defendants asked for a change of venue to Cortland County. There is no record of what happened in this case, the parties apparently settling out of court. Legally, Mary Wait was not liable for the debt if it was her husband and not she who was a partner in the firm. One wonders if the plaintiff was accurate in reporting that her husband had said that she was the real partner. If so, it is possible that she was in fact Ferguson's partner, but that, following the custom of the day which regarded men as more savvy in business matters than women, her husband signed his name to the papers. He may have described her as the real partner because she was the one who made the business decisions. But when the firm was being sued, it was to her advantage not to be seen as partner. Like Mary Trust, she may have been playing the role of conventional wife in order to win her case, a role that judge and jury would find credible because it would fit into the familiar frame provided by society's image of domestic womanhood. Yet as Fanny Fern commented in 1853, many nineteenth-century women did the real work for which men received the credit. Referring to the invisible role that women often played, Fern noted that many a minister's sermon was written by his wife.[5]

In addition to being sued for outstanding debts, women were taken to court in the foreclosure of mortgages. Women defendants figured in three types of foreclosure suits. The most common suit was that in which a mortgage was foreclosed on a widow after her husband died. It is not without reason that this story is such a familiar one. Usually the holder of the mortgage foreclosed soon after the death of the breadwinner because the new widow did not have the money to keep up the mortgage payments. In 1854 the Franklin Building Association, a "building, mutual loan and accumulating fund association," foreclosed on Barbara Becker, widow of Conrad Becker and mother of seven minor children, ages eight months to seventeen years. Her family lived in the house on 106th Street that she had inherited from her mother, Anne Rogers, but in 1853 her husband, Conrad Becker, had taken out an $800 mortgage on the property. On May 18, 1854, he died. Barbara could not keep up the monthly payments, and the Franklin Association took her to court in December 1854. At that time she owed $74.84. The case was submitted to a judicial referee, who concluded in August 1856 that the property could be divided and one section of it sold to pay the mortgage payments then owed. By then Barbara owed $240.79. Consequently the property, which measured one hundred feet by thirty-eight feet, was divided, and the lot adjoining the house was sold at auction in 1857. The money was used to pay the court costs, the judicial referee, and the mortgage payments. No money went to Barbara, who remained in the house with her children. However, she still could not afford to keep up the mortgage payments, and in 1863 the Franklin Building Association, after several years of legal maneuvering, petitioned the court to sell the balance of the property at auction. In this case, the widow had been fortunate in that the property could be divided initially rather than the whole being sold at once. The sale of part of the property and the slow movement of the court procedures — the petitions, the multiple hearings, the three submissions to a judicial referee — gave her some breathing time. It was not until ten years later that the house itself was finally sold, and by then many of her children were grown. This was one case in which the slow turning of the legal wheels acted to the defendant's benefit.

In other cases the widow did not have the option of dividing the property for sale. For example, Peter Hegeman in 1859 foreclosed on the property of Catharine Gavigan after her husband, Andrew Gavigan, died, leaving her with seven dependent children, ages seven to sixteen, and a mortgage on her home at 133 West Thirtieth Street. Another foreclosure on a widow with dependent children was the 1863 case of *C. Bainbridge Smith v. Rachel A. Kennedy* and her four children. Rachel's husband, William D. Kennedy, had died two years earlier, leaving her with a mortgage of six thousand dollars plus interest on her home at 33 Hammond Street. In most cases of this type, the sale of the house left the woman and her dependent children with no place to go. If the sale realized more money than was needed to pay off the mortgage, the interest, and the attorney's fees and court costs, the widow and her children would be entitled to the surplus money—unless it was claimed by other creditors, which often was the case.

In all of the above mortgage cases, there is no indication that the widow was actively involved in the case. Since she did not testify or submit a deposition, unlike in other types of cases, we never hear the woman's voice. The image of the "widow with dependent children" that emerges from these cases seems to fulfill the stereotypical image of the suffering female victim helpless in the hands of the callous holder of the mortgage. Of course, we don't know how active the defendant was behind the scenes. Did she attempt to direct the lawyer's actions? Did she make it her business to understand what was involved? Or was she too busy taking care of her children and wondering how she would get through each day to be able to concern herself with the lawsuit? Sometimes, however, in spite of the cut-and-dried format of the foreclosure cases, there are indications that the widow is a presence. Elizabeth Carroll was one woman who made her voice heard. In 1864 the Aetna Fire Insurance Company foreclosed on the mortgage on the home of Elizabeth Carroll after the death of her husband, William Carroll. On November 18, 1864, her house at 257 West Thirty-fifth Street was sold. Elizabeth, who had come to the United States from Ireland and was Carroll's second wife, had three living children, in addition to nine others who had died in infancy. William Carroll had had three children by his first wife, one of whom, Mary, had died along with her children. When the house was sold, Elizabeth refused to move out of the house. On December 20, the purchaser, Jeremiah Pangburn, submitted a petition to the court claiming that when he had "demanded possession" of the house, Elizabeth refused to let him have it. "She is damaging the premises by sawing down partitions, etc.," he complained. "She is collecting rents."

The judge ordered Elizabeth to "show cause why Pangburn should not evict her." In the meantime, he said, "she must desist from mutilating and damaging the premises or collecting rents or interfering with rents." Elizabeth's actions were futile, of course. Pangburn obtained legal help and she was forced out. But her actions are indicative of the desperation that must have overcome many of the widows in her position.

Fortunately, Elizabeth did not have to walk away completely empty-handed. There was a surplus after the house had been sold, and the referee recommended that the surplus money be divided among Elizabeth and the children, including Patrick Ahearn, the husband of her deceased stepdaughter, Mary Carroll. Elizabeth opposed the awarding of any of the surplus to Ahearn, but her objection was overruled. However, when the money was distributed, Ahearn received less than the other children; he won $248 while each of the other children received $502 in trust to their court-appointed guardian. Elizabeth was awarded $420.

It was not only widows who lost their homes to mortgages, of course. Married couples also defaulted on their mortgage payments. In 1859 Henry Camp took out a $4,000 mortgage on his property at 86 Twenty-ninth Street, on which he already had a prior mortgage of $5,000. Three years later William Nelson brought suit against "Henry Camp and wife" for the $4,000 mortgage. Throughout the proceedings, Camp's wife's first name was never used. This was not uncommon in nineteenth-century foreclosure cases. The lawsuit was really against the husband, but the wife's name had to appear on the mortgage papers because, according to common law, she was entitled to one-third of the husband's real estate as her dower. Thus, when he mortgaged or sold the property, she had to sign the papers agreeing to the transaction. The law existed for the wife's protection—so that she would not be left a penniless widow—but most women probably simply signed the papers that their husbands told them to sign. All of the widows discussed above had similarly signed papers agreeing to mortgage their homes. As Fanny Fern noted, most married women—including Fern herself in her first marriage—signed "business" papers that their husbands asked them to sign without thinking or asking questions, often without even knowing what the paper was for. It was only after her husband died in debt, having lost the house and all of their assets, that Fern realized the mistake she had made.[6]

In British common law, the dower law included a stipulation that required the judge to meet privately with the wife in order to give her the opportunity to ask questions and to make certain that she understood the significance of what she was doing. It was also a way to make sure that she was not being coerced into signing.[7] But this part of the law was not adopted in the United States. In the case cited above, *Nelson v. Henry Camp and wife*, the plaintiff complained that Camp was irresponsible and pointed out that there were other judgments against him. Nelson asked that a receiver be appointed to collect the rents and that Camp and his wife be evicted. On June 25, 1862, the judge ordered a receiver appointed to take control of the property. Camp's wife had signed the mortgage paper relinquishing her claim to the house, and due to her husband's irresponsibility, she was to be evicted. And we do not even know her name.

We do know Jane Coar's name, but her fate was the same. In March 1863 the same William Nelson brought suit against "Joseph Coar and Jane his wife" to foreclose a mortgage on their house on Forty-ninth Street. Nelson apparently was a speculator in mortgages, buying mortgages and foreclosing. On March 19 the premises were sold, and after Nelson's mortgage claim was satisfied, there was a surplus of $1,494.95. However, none of this money went to the Coars. On March 23 Elizabeth Horn came forward with a claim for $1,063 for a second mortgage that she held on the property, and on April 3, Thomas Kennedy came forward with a claim of $725 for a mortgage that he also held on the property. After these mortgages were also paid, there was no money left for the Coars. Interestingly, there were two women involved in this suit, one loser and one winner: Jane Coar, along with her husband, lost all of the equity in their house, including her dower money, but Elizabeth Horn, who had sold her mortgage on the property, gained from the mortgage. Like Nelson, Horn was apparently a speculator in mortgages. She was a married woman, but after the property act of 1860 she was entitled to buy and sell property. As mentioned in an earlier chapter, speculation in mortgages was one way that women could earn money of their own.

In a final mortgage case in which both husband and wife were defendants, the wife was wholly discounted while her husband engaged in nefarious business tactics. This was not a case of the family homestead being mortgaged but of a scheme in which her husband and two other men had conspired to purchase building lots and have houses built on them and then, through fraudulent mortgages, escape having to pay their creditors, including the building contractor who had built the houses. In 1859 the Gebhard Fire Insurance Company brought suit against George Leeds and Harriet, his wife, and others to foreclose on a $9,000 mortgage on property on Fourth Avenue at Thirty-fourth Street. Daniel Whitney, a builder, testified that in 1857 he had contracted with one Warren Beman to build houses on four of the lots. Whitney had not been paid for his work or for the materials and was owed $8,000, $2,000 of which was for the house he built on the lot in this suit. Joseph Burton was at that time the owner of the premises, and Beman was his agent. Whitney testified that Burton, Beman, and Leeds "conspired together and made an arrangement so that the said Burton conveyed the said premises to the said Leeds and said Leeds made and delivered to said Burton . . . the bond and mortgage set forth in the complaint herein, and the said conveyance and the said bond and mortgage were each and all made and received without any consideration therefore and for the purpose and with the intent of thereby hindering delaying and defrauding creditors." Altogether, Burton bought eight lots, and his plan, apparently, was to give them to Leeds in a pretended sale. Then Leeds would mortgage them at a price greatly exceeding their value, but again no money would change hands. According to Whitney, the plaintiff in the case was in on the fraud and stood to gain a sizeable fee for participating in the pretended mortgage. The foreclosure of the mortgage would force the sale of the property, Burton would take the mortgage money (paying the plaintiff, Leeds, and Burton for their part in the fraud), and there would be no surplus money with which to pay the creditors, including Whitney, who would receive nothing for building the houses. Whitney asked that the mortgage be declared void and his claim established. He wanted the property sold at auction and asked to have first claim to the purchase money for the $2,000 owed to him for building the house. Harriet Leeds's role in all of this is nebulous. She may have actively conspired with her husband and his associates, but it is more likely that she did not know what her husband was doing. She would have had to sign the mortgage papers because of the dower law, but her husband need not have told her of the fraudulent scheme. Given the cultural discounting of women with respect to money, she may not even have known what she was signing other than that her husband needed her signature on some "business papers."

In all of the above cases, the mortgage was brought against a married couple or a widow. Except in the case of recent widows, there were few cases in which the defendant in a foreclosure was a woman alone. Obviously this was because few women owned property in their own right, and if they did so, they were wealthy enough to hold on to a house that they had inherited without encumbrances. Few women were in a position to buy houses of their own. When Fanny Fern bought her own house in 1856, there was quite a stir. She was married to James Parton at the time, and the fact that it was *she* who purchased the house and not her husband caused comment among her contemporaries. In 1856 in New York the wife's money would have legally belonged to her husband. However, Fern and Parton had signed a prenuptial agreement prior to their marriage that made certain that her money belonged to her for her own separate use.[8]

The few cases that I did find in which a foreclosure was against a woman alone who was not a recent widow were all in the later part of my study. In March 1873 Samuel B. H. Judah (the same Samuel Judah who, as a young attorney many years earlier, was helpful in the lawsuits of his mother, Elizabeth Judah; see chapter 4) brought suit against Laura Nickerson for an $8,100 mortgage. Nickerson had the money to pay the mortgage and the interest, but the case languished for several months because the two parties disputed the costs. The plaintiff claimed costs of $161, but Nickerson's attorney insisted that that amount was $60 "in excess of what it should be." The house was ready to go on sale, but the plaintiff's attorney appeared in court on August 30, 1873, and declared that the plaintiff would agree to an adjustment in costs and accept the defendant's payment of the mortgage if the defendant would pay the referee's fee. The judge ordered the costs reduced from $167.81 to $127, and Nickerson paid the full amount of the mortgage along with the referee's fee. Obviously, Laura Nickerson was a woman of wealth if she was able to come up with $8,100 to pay off the mortgage. Yet she was so adamant about what she regarded as an unfair charge that she held out until the last minute and ultimately managed to have the charge reduced. Either she or her lawyer or both were very strong willed. It was probably she who insisted on holding out until the charge was reduced, since it is doubtful that her lawyer would have taken the risk that she would lose her house simply in order to gain a point and save $40. After all, she had more than $8,000 to pay off the mortgage, and the extra $40 was not as great a hardship as it would have been to a poor woman who had to count her pennies. All of the evidence suggests that Laura Nickerson was a strong-willed, independent woman, like Eliza Huell in Elizabeth Stoddard's 1863 short story "Lemorne *versus* Huell," discussed in chapter 7.

Eugenia Hargous was also a woman of wealth. However, she, or her family, had mortgaged her extensive property to such an extent that she was unable to maintain it. She owned a large house with an adjoining lot at 76 Fifth Avenue and a stable on Thirteenth Street. In 1870 Hollis Powers threatened to foreclose on three mortgages totaling $18,700. There was also a previous mortgage of $40,000 by the Equitable Life Insurance Company. Altogether, with interest, she owed a total of $83,375.10. On October 12, 1870, Eugenia's son, Peter A. Hargous, acting as her attorney, went to see the attorneys for the plaintiff, Gleeson and Babcock, and asked for a two-week delay on the sale of the property. He promised to have the money within that time. The plaintiff's attorney, Babcock, testified in a subsequent case that they agreed to the delay and postponed the sale to October 26. But, he said, two weeks elapsed without Hargous's making good on his promise.

What followed in Babcock's testimony provides us with an interesting look at the New York law scene in the 1870s. Babcock reveals his tendency to take unfair advantage of people as well as his anti-Semitism. He testified that "late in the afternoon of the last day, to wit, October 25, 1870, a Real Estate and Loan Broker by the name of Harry M. Lowenstein accompanied by three persons two of whom were apparently German Jews—whose names deponent does not recall—and one of whom was a person who said his name was Glover and that he was a lawyer, but who never appeared in these suits nor on any matter relating thereto except at said interview, . . . —came into deponent's office." According to Babcock, Lowenstein said that as broker he had negotiated a sale of the Hargous Fifth Avenue house and lot to one Hartman. This sale, if carried out, would give Hargous the money to pay off all of the mortgages. And, noted Babcock, "it would also enable Lowenstein to earn a handsome commission and their client the proposed purchaser to obtain a handsome bargain." Lowenstein asked for a further delay in the sale of the Hargous property, and Babcock, seeing that Lowenstein was eager to make the sale, cannily said that he did not "feel disposed to do anything farther in the matter without compensation." If Lowenstein's statements "were true," he suggested, "the adjournment was worth a considerable sum to him." Taking advantage of Lowenstein's eagerness, Babcock said he would delay if Lowenstein agreed to pay him a fee of $100 plus the printing and auctioneers' bills, a total of $580. Lowenstein agreed to all of this, and on November 9 he came again to Babcock's office with the other men, along with Hartman, the purchaser of the property. Attended by a "Mr. F. Tillore," whom Babcock described as "a respectable lawyer of this city," they paid off the mortgages and all of the additional fees Babcock had required. Babcock's glowing description of Tillore, who apparently was not Jewish, as opposed to his contemptuous description of Lowenstein and his associates, including their lawyer, "a person who said his name was Glover," reflects Babcock's prejudices. It is significant, also, that when he refers to Tillore, he gives him the title "Mr.," although he does not do the same for Glover and Lowenstein.

But this is not the end of the story. On December 19, 1870, Peter Hargous, acting for Eugenia, took Babcock and Gleeson to court, claiming that they had charged exorbitant fees in the settlement. Hargous maintained that the one-hundred-dollar fee charged to Lowenstein, the printing and auctioneers' fees, and the referee's fee were coerced. He demanded that Babcock and Gleeson be ordered to refund the money, which, he said, was "paid under protest and under no right whatever except the refusal of the plaintiff's attorneys to settle said suits without payment of the same at once, there being no time to have them adjusted, so that the sale made by deponent could go through." Babcock and Gleeson claimed that the fees were just, but their objection was overruled. On December 21, the judge ordered them to refund the fees: "The sum charged by plaintiff's attorney must be refunded as there seems to have been a mistake." The word "mistake" was a euphemism, of course; the only "mistake" was Babcock's greed in treating with contempt people whom he considered inferior because they were different from himself.

And what of Eugenia Hargous? Again, one does not know to what extent she was involved in the negotiations. Peter Hargous handled her business affairs for her, and Babcock's attitude toward the "German Jews" suggests the extent to which negotiations seem to have been a matter for "the club," i.e., Christian white men. As a woman, she too would have been excluded. Nevertheless, she owned the house in her own right; the deed that she turned over to Hartman was in her name alone. It was in her interest to make the best deal possible. Certainly, a sale at auction would not have realized as much money as a private sale. Ultimately, she sold the property for $103,000. Thus, after the mortgages and court costs were paid, she realized a profit of almost $20,000. It is possible that she discussed the affair with her son and lawyer, Peter Hargous; in fact, it might have been she who, when she heard about the exorbitant fees that Babcock had charged, insisted that Peter go back to court to demand a refund. As Babcock pointed out, Peter had not objected to the charges earlier. He might not have objected only because he wanted to make sure that the deal would go through; but it could also have been that when his mother heard about the overcharge, she felt strongly enough about the injustice of it that she sent her son back to court. However, whatever happened behind the scenes, in the public negotiations it was Peter Hargous whose voice was heard.

One female defendant who successfully fought against the foreclosure of a mortgage was Augusta Woodworth, who was able to win her case in 1860 after five years in the courts. Her story is a particularly interesting one, and although she was not a typical businesswoman, she does provide an example of one type of business open to a nineteenth-century independent businesswoman: Woodworth was the proprietor of a house of prostitution. She had first rented the house from Thomas Emmet on May 1, 1849. Early in 1855 she purchased the house, obtaining a mortgage from Emmet, but on October 3, 1855, Emmet brought suit against her to foreclose on the mortgage. He claimed that she had not paid the full amount of the mortgage payments and maintained that he had not known "that it was the defendant's intention to continue to keep such house of ill fame and of prostitution." He would never have sold her the house, he piously asserted, if he had known that the mortgage payments were to be made "from the profits of said premises." She replied that he certainly did know that she ran a house of prostitution. In fact, she said, it was because he knew that she ran a house of prostitution that he had charged her over "$2,000 more than the premises were worth," and she had refused to pay the exorbitant charges. Emmet's lawyer made a motion to have her answer stricken out as "frivolous," but the judge denied the motion and set a date for trial. Five years later the parties settled out of court. Unfortunately, there is no record of the terms of the settlement, but it is clear that by going to court, Woodworth prevented Emmet from taking advantage of her. Obviously he did not expect that she would do so. He had sought to take advantage of her, yet she fought back in the courts and won—or at least was not required to pay the exorbitant rates that he thought he could get away with charging because of her vulnerability as a woman and brothel keeper. In the case of *Emmet v. Woodworth*, we do hear the woman's voice.[9]

The fact that one of the few women who was not afraid to project a high profile in court was a brothel keeper confirms the evidence I have found among women writers. As indicated in chapter 2 and discussed more fully in chapter 9, because of cultural associations of economic independence with sexual promiscuity, the only white women writers who spoke publicly and unequivocally in favor of economic independence as a lifelong goal for women tended to be those whose reputations were already tarnished, women who had nothing to lose. Whereas "respectable" women might be afraid of the criticism they would invite by overstepping cultural boundaries, a brothel keeper would not have to fear losing her "good name."

The third type of case that involved women as defendants was the inheritance case. One of the most onerous types of inheritance cases in which a woman was the defendant was the case in which the woman's husband had died and her adult child or children brought suit to force her to sell her home so that they could collect the money due them in their inheritance. A woman's dower right entitled her to a lifetime interest in one-third of the real estate that her husband owned, and if the only real estate that he owned was her home and her children wanted their two-thirds in cash and did not want to wait until she died, they could bring suit to force her to sell her home.

One example of a son who dispossessed his mother is found in the case of *Horatio Judah v. Rebecca Judah*. Although Samuel Judah (whose assistance in the lawsuit of his mother, Elizabeth, was discussed in chapter 4) was helpful to his mother, Rebecca Judah's son was not so helpful. In 1859, after the death of Rebecca's husband, Uriah (Uriah was the son of Henrietta Judah, who was also discussed in chapter 4), Uriah's son Horatio brought suit against his widowed mother, Rebecca Ann, and sister, Anna, a minor, in order to force the sale of the family home. Although the inheritance laws at the time gave a widow only one-third of her husband's real property, Uriah Judah's will specifically stated that his wife was to have the use of the house during her lifetime: "No house owned by me in which my said wife Rebecca Ann Judah may reside at the time of my death shall be sold during her life unless by her particular request and sanction." One suspects that Uriah did not trust his apparently mercenary son any more than the elder Bellmont had trusted his vicious daughter-in-law and weak son when he established a trust guaranteeing his daughter, Abby, a lifetime claim to residence in the "white house" in Wilson's *Our Nig*.[10] Unfortunately for Rebecca Judah, however, her son refused to accept the terms of his father's will and challenged it in court. Rebecca testified that the house she lived in at 241 West Seventeenth Street was the only house her husband owned and that she did not want to have it sold, that she wanted to remain living in it with her dependent daughter. Nevertheless, her son wanted his inheritance, and, disregarding his father's wishes so clearly stated in the will, he pursued the case. The court found in his favor, and the house was ordered sold on March 5, 1860. Rebecca and her daughter, having been evicted, went to live at the boardinghouse owned by Rebecca's widowed mother-in-law, Henrietta Judah (who figured in mortgage cases in chapter 4), at 240 West Forty-eighth Street. This case provides a good example of the difference between the middle-class woman who had relatives to rely on in time of need and the working-class woman, like Frado in *Our Nig*, who was without such a safety net.

Sons were not the only men who used the law to dispossess a female relative. In 1851 William B. Moneypenny brought suit against his widowed sister-in-law, Mary Ann Moneypenny, and her four children. His father, John Moneypenny, had died in 1821, and in 1826 William had brought suit in the then-existing Court of Chancery against his mother, Mary Moneypenny, and his brother, Robert Moneypenny, then a minor. The court ruled that William and Robert were each entitled to one half of their father's real property, subject to their mother's right of dower, but she could not be dispossessed of the house in which she lived because, unlike Rebecca Judah, she owned it in her own right for the duration of her lifetime. It was determined that her "right of dower in the said real estate was $271.60 per annum," and the court ordered her to pay to the register of the court the sum of $4,620 from the personal estate of her husband (which was then in her hands as "administratrix" of the estate). The sum was invested at 6 percent, and it was calculated that the interest would pay her the sum necessary for her dowry. However, instead of giving the court $4,620 in cash, she took out a mortgage for that amount on the house. She assigned the mortgage to the court register and paid the amount due on the mortgage for two or three years, but afterward she paid nothing, and the court allowed the lack of payment "in lieu of her dower." When her son Robert died in 1841, his widow, Mary Ann Moneypenny, and their five children came to live with her in the Chambers Street house. Mary Ann opened a small grocery store at the site in order to support herself and her children. In 1850, however, Mary Moneypenny died, and in 1851 her son William again brought suit, this time against Mary Ann and her four surviving children, forcing the sale of the house. Mary Ann countersued, but the court ruled that the house must be sold and the profits divided. William was entitled to one-half the money from the house and Mary Ann to her dower right—one-third of her deceased husband's one-half—and her children were entitled to the remainder of their father's half. When the house was sold at auction, William Moneypenny bought it himself for $30,000, and when his sister-in-law and her minor children did not move out fast enough, he obtained a writ of assistance directing the sheriff to evict them. Mary Ann and her children then sued for their share of the $4,620 mortgage that Mary Moneypenny had taken out. The court ruled that the money, plus interest, should be divided equally between William and the estate of

Robert, subject to Mary Ann Moneypenny's right of dower (one-third of Robert's half).

The story of the Moneypennys reveals the vulnerability of women under mid-nineteenth-century inheritance laws. Entitled to only one-third of her husband's real property (whereas a man was entitled to the whole of his wife's) and to only a lifetime estate (and thus prevented from willing the property as she chose), a woman was vulnerable to the wishes of a son, brother, or brother-in-law who was eager to receive his inheritance. (In the cases that I studied, the plaintiff in such cases was always male except when the man's wife was named as joint plaintiff due to dower laws.) If the property was extensive enough to be divided among the heirs, the woman might be permitted to remain in the house in which she lived. But if the real estate property consisted only of the house in which she lived and that property could not be partitioned, the male relative could force the sale of the house in order to obtain his inheritance.

But the Moneypenny story also reflects some of the ways in which women, in spite of the inequities of the law, were able to function economically. Mary Moneypenny owned her home in her own right; thus she was able to retain it for her lifetime in spite of her son's suit in 1826 and was able to use a mortgage on her property to circumvent the court's ruling that she give up $4,620 of her deceased husband's personal estate. She was also able to provide a home for her widowed daughter-in-law and five minor children, the youngest of whom was an infant when their father died. However, because she owned only a lifetime interest in the house, she could not will it to her daughter-in-law or grandchildren as a man might have done, under the circumstances, to protect the house from William Moneypenny's lawsuit. Her daughter-in-law, Mary Ann Moneypenny, also demonstrated a certain amount of independence. She supported herself after she was widowed by opening a grocery store in her mother-in-law's home, and she actively (although unsuccessfully) fought her brother-in-law's suit when her mother-in-law died.

Sometimes a woman's other relatives helped her to keep her home. In 1855, after the death of his father, James F. Hartnett and his wife Catherine brought suit against James's mother, Mary Hartnett, and his six brothers and sisters and orphaned niece and nephew, the latter two of whom were minors, to force his mother to sell the house she was living in so that he could obtain his inheritance. The court ordered that the house be sold, but Mary—apparently with the help of her other adult children —was able to pay the purchase price of $6,800 so that she and her children and orphaned grandchildren could remain in it. After the attorneys' fees were paid, the remaining $6,190.50 was divided into eight equal parts, and each of the Hartnett children received the sum of $773, the two grandchildren each receiving half of that amount. It was for this $773 that James Hartnett had attempted to dispossess his mother, his siblings, and his infant niece and nephew.

In all of these cases, the real property that the male relative wanted to have sold in order to obtain his inheritance consisted solely of the family home. However, when the property was extensive, consisting of much more than the house that his female relative lived in, a man did not need to dispossess a female relative when he brought such a suit. If the real property was extensive enough, the court would rule that the property could be divided between the two parties. For example, in 1850, according to the will of their aunt, Lucretia J. Winvall, Martin Ficken and Harman Kattenhorn inherited a large tract of land in New York City—most of the property between Second and Third Avenues extending from Seventy-ninth to Eightieth Street. Kattenhorn died two years later, however, leaving a deathbed will giving his wife, Betha, "every portion of his estate both real and personal for her use and benefit forever." Martin Ficken brought suit against his cousin's wife, Betha, asking for "a fair partition and division" of the property; or, if it was impossible to make such a partition "without great prejudice" to either party, he asked "that the said premises may be sold by auction." Betha did not contest Ficken's suit; in fact, it is not unlikely that her husband's deathbed will giving her all of the property was made at her instigation. The court ordered that "three impartial men" be appointed to have the land surveyed and divided into two equal parts. If the parts were not wholly equal, said the judge, the commission would "set monetary compensation to be made by one party to the other" to make up the difference. In this suit, neither party would be evicted. Betha Katterhorn was apparently as eager to have the division made as was Ficken. But such luxuries were available only to the very rich.

A final inheritance case involved a suit for the construction of the will of the deceased. In 1856 James McBrair died leaving much property, including buildings on Wall Street and Water Street and undeveloped land on Fifth Avenue at Fortieth Street. In his will he specified that all of his property was to go to his son John and John's children. He also specified that the property should not be sold during the lifetime of John and his children but should be leased. John had four living children: James, Eliza, and Margaret, as well as Henry Clay, who was still a minor. His daughter Lucretia had died, but her husband, Abraham, and son, John, were among the defendants. The other defendant was John's wife, Deborah, who, along with their adult children and son-in-law, apparently disagreed with John regarding his father's will. In 1859 the court ruled that the terms of the will must be upheld: the property could not be sold. John was appointed trustee to execute leases for the premises. However, when the leases were drawn up, John's adult children refused to sign them. Margaret used avoidance tactics. When the lawyer called, she remained "busy elsewhere in the house, superintending cleaning and repairing her home." Interestingly, the lawyer did not ask to see her; he talked only to her brother. The next time the lawyer called, she was out and remained away from home from 8 A.M. to 6 P.M. "Entirely accidental," she said, when she was threatened with contempt of court. The lawyer gave her a copy of one of the leases, but, she said, "it would have been utterly impossible for me to read the lease and understand and compare it to the judgment of the court without several hours time and the aid of counsel or other person of experience." Her husband, she said, was out of town. She conceded that if her brother and sister signed the lease, she would. On October 5, 1864, the court ordered James, Eliza, and Margaret to sign all of the leases within fifteen days, which they did. However, John McBrair died the following year. He left all of his real estate to his wife with the remainder of his property to his son Henry Clay McBrair, now of age, and his grandson, John Rose, a minor. After John McBrair died, Deborah, his widow, along with her son-in-law, Abraham, went to court and obtained an order to sell the land, even though according to her father-in-law's will the land was not to be sold. In March 1869 the land was ordered sold at public auction. James McBrair's will was broken by his son's wife.

As we have seen, sometimes the woman defendant was an independent businesswoman or strong-willed participant in the legal cases in which she was involved. At other times, as with John McBrair's daughter Margaret, a woman conveniently used conventional gender roles to avoid legal confrontations. In many of the cases, however, the woman defendant played a passive role in the litigation, or if she was actively involved, her actions are not clear from the public record. Even more voiceless were the women who were used as pawns by the male defendants in the case.

One way in which a woman was made a pawn is evident in the case of *James Reed v. Leopold Mark and Jane Tisdale.* In 1858 Tisdale was taken to court and found in contempt for failing to answer the summons regarding nonpayment of a promissory note that she had endorsed for Mark. She claimed that when she received the summons, Mark had told her not to concern herself about it; he said that he would take care of it, she said. Moreover, she explained, "she had no acquaintance with legal proceedings" and was "in a disturbed state of mind." She insisted that she had no knowledge of the bank's "refusal of payment, or that said note was not paid." She asked that the judgment against her be dismissed and the costs charged to the plaintiff. On July 9 the court ordered that Tisdale be allowed to defend herself but charged her ten dollars in costs. There is no record of the conclusion of this case; the parties probably settled out of court, with, in all probability, Tisdale paying the amount of the note. Nor does the case reveal the relationship between Tisdale and Mark. Whether he was a lover, a friend, or a relative is unknown. But he obviously was more knowledgeable than she. Tisdale could, of course, have simply been a good actress pretending innocence in court. But the picture that emerges from her testimony is of an unsophisticated woman who had been taken advantage of.

Jane Tisdale apparently endorsed Leopold Mark's promissory note of her own free will; she was not coerced. However, in 1861 Esther Lichtenstein was sued by Rebecca Barnett for a promissory note that she claimed she had made out "under coercion." Lichtenstein owned separate property in her own name, a house at 207 West Forty-eighth Street, a house at 10 Greene Street, and other real estate "of great value," from which she collected rent. When the bank refused to cash her note, Barnett took her to court, demanding that her property be sold in order to pay the debt.

Barnett asked that "the court make a charge and lien upon the separate real and personal estate of the defendant and that the same be directed to be sold and the proceeds applied to payment of the plaintiff." Esther Lichtenstein had written the promissory note to Barnett because her (Esther's) husband, Marcus, had owed Barnett $152.17, and, unable to pay the debt, he had gotten his wife to write a note for the amount. Esther testified that she had not wanted to write the note but was forced to by her husband: "Her husband requested her to make the note to the plaintiff on account of his indebtedness, which she refused to do, but under coercion of her husband, she made the promissory note to him." Barnett's brother, John Barnett, testified that he had gone to the Lichtenstein house to collect the debt for his sister. He brought with him, he said, a "blank form of note" for Marcus to sign. But instead Marcus called his wife. When Esther was questioned in court, she said her husband "called me to sign this and said he should be sued if I did not sign." Marcus's testimony confirmed this. "I told her she must sign it," he said.

In a judgment in November 1861, the court found for the defendant Lichtenstein, charging Barnett with costs of $57.85. The judge used a very traditional argument: "The note is void as the act of a *feme covert*, who cannot enter into contracts binding to her personally." However, he denied that she had been forced, maintaining that it would be impossible to "force" a woman to help out her husband; she would help him as a matter of course. The judge ruled: "The said making of the note was not procured by or under the coercion of her husband; the same was done at the request of her husband and for his benefit and as his surety." Consequently, he said, the note did not create a charge upon her personal estate. And in a reference to the Married Women's Property Act, he used the argument that "the assent of her husband is not given in pursuance of the act of 1860." The act stated that, although a wife could own real property in her own right and could buy and sell (the latter ability had been denied to her in the 1848 act), "no such conveyance or contract shall be valid without the assent, in writing, of her husband."[11] Thus, using a conservative interpretation of the restrictions of the law regarding married women, the judge declared that Esther Lichtenstein was not liable for the note. Here was a woman of separate property who came to court after the 1860 law, yet ironically, her property was saved by the use of traditional legal arguments that circumscribed her rights. In effect, the court ruled that it was acceptable for her husband to coerce her into signing the note because a wife must be expected to save her husband, yet concluded that her actions were invalid because a *feme covert* could not sign contracts or make real estate transactions without her husband's permission in writing.

Barnett appealed in January 1862, but the appeals court upheld the judgment of the Supreme Court. Then, in May 1862, the defendant's lawyer appeared in court and asked that the liens be lifted against Lichtenstein's property. The court granted her attorney's motion that her property be "forever released and discharged of and from the effects" of the action. It is in the attorney's plea that we discover the extent of Esther Lichtenstein's holdings. Her attorney listed the premises affected by Barnett's lien. Since the lawsuit, she had purchased a "farm in Westchester valued at $12,000, under a mortgage of $2,500," and she sold "property in 22nd Street and in 32nd Street." Moreover, "the other property on 32nd Street which she still owns was purchased for $7500 with a mortgage for $4250; the property in 48th Street cost $8500 and has a $5000 mortgage; and the property in Eighth Avenue cost $14,000 and has a mortgage of $7500." Clearly Esther Lichtenstein was a "woman of property" as much as Soames Forsyte was a "man of property" in John Galsworthy's 1906 book by that title in the *Forsyte Saga*—yet she could not buy and sell her property without her husband's permission in writing.

The other woman in this story, of course, is the plaintiff, Rebecca Barnett, who pursued this debt to the very end. Why Marcus Lichtenstein owed her $152 is never spelled out in the narrative of the case. It is interesting to see how these two independent women found themselves pitted against each other because of a man's irresponsible actions, a scenario that modern thinking about nineteenth-century gender roles would not have envisioned. In the conventional view, it was the "weaker sex" that was irresponsible and ignorant of money matters. But as some of these cases make clear, the *pater familias* did not always handle finances with a steady hand and rational head.

One last case in which a woman appears to be a pawn is the 1866 suit of Friedrich Neudorffer and Adolph Ehret against Benjamin Lee, Ann

Elizabeth Douglass, and James Rattigan. In 1863 the plaintiffs had leased from Lee the first floor of property at 88 Broad Street, where they were partners in a restaurant. The lease was to expire on May 1, 1866, but in 1865 Lee had signed an agreement with Neudorffer and Ehret entitling them to renew for three more years. However, when they tried to renew the lease, Lee refused to renew on the ground that his twenty-one-year title to the property was up and the owners of the property had leased the property not to him but to his widowed daughter, Ann Douglass, for the term of six years. Neudorffer and Ehret said they "asked for Mrs. Douglass but Lee said she was ill and could not be seen." The plaintiffs claimed that at the time she signed the lease, Douglass knew of the plaintiff's option of renewal. They insisted that it was really her father who held the lease and that taking the lease in her name instead of her father's "was concocted and contrived with intent to cheat and defraud the plaintiffs out of the interest acquired by them and their right to a renewal according to the agreement of March 24, 1865." Lee, they said, wanted to oust them in order to rent the whole building at a higher rate. Their lease was for $400 a year, but Lee, using Douglass, had rented the whole premises instead to James Rattigan for $2,500. The plaintiffs said that they had contacted the attorney who had drawn up the 1865 agreement in which Lee had promised them three years' renewal, and in April 1866 they went with the attorney to see Lee. Because of Lee's deafness, they said, Ann Douglass "conducted the whole conversation." The month before they had gone to see Douglass alone. She said that because of the assignment of the lease to her, the renewal made by her father was not binding. Clearly, Ann Douglass knew all about the renewal and its terms.

On April 28, 1866, the plaintiffs obtained an injunction order against Douglass and Rattigan to prevent them from "disturbing the plaintiffs in the possession of the premises and from commencing proceedings to dispossess them." They asked that the court order Lee/Douglass to renew the lease, claiming that they had put a lot of money into renovation of the site in anticipation of renewal. At the trial Lee denied that he had contrived with Douglass to cheat the plaintiffs. He said he had "no further interest in or control of the matter." Douglass claimed that the plaintiffs knew that they should not expect renewal and reiterated that she had not "contrived to cheat them." She had rented the building to Rattigan, she said, as she "had a good and lawful right to do." The attorney for the owner of the property testified that when Lee requested that the new lease be drawn up to Douglass instead of himself, he (the lawyer) insisted that Lee produce evidence of her ownership. Before the document was signed, Lee produced such a document, but it seemed to have been done after the fact. "I had the impression," testified the attorney for the owner, "it was made simply to pass the legal title into Mrs. Douglass in order to satisfy my requirements." The plaintiffs' lawyer moved that Douglass be compelled to execute the plaintiffs' lease. There are no further records. Apparently the case was settled out of court, and the terms are unavailable. Everything indicates that the plaintiffs either won their renewal or reached some compromise arrangement. It seems clear, however, that Lee transferred the title to the property to Douglass as a way of avoiding having to make good on the promised renewal to Neudorffer and Ehret. The question is, was Douglass an active participant in this scheme, or was she simply being used by her father? Was the lease—and the rent money that came with it—hers alone, or was it her father who made the decisions and would collect the rent? The fact that Douglass was knowledgeable about the leases, that it was she who discussed the issues with the plaintiffs and their lawyer, suggests that she was not a passive participant. But we have no way of knowing whether or not it was she or her father who was truly in control. One thing is certain: if she was a pawn, she was no Lucy Bates, running from room to room closing doors. Nor was she an Ann Tisdale, who had "no acquaintance with legal proceedings."

In addition to appearing as debtors and heirs, and in addition to being used as pawns by male litigants, women defendants appeared in numerous types of miscellaneous cases. In order to round out the portrait of the woman defendant within nineteenth-century culture, I will end with a discussion of one of these varied cases. The 1864 case of *Heermance v. Heermance* is, on the surface, a custody case. But the issues are both economic and social, and the case reveals much about cultural attitudes toward gender. Frazier Heermance brought suit against his wife, Kate, to obtain custody of their child, also named Kate. They had been married around 1857, and when he could find work, he worked as a baggage master on the Hudson Railroad. In 1858 they had gone west to Illinois where her parents lived, but Frazier had quarreled with her father because he did not get the money he (Frazier) expected from him. Kate said that Frazier had "abused her father." They returned to New York with their child, Kate, and Kate senior got a job in the Stotts factory in Stockport. Then, in April 1861, Frazier enlisted in the army (the Civil War had begun) and did not see his wife or daughter for two and a half years. She testified that at the time he was unemployed and he had borrowed the money from her to go to camp. She also said that she had paintings that she had done, but her husband "reckoned up the prices of my pictures which I painted in Poughkeepsie and he sold them amounting to $50. He took the money."

After Frazier went into the army, Kate went to her brother's in Canada, where she said she worked "doing his housework for board of myself and child." In October 1862, she left her brother's and went with her daughter to her parents' home in Illinois, where she stayed for two years, helping her mother and working for her board. During all of this time, she said, she received very little money from her husband—a total of one hundred dollars in two and a half years. To earn some money while she was in Illinois, she worked as a domestic in a neighboring family. She shared a bedroom with a twelve-year-old girl, but they had separate beds, and a hired man named Eliott North slept in the adjoining room. He had to pass through their room to get to his. She had been suffering from headaches, she said, and he gave her some "medicine" to take before going to bed. On three occasions, she said, after she had taken the medicine, he came into her room and forced himself on her. She reported that she tried to stop him but could not: "I resisted him at my very utmost all three times. I did not holler—did not holler because I thought I was in his power." After this she became pregnant, and early in the pregnancy she visited her husband at Camp Parole, not telling him that she was pregnant. Soon afterward she and Kate went to her brother's in Canada, where she stayed until her baby was born. Frazier testified that when he got out of the army, she had a baby a few weeks old. Her visit to Camp Parole was approximately seven months before the child was born, and she told him the baby was premature. But he was suspicious, he said, because the baby had weighed ten pounds at birth. She denied that she had been unfaithful, but in order to find out the truth, Frazier went to Canada where the child had been born. He came home, he said, "satisfied of her infidelity" and demanded that Kate tell him the truth. She told him about Elliott North, and he set out for Illinois to "ascertain the facts." Meanwhile, Kate went with her two children to the home of family friends, the Dingmans, where she obtained a job in a factory. At the hearing, Caroline Dingman, who had known Kate since she was a child, and other witnesses testified that Kate was a person of "good character." When Frazier returned from Illinois, he said that he did not believe Kate's story, but he told her that he would take her back if she would "dispose of that baby where she would never see or hear from it." The Dingmans offered to take the baby, but he did not want the baby to be placed with friends. Kate testified that he had her arrested in New York and "carried before the police justices." Moreover, she said, he was abusive: "He knocked me down. I got up and he struck me again on the breast and knocked me down." At this point, he forcefully took six-year-old Kate away with him. The Dingmans testified that young Kate "screamed and hollered" when he took her away. Before that, they said, they had heard the child talk about hiding when her father came for her, and a neighbor testified that she "heard the child tell us to lock the door so her father couldn't get her." Dr. William Pitcher testified that young Kate was too ill to be moved, the events of the past week having caused a nervous condition. Kate testified that she was fully capable of supporting her children. However, Frazier obtained a writ of *habeas corpus* for custody of the child Kate.

The modern reader in reading the facts of this case might be appalled at so much that was passed over without comment by the justices: Frazier's violent temper and physical abuse of his wife, his abusive treatment of her father, his veritable desertion of his wife while he was in the army, his having her arrested on trumped-up charges, his theft of her paintings and money, his relentless attempts to find out the truth about her fidelity—traveling to Canada and then to Illinois—and his insistence that she "dispose" of her baby. All of this seems to have been regarded as acceptable male behavior. It was Frazier's narrative of "a husband wronged by an unfaithful wife while he was fighting for his country" that mid-nineteenth-century justices found most "believable." Kate's story, on the other hand, did not fit into any acceptable frame. Her apparent rape and her struggle to support herself and her daughter throughout her marriage counted for nothing in this case; her husband's abuse and the theft of her paintings were not regarded as crimes. The only thing that seemed significant in the trial was the fact that Kate had committed adultery; it didn't matter whether it was consensual or not. The picture of Kate that emerges from this narrative tells us a lot about nineteenth-century gender expectations. On the one hand, she seems passive and acquiescent to male rule: she felt she was in the "power" of the man who forced himself on her and did not cry out or report the incident. On the other hand, she was self-reliant and self-supportive. She was economically independent, and although it was a hard struggle, she was proud of it. Testifying at the trial, she asserted confidently: "When I worked at Stotts [factory] I worked for my board and that of my child. I can average from $25 to $30 per month. I can paint and sew. I can take care of myself and of these two children with all ease. All I wish is to be left alone." A twenty-first-century woman might say the same.

The accumulation of these cases is revelatory. The principal insight that emerges from the narratives of these many women is the realization that there is no one theory to explain nineteenth-century female defendants. If, on the one hand, some women defendants were only passively involved in economic issues as the widows of men who died in debt, as holders of mortgaged property, or as pawns in legal cases, others were actively involved in economic matters in taking out loans, in purchasing goods, in running their own businesses, in working for a living, or in playing the role of invisible partner. The narrative of these cases underscores the fact that whether a woman was active or passive, and whether she knew it or not, money was a part of her life. A number of women writers at the time reflected this reality in their fiction. In the next chapter we look at some of the ways in which money and the law coalesce in specific works of fiction by nineteenth-century women writers.

chapter seven

ECONOMICS
AND THE LAW
IN FICTION

FERN, TYLER, OAKES SMITH, CHESEBRO',
PHELPS, STODDARD, CHILD, DAVIS, RUIZ DE BURTON,
AND WINNEMUCCA HOPKINS

Although nineteenth-century American women were proscribed from active involvement in the law in an official capacity—they could not practice as lawyers, obtain judgeships, or serve on juries—nevertheless, as the court cases in this study indicate, many women were involved in legal matters. Since nineteenth-century culture constructed women as acquiescent and domestic, outside the marketplace or "public sphere," and since only high-profile legal cases would have received much publicity, to what extent were women in general aware of or interested in legal matters? Of course there is no way to obtain a statistical count by doing an opinion poll as one might today in order to determine the consciousness level or attitudes of a particular demographic group on an issue. However, it is possible to obtain a sense of what at least some women were thinking. One way in which we can gain insight into women's consciousness of and attitudes toward legal matters is to look at women's fiction. This chapter is intended as only a partial survey, of course, but, taken together, these texts—representing different perspectives, deriving from a broad span of time, and looked at in conjunction with the texts already discussed—provide a useful barometer of some contemporary women's ideas respecting the law and its relationship to women and money.

This discussion of law in literature reveals how closely conjoined legal and economic interests were for nineteenth-century women, even when the connection was carefully hidden away underneath the conventional rhetoric of femininity and domesticity, as in Susan Warner's *The Wide, Wide World*, in which all of the action ensues from the loss of a lawsuit and the consequent loss of money. The law was not a prominent theme in most women's fiction—which is consistent with cultural proscriptions and the social construction of womanhood—but a number of works include significant portrayals of and references to legal matters that were specifically of importance to women, and other works raise legal questions that affected both men and women. The fact that women writers tackled these subjects at all indicates that some women—both the writers and their readers—were aware of and interested in legal questions. And in all of these works, whether the focus is on legal or economic concerns, the two are clearly related, either directly or by implication.

Legal questions appear in these fictional works in principally three ways. The most common way centers on women's vulnerability before the law because of their ignorance of the law, because of the negative impact of laws on women, and because of specific legal restrictions based on gender. The second—and least common—way in which women writers treat the law is to portray women's active involvement in legal issues either as plaintiffs or defendants. And the third way in which the law figures in fiction is in the portrayal of injustices of the law in relation to issues that are not gender-specific, for example, in relation to slavery and issues of class or ethnicity.

The issue most often portrayed, particularly before the passage of later Married Women's Property acts that gave women control of their own money, was the question of women's vulnerability under the law. One of the most salient nineteenth-century fictional treatments of the dangers of women's legal ignorance and vulnerability appears in Fanny Fern's *Ruth Hall* (1855), which reflects Fern's own metamorphosis from an ignorant innocent with respect to both legal and economic questions to a savvy businesswoman who makes it her business to know her legal rights. Ruth has several encounters with legal issues, and Fern shows how she becomes more knowledgeable about the law as she becomes more experienced. Immediately after Harry Hall's death, when Ruth is at her most vulnerable, her husband's friend Tom Develin takes advantage of her ignorance of the law. Her father-in-law has requested Harry's clothes, and although legally the widow is entitled to her husband's personal effects, Develin wants to please Dr. Hall because Hall is wealthy and influential whereas Ruth is a poor widow with no influence. Develin's thoughts run thus: "The law is on her side, undoubtedly, but luckily she knows no more about law than a baby; she is poor, the doctor is a man of property; Ruth's husband was my friend to be sure, but a man must look out for No. 1 in this world, and consider a little what would be for his own interest."[1] Here Fern portrays a phenomenon that we saw in numerous court cases in which a male relative or family friend, looking out for "No. 1," took advantage of a woman's ignorance and/or vulnerability in order to obtain money or property for himself—from the son who used the law to force his widowed mother and minor siblings out of their house to the brother-in-law executor who defrauded his brother's widow and children of their inheritance. As we also saw, not all men were guilty of such behavior, nor were all women so passive or ignorant as to allow themselves to be taken advantage of without a fight; nevertheless, there were enough of these cases to show that Fern's portrayal is an accurate reflection of an unfortunately not-uncommon occurrence—and we saw only the cases that came to court.

Ruth learns more about the law when she visits the insane asylum where her friend Mary Leon has died, and the chapter calls attention to the vulnerability of women under the law. First of all, as numerous court cases show, the laws were so loose in the mid-nineteenth century that, if a woman did not have friends and family to speak up for her, it was possible for a man to have his wife committed even if she was not insane simply because her husband wanted to get her out of the way. At that time in New York State, for example, a person needed only one signature to have someone committed. In her "Reminiscences" Elizabeth Cady Stanton tells how in 1861 Susan B. Anthony succeeded in helping in the escape of a fugitive mother who had been "incarcerated by her husband in an insane asylum for eighteen months," although everyone who knew her then and afterward testified that she was not insane. Since Anthony was breaking the law in refusing to divulge the hiding place of the woman, Stanton compares the case to that of a person aiding a fugitive slave: "In both cases an unjust law was violated; in both cases the sup-posed owners of the victims were defied." Stanton concludes: "Could the dark secrets of these insane asylums be brought to light, we should be shocked to know the countless number of rebellious wives, sisters, and daughters that are thus annually sacrificed to false customs and con-ventionalisms, and barbarous laws made by men for women."[2]

Also significant is the fact that child custody laws favored the man throughout most of the nineteenth century. While in the asylum Ruth hears a woman screaming for her child. The matron tells her that the woman's husband had taken the child away from her "to spite her." The woman "went to the law about the child," says the matron, "and the law, you see, as it generally is, was on the man's side" (111).[3] The economics of these two situations are implicit rather than explicit and will become clearer in chapter 8. As the divorce cases I will discuss there indicate, the woman whose moneyed family stood behind her could not be incarcer-ated simply on her husband's say-so, and the woman who had money of her own when her husband did not was able to retain custody of her chil-dren. Without money, a woman was doubly vulnerable to the law.

Just as Ruth learns about the law, so Fanny Fern herself became more astute in legal matters. In *A New Story Book for Children* (1864), Fern de-scribes how during her first marriage she had ignorantly signed papers that enabled her husband to mortgage their home and other property beyond his means to pay. Since, as we saw earlier, under common law a wife was entitled to her dower share of one-third of all real estate her husband owned, a man could not take out a mortgage on or sell real property without his wife's signature. Fern writes of how her mother tried to warn her of the need to pay attention to what she was signing, but she ignored her warning.

> [A] law paper was sent for my wifely signature. . . . "Stay! child," said my mother, arresting my hand, "do you know what that paper is about?" "Not I!" was my laughing reply; "but my husband sent it, and on his broad shoul-ders be the responsibility!" "That is wrong," said she, gravely; "you should never sign any paper without a full understanding of its contents." It seemed

to me then that she was over-scrupulous, particularly as I knew she had the same implicit confidence in my husband that I had. I had reason afterward to see the wisdom of her caution.[4]

Fern's husband, Charles Eldredge, had undertaken a construction project that sapped him of all of his assets and left him hopelessly in debt. When he died he had lost a lengthy lawsuit and was working on an appeal. He owed $50,000 that he could not pay, and he had lost their house. In 1839 he had taken out two mortgages on the house, one for $3,000 and one for $4,000, and in 1840 he purchased property for $21,000, of which he paid approximately $6,000, agreeing to pay the balance of $15,000 in a year. Fern's signature — Sara P. Eldredge — is on all of these documents.[5] When Charles Eldredge died in 1846, Fern and her two children were left penniless. Looking back on her own ignorance and the catastrophe that resulted, Fern came to realize how important it was for a woman to understand the law. In case after case that I looked at, women who, like Fern, had signed the mortgage papers found themselves without a home to live in.

That Fern had gained a better understanding of the law by 1853 is apparent from the fact that when she began making substantial money from her writing, she made certain to ascertain whether or not her second husband, Samuel Farrington, had any legal claim to her money after their divorce. Farrington had obtained a divorce from her in Chicago in 1853 on the grounds of desertion, and when her first book was published later that year, she dispatched a lawyer to Chicago to discover whether or not Farrington could claim her earnings. She must have been relieved when the lawyer, after meeting with Farrington's lawyer and reading the divorce papers, reported that the divorce was absolute and that her former husband had no claim to her "person or property."[6] It is possible that Farrington, when he learned of her monetary success as a writer, had attempted to browbeat her into believing that he was entitled to her money. In Fern's 1856 novel, *Rose Clark*, John Stahle, who is based on Farrington, confronts his former wife, Gertrude, whose success, like the author's, had come after her husband obtained a divorce. He demands money from his former wife, planning to take advantage of what he presumes to be Gertrude's ignorance of the law. In the following exchange, his friend has asked him how he expects to get money from her since they are divorced and the law will not allow him to "touch any of her earnings." Stahle gives this reply: "All women are fools about law matters. She don't know that. . . . I'll frighten her into it. . . . I'll have some of her money."[7] If this incident is based on a real-life confrontation with Farrington, he, like Stahle, was foiled; at this point in her life, having learned from her past experiences, Fern had made it her business not to be ignorant of the law. And when she married her third husband, James Parton, in 1856, she had him sign a prenuptial agreement stating that all of the money that she earned before and after their marriage would be hers alone.[8] Fern's portrayal of women's experiences with legal questions, based on her own experience, makes very clear that ignorance and vulnerability led not only to sentimental loss but also to real economic loss.

A particularly devastating portrayal of woman's vulnerability under the law is found in another autobiographical novel, *A Book without a Title: or, Thrilling Events in the Life of Mira Dana* (1855) by Martha W. Tyler (1819-?).[9] Published soon after *Ruth Hall*,[10] Tyler's novel tells the story of a former factory worker whose tyrannical and abusive husband took possession of her three young children and what limited property she had—all of which he was legally empowered to do. Tyler states in the preface that her purpose is to "draw public attention to those acts of oppression, earnestly imploring those wise legislators who make our laws, to devise some means by which . . . [women] can be liberated from a bondage so painful" (viii). Although the feisty Mira fights back against her husband's oppression with the same spirit and intelligence that made her a leader in the 1836 strike at the Lowell textile mills where she worked before her marriage, she does not win, because, as she discovers in the course of the novel, the law is against her. The book follows pretty closely the details of Tyler's own life and is an angry indictment of the laws that, as Tyler says, make woman "a cipher" (285).

Interestingly, Tyler does not discuss the legal system in the book's earlier chapters, which deal with the mill strike; in those chapters, the law is only mentioned once in passing: when Mira goes to collect back pay for the strikers, she tells the recalcitrant paymaster that if he does not pay her what is required by law, her "legal friend at the door" will help her gain what is due the workers (30). But Tyler never discusses the possibility of legal redress for the long hours, poor working conditions, and meager pay that the factory operatives endure. Nevertheless, it is apparently her experience in the strike that gives Mira (like the author) the confidence, assertiveness, and know-how to challenge her husband's authority. In fact, Tyler uses the same rhetoric to describe the oppression of the mill girls that she later uses to describe Mira's situation as a wife. The Lowell operatives go on strike for their "independence and liberty," she says; they are not "cringing slaves" to "meekly submit to wear the galling chain of oppression" (22, 24). Similarly, when Mira's husband, Herbert Tyrrell, attempts to force her to his will, the author tells us, "Mira Tyrrell can die; but she cannot bow her free soul to the galling yoke of slavery" (268).

Since Tyler's narrative so closely follows her own life, it is not surprising that the details of Mira's legal problems parallel the stories told in actual court cases under study here, not only in many of the divorce cases discussed in the next chapter but most specifically in the case of *Trust v. Trust* in chapter 1. Herbert Tyrrell's motivation is the same as that of Joseph Trust: in both instances, the husband is frustrated by the independent spirit of his wife and is determined to humble her. What seems to infuriate Mira's husband more than anything else is his inability to break her will. Early on he vows: "I'll break her to the 'traces' yet, and teach her *my* purposes are not to be thwarted by such as *she*" (138). Later he comments that he wants to see her "well humbled" (213), and when she writes him a letter demanding that he support her as required by law, he asserts, "If she had written me a *good* letter, showing her submission . . . , I would send her some clothing, but the haughty creature has got too much *spunk*; but . . . I'll break her" (224). He employs various means to accomplish his purpose. Like Joseph Trust (in testimony corroborated by the Trusts' daughter Constance), Tyrrell inflicts on his wife a constant barrage of cruel and vindictive treatment (118, 140–141). Also like Trust, he calls the police on false charges against his wife. And just as the police in *Trust v. Trust* sympathize with Trust's attempt to make his wife obedient, the constable in Tyler's novel takes the husband's part, commenting, after feeling the sting of Mira's "biting sarcasm and lashing reproof," "I don't wonder her husband is afraid of her" (278–279). He ends by telling Tyrrell to bring her down to the police station, where they will "settle the matter to your satisfaction" (179). Like Joseph Trust, Tyrrell succeeds in driving his wife out of the house. Tyrrell goes even further, inviting his disreputable sister to live with him in order to make it impossible for Mira to return without humiliating and compromising herself, and he determines that he will attempt to drive her crazy, hoping that she will do something desperate so that he can have her committed to an insane asylum or to jail (251, 282). When this fails, he appropriates all of her furniture and gets a court order to take her trunks containing her clothing, commenting as he plans the latter, "I have always said that I would humble that proud woman" (251). And as he takes possession of her trunks, he avers, "I'll show that woman that . . . the husband is her lord and master" (254).

Both husbands engage in smear tactics, attempting to sully the reputations of their wives. Joseph Trust characterizes his wife as a brothel keeper, and Tyrrell accuses Mira of committing improprieties with his friend. As Tyrrell's lawyer tells him when he advises him on this course, "It is an easy matter to throw dirt" (189). Ultimately, like Joseph Trust also, Tyrrell exercises his legal right to take Mira's children; just as Trust obtained a writ of *habeas corpus* and forced Mary to give up her children, Tyrrell takes Mira to court, where she is forced to sign a document giving up all control of her children (284–285). Tyrell and Trust are both ordered to support their wives, and in both cases, they find such a ruling galling and vow that they will never pay. Both plead poverty. Trust avoids being required to pay by declaring that he is not legally married to Mary, and when the court orders him to pay, he refuses until he is threatened with jail. Tyrrell uses a method of escape seen in other court cases: he places all of his assets in the name of a friend so that he will appear poorer than he is (188, 190).

Mira's conduct is also similar to that of Mary Trust. Both had been earning their own living before marriage, which may help to account for their refusal to accept the subservient position their husbands demanded. Both are independent women with sharp tongues. Both seek help from the law and determine to triumph over their husbands. They institute divorce proceedings initially in order to gain monetary support, and for both, the overriding concern is economic: having been forced by law to give over all of the money and possessions they brought into the marriage and angered by the injustice of their husbands' treatment of them, they are determined to obtain money from their husbands. After leaving her husband, Mary Trust was much more successful at supporting herself than was Mira Dana, who sought the help of relatives until she, like her creator, decided to write a tell-all novel. However, unlike Fern, Tyler did not obtain a publisher and had to publish the book at her own expense. Although she sold copies of her book, it was not a bestseller like *Ruth Hall*. Tyler was able to bring out a second edition in 1856 as well as another book the following year, but she did not continue in a writing career.[11] As we saw in chapter 1, Mary Trust ultimately succeeded in obtaining a generous settlement; Mira, however, was able to obtain only two dollars a week. When the Tyrrells go to court, says Tyler, the question was "debated whether a woman could live on two dollars per week" (283), and the court decided that she could.

Tyler's portrayal of the law with respect to women in *A Book without a Title* is not a positive one. The lawyers are given Dickensian names that reflect the author's opinion of them: Mira's lawyer is Squire Foolsome; her husband's lawyers are S. W. Cheetman and Lawyer Renown (180–181, 165–166, 188–189). Renown, who basks in his own prestige, tells Tyrrell his goal: "The law is very hard with us husbands sometimes; it *compels* us to provide food and clothing for our wives, if they are ever so undeserving. But *I* intend to have *that law* brought *before the legislature* and altered" (206–207). When the divorce court makes its final determination taking Mira's children away from her, Mira addresses the court: "Is this the boasted justice which you stand here to dispense . . . ? Tell me, in God's dear name, if this arrangement is made in accordance with the laws of my country?" (284–285). Assured that it is, she declaims, "O land of liberty! A foul blot is upon thy fair escutcheon" (286). Tyler's novel is not only one woman's painful story; it is a call for change and a detailed representation of the impact on women of the inequities of the legal system.

Another outspoken writer in mid-nineteenth-century America with respect to woman's relationship to the law was Elizabeth Oakes Smith (1806–1893). A prolific writer of poetry, novels, and nonfiction and a lecturer on social issues, Oakes Smith never gained the popularity of Fern, but she was able to support herself and her family with her varied writings, some of which gained wide recognition. Her 1854 novel, *Bertha and Lily; or, The Parsonage of Beech Glen*, critiques the unjust legal restrictions on women and reflects the polemic in Oakes Smith's nonfiction. "Human legislation" has decreed that men and women should have different spheres, says Bertha, the novel's protagonist, but, she says, the only measure of a person's sphere should be his/her "capacity."[12] Bertha enjoys her independence: "[I am] entire mistress of myself, going and coming at mine own will and pleasure, expending money, buying and selling at the dictation of no one" (26). In marriage, she says, man and woman "should be entirely independent of each other in money matters" (27). The fact that the law recognizes woman only as the "property of her husband" (25), Bertha says, has serious consequences; not only does it determine the character of a woman, making her manipulative and wheedling, but it also can result in her impoverishment. Ernest Helfenstein, the parson of Beech Glen, describes the hypothetical case of a woman whose husband lost all of their money and left her a penniless widow to die in the poorhouse: "Her property, by that act of marriage, passed out of her hands into those of her husband. He became a spendthrift, an inebriate, a gambler—she had no redress. He squandered her whole estate. . . . His wife . . . [died in] the alms-house" (129). In contrast to this dependent wife, Bertha, as an independent woman, is a woman of "sound sense" who can take care of herself financially. As Helfenstein observes, "She has invested her money in good stocks, in a manly way. She cultivates her ground, and employs workmen, and knows how to make her funds productive" (132).

The solution to woman's problems, Oakes Smith says in her nonfictional manifesto, *Woman and Her Needs* (1851), is to change the laws. Men have all the power over women, she writes, and it would be a "miracle" if they didn't abuse it. This country has restricted the power of tyrannical civil governments, she points out, because "men could not be entrusted with unrestricted power over each other; and can the case be any better when the power is unlimited over our own sex?"[13] Woman, she said, is held as an "infant" in society; she "never reaches her majority" (71). For Oakes Smith, law was the key to the betterment of women's position: "We find her treated in law as a child and an idiot; we find public opinion, leading and led by the law, regarding her very much in this light"

(49). Woman, she said, "has had no voice in the law, and yet has been subjected to the heaviest penalties of the law" (20). What is needed, asserts
Oakes Smith, is to "raise the legal liabilities" of women (71).

A married woman's impoverishment due to a husband's legal and
financial troubles, which Fern and Oakes Smith warn about, was a not-
uncommon problem for nineteenth-century women, both in life and in
fiction. A principal reason why many women were left penniless when
their husbands lost their money was, as indicated in chapter 2, the common law restriction that a married woman's property belonged to her
husband. Thus her financial fate was tied to his. Numerous law cases in
the preceding chapters illustrate the frequency of occurrence of this
phenomenon, and a number of the works discussed in earlier chapters
make the vulnerability of wives to their husbands' legal difficulties the
catalyst for the ensuing action in the narrative: Mrs. Montgomery in Susan Warner's *The Wide, Wide World*; Hagar in Southworth's *The Deserted
Wife*; Mrs. Shelby in *Uncle Tom's Cabin*; and Mrs. Vincent in Crafts's *The
Bondwoman's Narrative*.

If the focus on inequities for women due to the married women's
property laws was a not-uncommon theme in nineteenth-century novels
by women, especially before the Civil War, a less common theme centered on a different legal question, the legality of which was ignored—
even deliberately avoided—by almost all nineteenth-century fiction
writers, both men and women: the question of the out-of-wedlock—"un-
lawful"—birth of a child. Almost no writers questioned the civil law that
made such a birth illegitimate, the moral law that made the action a sin,
or the custom that made it impossible for such a woman ever to compensate for the lapse. If a writer treated the phenomenon, it was to portray
the mother as a fallen woman who must be punished: the character is ostracized by society within the context of the work, and/or she is killed
off by the author. Even if the author sympathizes with the woman's
plight and portrays the woman as a victim of a predatory male or an unfortunate casualty of the sexual double standard, the author does not
question the law. In accordance with the pattern established in late-eigh-
teenth-century novels like Susanna Rowson's *Charlotte Temple* (1791) and
Hannah Foster's *The Coquette* (1797), the erring character dies, and the
book provides a sad warning to other women. If the character does not

meet an early death, she, like Hester Prynne in *The Scarlet Letter* (1850), spends the rest of her life in expiation of her sin.

Elizabeth Oakes Smith is one of the few authors who allows her protagonist to have an illegitimate child without having to die or to wear a hair shirt for the rest of her life. At the end of *Bertha and Lily*, we find that the protagonist had had an illegitimate child, Lily, who resides in Beech Glen. In a daring defiance of convention, Oakes Smith does not "punish" her character by having her killed off or ostracized like other transgressing female characters in nineteenth-century novels. Instead, Bertha becomes a pillar of society whom the author portrays as preferable to Julia, the alternative heroine. Bertha even gives public readings, *instructing* other women who, the author says, "learned much that women should learn from the lips of woman only" (333). And at the end of the novel she marries the minister. This unconventional ending—allowing such a character to have an honorable marriage—is rare in nineteenth-century American literature. Even in novels that attempted to show that a "fallen" woman could be rehabilitated, the character was not allowed to marry. In *Hedged In* (1870) Elizabeth Stuart Phelps (Ward) goes further than other authors, rehabilitating Eunice (Nixy) Trent, allowing her to become a respectable teacher, pointing out that her youthful error was environmental, and urging tolerance of her "difference." But she does not permit her to marry. As Eunice realizes when the alternative heroine, Christina Purcell, tells her that she is going to be married, "The sacredness of that white thing, a woman's happy love," is not for her.[14] Instead, Eunice, who has succeeded in becoming a "good woman," nevertheless dies an early death on the night of Christina's wedding. Even in *Isa, A Pilgrimage* (1852), by Caroline Chesebro' (1825–1873), which permits the heroine to live in unwedded atheistic happiness with her lover, the heroine is "punished": she and her lover lose their money, their child dies, and then Isa dies. Moreover, the author implicitly criticizes her heroine's behavior, framing the novel with a preface and a conclusion that extol the Christian life that the heroine eschews.[15]

In contrast to the authors of these works, Oakes Smith makes clear in *Bertha and Lily* that a woman who becomes pregnant outside of marriage and thus breaks a civil and a moral law can, if she is a good person, live a happy and fulfilling religious, intellectual, economic, and domestic life.

This is very different from the fate of the fallen woman in most nineteenth-century fiction, and apparently in nineteenth-century life as well. The social isolation and impoverishment of Mag in Wilson's *Our Nig* because of her initial pregnancy was probably a more common occurrence, although once again class markers must be factored in: Bertha is clearly well educated and higher on the social scale than Mag. Still, what is significant is that Bertha is not criticized by the author: she is not killed off; she is not ostracized; and at the end of the novel she, not the alternative heroine, marries the male protagonist in a joyous wedding celebration in a church "garlanded with flowers" (335). This is a radicalized sentimental ending which asserts that the "fallen" woman can pick herself up and become a respected member of society. She can also live a productive life; she does not have to have her economic livelihood terminated by a youthful indiscretion. It is significant that Bertha is not only "good" but is also an astute economic manager of her money.

Whereas Fern, Tyler, and Oakes Smith overtly challenged legal inequities for women, many other women writers, if they did not center legal questions in the plot of the story, introduced questions of law either as background or in relation to the development of plot. This was particularly true of works published later in the century after the passage of many of the married women's property laws. These references to legal matters were almost invariably related to the role of women and questions of money.

Elizabeth Stuart Phelps (Ward) (1844–1911) in *The Story of Avis* (1877), for example, only touches on legal questions, but although they seem not to be central to the narrative, they are important to the textual development of the novel. One such reference is the information about Susan Wanamaker's unhappy marriage. She tells Avis that her husband wants to go to Texas and that she must go with him: "The law compels me to go with him, as if I were a horse or a cow."[16] Also significant is the fact that she is subject to beatings for which the law does not provide any recourse. One character says this of Susan's injuries: "We are not to understand that she was knocked down, and trampled on. She fell. It is surprising how insecure of foot women with drunken husbands are found to be" (160). Susan is not a major character in the novel, but she is important in providing damaging information about Philip's past, thus contributing to Avis's growing disillusion with her husband, Philip, and with marriage. But even more important is the way in which Susan's unhappy marriage foreshadows and reflects Avis's own unraveling marriage. Susan says of her forced move: "Women don't think of such things when they marry" (161). Later Avis will realize that there were many things she did not think of before she married, and by the end of the novel—after Philip loses his job, accumulates debts, abdicates family responsibilities, goes back on all of his promises to support her art, flirts with Barbara Allen, and saps Avis of all of her creative energies—she seems to echo Susan's words when she thinks of how her marriage to Philip had "eaten out the core of her life, left her a riddled, withered thing, spent and rent" (244).

Another reference to the law in *The Story of Avis* occurs after Philip's departure for Europe, when Avis is struggling to support herself and her two children. She has reluctantly sold her painting *The Sphinx*, and when she finds that Philip's old college debts have still not been paid, she pays them by selling some bonds "of her own, upon whose proceeds the family were in part dependent for the coming year" (205). Phelps adds the following: "Fortunately she had not to deal with stock or real estate, which the wife cannot sell without the husband's consent. Avis did not know this. She knew nothing, except that she was grieved and shamed" (205). Phelps's comment reveals Avis's ignorance of the law as well as her struggle to "cover" for her husband's deficiencies by paying his debts. In this sense, she is comparable to Susan, who "covers" for her husband's drunkenness and brutality by allowing people to believe that she "fell" when in fact he had beaten her. Thus Phelps's mention of the law seems peripheral, but it relates in important ways to women's role and the development of the narrative. Moreover, Phelps's description of the legal impediments to women's sale of stocks and real estate calls attention to the fact that in 1877 married women were still legally restricted in their economic dealings.

In *The Morgesons* (1862), Elizabeth Stoddard (1823–1902) includes a number of specific references to the law; legal matters are closely tied to economics, and their significance for women is an important theme in the book. At first the references to the law seem peripheral, but they provide a background for the legal-economic theme that builds as the novel progresses. The author tells us that the families of most of the girls in the fashionable school Cassandra attends for a year acquired their money from a grandfather who was involved in illegal and/or shady business practices.[17] None of the girls has any knowledge of the disreputable practices by which their grandfathers gained the fortunes that buy the girls' clothes. As the narrator says, "Elmira Sawyer . . . never heard that her grandfather 'Black Peter,' as he was called, had made excursions . . . on the River Congo. . . . Neither was Hersila Allen aware that the pink calico in which I first saw her was remotely owing to West India Rum. Nor did Charlotte Alden, the proudest girl in school, know that her grandfather's, Squire Alden's, stepping-stone to fortune was the loss of the brig, *Capricorn,*" due to "the hole bored through her bottom" in accordance with Alden's instructions (34–35). Thus Stoddard underscores the role of money and the law in the lives of women even if the women themselves are ignorant of it.

Another law-related reference is made when Cassandra goes to stay with Charles Morgeson's family in Rosville. The narrator comments that, since the courts were held there, there were "several lawyers of note who had law students, which fact was to the lawyers' daughters the most agreeable feature of their father's profession" (73). On the one hand, this reference furthers the plot in that it prepares us for Cassandra's meeting with Ben Somers, but it also provides an indication of gender divisions and the limitation of women's opportunities in nineteenth-century society, which is a major theme of the novel. The young women look to the budding lawyers as potential husbands since they cannot become lawyers themselves.

A further reference to the law in *The Morgesons* concerns the disposition of money in a man's will. According to the terms of Ben and Desmond Somers's grandfather's will, his grandchildren will inherit a sizable fortune when their youngest sibling turns twenty-one (169). Desmond is twenty-nine when his mother has a new baby boy, which means that if the child lives to maturity, Desmond will be fifty years old before he will be independent. He does not ask Cassandra to marry him until after the child dies prematurely. The terms of the will thus serve to extend the time before Cassandra gets married; they also allow the profligate Desmond sufficient time to reform. In the Morgeson family, the arrival of a boy baby is portrayed as eventful for economic reasons also. His grandfather leaves him ten thousand dollars in his will, although he leaves nothing to his granddaughters. When Arthur is born, the housekeeper says that their father "ought to have a son to leave his money to" (25). Temperance comments: "Girls are thought nothing of . . . ; they may go to the poor house, as long as the sons have plenty" (25). These events and the servants' comments illustrate society's assumption that it is the men who will handle the money. It is also an illustration of the way in which women were left without money of their own because they were expected to find a husband to depend upon for support. By providing these two examples of male-authored wills, Stoddard calls attention to the way in which cultural assumptions are given legal power and have a significant impact on women's economic lives.

Despite this emphasis on the male-dominated nature of money matters, the movement of the novel takes us in a counterdirection from this accepted wisdom, with multiple threads leading to the assertion that it is a mistake to exclude women from economic responsibility. For example, when Cassandra's father says that she will probably marry, Alice Morgeson says, "If you leave her a fortune, or teach her some trade, that will give her some importance in the world" (101). And when Alice's husband dies, she herself takes over the management of the mills (125). Also, it is *Mrs.* Somers who has the money in the Somers family: she has a separate estate that is legally her own; she doles out her sons' allowances and decides what her husband shall spend (169, 203, 233). The possession of money gives her an inordinate amount of power in the family, although it also makes her tyrannical. On the other hand, when Cassandra and Veronica were growing up, they and their mother were "ignorant of practical or economical ways." Cassy says, "We never saw money." Her father, Locke Morgeson, makes money in his business and does all of the spending, while her mother is "indifferent to much of the business of ordinary life" (23). Thus Cassandra looks up to her father as the person who handles the money. However, when she is grown and Locke's business fails due to his irresponsible behavior, she becomes disillusioned with him. He tells her that most of his creditors are women: "Half the widows, old maids, and sailors' wives" in town are his creditors; they trusted him more than they did the bank (221). Cassandra says that she "felt a cold twinge" at that news, realizing that her father's poor management has lost the money even of poor servant women. He had been "insolvent for five years" (231), but the public had not known it. Her father's behavior is disturbing to her: "I perceived a change in my estimation of father; a vague impression of weakness in him troubled me" (232).[18] Legally, Cassandra's father is liable for other people's money as well as the money of his own family; his creditors sign legal papers giving him three years to repay his debts or they will claim all of his remaining property (231). In this novel, the law and economics constitute the frame underlying all of the action, and the author makes clear that women are involved in such matters whether they know it or not.

The second way in which legal questions are treated in nineteenth-century women's writing is in the portrayal of a woman who actively uses the law for her own purposes, either as plaintiff or defendant in a lawsuit. This category has few representatives in nineteenth-century American fiction. Tyler's novel discussed above downplays the fact that Mira Dana is a litigant and focuses instead on her husband's machinations. When a woman is overtly portrayed as a litigant, the portrayal is generally a negative one. One of the few such women in men's writing of the period is Mary Monson in James Fenimore Cooper's *The Ways of the Hour* (1850), which Cooper wrote deliberately to oppose the Married Women's Property law in New York. When she is falsely accused of murder, Mary Monson actively takes part in the conduct of the case, cross-examining the principal witness against her and ultimately proving her innocence despite the ineptitude of her lawyers. Instead of portraying her independent use of the law as an astute way of saving herself from hanging, Cooper condemns her behavior as "unfeminine" and labels her a "discredit" to her sex; the "true woman," he says, is gentle and self-effacing, not self-willed and self-assertive.[19] That Cooper can take such a strong stand for "proper" feminine behavior in view of the fact that if Mary *had* behaved like a "true woman" she would have been executed is an indication of the powerful condemnation of women who concerned themselves with legal matters that was current in traditional society at midcentury. It is perhaps because of this attitude toward women's "going out of their sphere" that so few women (or men) writers portrayed women's active involvement in legal questions, even though we know from the court cases that many women did, in fact, pursue legal matters in court as litigants.

Even when a woman writer portrayed a legally active woman, that woman was seldom portrayed sympathetically. In Elizabeth Stoddard's 1863 short story "Lemorne *versus* Huell," Eliza Huell is crass and manipulative, a woman who, in effect, sells her niece in order to win a lawsuit. If woman's unwitting involvement in legal and economic questions is the underlying thread in *The Morgesons*, it is the principal theme of Stoddard's short story. In this story, Stoddard portrays two women, one of whom uses the law for her own purposes while the other unknowingly becomes a tool of the first. When Margaret Huell's wealthy Aunt Eliza asks her to come to Newport with her, twenty-four-year-old Margaret, who lives with her poor mother and teaches piano lessons for a living, agrees to go because her mother urges it in the hope that they will benefit from Eliza's money. The imperious Eliza is not an easy person to get along with, however, and treats Margaret like the poor relation that she is, ordering her about like a servant.[20] Acting as narrator, Margaret laconically and sarcastically describes her two-month ordeal as the passive instrument of her aunt's whims.

Eliza Huell has been involved in litigation for three or four years concerning a "tract of ground in the city" that has "become very valuable" (269). Although Eliza is determined to win the case at all costs, Margaret is ignorant of the law and of the particulars of the case. As she says at the beginning of the story, "I never felt any interest in it" (269). When she meets Edward Uxbridge at Newport, she is attracted to him, and when he asks her—or rather commands her—to marry him, she acquiesces just as passively as she has in the performance of her duties for her aunt. As she says of her engagement, "I was not allowed to *give* myself—I was *taken*" (280). The Uxbridges are the lawyers for Aunt Eliza's opponents in "Lemorne *versus* Huell," and Edward Uxbridge is, as Aunt Eliza says, "the brain of the firm" (271). It is not until after Margaret is married and hears that her aunt has won the court case that she realizes she has been used as a pawn. She recalls a conversation between her aunt and Uxbridge and realizes that her aunt (who previously planned to leave her money to charity) had told Uxbridge that she would give Margaret sixty thousand dollars if Uxbridge agreed to "throw" the case—which he does. By marrying Margaret, he acquires sixty thousand dollars without any money changing hands suspiciously. Of course, such a plan is feasible only because the money belonging to his wife will be his also. Although the New York Married Women's Property acts of 1848 and 1860 would technically give the wife full possession of the money, the assumption is that since Margaret is so passive in everything, he will be the one who will handle the money. Moreover, since Uxbridge is a lawyer, he would be fully cognizant of the courts' conservative interpretations of the laws, in most cases giving the husband control of a wife's money unless the husband had abandoned his wife or could be proved incompetent.[21] The conversation between Eliza and Uxbridge had taken place in Margaret's presence, but as if she were not there. As Margaret says, no one has ever respected her individuality: "Every person's individuality was sacred to me, from the fact, perhaps, that my own individuality had never been respected by any person with whom I had any relation—not even by my own mother" (277). It is not until the end of the story that Margaret "wakes up" and realizes what has happened. The story closes with her epiphany: "That night I dreamed of the scene in the hotel at Newport. I heard Aunt Eliza saying, 'If I gain, Margaret will be rich.' I heard also the clock strike two. As it struck I said, '*My husband is a scoundrel,*' and woke with start" (283). What she will do with this realization is not spelled out, and perhaps Stoddard's implication is that she will do nothing with it. She is like the majority of women who, as Stoddard suggests in *The Morgesons*, have wittingly or unwittingly been very much involved in legal and economic matters.

The third way in which the law figures in women's fiction is in relation to issues that are not gender specific—slavery and issues of class and ethnicity. With respect to women fiction writers' critiques of the laws that legalized slavery, we have already looked at Harriet Beecher Stowe's *Uncle Tom's Cabin*, as well as at Hannah Crafts's *The Bondwoman's Narrative* and the nonfictional autobiography of Harriet Jacobs, *Incidents in the Life of a Slave Girl*. One of the earliest and most outspoken critics of slavery was Lydia Maria Child (1802–1880), who wrote the introduction to Jacobs's book and had written the nonfictional *An Appeal in Favor of That Class of Americans Called Africans* (1833) and several short stories for children in the early 1830s. A decade later she published two important stories, both of which portray the injustice of slavery and its particular impact on women. Her 1843 "Slavery's Pleasant Homes," a starkly realistic story, proved palatable only to the already converted, but her 1842 short story, "The Quadroons," was written in a more sentimental style and had a wider appeal.[22] In the latter story, Child portrays the situation of a light-skinned slave woman and her daughter who are the "wife" and daughter of a white Georgian. But marriage between the races was "unrecognised by law" in the South, Child points out, and after ten years, the man, "unfettered by laws," marries a white woman, the daughter of an influential man who, he hopes, will promote his political career. When he dies prematurely, his slave wife and daughter are vulnerable to the "law of property," which brings about the early death of the mother and causes the beautiful and virtuous fifteen-year-old daughter to be sold at auction as a sexual slave to the highest bidder. Child concludes her narrative with an address to the reader: "Believe me, scenes like these are of no unfrequent occurrence at the South."[23] Her paradigmatic tale foreshadowed similar stories in later antislavery fiction. Stowe, for example, used a similar story in *Uncle Tom's Cabin*, and William Wells Brown used the same story, with heavy borrowings, in *Clotel, or, The President's Daughter* (1853). The sexual use of women and young girls, which was not foregrounded in most men's writing, is prominent in much of the antislavery literature by women. Such stories appear, for example, in Crafts's *The Bondwoman's Narrative*, Jacobs's *Incidents*, and Harper's *Iola Leroy*, among others. By calling attention to the sexual use of women made possible by a law that legalized the buying and selling of human beings and by the corollary law that outlawed legal marriage between whites and blacks, women writers thus forced their readers to examine the law in relation to moral questions prioritized by their culture. The average Northern reader who did not own slaves might be persuaded that it was all right to buy a person for labor (there was a precedent for it in the apprentice system or in the use of indentured servants), but he/she would have had a more difficult time accepting the idea that the law allowed a man to buy an innocent girl for sexual purposes.

In addition to the portrayal of the injustices of slavery, some women writers dealt with injustices with respect to issues of class. In "Life in the Iron-Mills" (1861), Rebecca Harding Davis (1831–1910) portrays the way in which rigid class divisions rendered poor, uneducated factory workers vulnerable before the law. When Hugh Wolfe, a Virginia ironworker, is wrongly convicted of stealing a journalist's wallet, he is sentenced to nineteen years of hard labor. The jailer says, " 'Twas a hard sentence, — all the law allows; but it was for 'xample's sake. These mill-hands are gettin' onbearable." And Doctor May, who earlier is portrayed as all heart, remarks, "Scoundrel! Serves him right."[24] Yet, although Davis recognizes and calls attention to legal injustice in this respect, she does not overtly advocate legal redress for the poor working and living conditions that she portrays. Davis humanizes her working-class characters in a way that had seldom been done before in American fiction, however, calling upon her middle- and upper-class readers to identify with the working-class "other" in the same way that Harriet Beecher Stowe or Harriet Jacobs, for example, forced their white Northern readers to identify with the racial "other." But whereas Child, Stowe, and Jacobs specifically urged a legal remedy (the elimination of slavery), Davis vaguely looks forward to "the Hope to come," concluding her tale with the inspiring but non-specific image of the sunrise in the east where "God has set the promise of the dawn" (14, 65). The same spiritual solution is the only solution offered in her novel *Margret Howth* (1862).[25]

Similarly, Elizabeth Stuart Phelps (Ward) in *The Silent Partner* (1871) does not look to the law for answers to class exploitation. This is particularly surprising in view of the fact that the novel's exposé of the exploitation of factory workers reveals so many specifics about the appalling working and living conditions of the workers that today have been amended by law. The law is mentioned in relation to only two matters: the use of child labor and the need for a shorter workday. The upper-class protagonist, Perley Kelso, is horrified to discover that eight-year-old Bub Mell is illegally employed in the mills and that the mill owners and managers look the other way in order to profit from child labor. The law in Massachusetts at the time stipulated that a child under the age of ten could not work in the factory.[26] The second mention of the law refers to the need for a shorter workday. American millworkers were

working a thirteen-hour day, but as Bub Mell's father points out, a national "ten-hour bill" had been passed in England. Since working in the
New England mills, Mr. Mell, who emigrated from England, had been
"turned out o' mills in this country twice for goin' into a ten-hour strike"
(110–111). Similarly, Bijah Mudge is fired and then blacklisted in all of the
mills in Massachusetts and New Hampshire for testifying in favor of a
ten-hour day (121, 167, 173). This piece of information—that employees
who ask for a ten-hour day are fired and blacklisted—indicates that one
cannot rely on the mill owners' "good will" or "Christian charity" and
suggests that the only redress is government legislation.

Although Phelps apparently recognizes that fact in this instance, she
does not carry over this thinking into her discussion of factory conditions. The novel is filled with descriptions of the horrors of mill life; the
list includes working in temperatures of 110 to 116 degrees Fahrenheit
with no ventilation and the risk of being fired for opening a window,
working with a literally deafening noise, handling wool that can cause
permanent blindness, inhaling cotton fibers all day that cause a chronic
cough, and not being able to lay by any money for old age (96, 113, 114,
186, 82, 178–179). When eight-year-old Bub Mell is pulled into one of the
machines and killed, his father says to himself, "What damages do you
think the mills'll give me? I'd ought to have damages on the loss of the
boy's wages" (220). The implication is that he will get no compensation
whatsoever, and Phelps does not comment on the need for a law that will
protect workers from unsafe conditions. Instead, with respect to this
and other horrific working conditions, she simply describes the situation
and appeals to the need for Christian charity and compassionate humanity on the part of the mill owners. Not only are the working conditions
appalling but the living conditions are no better. The tenement in which
the Mells live has broken stairs and falling plaster that cause dangerous
falls and injuries. It also has a permanent stench and unhealthy damp-
ness because the river water floods the cellar every spring, bringing with
it the offal from the mills. The owner (who, Perley discovers to her
shame, is her then-fiancé, Maverick Hayle) never cleans up the building
or makes any repairs; in fact, he has never seen the building (110). All of
these working and living conditions today are subject to legal restrictions, yet it does not seem to occur to Phelps (or to many of her contem-

poraries) that the law could be used to redress these problems; or if it did, she does not say so. This is true also in her story "The Tenth of January" (1868), in which she describes the conditions in the mills of Lawrence, Massachusetts. The story derives from an actual event, the fire in the Pemberton Mills on January 10, 1860. In Phelps's story the building collapses due to faulty construction, burying seven hundred and fifty workers, of whom eighty-eight were killed, yet Phelps does not suggest that legal measures might help to prevent such catastrophes.[27]

Phelps and Davis show us the injustices of class disparities and attempted to show middle-class readers the humanity of working-class people in order to give such readers an understanding of what other people's lives were like. As Phelps said in *The Silent Partner*, people have to "know" in order to "care" (128). Implicit in this is the suggestion that if people knew, they would do something to alleviate the appalling conditions. But Phelps and Davis did not think in terms of specific legal solutions. All that Perley Kelso can do in *The Silent Partner* is to act the Lady Bountiful and feel compassion for her working-class friends, helping out when she can. Perhaps the fact that women did not have political and legal power themselves is one reason why these writers did not think in terms of legal restrictions to address the wrongs they portrayed. Or perhaps their own class identification stood in the way of their conceiving of activist work to produce legal inhibitors of business.[28] But Martha Tyler in *A Book without a Title* did not discuss legal reform for working-class inequities either, even though she addressed the question with respect to women. A more comprehensive explanation is that the idea of making laws to interfere with business practices was too new a concept at the time. It was not until the Progressive reform movement at the turn of the century that the concept of looking to the law for the protection of workers in the workplace gained more widespread acceptance.

· ❦ ·

After slavery and issues of class, the remaining type of non-gender-specific legal injustice as portrayed in women's fiction is in relation to ethnicity. Two groups that received particular attention were Mexicans and Native Americans. In *The Squatter and the Don* (1885), María Amparo Ruiz de Burton (1835–1895) describes the legal quagmire that resulted in the appropriation of Mexican land after the Mexican-American War. The Treaty of Guadalupe Hidalgo, signed in 1848, guaranteed that Mexicans who lived in the territories the United States had taken from Mexico would retain the right to their land and would have the rights of American citizens. However, American settlers were eager to acquire possession of the land, and squatters moved onto the Mexican land, just as for years they had homesteaded on Indian land. Laws were passed retroactively withdrawing the promise of the treaty and essentially enabling the squatters to appropriate the land. As Ruiz de Burton writes, "to win their votes . . . our representatives in Congress helped to pass laws declaring all lands in California open to preemption."[29] A "land commission" was established to examine the Mexicans' titles to any disputed land, but while the litigation dragged on, the squatters settled on the land, built houses, planted and harvested crops, and killed the Mexicans' cattle with impunity. To add insult to injury, during the litigation the Mexican landowner had to pay increased taxes on any land the squatters cultivated or built on. The economic implications of these laws, then, are clear, and the novel spells out the economic effects both for the squatters and for the Mexican landowners.

Ruiz de Burton was in a good position to write of these inequities. A Mexican American, she herself had spent ten years in litigation, only to ultimately lose her money and all of her family's land.[30] Moreover, although she grew up in Mexico, she married an American general after the Mexican-American War and, after her marriage, lived for a time in the Northeast, where she and her husband were very much a part of government circles and upper-class society in Washington and Virginia. As Amelia de la Luz Montes points out, an understanding of Ruiz de Burton's work complicates literary history in that it provides us with the voice of an educated Mexican American woman to set against the voices in Anglo frontier literature that erase the Mexican presence except in stereotypical portrayals of lazy men and loose women.[31] Thus, Ruiz de Burton, writing from the point of view of a Mexican American who has gained the literary and political sophistication of the eastern elite, calls attention to the injustices of American law in relation to Mexican Americans, and in the process she forces her readers to revise their image of the Mexican "other." As the editors of *The Squatter and the Don* note, however, the novel is not written from the point of view of the other because the Mexicans are not seen as "other."[32] In this sense, the book accomplishes what we have seen in works by authors from other formerly marginalized groups: by making her/his otherness the default, the author dramatizes the injustice. In the context of the book, the injustice is not perpetrated against "them" but against "us." And the psychological effect of this relationship with the reader renders the protest against unjust laws more powerful.

Although Ruiz de Burton presents the case for Mexican Americans, she discounts the claims of the Native American Indians. She accepts the white perception of Indian land as "public land" that is open for exploitation.[33] Other women writers, however, wrote of white injustice to the Native Americans. One of the most comprehensive and compelling narratives of white treatment of the Native Americans is Sarah Winnemucca Hopkins's autobiographical *Life among the Piutes* (1883), which deals with the failure of American law to protect Native Americans and highlights the economics of that failure. Unlike other Native American women who told their stories in print—for example, S. Alice Callahan (1868–1894) and Zitkala-Sa (1876–1938)—Hopkins (1844–1891) did not have white antecedents, nor did she grow up on a reservation. Her autobiography begins with her childhood in the territory that is now Nevada and tells of the tribe's first contact with whites and how a portion of the Piute tribe was forcibly moved to the Yakima reservation in Washington territory in midwinter, which caused many deaths among the Indians and the painful separation of families. At Yakima the Piutes were cheated by the agent, who pocketed the money the government allotted for food and supplies. Hopkins became an interpreter for the army and later traveled to Washington, where she met with President Hayes and the Secretary of the Interior to plead for her people. Her principal request was that the Piutes be allowed to return to their land on the Malheur reservation in Oregon. The president promised to help, but nothing was ever done. Her book contains a copy of her petition to Congress stating that the Piutes had been illegally deprived of their land "decreed to them by President Grant" and asking Congress to allow them to return to Malheur.[34] The book concludes with a note by Mary Peabody Mann urging people to sign the petition. Hopkins's heartfelt plea, which caused Mrs. Hayes to weep (246) and also moved audiences on her lecture tour, was answered by personal attacks on Hopkins and denials from the Bureau of Indian Affairs. For the literary historian, however, Hopkins's book provides another "voice" in American literature, a voice that once again dramatizes injustice by putting the reader in the place of the "other." Particularly compelling in this respect are the scenes from Hopkins's childhood in which white-oriented tales of Indians are reversed as the Indians run in terror from the white "savages" whom they fear as cannibals and murderers (e.g., 11–17, 22).[35] Certainly, after reading her book, today's reader has no doubt of the answer to the rhetorical question asked by S. Alice Callahan in her novel *Wynema* (1891): "Will history term the treatment of the Indians by the United States Government, right and honorable?"[36]

In all of these works, then, the authors wrote about the importance and interdependence of legal and economic matters. In the earlier works of fiction, before the passage of many of the married women's property laws, women writers who treated legal questions focused on the inequities of the existing laws with respect to married women. Women's vulnerability before the law and gender-specific restrictions are in some works referred to implicitly while in others they become part of a polemic. Ironically, however, even though many women were aware of and some writers challenged these unjust laws, few women writers actually portrayed women who were litigants. Since we know from looking at the New York Supreme Court cases that there were many women involved in litigation, the absence of such women from the pages of American fiction suggests that writers were reluctant to portray a heroine in what would have been regarded as an "unfeminine" role. Stoddard's "Lemorne *versus* Huell" is one of very few works that portrays a legally active woman, and it is not a sympathetic portrait. Conventional attitudes, which defined women as acquiescent and self-effacing, apparently made it difficult for women writers to write about and have published works portraying the heroine as a litigant; the word itself connotes contentiousness—certainly not the quality most admired in a nineteenth-century woman. The cultural proscription against women's taking an active role in legal matters provided an insidious way of containing women's economic threat: as long as women were afraid to speak out and remained ignorant of their rights, men could keep the money in their hands. The "ideal" woman was like Mrs. Montgomery in Susan Warner's *The Wide, Wide World*. Although her husband's lawsuit is the catalyst for all of the action, she neither questions his behavior nor complains about the catastrophic results, even though the full burden of the economic damage falls upon her and her daughter. This is the narrative that midcentury American culture found believable. The narrative of woman-as-litigant or woman-as-legal-questioner seldom appeared in American fiction.

The final category in which legal matters are referenced contains works that deal with non-gender-specific injustice—slavery and issues of class and ethnicity. In these works, the legal issues are specifically related to economics—whether it is the traffic in human "property," the economic deprivation of workers and the enrichment of the factory owners, or the one-sided laws that enabled appropriation of land from Mexicans and Native Americans. Whereas antislavery writers focused on a specific change in the law—the elimination of slavery—and Ruiz de Burton's and Winnemucca Hopkins's works are specifically focused on legal-economic questions, writers who dealt with class issues tended not to think in legal terms, even though today many of the conditions that they wrote about have been subjected to legal restrictions.

Although the focus in these works varies and the legal questions range from specific to general, and even when the writer was not sure herself when and how to propose legal remedies, it is clear that for many nineteenth-century women writers and their readers legal questions and their economic corollaries were very much in their consciousness. It is also clear that not all nineteenth-century women were "fools about law matters," as John Stahle claimed in Fern's 1856 novel *Rose Clark*.[37]

————•<∞>•————

chapter eight

THE
ECONOMICS
OF DIVORCE

At a time when women were expected to be ignorant of money matters, divorce was to many women the catalyst that dramatized or called attention to the importance of economics in their lives. In the cases that I read from the New York Supreme Court from 1845 to 1875, 23 percent of the cases involving women were divorce cases. In the large majority of divorce cases, it was the woman who initiated the suit. Seventy percent of the divorce cases had a woman as the plaintiff; in only 30 percent was a man the plaintiff. As will become clear, the reason for this disparity was economic. Divorce cases provide an important measure of how important economics was in nineteenth-century women's lives. Raised to be dependent upon men and conditioned to have—or to pretend to have— little or no understanding of money matters, women involved in divorce proceedings were forced to mention the unmentionable. The wife whose husband took care of his family financially (as his society said that he would) could comfortably accept the culture's definition of money as a "vulgar" subject for a respectable woman to discuss. But the wife who had been abandoned by her husband, or who had been driven to leave him because of his abuse, or who had never been supported by him in the first place had to talk about how she was going to eat, and if she had children, how she was going to feed them. If she had brought property into the marriage, or if she had earned money during her marriage, she wanted to know if she could regain any of it, and if she had a means of earning her living, she wanted to be able to retain her own earnings. Even if she had family to help her, unless they were very wealthy, the woman separated from her husband needed to think about dollars and cents.

In nineteenth-century New York the only ground for an absolute divorce (*a vinculo matrimonii*) by either party was adultery.[1] And if one party was found guilty of adultery, he or she (the guilty party) could not remarry, but the innocent party could remarry. In New York it was possible to obtain a separation or limited divorce (*a mensa et thoro*)—after which neither party could remarry—on grounds of abandonment, desertion, or cruel and inhuman treatment. Men seldom sued for divorce on these grounds; in fact, *all* of the male plaintiffs in the cases that I read brought suit on grounds of adultery. On the other hand, only a quarter of the women plaintiffs sued for divorce on grounds of adultery. The principal reason why women sued for divorce on other grounds—abandonment or cruel and inhuman treatment, including physical abuse—when all they could obtain was a limited divorce or legal separation without the ability to remarry was to obtain monetary support. Since men usually did not need economic support from their wives, they sued for divorce only in order to get rid of an unwanted wife and/or to be free to remarry, which in New York State they could not do on any other grounds than adultery. Later in the century, divorces were sometimes collusive, that is, one of the parties pretended to have committed adultery so that both parties could obtain a divorce.[2] However, in New York in the mid-nineteenth century, although one might be eager to prove adultery against one's spouse, one would be unlikely to feign adultery oneself, since the party found guilty of adultery could not remarry, and if one wanted a limited divorce (which did not permit remarriage), one could obtain it on other grounds.

Because of the social stigma attached to divorce, particularly for women, most women did not seek a divorce unless they had to. The working- or middle-class woman who was abandoned by her husband or who left him because of his abuse, needed to make the separation legal, if she did not have family to take her in, so that the court could compel her husband to support her and her children. Economic desperation was her principal motivation in seeking a legal separation or limited divorce. Under common law, if a man deserted his wife or if she left because of ill treatment, he was required to continue to support her.[3] Job opportunities were few for women, and wages in all occupations were considerably lower for women than for men. Unless a woman had a safety net of relatives who could afford to support her (and her children) if she and her husband were unofficially separated, she was dependent upon her husband's good will—which was not a dependable resource, considering the hostile circumstances under which such separations often took place. Some women were able to support themselves or had family to support them, but for the majority, separation from a husband meant poverty, unless he could be compelled by the court to pay her adequate alimony and/or child support.

Just how much of a social stigma was attached to divorce in the nineteenth century is evidenced by the ambivalence and divided opinions on the subject evinced even by people in the women's movement. Although a resolution at the Woman's Rights Convention at Seneca Falls in 1848 had raised the question of divorce,[4] feminists were divided on the issue. Many believed in the sanctity of marriage, and others were reluctant to speak out because of the fear of being perceived as antifamily. Although Elizabeth Cady Stanton spoke out strongly on a woman's "right" to free herself from the "bonds" of marriage, few women followed her example. She maintained that marriage was a "contract" and that if the husband did not fulfill the terms of the contract (e.g., he was a drunkard or a wife beater) the wife had the right to dissolve the contract.[5] Some feminists were appalled at Stanton's application of the commercial and legal theory of contract to what they regarded as a permanent Christian relationship; others were afraid that her stance on divorce would prejudice people against the campaign for suffrage.[6] That few of Stanton's contemporaries shared or were willing publicly to espouse her view is apparent from the results of the writing contest she sponsored in the temperance magazine, the *Lily*, in 1853. When she offered a ten-dollar prize for the best essay on the subject "The Duty of the Drunkard's Wife," not a single contestant suggested legal divorce as the solution; they considered only such resolutions as separation or death or (optimistically) the reformation of the drunkard.[7]

Although Stanton's contemporaries criticized the concept of liberal divorce for many reasons, few of them dealt with what was in the nineteenth century the principal problem with liberal divorce—the economic impact on women. Only a few reformers recognized this problem. In the abstract, a woman newly liberated from a cruel husband would be free to support herself; what was important to the reformers was that she was "free." But given the dearth of job opportunities for a nine-teenth-century woman, particularly if she had children, her freedom could also mean that she was free to starve. Middle-class reformers did not address the plight of the working-class woman suddenly thrust into the job market with several children in tow and no family or other resources to rely on. Only the Boston branch of the women's movement spoke out on the economic problems inherent in liberal divorce. Pointing to the economic realities of the time, an 1870 article in the *Woman's Journal* declared that "a wife with children, who has lost the help of her husband, has undertaken a contest with fortune against heavy odds." Moreover, in looking at the problem from the point of view only of the wife, most reformers did not consider that easy divorce would also enable a husband to free himself from the encumbrance of an unwanted wife, thus throwing her on her own resources. As the *Woman's Journal* again pointed out in 1874, free divorce meant, "practically, freedom of unworthy men to leave their wives and children to starve, while it could not give similar freedom to mothers to leave their children."[8]

During the years included in this study, there was no easy divorce in New York State; the only ground for an absolute divorce remained adultery. However, the above observations are an important reminder of the economics of divorce. Money questions constituted the principal factor in almost every one of the divorce cases under consideration here. In order to understand the importance and character of those questions, we need to look closely at the stories of the women who, whether working class, middle class, or wealthy, and in spite of the stigma and shame attached to divorce, found themselves in the divorce courts in the nineteenth century.

In 1848 Julia Harvey, who gave her occupation as "maid," and signed her statement with an *X*, petitioned "for leave to sue as a poor person."[9] She had been married in 1839, but, she maintained, her husband had deserted her and had been "living in open adultery with one Ann Harvey in the city of New York" since 1845. She wanted to sue for divorce but could not afford a lawyer: "Your petitioner is not worth the sum of twenty dollars exclusive of her wearing apparel and furniture." Harvey asked that the court assign James T. Boyd as her attorney. The court appointed

Boyd to represent her, and she was able to sue for an absolute divorce and for support.

Even though the court granted her a divorce and ordered her husband to pay her support money, whether or not Julia Harvey was able to obtain support money from her husband is another question. If a man failed to pay court-ordered alimony, he could be put in jail. However, in some circumstances even this threat was not effective. In 1850 Erina Maginn obtained a divorce from her husband, Daniel, on grounds of adultery. She was granted the right to remarry if she chose and the right to assume her maiden name, Erina Richardson, although Daniel, as the guilty party, was not allowed to remarry until or unless Erina should die. He was ordered to pay her costs in the suit of $73.63, $30 to her attorney, and $2 a week support, for which he was required to pay $250 security. He refused to pay anything, and the judge ordered a police officer to "demand and secure from Daniel Maginn" the money he owed. But the officer reported that when he visited Maginn, the latter "replied that we might lock him up and he claimed to us that he had got no money and would not pay it." The judge cited Maginn for contempt for not complying with the order of the court and ordered his arrest. But again, we do not know whether or not his wife was ever able to collect her support payments.

In the case of *Trust v. Trust*, the threat of jail forced Joseph Trust to pay the court-ordered payments, and Mary Trust had the money and apparently the know-how to go to court when he failed to pay. Many women, lacking money and knowledge—or knowledgeable friends—gave up on receiving support money regularly or at all. Moreover, a man who was not established in the community could easily leave town rather than pay support payments. Joseph Trust had a successful business in New York City and was not in a position to disappear. But for a man with no professional roots—a laborer, itinerant worker, or unsettled businessman—in the nineteenth-century's fluid society and before the advent of traceable driver's licenses or IRS records, it was easy enough to disappear "out West" or even into another city. Many women in their suits for divorce said that their husbands had left New York and simply gave the name of a city, state, or territory that was the last place they had heard that the man had gone to—Chicago, or Boston, or Michigan, or California. The court ordered that a summons be mailed to the man in care of the post office in the place cited and an advertisement placed in the local newspaper as well as in two New York papers. Considering the number of "deadbeat dads" there are today even with modern record-keeping, one is not surprised to find that the husband whose whereabouts were thus vaguely described was never heard from again and consequently that he never paid any support payments.

Sometimes a husband could disappear in New York City itself. On July 23, 1859, Christiana Neideck brought suit against her husband, Lorenz Neideck, for divorce on grounds of adultery. Her husband did not answer the complaint, and the case was sent to a judicial referee who conducted hearings to determine the accuracy of her charges. He "reported that all the material facts charged in the complaint were true" and recommended that the divorce be granted. The judge, however, denied the motion for divorce and sent the case back to the referee to "take additional proof of the facts of adultery." Meanwhile, Lorenz Neideck had told his wife that he was going "out West" and said that he would write to her and tell her where he was. She never heard from him, however, and gave up hope of ever hearing from him again, suggesting how common such a disappearance was at the time. Then, four years later, in 1863, she found that he had not gone West at all but was living in New York City "in open and notorious adultery" but under a different name. Christiana wanted to continue the suit, but she had no money, she said, "or any means of supporting herself except by her own labor." When she began the suit four years earlier, she had had two hundred dollars she had received as an inheritance from her relatives in Germany, but the money was all gone. She asked that the court order her husband to pay her support during the pendency of the suit as well as her attorney's fees.

Christiana worked in a shoe factory, earning no more than a dollar fifty a week, and, she testified, that was all she had "for rent, food, and clothing." Her husband's trade, she said, was "making rollers for lithographic presses," which she characterized as a "very good business." Moreover, she said, "he has constant work and supports the woman with whom he lives, and keeps a small beer saloon in addition to working at his trade." She, on the other hand, was in debt for two months' rent, "to wit the sum of four dollars," and she was further indebted to her employer for money advanced to her. Her employer, Samuel Mann, testified that he was a shoe manufacturer and that she worked for him binding shoes, that she never earned more than a dollar fifty per week, and that she generally earned less. He said that she had worked for him for a year and that she was "a respectable industrious woman."

Although Lorenz Neideck had not answered his wife's first complaint in 1859 and had disappeared instead, in 1863, having been found out, he testified in court, denying her accusation that he had committed adultery. He also used the ploy that Joseph Trust used when he wanted to get out of paying alimony: he said that he had never been married to her. Christiana's lawyer did not respond to the denial of marriage except to discount it, but in response to Neideck's denial of adultery, he produced a witness, Ann Loughlin, who testified that during the year 1862 Lorenz Neideck had rented the lower level of her house at 308 Stanton Street. Going by the name of Wills, he had lived in the apartment for seven months with a woman whom he represented as his wife. He seemed to have plenty of money, Loughlin said. He paid twelve dollars a month for the rooms, and on one occasion, after giving her the rent money in advance, he gave a handful of bills to his presumed wife, Mrs. Wills, saying, "There you have sixty dollars, and there is over thirty dollars coming to me" for a job he had just completed.

Lorenz responded in court that he had rented the rooms for Mrs. Wills "as an act of kindness." He did not explain why his act of kindness included living in the rooms with her. Moreover, he testified, he was without any means to support Christiana since his business had not been good lately. Elenore Wills submitted testimony denying that she had committed adultery with Neideck. She signed her statement with an *X*. Citing prior cases (*Smith v. Smith*, 1 Edeo 25; *Deuton v. Deuton* 1 John Ch.R. 364), the plaintiff's attorney pointed out that "an allowance may be granted almost as a matter of course, and even though the marriage be denied." The court ordered that Lorenz Neideck pay Christiana the sum of two dollars a week, along with counsel fees and court costs.

In reading of the respective finances of the husband and wife in this case, the modern reader is struck by how much has *not* changed. According to recent studies, the lifestyles of a man and woman after divorce today are often very different from each other, with the standard of living for a woman declining considerably after her divorce while the standard of living for the husband rises or continues at the same level.[10] After their separation, Lorenz was paying $12 a month for an apartment, while Christiana was paying $2 a month for a rented room—and she was in debt for two months' rent, a total of $4, while he had $60 to give to Mrs. Wills after paying the rent. He had a lucrative business, while she earned no more than $1.50 a week working in a shoe factory. Today women have more opportunities to earn money, yet they still earn at best only 76 percent of what men earn.[11] And their limited skills, lack of experience, and, in many cases, interrupted careers while on the "mommy track" determine that a divorced woman's income will generally be lower than that of her husband. One difference between the Neideck case and that of a case today is the greater facility of checking records today. Certainly, the marriage records could easily be checked so that Neideck could not claim that he had never married. Moreover, although a husband today could claim that business was not good, and he could hide some of his profits from the IRS by working "off the books," there are records of his declared income, whereas the court had no way to trace Lorenz Neideck's income. He did not work for wages and consequently did not have an employer to testify as Christiana did, and there were no IRS records to consult.[12] If a nineteenth-century husband credibly claimed that he did not have much money, the court would award his wife a small settlement, proportionate to the amount of money that the man said he earned.

In some cases, the court would award no settlement at all. In 1859 Josephine Baugh sued her husband, James Baugh, for divorce on the grounds of his "improper conduct." She asked for support and counsel fees, maintaining that he earned forty dollars a month and had other money and property. She had left him on September 15, 1856, taking with her their child, Daniel Nelson Baugh, and, he claimed, the household furniture, worth two hundred dollars. Since then she had been working as a seamstress and chambermaid. She said he had not given her anything for her or the child's support in three years, though she had often asked him to. He claimed that he had asked her to come back and live with him and had offered to take the child, but she had refused both. He was currently working as a waiter at the Delavan House in Albany, where, he said, he earned only fifteen dollars a month. He insisted that he had no other money or property except his wearing apparel and claimed it would be absolutely impossible to support her or pay her fees during the suit. The court denied her motion for support.

In this case, the man's assertion that he did not have the money to pay her support, coupled with his claim that he wanted her to come back to him and his apparent willingness to take custody of the child, led the court to deny her any support money, in the belief that the couple would be better off if they reconciled. The court apparently believed James Baugh's assertion that he only made fifteen dollars a month—although as most people know today, a waiter's principal source of income is his tips, and there is no way to ascertain how much he makes from tips. One suspects that James Baugh's income was much higher than he pretended, since as Josephine Baugh testified, when she was living with him he earned forty dollars a month. However, Josephine was left with three alternatives: continue to attempt to support herself and her child as a seamstress and chambermaid; reconcile with James; or give up her child to her husband. Since she had brought suit on grounds of "improper conduct," which most often meant physical abuse and/or drunkenness, her alternatives were not attractive.

One way that a man could avoid having to make support payments was if he could prove that his wife had committed adultery: the court would not require him to pay support to an adulterous wife. In February 1864 William Gaynor brought suit against his wife, Helen, for divorce on the ground of adultery. He had deserted her and their two children two years earlier and was himself living in an adulterous relationship with a Miss Lucas. Helen testified that she was destitute because of the loss of one of her hands and could not work as a seamstress, which she had done before and during her marriage. She had had to put the two children in a home for indigent children and poor orphans on Randal's Island, she said. The court apparently did not give credence to William's trumped-up adultery accusation and ordered him to pay her six dollars a week during the pendency of the suit, plus fifty dollars for her attorney's fee.

Then follows a tale of outrageous behavior on the part of William Gaynor and his attorney, H. Daily. Having failed in his attempt to claim adultery against his wife and unwilling to pay her any support money, Gaynor and his lawyer, who appear to have been the ultimate scoundrels, lied and attempted to intimidate Gaynor's wife into silence. On April 14, 1864, Helen's lawyer, Joseph C. Ashley, served a copy of the court order for support and attorney fees on her husband, after Gaynor and Daily told Ashley that the lawyer (Daily) was no longer working for Gaynor. Gaynor never paid any of the money, and when an order was given for his arrest for contempt of court on June 2, 1864, he appeared in court and swore that the notice had never been served on him. His lawyer, Daily (who apparently was still working for him after all), demanded that the order be declared void since the notice had not been served on him (Daily) or his client. Ashley swore that he had served the notice on Gaynor, after being told by both Daily and Gaynor that Daily was no longer working for Gaynor. Helen Gaynor testified on June 6 that for the past eighteen months to two years her husband had given her a total of only eighteen dollars for herself and the two children. She said that on April 25, 1864, eleven days after the court order for alimony had been served upon him, she had called on him at the saloon that he owned and asked him for the alimony money. He said he would never pay her "one cent" of it but finally gave her five dollars as a "loan." On June 3, after his arrest had been ordered, he sent for her to come to see him at his saloon. She waited outside on the sidewalk, and when he came out, he asked her to vacate the arrest order. She said she would if he would pay her part of what he owed her. He told her he had no money to give her and said that he and Miss Lucas were going to go to California as soon as he could get away. At that point Daily, her husband's attorney, came up and with "profane language" told her that if she came there again he would have her arrested and "forced her rudely off the sidewalk with his fist." The next day Gaynor sent for her to come to his saloon again, saying that he wanted to settle this "troublesome matter." She waited outside on the sidewalk, but her husband sent out a "rough looking man," who struck her on the face and ran off. She went inside and saw her husband and Daily laughing. Daily dragged her out and said he would have her arrested if she came to the saloon again. This behavior is despicable enough in itself, but it is even more so when we remember that Helen Gaynor only had one hand.

Apparently William Gaynor had sufficient money to support his wife and children if he wanted to. On June 7, 1864, Joseph G. Woolley testified that on May 29, 1864, he was asked by Helen to go to see her husband and ask for her court-ordered support money. Gaynor gave him three dollars and told him he planned to sell the saloon, which, he said, was "making good money." He said he would sell it for two thousand dollars and asked Woolley to ask his father if he wanted to buy it. Woolley said that Gaynor told him he was making more money on Wall Street than in the saloon, that he had "made $2,000 yesterday" in the stock market. Ashley testified that when he served the order for alimony on the plaintiff, Gaynor had told him that his wife would never get anything from him. Then he had torn up the papers and thrown them in the fire, saying, "That is all she will ever get." The judge issued an order on June 7 denying William Gaynor's motion to vacate the order to pay alimony and fees. So Helen Gaynor received justice in the court. But did she receive her money? Was she able to take back her children? Or did William Gaynor sell his saloon and take off for California without ever paying her "one cent"? There is no way to know.

Another husband who resorted to the adultery ruse in order to avoid court-ordered support payments for his wife and children was James Torrey. In June 1850 Louisa M. Torrey brought suit against her husband, James D. Torrey, for a limited divorce on the grounds that he had deserted her and their three young children the month before. She asked for custody of the children, for alimony, and for court costs. She said that she had no livelihood or means of support for herself and her children, the youngest of whom was but five weeks old. Her husband had refused to support them, she said: "The utmost he has expressed a willingness to supply was the sum of five dollars per week for the four, which is not sufficient for their support and maintenance." He had required that they move from a "respectable boarding house kept by Mrs. Allison at No. 70 Greenwich St., and where he was paying at the rate of nine dollars per week, to a place selected by him at No. 39 Walker St.," a basement room that only cost him five dollars and was "chilly and damp" and unhealthy for herself and the children. She pointed out that her husband was a master printer with a business at 12 Spruce Street in New York City, that he had a number of men in his employ and several printing presses, and that his business was "extensive and lucrative, yielding him an income of about $2,000, or some such sum a year." James Torrey consented to the complaint, and the judge ordered him to pay immediately $25 for clothing for her and her children, $50 in attorney's fees, and $7 a week during the suit. At this point, and apparently alarmed at the possibility that he would have to pay her permanent alimony and child support, James Torrey attempted to prove adultery.

Because of her husband's harassment and meager support, in October 1850 Louisa and her children had moved in with her newly married sister, and in May 1851 she and the children moved to a rented house in Brooklyn with her mother. James Torrey had her followed and set up a stakeout outside her mother's house in Brooklyn. Thinking that he had found the evidence he needed, on June 30, 1851, he returned to court and asked that his answer to her complaint be amended: instead of consenting to her accusation of abandonment, he now wished to claim that she had committed adultery with a man named Brown. Louisa Torrey denied his accusation and testified that the only persons she knew by the name of Brown were her sister's husband and his brothers. Her mother, Catharine Ackerman, testified that the charges made by James Torrey were false. She claimed that she was her daughter's "bed companion." She said that for some time she and her daughter had been alarmed that Torrey had hired thugs to spy on their house. On June 26, she said, they saw some strange men again lurking outside the house. Fearing violence or that Torrey would attempt to "get possession of the children," she mentioned their fears to Albert Brown, her son-in-law's brother, and "entreated" him to come to their house and stay with them to protect them should Torrey threaten violence. Albert Brown testified that he had indeed come to their aid the next day, that he remained in the house that evening, and that at three o'clock in the morning four men knocked loudly at the door of the house, threatening to break down the door. One of the men claimed to be a policeman and said that there had been a report that there was a thief hidden in the house. The men demanded that they be allowed to search for the thief, said Brown, "which they did, much to the terror and alarm of the family." Brown denied that he had ever had adulterous intercourse with the plaintiff and said that she had always "conducted herself since he has become acquainted with her as a chaste and virtuous woman."

After hearing the testimony of Ackerman and Brown, James Torrey's attorney must have recognized the difficulty of proving adultery and probably would have withdrawn the proposed amendment. But just in case Torrey was determined to continue to allege adultery, Louisa Torrey's attorney pointed out that the amendment (claiming adultery) would introduce a new issue into the case and would involve more time and expense. He noted that the case had already been much delayed by the defendant and that he (the attorney) thus far had only received seventy-five dollars from the defendant for over a year's work. Consequently, said the attorney, if the court allowed Torrey to amend his answer as proposed, "a further allowance of one hundred dollars will be absolutely necessary to enable the plaintiff to meet the expenses of trying the question." At this threat of further payments and with every indication that his adultery charge was untenable, James Torrey withdrew his proposed amendment and Louisa obtained her divorce settlement: permanent alimony and child support for her three children.

What are we to make of this story? It is possible that Louisa Torrey was having an adulterous affair and that she, her mother, and Brown all perjured themselves. However, it seems more likely that James Torrey, desperate to get out of paying more than five dollars a week to his wife and children, did indeed hire thugs to watch her house, looking for an opportunity to prove adultery. He apparently did not know that her sister had married a man named Brown in the year since he had left Louisa, and, when his spies reported that a man named Brown was in her house overnight, he thought he had caught her "red-handed" and planned to use his spies as witnesses. If she had been without friends or relatives to help her, she, like other women in her position, could easily have been put into a compromising position which, with witnesses to testify to the presence of a man in her house overnight, would have enabled Torrey to avoid paying her any support. The story gives an indication of a nineteenth-century woman's vulnerability. If she had not had a married sister or a mother to take her in, she would have been left in the basement room, and she would have had to face her husband's harassment alone, which would not only have been frightening but would have left her without witnesses to prove her "chastity."

Today's reader might ask why Louisa Torrey's lawyer did not ask other questions: Was the policeman really a policeman? Where was his search warrant? How were four men able to force their way into her house at 3 A.M.? Would the court follow up on this story, and if so could it prove that James Torrey had hired men to gain entrance into his wife's house under false pretenses? The fact that these questions were not asked suggests that what was important was not the legality of a husband's tactics but the question of a wife's fidelity: the only point at issue was whether or not she had committed adultery. This was the crux of the matter, and it was so important that it dwarfed all other considerations. This was the telling narrative. In fact, it was so important that if she had been proved guilty, her husband would not have had to pay her a cent—and he would have gained custody of the children if he had wanted them.

Another case that involves the question of whether or not a husband attempted to prove adultery in order to escape having to pay alimony is more complicated. A second reason for falsely claiming adultery on the part of the spouse was to enable oneself to remarry. In November 1853 John Goldsmith brought suit against his wife for divorce on the ground of adultery, claiming that she had committed adultery with his former partner, Henry Parsons. Mary Goldsmith responded that at the time her husband claimed that she committed adultery with Parsons she did not even know Parsons, that she was only introduced to him by her husband much later. She denied the accusations of adultery, maintaining that it was her husband who had committed adultery. He had abandoned her and their three children on August 27, she said, after she had confronted him about his adultery. She claimed that he had made the adultery charge against her in order to harass her, to get out of having to support her and the children, and to prevent her from interfering with his plans to remarry. Her lawyer contended: "He has determined to rid himself of the support of her and her children, with a view to a new marriage." She said that she could prove that he had committed adultery "with a servant in their house" and with other women. During their marriage, she said, he had joined an amateur theater group, and he stayed out until three o'-clock in the morning several nights a week. He had joined the troop, she contended, "solely to be intimate with loose women," one of whom she named as his principal adulterous partner. Moreover, since her marriage to him, she said, she had discovered that his first wife had divorced him on the ground of adultery and that he had been forbidden to remarry.

Maintaining that her husband had left her destitute, Mary Goldsmith asked for alimony and court costs. She said that while she had no money to support herself and her children and was "dependent on friends and on her needle," he was living luxuriously "at the best hotels and watering places." Her husband, she said, was a cutter and foreman in the clothing business with Dringold and Prosel Clothing on Fulton Street, where he had an interest in the business or was on salary. His previous salary, she said, was twenty-three dollars per week. Although he claimed to have no money, she said she knew that he had concealed assets. When Mary's lawyer made a motion for alimony and counsel fees on December 2, 1853, her husband's lawyer moved that the request be dismissed "on the grounds that no next friend had been appointed for said defendant." She submitted a petition pointing out that it was not until she asked for alimony and fees that he objected that she did not have a "next friend." Although technically she did require a next friend (it was not until 1860 that a woman in New York State was able to sue or be sued in her own name), her husband's belated objection on these grounds was clearly a delaying tactic. Her lawyer moved that Laurence Tunison be appointed her next friend, and the suit continued.

In response to Mary's request for support, John claimed that he had no money. He denied that he had any concealed assets and said that he did not live luxuriously but had many creditors. Moreover, he said, his wife was able to support herself: "She has two sewing machines and five or six girls in a vest and pant making business in his house. She makes thirty to forty pairs of pants a week at one dollar a pair." He also brought in three witnesses, including his nineteen-year-old daughter, Susannah, from his previous marriage, to testify that they had been present at a conversation on October 21 when Mary Goldsmith stated that she did not need her husband's help, that she was proud to be able to support herself. The witnesses testified that she said that "she was willing and able to support herself and could make money enough, . . . and would never touch one cent of plaintiff's money, and further that she had made eighteen vests that week already by aid of a sewing machine."

John Goldsmith's claim that his wife was self-supporting is reminiscent of Joseph Trust's exasperated—but unproved—claims that his wife was a physician. But even more interesting is Mary Goldsmith's attitude.

If we can believe her husband's witnesses, she was proud to be self-supporting; and although they were his witnesses, given that three people all testified to hearing her say the same thing, I think that we can assume that she did say something to that effect. But although she must have felt pride in being independent of a husband who had treated her so shabbily, the reality was that she was not wholly independent. Unlike Torrey, who had put his wife and three children in a rented basement room, Goldsmith had left his wife and children in their rented house and had continued to pay the rent. The house, he pointed out, was well furnished and his wife could sell the furnishings if she needed money. He also noted that she had put up a sign advertising for boarders in addition to earning money from her vest and pants business. Clearly, Mary Goldsmith was not as hard up as Helen Gaynor, Josephine Baugh, or Erina Maginn. Although she asked for support payments, she was not in immediate danger of starvation. However, as she must have realized, her husband could stop paying rent on the house at any time and could reclaim the furniture, which, as he pointed out, was his property. Consequently, she was in a precarious position: her ability to earn money through her business and by running a boardinghouse depended upon her having possession of the house and its furnishings. Unless or until she was able to save enough capital to be able to buy or rent other quarters, she needed a court-ordered guarantee that her husband would continue to support her.

Determined to prove adultery, John Goldsmith brought in testimony from his daughter Susannah that she had seen Mary Goldsmith and Henry Parsons in a compromising situation, and he claimed that Parsons was the father of two of Mary's three children. The court, however, apparently did not accept his charges. Whether she had committed adultery or not is impossible to know. However, Parsons's actions in the case seem to be those of a friend rather than a lover. On December 10 Goldsmith was arrested and taken before the judge for abandoning his wife, and his lawyer claimed that it was Parsons who "instigated the arrest." Goldsmith complained that Parsons "wrote a nasty letter" to his employers and threatened to "cowhide him." Parsons apparently regarded Goldsmith as a scoundrel and was disgusted with his treatment of his wife.

In this case the accusations and counteraccusations make it difficult to know who was guilty of what. The court, however, found neither party guilty of adultery and granted a limited divorce, which meant that neither party could remarry. John Goldsmith was ordered to make support payments to his wife and children and to pay her court costs. Thus, if he had falsely accused his wife of adultery in order to obtain an absolute divorce so that he could remarry, or in order to avoid paying support for her and the children, he was foiled.

For all of the above women, support payments were the principal economic concern. Even for Mary Goldsmith, who was able to earn a good living, support payments were important. In some cases, however, the question of support was not as important as other considerations, both economic and noneconomic. In 1855 Elizabeth Romertze obtained a limited divorce from her husband, Henry Romertze, who, she claimed, had beaten and threatened to kill her and had prevented her from earning a living. The court ordered him to pay her one hundred dollars a year in support, but the support payments were not her principal concern since her husband had never supported her anyway. She had supported herself. Elizabeth Romertze operated a small business; she made shirts, which she sold out of her house, and was able to earn enough to support herself and her two children. The house, which she had owned prior to her marriage, was her own "separate estate." Unlike Louisa Torrey, forced into a basement room, and unlike Mary Goldsmith, living in her husband's rented house, Elizabeth Romertze was not dependent upon her husband's largesse. Her husband, she said, did not have steady employment but depended upon her earnings, which he forcibly took from her.

When Elizabeth obtained her divorce, the decree contained a restraining order, which stated the following: "It is further ordered and decreed that the defendant refrain from interfering with, molesting, ill treating, beating, visiting, remaining with, or annoying the plaintiff, and from calling on her at her residence, or place of business, and also that the defendant refrain from interfering with, selling, disposing of, conveying, assigning, transferring or molesting the business of linen ware, the stock in trade and fixtures of the plaintiff, and also from collecting and receiving any monies that may be due to her, arising out of her said business."

In spite of this clear order, Henry Romertze continued his abusive behavior. The police were called on two occasions, and he was arrested but released on bond. A month after the divorce decree, Elizabeth was back in court asking to have her husband arrested and put in jail. She brought a witness who described how he had broken into the house and beaten her. Elizabeth said that he had returned to her house almost every day, assaulted her, verbally abused her, and threatened to kill her. She said that he extorted money from her, threatening that if she did not give him what he wanted he would break her furniture and destroy property in the store or worse. Finally, she said, his behavior had been so violent toward her and toward her customers that her customers had become afraid to come to her house, and she had had to give up her business. She had no relations or friends to help her, she said, and "without some restraint can be put upon him, she will from necessity become a charge upon the public as her own means are entirely exhausted and having two children to support." The court ordered that Henry Romertze be arrested and made to answer for his misconduct and contempt. His bond was set at five hundred dollars, a sufficient amount to make certain that he would not be on the streets soon.

The most tragic aspect of this sorry tale is that it could have occurred today: we are all familiar with stories about the abusive husband or ex-husband, who in spite of restraining orders physically assaults his wife, sometimes murdering her. There is a major difference, however. Whereas today the man's principal offense would be the physical abuse of his wife, in 1855 his principal offense was economic. Although Elizabeth had complained of his abusive behavior twice before and he had been arrested, the court did not hold him. It was only when she made an economic argument that the court took sufficient action to hold him: she demonstrated that he had destroyed her business and said that unless the court confined him, she and her two children would become public charges who would need to be supported at public expense. Whether these claims were true or not, they apparently were effective. Wife beating was not a serious crime in 1855, but once Elizabeth Romertze was divorced from her husband, it was illegal for him to take her money, terrorize her and her customers, and vandalize her business. And the suggestion that three people would become public charges was an effective threat.

Another difference between Elizabeth Romertze's story and the story of an abused wife today, however, is that in the 1850s, before Elizabeth Romertze obtained a divorce, her husband was legally entitled to all of the money that she earned from her shirt business. The Married Women's Property Act of 1848 did not protect a wife's earnings; it protected only her unearned money—money or property that she received as a gift or bequest. The money that she herself earned—money that she earned as wages, or from keeping a boardinghouse, or through the sale of items that she made—legally was the property of her husband. It was only after Elizabeth Romertze obtained a divorce from her husband— and he was no longer her husband—that the court ordered him not to take her money.

Sarah White was not protected by the Married Women's Property Act of 1848 either. Like Elizabeth Romertze's money, the money that she acquired during her marriage came from her own earnings. Unlike Romertze, however, she lost everything. Her husband not only destroyed her business and physically abused her, but, to add insult to injury, he cheated her in an underhanded separation settlement and then tried to frame her in an adultery suit. Married to William White in 1834, she was abandoned by him in 1855 when she had three children and was pregnant with the fourth, a baby who died six months later. In October 1855 she petitioned the court to appoint Edmund Martin as her "next friend" so that she could sue her husband for a legal separation. She claimed that he drank and abused her and the children. He had knocked down her ten-year-old daughter Adeline three times, she said. Her father, Peter Goetchius, had arranged a settlement with her husband's lawyer, but, she said, she had not understood the details of the settlement and it had proved to be disastrous for her. (Her husband's lawyer was clearly more astute than her father was.) During her marriage to White, she had taken in boarders at two separate houses and had saved enough money to purchase the houses with the help of her husband. However, legally the houses were in her husband's name alone. In the separation settlement, her father signed a quitclaim to any support from her husband and arranged to have her husband sign over the two houses to her so that she could support herself and the children with the profits. On the surface, this sounds like an equitable arrangement. However, William White had heavily mortgaged both properties (a detail that her father apparently did not know or did not realize the significance of), and one of them was mortgaged to William himself via his lawyer. After the separation, Sarah was responsible for paying off the mortgages as well as maintaining the properties and running the boardinghouses. She says she worked very hard to pay off the mortgages: she took in boarders, did people's washing, cleaned people's houses, and ran a store. She did everything she could, she said, and raised her children by herself, but in 1862 the mortgages were foreclosed.

Immediately after the foreclosure of the mortgages, William White brought suit against Sarah for a divorce on the ground of adultery. He claimed that she had committed adultery with one of her boarders, Charles Williams, and called in three other boarders to support his claim. Sarah, Charles Williams, her brother, and her by-then-adult daughter, Adeline, all denied the accusation and pointed out that the three "witnesses" that William had called in were all disgruntled former boarders who owed Sarah or her brother money. Sarah stated that she slept in the same bed with her youngest son, ten-year-old Alpheus, and said this of her husband's suit: "His pretenses of adultery are wholly false, and malicious, and this suit has been brought at a time when he supposed this defendant not to have sufficient means to defend herself and when she was much depressed, and afflicted by the foreclosure and sale of said property." She claimed that her failure with the boardinghouses was due to her husband's deliberate interference: he and his agents prevented the collection of the rents and spread stories about her to her tenants that caused them to leave. Her attorney summed up the situation: "She was engaged in keeping boarders, and laboring hard for a living, but by this evil report spread by said plaintiff, and his pretenses of misconduct between her and her boarders, which are wholly without foundation, he has succeeded in breaking up her business, and she is now compelled to support herself and younger child by her daily labor." By 1862 Sarah's father had died, but her brother William Goetchius, a carpenter, was trustee in her father's place. He testified that he had been unable to prevent the sale of the property and confirmed that William White had deliberately destroyed her business: "Much of the rent of said premises was lost in consequence of the interference of the plaintiff and his agents with the tenants."

Williams, age sixty-four, was a bible salesman, and he and Sarah sometimes went to prayer meetings together. Calvin Lathrop of the Soldier's Relief Association said they attended religious meetings at his organization and that Sarah distributed tracts for him. He had thought she was Williams's wife, he said, until she appealed to him for relief because of her son, James White, who was in the army. She appealed for relief in 1862 after the mortgages had been foreclosed and she was without means of support. (In 1862, the Civil War was raging, and the Soldier's Relief Association was a charitable organization that provided help to the needy wives and mothers of Federal soldiers.)

It appears that William White's claim of adultery and his decision to sue for adultery were motivated by the desire to obtain an absolute divorce. Perhaps he wished to remarry. He had deliberately destroyed his wife's ability to earn a good living, and he brought the suit at a time when he apparently believed that she would be financially (and perhaps emotionally) unable to contest it. Sarah's attorney pointed out that Sarah was now forty-six years old and destitute because of her husband's interference with her business, while her husband was in possession of one of her properties (the mortgage having been made out to his attorney for his own benefit), earned twelve to fifteen dollars a week in his business (he was a cartman), and was worth "upwards of $6,000." She asked for alimony and costs. Her request for alimony was denied (because of the quitclaim her father had signed), but her husband was ordered to pay her costs and attorney's fees. Although the judge did not award her alimony, he also refused to grant William White a divorce on the ground of adultery. Sarah White gained a moral victory but suffered an economic loss: the law had refused to brand her an adulteress, but all of her earnings and the property she had bought with them were lost to her. She would need to continue to support herself by cleaning other people's houses and washing other people's clothes.

Elizabeth Romertze and Sarah White had sought to gain control of their earnings or the property those earnings had bought. Another way in which economic issues other than support payments were crucial to a woman's divorce action is made clear in the attempt of the wife to gain control of unearned money that belonged to her, money that had come to her as a gift or bequest. In 1850 Elizabeth R. Moulton, of White Plains in Westchester County, represented by her "next friend," Lucius Pitkin, and her attorney, H. P. Hastings, sued her physician husband, Peter Moulton, for a separation. She not only sought support payments (she was awarded three hundred dollars a year) but also claimed the interest on the money that had been invested for her according to the terms of her father's will. In his 1840 will, her father had stated that upon his death, his property should be sold and, after one-third of the money was set aside for his wife's dower, the remaining money should be divided equally among his two sons and two daughters. However, in a codicil to his will, he wrote that Elizabeth's share of the estate should be invested for her rather than paid to her all at once, "the interest to be paid to her semi-annually, during her lifetime, and at her decease the principal to be equally divided among her children." Obviously, Elizabeth's father had become aware of something not quite right about his son-in-law and did not want all of Elizabeth's share to fall into her husband's hands, since in 1840 the law specified that any money belonging to a man's wife was legally her husband's property. Elizabeth's father sought to protect her share of his estate by having it invested for her. If the money had been given to her outright after her father's death, her husband would have owned it and she could not have reclaimed any of it when she sued for a separation. In fact, in her attorney's statement of her husband's assets, he included other property "that the defendant has received by his wife," and this property was lost to her. But because her father's codicil had caused her inheritance to be invested for her, her husband could not claim it, although during most of their marriage he had been able to claim the interest.

The reason Elizabeth Moulton's husband could not claim her inheritance when she sued for divorce was that by 1850 her inheritance was protected by the 1848 Married Women's Property Act. The act was not retroactive (the retroactive section had been ruled unconstitutional), so that if her inheritance had been given to her *in toto* before the new law was passed, it would have been the property of her husband and she could not have later reclaimed it. But the law stated that "it shall be lawful for any married female to receive, by gift, grant, devise or bequest, from any person other than her husband and hold to her sole and separate use, as if she were a single female, real and personal property, and the rents, issues and profits thereof." Consequently, she was entitled to the profits that she was then receiving semiannually from her share of her father's estate, although she could not reclaim from her husband any of the profits that he had appropriated during their marriage and before the 1848 act. When she sued to claim the interest as her own, the court ruled that "the plaintiff is entitled to have and receive the income or interest so given to her by said will, as her separate property and that *the same be paid to her by the executors of the said will, as though she were a single woman.*" This segment of the court ruling is underlined in the original and reflects the words of the 1848 law. Thus, although Elizabeth Moulton was disadvantaged by legal restrictions—she was treated as a minor in the courts, she could not obtain an absolute divorce, for years her husband had claimed her money as his own, and she could not reclaim any property that her husband had acquired through her—in the end, because of her father's codicil, she profited from the 1848 law, which enabled her to claim the interest from her inheritance. Her father could not have foreseen that the Married Women's Property Act would be passed eight years after he wrote his will, but he knew that if she acquired the whole amount of her inheritance at the time of his death, her husband could take it from her.

Margaret Moncrief also profited from the 1848 law. She had brought to her marriage property in which she owned a life interest—property on West Eighteenth Street that she had inherited and was, according to the 1848 law, her separate property. On November 1, 1859, she brought suit against her husband for a limited divorce on the ground of cruel treatment. She testified that he was worth between $15,000 and $20,000 and owned a "*large*" amount of real estate in New York (her italics). He had collected the rent from his many properties as well as from her property on West Eighteenth Street. Prior to their separation, she lived with him in her building on West Eighteenth Street. He collected rents for the units not occupied by them and mingled that money with the money he collected from his property. He had money in a savings account in the

Greenwich Savings Bank, a large portion of which belonged to her, she said, and he refused to give her her money. In addition, when they separated, he took with him in cash around $160 from the rent for her property, and he had not returned it to her.

Fearful that her husband would withdraw all of the money from his bank account before she could get a court order to force him to pay her the money due her, she had held on to his passbook. On March 8, 1860, she obtained a limited divorce and a court order requiring him to pay her $322 from the savings account as well as $5 a week alimony and $50 in attorney's fees. John Moncrief refused to pay any of it. The court ordered his arrest three times, but each time he could not be found. He apparently had fled the state and moved to Hoboken, New Jersey. He was cited for contempt and his arrest ordered again, this time with bond set at $100. He appealed the order but it was reaffirmed, and in June he appeared in court, maintaining that he could not pay until the plaintiff returned his passbook to him because, he said, he did not have any money. His lawyer made a motion that Margaret be ordered to return the passbook. However, her lawyer pointed out that he and his agents had continued to collect the rents from his real estate properties during all of the time that the case had been in the courts. She provided the addresses and the amount of rent he received for each property. His motion was denied, and on September 18, 1860, the court ordered that a receiver be appointed to collect the rents from his real property, out of which Margaret would be paid alimony and attorney's fees as well as the $322 that he owed her. In addition, he was required to pay all of the costs that had accumulated from the litigation and arrest orders. She retained ownership of the Eighteenth Street property as well as the right to any "rents and profits" from it. Prior to the 1848 law, her husband would have had the legal right to all of the rents he had collected from her property.

Thus, Margaret Moncrief benefited from the married women's property law. But it is important to note that the law alone could do only so much. In order to profit fully from the law, a woman needed to know what her rights were and she needed to be fully cognizant of her family's finances. What helped Margaret benefit from the law was the fact that she herself was savvy about money. Unlike many women of the time, she was not ignorant of her husband's and her own finances. She knew her husband's worth, and she even knew the addresses of the properties he owned and the amount of rent he realized from each of his properties, as well as the exact rent due from her own property. It was her involvement in economic matters that enabled her to save her rent money when her husband left. By holding on to the passbook, she prevented him from withdrawing the money from the bank before she could obtain a court order for it, and by her knowledge of his finances, she was able to undercut his claim that he did not have any money.

That Elizabeth Moulton and Margaret Moncrief profited from the 1848 Married Women's Property Act confirms the judgment that the law was written to protect the property of wealthy men and not that of working-class women. Margaret Moncrief owned a life estate in a building with several rental units in it, property that a working-class woman would not possess. And Moulton came from a family wealthy enough to have money invested for her. Of course, in protecting the man's property, the law also benefited the woman. The money that came to Elizabeth Moulton from her father and the rental property that Margaret Moncrief had title to gave each woman the economic independence that made it possible for her to seek a divorce. Neither was wholly dependent on the support payments that her husband was compelled to pay.

Looking at the above cases suggests the importance of class in the economics of divorce. The working-class woman was the most vulnerable, particularly if she did not have family support. Working as a maid, seamstress, and shoe factory operative, Julia Harvey, Erina Maginn, Josephine Baugh, Christiana Neideck had no capital and no resources but their own poorly paid labor. In order even to sue for divorce or separation, they were dependent upon court-appointed attorneys or the court's willingness to compel their husbands to pay attorney's fees. Middle-class women sometimes had family support (Louisa Torrey) or the ability to support themselves comfortably (Elizabeth Romertze and Mary Goldsmith). They were often also dependent upon the court's willingness to force their husbands to pay attorney fees, but they sometimes had knowledgeable friends who could help them in selecting a lawyer or in pursuing their case. However, the woman who came from a wealthy family was in a better position to obtain a favorable divorce than the woman from a working-class or middle-class family. One reason was simply that a person from a wealthy family would be in a better position to obtain the best legal help. Little has changed in this respect today; in any court case, the person with money is better able to obtain a "dream team" of lawyers. Certainly, Elizabeth Moulton's wealthy father had better legal advice than Sarah White's artisan father. Both fathers sought to protect their daughters, but Moulton's father's codicil was more effective than White's father's acquisition of heavily mortgaged houses for his daughter. If an upper-class woman's family supported her in her decision to seek a divorce, she had three advantages that came with the possession of money: the money gave her the independence she needed to seek a divorce; it made the process easier because she had access to the best legal help; and it could help her obtain custody of her children because, although the father was usually given custody by the courts if he wanted it, the court also considered the economic means of the guardian in determining custody.[13]

All of the above factors are evident in the 1859 case of *Hollins v. Hollins*. In June 1859 Elizabeth C. Hollins sued her husband, Frank Hollins, for divorce on the ground of adultery. He denied her charges. However, she had the money and the legal know-how to obtain the evidence needed. Her attorneys placed Hollins under surveillance over a period of time, and they prepared a very specific list of charges, citing seven instances of adultery. In a list of questions, they asked, for example, did the defendant have "carnal connexion and commit adultery with any woman or women named or described in the complaint, in a house of prostitution in Mercer Street, between Spring and Prince Streets in the city of New York?" And did he have intercourse "with a woman named Isabella Jones" in April 1859 at 178 Christie Street or in May 1859 at 162 Orchard Street; and did he have intercourse "with a woman named Maggie" at 76 Elm Street? Frank Hollins apparently had not expected his wife to have proof of adultery, and when he heard the specific charges—including names, dates, and addresses—he withdrew his denial of adultery. The judge found him guilty and awarded Elizabeth a divorce.

But Elizabeth Hollins was not finished. The following October she petitioned for custody of their six surviving children, ranging in age from two to twelve years. She had not asked for alimony and she did not ask for support payments; she knew that Frank could not pay anything, and she did not need money from him. She and her husband and the children had lived with her mother, Eliza Morris, who supported them and who apparently had the money to bankroll Elizabeth's ventures into court. In her petition for custody, Elizabeth pointed out that she and her mother had a large enough fortune to support and educate the children, while Frank Hollins was dissolute and destitute. Her objective was to gain legal custody so that he could not take the children away from her.

> The said Eliza F. Morris is a lady of the highest respectability and of large fortune, and is able and anxious to continue to support your petitioner and her said children and to educate and provide for the said children in a manner suitable to their present position in life and their future expectations. And your petitioner further shows that the said defendant is a man of grossly intemperate and licentious habits. . . . That he was once possessed of a fortune of about $20,000 which he squandered or lost in a very short time, and that for several years past he has been hopelessly insolvent and is now in utterly destitute circumstances. . . . [He] has made repeated attempts to get possession of the children, and your petitioner greatly fears that he may again attempt to interfere with her right of custody of said children unless the same is secured by an order of this court.

Elizabeth Hollins was granted custody of her children, just as she had been granted the divorce. Her mother's money had enabled her to develop an airtight case against her husband. The adultery conviction, together with evidence of Frank's impecunious circumstances, persuaded the court that she and her mother should be the preferred guardians of the children. Clearly in this case, money trumped gender.

Money did not make a woman invulnerable, however. One of the most poignant cases is the case of *Agnew v. Agnew* in 1860. Mary and John Agnew were a wealthy couple with two children. He was in business with his brother, who conceded that John Agnew was worth at least fifty thousand dollars (although he was clearly worth a lot more, and his brother was trying to portray him as having less money than he did in answer to Mary Agnew's request for support payments). The family lived in a comfortable house on Nineteenth Street with many servants. In the fall of 1854, several of those servants confided to Mary's brother, Charles Bostwick, Jr., that John was physically abusing Charles's sister. They told

Charles of specific incidents, portraying a story of private horror that was hidden from public view, and they indicated that it had been going on for some time. The couple had been married in 1845. Charles was angered by the story and asked the servants if they would put their allegations in writing, which they did. He then showed the document to John's brother and business partner, Alexander Agnew, who claimed that the servants must be lying. Charles next went to their minister, John McLeod, and told him about the servants' allegations. The minister was shocked at the suggestion that John, whom he said he had known from birth and whom he thought of as a religious man, would abuse his wife. The minister went to see Mary and asked her if the story was true. Mary became very upset and admitted that she did not "live happily" with her husband, but she denied the beatings and pleaded with McLeod not to say anything to her husband. Her brother-in-law also went to see her, and again she denied the beatings and urged him not to tell her husband. At this point, Mary's father, Charles Bostwick, Sr., went to see her husband and asked him point-blank if he had been using "personal violence" against his daughter. John Agnew vigorously denied any wrongdoing and said that it was "scandalous" that anyone should say such a thing about him.

Three years after these denials, however, in May 1857, Mary Agnew left her husband's house one night and fled to her parents' house on Twenty-second Street in a "distracted state." Her husband came to reclaim her, but she refused to go with him. He talked at length with her father and persuaded him that what she needed was a rest and a "change of air." He said he would take her on a trip where she could relax and regain her health. Her father agreed to what seemed (to him) a reasonable proposal, and John and Mary set off on a "holiday." However, John took her, not on a vacation but to Northampton, Massachusetts, where he had her committed to an insane asylum. She remained in the asylum for two years until her parents ascertained her whereabouts, and in November 1859 her mother traveled to Massachusetts and "clandestinely" brought her out of the asylum. She went to stay at her brother's house in New York.

When John Agnew found that she had returned to New York, he sent his minister, John McLeod, to her brother's house to bring her home to him. Much to the minister's "surprise," she absolutely refused to return to her husband. Soon afterward she filed suit for a separation on the grounds of "cruel and inhuman treatment." In her complaint she stated that her husband had used "personal violence," striking her and subjecting her to "profane language"; that he had "deprived her of food"; that he "did not take her sufficiently into company"; and that "he required her to be too much occupied at home." She asked for support money and for custody of the children. John Agnew denied all of her allegations, claiming that he had been kindness itself. He maintained that he wanted her to come home and called as witnesses his minister, his brother, and his sister's husband, all of whom testified that they had never witnessed any brutal behavior by the defendant. They conceded that at times he was "irritable and nervous," due to an eye affliction, but they concluded that any problems between the couple were caused by Mary's "interfering mother." The doctor from the Springdale asylum in Northampton, Edward Denniston, was called to testify. He maintained that the patient's "mania exhibited itself in her dread of cholera and in the want of affectionate interest and care for her children and her domestic relations."

Was Mary Agnew insane? Her younger brother had died of cholera a few years earlier, so that her fear of cholera was not illusory. (Henry David Thoreau was convinced that he was going to die of lockjaw after his brother John died of that disease in 1842, but he was not institutionalized.[14]) Moreover, if Mary was being regularly beaten at home, it is not surprising that she did not exhibit an interest in her "domestic relations." And her attitude toward her children suggests that she was suffering from post–traumatic shock syndrome, in which the mind shuts down and the person experiences a kind of numbness—a common survival technique in cases of spousal abuse. Puzzled by her attitude on these subjects, Dr. Denniston concluded, "On all other subjects she appeared to be rational."

In numerous nineteenth-century works of fiction a woman is institutionalized who is not insane. Either a husband wants to get her out of the way (e.g., in Fern's *Ruth Hall*) or relatives want to reap her inheritance (Southworth's *The Hidden Hand* and Alcott's "A Whisper in the Dark"). British novelist Wilkie Collins uses the same theme in *The Moonstone* (1868). Today these stories might seem to stretch our credulity, but the story of Mary Agnew reminds us that they were not far removed from the truth. Chapter 8 discusses the case that Elizabeth Cady Stanton reported in which Susan B. Anthony "rescued" a woman from an insane asylum. And in 1873 Elizabeth Packard, whose husband had had her committed to an Illinois insane asylum in the 1850s, wrote a book describing how vulnerable she and other women were to the decisions of male legal and medical authorities.[15] Recent studies of nineteenth-century insane asylums have shown that women were committed at a disproportionate rate and for behavior that in a man would not have been considered insane. Moreover, it was not difficult to have a person committed. In New York State, prior to 1874 when the law was changed, a person could be committed on the basis of one person's testimony only. After 1874 no person could be committed without the certificate of two physicians.[16]

The case of Mary Agnew demonstrates that upper-class women were not invulnerable. In the end, however, it was her family network that rescued her, both from her abusive husband and from the insane asylum. Without her family, she would have had no recourse. Wholly dependent on her husband's money, she was worse off than the working-class woman who could support herself by working in a shoe factory or the middle-class woman who gained some autonomy by starting a sewing business or running a boardinghouse. In her divorce suit, Mary Agnew complained that her husband beat her, kept her confined to the house, and denied her food (as punishment, perhaps), yet it apparently never occurred to her to leave his house and support herself, as Josephine Baugh or Elizabeth Romertze or Sarah White had done. When she finally did leave, she went home to her parents. Elizabeth Hollins was the most economically powerful of the women whose stories we have discussed thus far, yet she too was dependent upon the support of her family. Without her wealthy mother's support, and with six children to care for, she would have been vulnerable before her dissolute and irresponsible husband. Even Elizabeth Moulton's power came from her family via her wealthy father's posthumous provision for her. The upper-class woman, then, unless she had family to support her, was vulnerable because she was the most removed from the world of economics. Her class position gave her power only when she had family behind her, or when, like Eliza Morris, Elizabeth Hollins's wealthy widowed mother, she was herself in charge of her wealth, either as a single woman or as a widow. Yet, as these divorce cases demonstrate so vividly, although the wealthy woman was removed from the world of economics in the sense that she did not think about ways to support herself, she was not really outside that world. Her apparent insulation from economic considerations was an illusion fostered by the society in which she lived. It was as if she were behind a one-way mirror: she could not see the economic machinations, but they were a part of her life nevertheless. Divorce tore down the mirror so that instead of seeing only herself, she saw the importance of money—not just for herself as a consumer but as a power wielder.

But what about the wealthy wife who already knew about money, who was herself economically independent before marriage? Even economic independence was no guarantee of invulnerability. A woman was vulnerable also because of her acceptance of society's construction of womanhood: the goal for women was marriage, and independent women could be brought to do foolish things in order to conform to society's image of woman. Delania Brainard and Edward Furber, two Americans traveling separately abroad, met in Liverpool, England, in 1861. When they met, she was thirty-six, a self-described "widow" (a designation that she as a professional woman had apparently adopted because it lent her an air of respectability), and he was a fifty-five-year-old widower with three adult children. She ran a successful dressmaking business in Washington and Philadelphia, which, she told him, was worth five to ten thousand dollars. A sea captain, he was then involved in a gold mining operation in Nicaragua. When they returned to New York, he took her to visit Ravenswood, an estate on Long Island that he represented as his own; he also said that he was the owner of three ships. After he asked her to marry him, he told her that his business in Nicaragua was in danger of failing if he didn't have money immediately. She loaned him the money that he said he needed. They were married in January 1862, but they kept the marriage a secret because he said he wanted to be able to inform his children, who were then abroad. She sold her dressmaking business, and they left for Nicaragua in April 1862. Once they arrived in Nicaragua, she loaned him more money for machinery. Soon afterward, she received word that she had to return to New York because of a lawsuit against her by a silk vendor. When she told Furber that she had to go to New York, he gave her an order for $745 to be paid by his agent, William Irving, in New York, which, he said, would be partial reimbursement for her loans to him. But when she presented the order to Irving, instead of paying her the money, Irving paid it to Furber's brother, William Furber, in New York.

After Delania settled the lawsuit, which was dismissed, and returned to Nicaragua, her husband told her that his mining business had failed and that he had lost all of his (and her) money. Already distressed by the loss of her money and suspicious of Furber because of Irving's refusal to pay her money to her, she made an alarming discovery. She found letters from her husband's brother telling him to divorce her. William Furber had written to her husband: "From your own letter to me I know that you despise your wife and I wish to God you would get clear of her by divorce. At all counts I would suggest that if I were in your place I would keep my affairs as close as possible, leave her under the impression that you are as poor as a church mouse and be as ugly as the Devil. In fact try to borrow some more money of her."

When Delania told her husband she had found the letters, he tried to get them from her. She refused and went to the American Consul for protection. They returned to New York separately, he refusing to pay her passage; she said she had to sell her jewelry in order to get back home. When they arrived in New York he refused to support her and went to live with his brother at Ravenswood while she stayed with friends.

On January 11, 1864, Delania Furber brought suit for divorce on grounds of abandonment and cruel and inhuman treatment. She asked for support and for reimbursement for the money she had loaned her husband. She claimed that he had appropriated $4,000 to $5,000 from her separate property. He claimed that she had given him only $1,500, that the money was not a loan, and that he had invested it in his business. In any case, he said, he now had no money. He maintained that he had been ill and was forced to depend on friends. He testified that the estate Ravenswood and the three ships were not his but were in his brother's name. The attorneys arranged a settlement in which Furber would pay his wife $1,000 if she would return the letters and $500 more if she returned other items. She returned all of the items and letters, except the documents pertaining to the $745 William Irving had paid to Furber's brother. She had begun a lawsuit against Irving and William Furber in an attempt to recover her money. Edward Furber then backed out of the agreement. The court threatened to arrest him if he did not pay, but he claimed that he had no money; his attorney confirmed that Edward Furber had no money, maintaining that he (the attorney) had not been paid and that the $1,000 Furber had agreed to pay his wife was from Furber's brother, not Furber. Furber claimed that it was his brother who had backed out of the agreement, because Delania had not returned the documents pertaining to the lawsuit against him and Irving. And, said Furber, his brother, who was also a sea captain, had already sailed and would not be back in New York for many months. In January 1866 the court dismissed the case.

Delania Furber lost up to five thousand dollars, her business, and four years of her life. Even with the 1848 and 1860 married women's property laws to protect her, she lost all of her money. She realized too late that she had been had—used. Furber had represented himself as a wealthy man—a sea captain, owner of ships, owner of a large country home, and proprietor of a gold mining operation. But any assets he had were in his brother's name. It seems clear that he had married her primarily to obtain the money to finance his mining operation. Perhaps if it had been successful, he would have reimbursed her. But—given that they had put nothing in writing—it is possible that he never intended to reimburse her. In view of the sentiments expressed in his brother's letters, and in view of the fraudulent draft he gave her for Irving, one suspects that he simply wanted the money. Had she proved to be pliable and acquiescent, he might have retained her as a wife. However, she was an independent woman, proprietor of a successful business, and unaccustomed to being treated as though she did not count. When she rebelled against his treatment of her, he apparently followed his brother's advice: he divested himself of his assets and did his best to alienate her and force her to seek a divorce. Of course, we cannot know whether his assets were originally in his brother's name or if he made the change only in order to prevent her from obtaining money from him. I suspect that the latter is closer to the truth. But the case makes clear that even an independent woman can be vulnerable.

Certainly, the situation that Delania Furber found herself in was not peculiar to the nineteenth century. There is no shortage of women today—particularly women of "a certain age"—who have been conned into giving money to a smooth-talking man who represents himself as well-to-do and who proffers marriage. Edward Furber, although he cried poverty when she was suing him for divorce, clearly gave the appearance of being a wealthy man during his courtship of her. Whether or not his assets were in his own name before he answered her divorce suit, he led the life of a wealthy man: he and his children traveled in Europe, he lived in a large estate on Long Island, and he operated a gold mining business in Central America. Delania Furber thought she was about to become part of a wealthy family, but she gave up her economic independence for a dream of marriage that was as illusory as the gold that Edward Furber sought in Nicaragua. She was, however, in a better position than Sarah White was when her husband took her two houses away from her. Delania had built up a reputation for herself in her dressmaking business and would have no trouble obtaining a new position. In fact, her husband, in claiming that she did not need support from him, said that she had told him she had been offered one thousand dollars a year to go to work in an establishment whenever she chose. Of course, it would not be her own business, and we do not know whether or not she had sufficient capital left to begin her business anew. But at least she would not need to support herself by cleaning people's houses, as Sarah White was forced to do.

Whereas Elizabeth Hollins and Mary Agnew were dependent upon their families for economic support and Delania Furber lost her money, other wealthy women were able to gain economic power for themselves. One example is the case of Charlotte Gaynor, who, like Mary Agnew, was the victim of physical abuse by her wealthy husband, Thomas Gaynor. Yet, unlike Mary Agnew, she did not resign herself to his abuse. Nor did she, like Delania Furber, allow herself to be taken advantage of. Although it took her many years to extricate herself from her husband's control, she was able to do so by making herself economically independent. Married in 1853 to a wealthy man who was increasingly violent, in 1862 and again in 1867 she brought suit for divorce. However, in 1863 and again in 1867 she had another child, and both suits were discontinued, probably because of the pregnancies. But in February 1869, when she had five children, ages two to fourteen years, she brought suit for divorce on the ground of cruel and inhuman treatment. This time she had prepared her case well. She claimed that her husband had committed many acts of violence against her and had threatened to kill her. She submitted a long list of specific instances of physical violence, a list that provides a hair-raising chronicle of abuse. For example, in June 1865 he "violently and cruelly assaulted, beat, hit and kicked the plaintiff"; in March 1866 he "threatened to choke and kill, and attempted to strangle this plaintiff, and threw her upon the floor and kicked her"; and on January 9, 1869, he "violently assaulted this plaintiff with a knife and tore the hair from her head." She maintained that it was "unsafe for the plaintiff to live, reside with or be under the control of the defendant" and asked for a limited divorce, custody of the five children, and support for herself and the children. She claimed her husband had an income of more than twelve thousand dollars a year in addition to a lucrative business and real estate property.

Thomas Gaynor contested the divorce, and although he did not deny that he physically abused his wife, he attempted to show by his counter-accusations that she had provoked his violence. His principal accusation was that she had "set up a store and place of business of the same kind as deponent had advertised in a different place and in every way tried to reduce and destroy deponent's business and has to a great extent succeeded in so doing." In other words, his main "beef" with her was that she had become a business competitor and a successful one. He went on to say that she was a "designing" woman, all of whose "words, actions, and conduct by threats, by coaxing or in some way tend to deprive this deponent of the balance of his property." He claimed that he had given her a house on Sixth Avenue and one on Fifth Avenue, that she realized rents of $6,000 a year, and that she had sold the Fifth Avenue house for $13,000 and had bought government bonds. Obviously, Charlotte Gaynor had not been wringing her hands in desperation while her husband had been abusing her. Like Mary Trust, who saved her money so that she could leave her husband and who apparently set herself up in business as a "female physician," Charlotte Gaynor had gained control of two pieces of property and had used the money to start her own business. Why he had signed over the property to her is not clear. Perhaps he did so in order to persuade her to discontinue her previous divorce suits.

Or perhaps she had inherited the property or it had been hers before marriage. The Gaynors were married in 1853, so that if she had inherited the property or brought it into the marriage, she would have been legally entitled to retain ownership of it under the Married Women's Property Act of 1848. If this was the case, when her husband "gave" her the property, he was only giving her what she already owned. However she gained control of the property, it was her possession of it that enabled her to start her own business and attain the economic independence that provided her with the money and confidence to sue her husband for divorce. The court granted her a limited divorce and ordered Thomas Gaynor to pay his wife $20 a week support money for herself and her children and $300 in attorney's fees.

What these cases show us is that it is as impossible to generalize about class as it is to generalize about individuals. Situations differ and personalities differ, and even within social class there are variations in resourcefulness as well as differences in situatedness. Of the four wealthy women discussed above, Elizabeth Hollins was able to obtain an absolute divorce and custody of her children because of her mother's money. Mary Agnew was vulnerable to her husband's abuse and seemed incapable of helping herself until she was locked up in an insane asylum and rescued by her parents. Delania Furber, a middle-class woman who married into a wealthy family, was deprived of her money by her charlatan husband because of her naïve belief in society's idealized domestic goal for women. But Charlotte Gaynor, through careful planning over the years and in spite of (or perhaps because of) frequent pregnancies and beatings, was able to make herself financially independent in order to escape her husband's abuse. It is impossible to say that "upper-class women do x or y." Similarly, middle-class women acted and reacted differently and with varying results. Louisa Torrey sought her family's help. Mary Goldsmith and Elizabeth Romertze successfully earned their own livings. Yet Sarah White's brave attempts to earn her own living were foiled by her husband and his lawyer. Working-class women also found themselves in differing circumstances. As indicated above, however, they were the most vulnerable, since they were less likely to have family who could take them and their children in, and they did not have the money to obtain the best legal advice. A poor woman's ability to win depended on three factors: if she could prove that her husband had committed adultery, she would be able to obtain an absolute divorce and a court-awarded settlement; if her husband was in steady employ, he would have the money to contribute to her support; and if he didn't "light out for the territory" when ordered to pay, she could collect her money for herself and her children.

The principal—perhaps the only—overarching conclusion that one can draw from all of these cases is that divorce was a catalyst that revealed how important economics were in any woman's life regardless of class. Women whose culture trained them to be ornaments or domestic "angels in the house," protected and provided for by their husbands, along with women who had already discovered the illusory nature of that assurance, found themselves thrust into an economic reality that underscored the importance of money for women as well as for men.

chapter nine

WOMAN'S ECONOMIC INDEPENDENCE

FERN, ALCOTT, AND GILMAN

Although all of the nineteenth-century women writers in this study recognized and dealt with in their works the significance of economics for women, only a small proportion of those writers publicly advocated woman's economic independence. In this chapter I will look at the arguments of three authors who emphasized financial independence for women, thus breaking with the dominant ideology of their society.

In their first significant works of fiction, Fanny Fern (1811–1872), Louisa May Alcott (1832–1888), and Charlotte Perkins Gilman (1860–1935) portrayed the terrifying effects of absolute dependence for women. In *Ruth Hall* (1855) Fern portrays the destitution that can result when a woman remains ignorant of money matters and wholly dependent on a husband whose death leaves her and her children penniless. In Alcott's novel *Moods*, first published in 1864 and then revised in 1882, Alcott portrays a young woman who suffers from moods of melancholia and malaise but who dreams of a life of experience and adventure, such as might be available to a man. After her marriage, she feels the loss of her individuality and finds herself increasingly tormented by the awareness that she is no more than a possession of her husband. And in "The Yellow Wallpaper" (1892), Gilman portrays a woman who goes mad because her husband, her doctor, and society as a whole insist that the "cure" for her depression is the total suppression of her individuality. She must not think for herself, and she must not "do" anything. Intellectual stimulation and productive activity are forbidden. Reduced to childlike dependence, she goes insane.

It is not surprising that all three of these works—*Ruth Hall*, *Moods*, and "The Yellow Wallpaper"—were misunderstood by their contemporaries; the secrets that they revealed about women and marriage were not publicly acknowledged, and their call for woman's independence was too radical for the time. Contemporary reviewers of *Ruth Hall* focused on the satirical aspect of the novel and the author's "unfeminine" writing, wholly missing Fern's emphasis on economic independence for women.[1] Similarly, early readers of *Moods* focused on the love triangle and failed to see Alcott's psychological exploration of a young woman's development; a theme focusing on the development of a woman's selfhood was invisible to critics who did not think that a woman had a self to develop or who regarded the female self as beside the point.[2] And for years, Gilman's "The Yellow Wallpaper" was regarded as primarily a Poe-esque horror story; the author's point regarding women's need for autonomy was wholly overlooked.[3] For these authors, the problem was to find an answer to a question that most of their contemporaries did not even acknowledge was a question: How can a woman gain economic independence in a society that denies autonomy to women and regards women and money as definitionally opposed? Their early works introduced the question, and in their succeeding works and in their own lives, Fern, Alcott, and Gilman attempted to answer it.

The central theme of Fanny Fern's 1855 novel *Ruth Hall* is woman's economic independence. I have discussed other aspects of this novel in previous chapters, and in this chapter I will focus primarily on Fern's newspaper articles. However, it is important to look first at her development of the theme of economic independence in the novel. In *Ruth Hall*, when the protagonist's husband dies, leaving her and her children destitute, and with only grudging help from her family, she must find a way to earn her living. Unable to earn enough money as a seamstress, and failing to obtain a position as a teacher, Ruth decides to attempt to support herself by her writing. She asks her editor brother, Hyacinth, for his help, and when Hyacinth refuses to help her, his denigration of her work only intensifies her determination to succeed. "I *can* do it, I *feel* it, I *will* do it," Ruth declares when she receives his cruel letter.[4] The italicized words in her assertion and the reiterated "I" indicate a significant break with the passive selflessness of traditional feminine behavior. Remembering her father's unkind treatment of her daughter when the child was dispatched to ask him for a dollar for the rent when Ruth was sick, Ruth determines that henceforth she will not seek the grudging assistance of hostile relatives but will try to support her family on her own: "She would so gladly support herself, so cheerfully toil day and night, if need be, could she only win an independence" (115).

Ruth perseveres, and when, after a hard struggle, she succeeds as a columnist and her popular articles are printed in a best-selling book, she thinks with pride and excitement of her newfound ability to support her children: "She would make her a new home. Home? Her heart leaped!—comforts for Nettie and Katy,—clothes,—food,—earned by her own hands!" (181). At the end of the novel, Ruth's father-in-law, ignorant of her success (her book and articles have been published under a pseudonym), threatens to take her children from her, citing the law: "The law says if the mother can't support her children, the grand-parents shall do it." But Ruth replies, triumphantly taking Katy away from her cruel grandparents: "The mother can—the mother *will*. . . . I have already earned enough for their support" (185). And later, as she looks at her sleeping children, she revels in her power: "How sweet to have it in her power to hedge them in with comforts" (197). This power is graphically illustrated by the photograph of the certificate for ten thousand dollars in bank stock made out to "Ruth Hall" which, as I mentioned in chapter 3, is printed at the end of the novel (209). Instead of concluding with the visual image of a handsome husband-to-be as might appear in a more traditional novel, *Ruth Hall* ends with a picture of the heroine's certificate for bank stock that she has acquired by her own efforts. That this is the only illustration in the book is indicative of its significance.

The novel *Ruth Hall* provides a dramatization of Fern's theme of economic independence, but in her newspaper articles her argument is explicit. In 1861 Fern critiqued in the *New York Ledger* the economic double standard that condemned women for attempting to make themselves financially independent: "There are few people who speak approbatively of a woman who has a smart business talent or capability . . . which would lift her at once out of her troubles, and which, in a man so situated, would be applauded as exceedingly praiseworthy" (RHOW, 318). Fern consistently opposed this double standard. On July 16, 1870, she wrote in the *New York Ledger*: "Why shouldn't women work for pay? does anybody object when women marry for pay?—without love, without respect, nay, with even aversion? . . . How much more to be honored is she who, hewing out her own path, through prejudice and narrowness and even insult, earns honorably and honestly her own independence." In the June 26, 1869, *Ledger* she had also asserted, "I want all women to render themselves independent of marriage as a mere means of support."

Conventional critics were shocked by Fern's independent stance in thus redefining gender and labeled her work "vulgar," "monstrous," and "abominable," condemning Fern as "unfeminine," "immodest," and "indecorous." Not only was Fern criticized by literary critics, but her private life suffered as well. "Respectable" people refused to be introduced to her, and her third husband's relatives treated her as if she were a pariah and attempted to break up her marriage.[5]

What enabled Fern to defy convention in this way, asserting her belief in woman's economic independence as a lifelong goal for women at a time when society defined women as dependent and acquiescent? There are three principal reasons for Fern's independent stance: (1) her own experience with economic dependency, (2) her change in class status, and (3) the attack on her reputation. With respect to the first of these categories, her own experience had shown her the catastrophic results of economic dependency. First of all, the death of her first husband had left her penniless, and she realized that her financial ignorance had left her unprepared to support herself and her children after his death; moreover, she had been kept unaware of and uninvolved in crucial financial decisions throughout her marriage—decisions that had resulted in her later impoverishment. In addition, during her second marriage, her abusive husband used economic leverage to force her to his will, and her economic dependency left her and her children powerless before him. And finally, after she left her second husband, her father-in-law used economic leverage to attempt to take her children from her, cruelly rewriting his will so that her children would inherit his money—but only if she agreed to give them up.[6]

All of these experiences made Fern aware of how vulnerable women were because of their dependence on men for economic support. She recognized the need for women to be informed and active in economic issues that affected them. "When you can," she concluded, speaking to women, "achieve financial independence. Freedom from subjection may be gotten by the fruits of your own labor," and financial independence, she said, was even more important than the vote.[7] After Fern left her second husband and began to earn her own living, she took an active part in business transactions—signing contracts, inquiring about her financial affairs, and making informed economic decisions. In her private life also, Fern made certain that her assets were protected. As I mentioned in a previous chapter, before Fern married James Parton, her third husband, in 1856, she had a prenuptial agreement drawn up specifying that she would have absolute control of all money and property that she brought into the marriage and that she acquired thereafter.[8]

Fern's experience with economic dependency taught her a hard lesson in the need for economic independence, but it was her change in class status that radicalized her and made her aware of the differences in gender identity. Her sudden descent into poverty showed her that middle-class definitions of womanhood were not universal. The shift from protected middle-class wife to working-class single mother had the effect of fracturing the concept of the universality of gender identity. The man who is a protector of women in his own class is often, Fern noted in the *Olive Branch* on May 29, 1852, a "highwayman" in relation to working-class women: he takes advantage of them, she said, *because* they are "alone and unprotected." Consequently, characteristics that had seemed to be essential to middle-class womanhood—dependency, delicacy, ingenuousness—were suicidal for the working-class woman, whose survival depended on her independence, strength, and knowledge of the world. It was this recognition of the fluidity of gender identity that brought Fern to her own definition of gender, a definition that included women's economic independence.

Thus, Fern's experience with dependency, coupled with her change of class status, led her to a recognition of the need for woman's economic independence and the fatuousness of rigid gender roles. But it was the attacks on her reputation that enabled her to speak out publicly. When Fern left her second husband, he and his brother circulated stories about her, falsely accusing her of promiscuous behavior. Thus, when she began to write, she had nothing to lose. Her reputation was already tarnished. Freed from the concern to protect her reputation that inhibited most nineteenth-century American women, Fern was not afraid to say in public what she believed in private—including her belief in economic independence for women.[9]

Louisa May Alcott urged women's independence, but she was less explicit and more circumspect than Fern in her public articulation of the need for woman's economic independence and the power that it won. In her first novel, *Moods*, Alcott focuses on the question of female dependency. In one scene, Sylvia's husband gives her a signet ring bearing the letter *M*. As he presses it onto her finger to hold on her wedding band, he says that it is "to signify that you are mine." Sylvia does not like his possessiveness: "She shrunk from him a little and glanced up at him, because his touch was more firm than tender, and his face wore a masterful expression seldom seen there."[10] Sylvia falls in love with another man, and the reader might be led to believe that with the other man she would be happy. However, Alcott answers that question by a repetition of the ring scene with her lover, Adam Warwick. He grasps Sylvia's hand and the signet ring falls off. Alcott says that Sylvia "felt Warwick's hold tighten as if he echoed the emphatic word uttered when the ineffectual gift was first bestowed" (161). The "emphatic word," of course, is "mine." Alcott concludes that marriage with no equality of opportunity or power is slavery. Sylvia visits a wise spinster, Faith Dane, and when Sylvia asks her which man she should go to, Faith tells her "neither." Faith warns Sylvia that Warwick "demands and unconsciously absorbs into himself the personality of others" (180). In both versions of the novel, Sylvia leaves her husband, and Warwick is killed. In the 1882 more conventional rewrite of the novel, Sylvia is reunited with her husband at the end; but in the original version, Sylvia dies.

Both versions of the novel provide a glimpse behind the mask of society's image of marriage. Alcott tells her readers of the secret unhappiness of women, which she indicates is more widespread than is publicly admitted. Sylvia, Alcott says, because of her own "household grief," "found herself detecting various phases of her own experience in others. She had joined that sad sisterhood of disappointed women; a larger class than many deem it to be, though there are few of us who have not seen members of it" (190). Such women include "unhappy wives," "mistaken lovers," women who make "a long penance of their lives for the sins of others," and gifted women who cannot fulfill their talents.

Louisa May Alcott was one of the few mainstream nineteenth-century women writers who recognized the need for work as a lifelong means to independence for women. In the 1882 edition of *Moods*, Adam Warwick advises Sylvia, articulating what was to become Alcott's credo: "My panacea for most troubles is work" (254).[11] Alcott wrote of herself in 1872, "Work is and always has been my salvation."[12] In her popular fiction, Alcott did not usually link her heroine's work to financial independence; work could mean simply becoming involved in useful and productive activity. In *Rose in Bloom* (1876), Rose Campbell says to her male cousin, "It is as much a right and a duty for women to do something with their lives as for men. . . . Would you be contented to be told to enjoy yourself for a little while, then marry and do nothing more till you die?"[13] In this novel, the heroine is an heiress, and she uses her money for philanthropic enterprises, such as providing housing for working women and healthy care for orphans. However, the other young woman in the novel, Phebe, works for a living. Phebe gives up her career when she marries, but Jo March in *Little Women* (1868) continues to write after her marriage to Professor Bhaer, although she will no longer write thriller fiction. In *An Old-Fashioned Girl* (1870), Alcott portrays working women who live together and support themselves. They are visited by the heroines, who admire them, and although the heroines will not follow the example of the working women, they all look forward to a happy future when women will be economically independent.[14]

Alcott's popular fiction, which was written for children, contains suggestions of her belief in women's independence, but it is in her pseudonymous and unconventional fiction for adults that Alcott gave full expression to her belief in autonomy for women. The thriller stories that were published pseudonymously focus almost wholly on the theme of female power. The subtitle of the most well known of these stories, her 1866 novella "Behind a Mask," is "A Woman's Power." Jean Muir, the female protagonist, is a puppeteer and entrepreneur who successfully orchestrates her own ascendance to wealth and power. As a character comments in "The Mysterious Key," a story published the following year, "I am tired of pity. Power is sweet, and I will use it."[15] "Pauline's Passion and Punishment" tells the story of a woman who seeks revenge, and "A Pair of Eyes" explains how "a sense of power" brings "exultation" to a woman.[16] In the story "Taming a Tartar," in many ways a rewrite of Shakespeare's *Taming of the Shrew* with role reversal, the heroine sets out to tame a man who has a "cursed temper" and a "despotic will."[17] She is triumphant in the power struggle, and by the end of the story he yields to her, humbly declaring, "I submit."[18] This bold assertion of female power never appears so explicitly in the fiction to which Alcott signed her name.

Particularly significant is her posthumously published novel, *A Long Fatal Love Chase*. Written in 1866, two years before the publication of *Little Women*, this novel, which was originally titled "A Modern Mephistopheles" (a title that Alcott later used for a very different novel), tells the story of a young woman who is willing to sell her soul to the devil in order to win her freedom. Because of the controversial subject matter, Alcott could not find a publisher for this novel during her lifetime, and it was not published until 1995. Living on an isolated island with an indifferent grandfather, eighteen-year-old Rosamond feels stifled by convention and declares, "I'd gladly sell my soul to Satan for a year of freedom."[19] She knows that there is nowhere for her to go on her own, however, since she is "a girl, young, penniless and alone" (4). Thus, when Philip Tempest wins her from her grandfather in a card game and agrees to marry her, she is glad to go with him. But instead of finding "freedom," she finds that she is the *possession* of a tyrannical man who is a murderer and a bigamist. She flees to Paris, where she supports herself as a seamstress for nine months until the obsessive Tempest finds her, "exultingly" attempting to reclaim her like a "master who has recovered a runaway slave" (96). Rather than return to him, Rosamond asks for a delay and escapes by climbing out of the window and dragging herself across the roof to the window of another seamstress, who agrees to help her get away. Cross-dressing to elude Tempest, she is taught to walk like a boy, "to take a larger stride, to look boldly up and swing her arms" (117). The novel becomes a power struggle between her and Tempest. She tells him early in the novel, "You might kill me but not bend me" (46). Tempest is determined to "see her proud spirit broken" (159), but even after he has her imprisoned in an insane asylum, and she is weak and ill, he realizes that "however weak her body might be her soul was unconquered still" (184). Alcott reiterates this assertion of Rosamond's strong will over and over throughout the text. In fact, Rosamond's yearning for freedom and independence is close to Alcott's own. Alcott wrote in her diary in 1856: "I love luxury, but freedom and independence better."[20]

Implicit in Alcott's focus on the search for power is the realization that the ability to earn money was in itself a source of power for women. In "Behind a Mask," it is Jean Muir's ability to gain enormous wealth that makes her invulnerable. Jo March, when she finds she can earn money for herself, is exhilarated by her newfound power: "She . . . began to feel herself a power in the house, for by the magic of a pen, her 'rubbish' turned into comforts for them all."[21] Alcott herself exulted in her own power of independence. In 1868 she wrote, "I want to realize my dream of supporting the family and being perfectly independent."[22] Her journal is simultaneously a record of her earnings and expenditures, entered with pride in the money earned from her writings and the money spent on items for herself and her family.[23] Alcott's capacity to earn a living from her writing made her father call her an "arsenal of powers"—which was particularly significant considering the lifelong power struggle between Alcott and her father.[24] When she was twenty-four years old and working to support herself in Boston, she wrote home to her father: "I think I shall come out all right, and prove that though an *Alcott* I *can* support myself. I like the independent feeling; and though not an easy life, it is a free one, and I enjoy it."[25] Considering the fact that her father was notoriously unable or unwilling to support his family, that her mother was the breadwinner in the family, this letter is clearly a put-down of her father; it is also an assertion of her joy at being economically independent.

Alcott's children's fiction hints at the need for independence; her pseudonymous fiction overtly asserts female power; but it is in her adult novel *Work* (1872) that she explicitly develops the connection between economic independence and female autonomy. *Work* begins with heroine Christie Devon's assertion of her strong need to be independent. "Aunt Betsey," she says, "there's going to be a new Declaration of Independence. I mean that, being of age, I'm going to take care of myself, and not be a burden any longer."[26] Christie insists that she is going to leave home and make her way in the world just as she would have been expected to do if she had been a boy. "I hate to be dependent," she says. "There is plenty of work in the world, and I'm not afraid to do it" (5). The rest of the novel chronicles her adventures in the various jobs that are open to a woman—servant, actress, governess, companion, seamstress, army nurse. After almost twenty years of work, she marries, is widowed, becomes a mother, and continues to work, establishing a women's cooperative business. As she says at the end of the novel, she has been a working woman all her life.

Although Alcott believed in the necessity of work for women, both philanthropic and wage-earning work, she was not able to reconcile women's need for economic independence with the concept of marriage. Christie is able to work after marriage only because her husband dies. Alcott herself never married. In 1868 she wrote an article for the *New York Ledger* entitled "Happy Women," in which she described the happy lives of women who had not married. Her message is similar to that of Frances Harper in her 1859 story "The Two Offers." Young girls, Alcott said, were so afraid to be old maids that they often rushed into marriage without realizing that the "loss of liberty, happiness, and self-respect" was a high price to pay.[27] One of the women she described in the article was a writer, "A," who is probably herself. Having seen much of the "tragedy of modern married life," "A" chose not to marry but found happiness because necessity taught "the worth of work" (205).

The problem for Alcott was how to reconcile marriage and motherhood with women's need for independence. In a society that did not grant equal power to women, she saw marriage as enslaving. In the novel *Work*, Christie refuses to marry a man whom she perceives as too possessive. "However much Mr. Fletcher might love his wife," Christie thinks, "he would be something of a tyrant, and she was very sure she would never make a good slave" (324). Instead, Christie chooses David Sterling, who is more nearly her equal. However, even in this companionate marriage there would be complications, Alcott feared, and she solved the problem in the novel by killing off David in the Civil War. As a widow, Christie can resume her independent work. Alcott's solution to the question of women's work is contained in her vision of female independence and unity, which appears at the end of the novel. *Work* concludes with this image: "With an impulsive gesture Christie stretched her hands to the friends about her, and with one accord they laid theirs on hers, a loving league of sisters, old and young, black and white, rich and poor, each ready to do her part" (442).

Alcott was painfully aware that the situation needed to be changed, but she could not conceive of a workable solution. The image in *An Old-Fashioned Girl* also looks to a visionary future. The sculpture of "the coming woman" reveals a "woman who is to stand alone, and help herself," a "strong-minded, strong-hearted, strong-souled, and strong-bodied woman" (257–258). All of the women, Alcott says, are helping to bring about the day "when their noblest ideal of womanhood should be embodied in flesh and blood, not clay" (263). But for the present, female independence was difficult to realize. The heroine looks at the woman writer in the group and wonders "if the time would ever come when women could earn a little money and success, without paying such a heavy price for them; for Kate looked sick, tired, and too early old" (263).

Alcott knew that the portrayal of woman as power seeker was not socially acceptable—particularly in a married woman, but even in an unmarried woman. In a revealing interview, Alcott once commented that the reason she did not write "lurid" material (she did not acknowledge that she wrote it anonymously) was because she did not want to forfeit the approval of the patriarch: "To have had Mr. Emerson for an intellectual god all one's life is to be invested with a chain armor of propriety. . . . And what would my own good father think of me if I set folks to doing the things I have a longing to see my people do?"[28] Alcott's periodical publishers attempted to persuade her to sign her name to her thriller fiction, but she adamantly refused. There were only two occasions when Alcott did agree to sign her name to her mystery stories, and it is significant that in those two cases the stories, although "lurid," did not involve a power-seeking woman as did most of her mystery fiction.[29]

Clearly, it was not simply because of the "luridness" of the material but because of her portrayal of the woman as power seeker that Alcott refused to publicly acknowledge her mystery fiction.

When protected by her anonymity, Alcott redefined female gender to include the power that comes with economic independence; but in the fiction to which she signed her name, she was more circumspect. Unlike Fern, she did not have nothing to lose; she needed to protect her "chain armor of propriety." In her anonymous works the heroine could assert her power, challenging the annihilating male will; there, Alcott portrayed the female power seeker as autonomous, shrewd, and unregenerate. But in the works to which Alcott signed her name, her heroine kept within the bounds of normative female behavior. Privately and anonymously, Alcott established new and radical performative acts constituting gender identity, but she was not willing to risk her own reputation by publicizing her redefinition of woman. Instead she looked toward a visionary future.

Fern, Alcott, and Gilman criticized what they regarded as the intolerable dependency of married women, and all of them recognized the need for women's economic independence. Only Gilman, however, was able to imagine a future that contained a realistic process by which it might be realized. Charlotte Perkins Gilman categorically stated her belief in the need for economic independence for women. It is significant also that, like Fern's, Gilman's reputation was already blighted when she spoke out for women's economic independence. She had left her husband, and that in itself was unconventional, but her principal crime came later when she voluntarily gave up her daughter to her husband and his new wife. Although she did so for her daughter's benefit, she was pilloried as an unnatural mother, and the scandal caused her a great deal of pain.[30] But it also put her in the position of having nothing to lose by speaking out.

"The Yellow Wallpaper" (1892) describes the rest cure of S. Weir Mitchell that Gilman had herself undergone, and the conclusion provides an indication of what Gilman believed would have been the result for herself if she had remained in a marriage that was so destructive of the self. Instead of accepting the definition of womanhood that destroys her protagonist, Gilman fractured the concept of gender to redefine womanhood. Having learned from her own experience the stultifying effect of passive dependence and nonactivity, Gilman, in her life and in her work, asserted woman's need for independence.

Whereas Alcott had difficulty envisioning a married woman's economic independence, Gilman was able to imagine a future that contained a realistic process by which it might be realized. Gilman's ideas are expressed in her fiction and in her nonfiction. Her most complete statement of her ideas is contained in her nonfictional work *Women and Economics*, published in 1898. She began with the assertion that human beings are affected more by "economic conditions" than by any other force.[31] In language reminiscent of Marx (although she was not a Marxist), Gilman pointed out that women's labor "is the property of another" (7). Like Marx also, she emphasized a historical imperative. For Gilman, however, this was not a class issue but a gendered social issue (138). Nor is the issue women's political freedom. Instead of focusing on the vote, she focused on economics: progress, she said, will come only when "both men and women stand equal in economic relation" (340).

How did Gilman reconcile women's work with marriage and motherhood? Unlike Fern, who ridiculed her critics into silence, or Harper, whose belief in women's self-sufficiency was complicated by a belief in the importance of the married woman's domestic role, or Alcott who could only look toward a visionary future, Gilman proposed a practical change in living arrangements. In *Women and Economics*, Gilman developed a plan in which families and individuals would live in kitchenless apartments or kitchenless suburban houses constructed around a central food-supply building. The food would be centrally prepared by professional nutritionists and served in community dining rooms. The dwellings would be cleaned professionally, and each complex would provide professional child-care services in nurseries within the building complex (241–245).[32] Women, thus freed of housework, cooking, and constant child care, would be able to have meaningful and fulfilling employment outside the home, from which they would derive financial remuneration that would enable them to be economically independent in the marriage relation. Moreover, said Gilman, her plan would enhance traditional values like marriage, motherhood, and the home; women would be better wives and mothers because of it (289–290, 312–315). On the one hand, such an assertion was Gilman's way of placating critics by demonstrating that the goal of her plan was not to destroy the institution of marriage. At the same time, however, it is a radical redefinition of gender identity: in Gilman's discourse the terms *wife* and *mother* no longer connote the discursive construction of the dependent "angel in the parlor." "The Yellow Wallpaper," then, although it is powerful as a repudiation of the Mitchell "rest cure," is even more powerful as a searing portrayal of the nineteenth-century middle-class woman's life, in which the woman was confined to the home sphere and treated like a child. For both Fern and Gilman, the solution to what they considered a madness-inducing situation was economic independence.

The concept of economic independence for women was a threat to traditional nineteenth-century society. And it is in dealing with the fears engendered by this threat that Fern and Gilman differ. Fern's method of dealing with her critics was assertion and argument, revelation and ridicule. She would assert what for her were obvious truths, present her case with terse but cogent arguments, and portray the folly and injustice of traditional practice, ridiculing with her scathing satire those whose shortsightedness, brutality, or selfishness prevented them from seeing the necessity for change. Fern was not a theorist; her ideas derived from the exigencies of experience and were practical "what-can-we-do-now" ideas. Gilman, on the other hand, was a theorist. She attempted to provide answers to the objections and developed plans to implement her theories. In this respect, Gilman, who was born fifty years after Fern, continued the deviant tradition, carrying it a step further—from assertion and ridicule to concrete plans for change.

Although Gilman's thinking has been characterized as utopian, she was not presenting a fairy-tale vision of society. In examining Gilman's thinking, we must recognize three important factors. First of all, she provided a concrete and in many respects workable plan that made it possible to conceptualize the economic independence of women as a real possibility. Second, she met the potential objections of her critics by incorporating into her plan carefully presented arguments demonstrating ways in which her plan not only would not attack but would in fact enhance traditional values like marriage, motherhood, and the home.

And finally, she portrayed her plan as part of the inexorable forces of history, which made her ideas not only desirable but necessary and inevitable.

Gilman begins her book with the observation that human beings "are the only animal species in which the female depends on the male for food, the only animal species in which a sex-relation is also an economic relation. With us an entire sex lives in a relation of economic dependence upon the other sex" (5). Women, she said, "work under another will, and what they receive depends not on their labor, but on the power and will of another" (7). Gilman also emphasizes a historical imperative. She says that the subjection of women has been necessary to socialize the male: history has forced the naturally aggressive and selfish male to be the caretaker of the female in order to teach him nurturing traits. Women, she says, should not be resentful of the centuries of subjection, because cruel as this dominance has been, it was necessary for the development of the species. Moreover, it will soon be over: "The period of women's economic dependence is drawing to a close, because its racial usefulness [i.e., its usefulness for the human race] is wearing out" (137–138). For Gilman, this is a social issue (138). The issue is not women's political freedom. "The woman's movement," she says, "proclaims 'equality before the law,' woman's start in political freedom; but the main line of progress is and has been toward economic equality and freedom" (144).

Gilman was very specific in outlining the ways in which the economically freed woman will be a better mother. The effect on children of having mothers who are dependent, limited, and demanding, is harmful, she said; the mother should be freed for several hours each day to be a human being "as a member of a civilized community, as an economic producer, as a growing, self-realizing individual" (289–290). Then she will return to her children with an "eager, ceaseless pleasure" (290). Moreover, said Gilman, it will aid in the uplifting of the species for children to see their mothers as producers instead of only as consumers. Our present family life breeds selfishness, she said, and our present retardation of women breeds timidity and passive characteristics into the human race: "The economically independent mother, widened and freed, strengthened and developed by her social service, will do better service as mother than it has been possible to her before. No one thing could do more to advance the interests of humanity" (293–294). With respect to marriage, women will choose their husbands for self, not for support (315), Gilman wrote, and women will not need to be manipulative and conniving in order to obtain their goals. Consequently, she predicted, marriage will be happier, freer—a partnership between two independent individuals instead of the current master-slave relationship that degrades women and corrupts both partners as well as their children. Even more important, maintained Gilman, women thus freed will contribute to the betterment of the human race. She concludes the book with these words: "Progress . . . will flow on smoothly and rapidly when both men and women stand equal in economic relation. When the mother of the [human] race is free, we shall have a better world, by the easy right of birth and by the calm, slow, friendly forces of social evolution" (340).

This is the plan as it is outlined in *Women and Economics*. Gilman's ideas are also clear from her fiction. In story after story, Gilman portrays the solution to women's dilemma: the woman needs to find something practical to do that will enable her to earn money of her own. As long as she is dependent, she cannot realize autonomy in her own life. In the story "Making a Change" (1911), the young mother and her mother-in-law were unhappy, and the wife was ready to commit suicide. Instead, they both begin separate careers, which results in happiness for all. Even the husband realizes the wisdom of the change. In the story "An Honest Woman" (1911), the deserted woman who has made herself financially independent and educated her daughter refuses to take back her errant lover. She has gained self-respect and dignity. In the story "Turned" (1911), the wife leaves her husband after he seduces their servant girl; she independently follows a teaching career and refuses to go back to her husband, whom she now despises because he has misused his power. In the short story "The Widow's Might" (1911), the grown children discuss the problem of caring for their newly widowed mother, wrestling with the question of who will take her and who will pay. Their mother surprises them by revealing that during her husband's long illness she had taken control of the estate and had earned so much money that she can now take care of herself. The widow will not be dependent upon the goodwill of her grown children; because she has money, she can call the shots herself.[33]

In *Benigna Machiavelli* (1914), a novel based on Gilman's revision of her own life, Gilman portrays a woman who asserts her independence. Her name suggests that although nineteenth-century patriarchal culture would regard such a woman as Machiavellian, Gilman believes her influence is in fact benign. Benigna tricks her cruel father into leaving the house and establishes her long-suffering mother in a successful business, which gives her mother autonomy and the strength of character and personality that were lacking when she was passively dependent. Then Benigna goes out into the world to educate herself "to grow." "I want to be a *worthy* person," she says. "To be a plus and not a minus. Not to spend my days wanting things and hanging on to other people."[34]

Some of Gilman's fiction specifically portrays aspects of the plan outlined in her nonfiction. In the novel *What Diantha Did* (1910), Diantha establishes a food supply and housecleaning business, which provides a model for the kind of centrally organized preparation of nutritional food and professional housecleaning that would be available to communities of people in the plan Gilman outlined in *Women and Economics*. Diantha herself is a model of the economically independent woman. She refuses to marry unless her husband will recognize the need for her to continue her successful business, and even after they are married and have children, Diantha continues to work. Her husband finally acknowledges the "brave, strong, valuable work" she has been doing.[35] Gilman's ideas for a new community are concretely portrayed in her utopian novel, *Moving the Mountain* (1911). People live in an apartment complex such as she described in *Women and Economics*. There are no household chores, and healthy food is prepared professionally. The reader, along with the narrator, John, who is visiting the new society, is shown the wonders of technology and planning that make the society possible. The narrator ultimately chooses to join the new society after becoming disgusted with the dirt, the tensions, the ignorance, and the badly cooked food of the old society. The difference for women is summed up in his comparison between his cousin, Drusilla, who has lived a wholly domestic life, and the women in the new society: "I thought of them, those busy, vigorous, eager active women, of whom no one would ever predicate either youth or age; they were just women, permanently, as men were men. I thought of their wide, free lives, their absorbing work and many minor interests."³⁶ At the end of the novel, he marries his Drusilla and takes her back to live in the new society, where he is astounded at her metamorphosis: "Nobody would know Drusilla now. She grew young at a rate that seemed a heavenly miracle. . . . I grew to find the world like heaven, too—if only for what it did to Drusilla" (290). Gilman's most well known utopian novel is *Herland* (1915). In this novel three men stumble upon a community of women in which children are born through parthenogenesis. The women have created a "perfect" society: there is no violence or inequality, and all members of the society contribute to the well-being of the community.³⁷

Like Frances Harper, Gilman devoted her life to cultural work. She wrote fiction and nonfiction, she edited and wrote most of the articles in her own periodical, *The Forerunner*, for seven years, and she lectured all across the United States and in Europe. All of her work focused on the theme that to her was crucial to humanity: the old patriarchal system of society was deteriorating and destructive and needed to be replaced by a system of gender equality. As she wrote in her autobiography, *The Living of Charlotte Perkins Gilman* (1935), there was no reason "to write, [or] to talk, without a purpose."³⁸

Today's reader, accustomed to dismissing as visionary and impractical the ideas represented in utopian fiction, might ask, How workable is Gilman's plan? Interestingly enough, the basic outlines of Gilman's plan are very workable indeed. In fact, although many of us might not realize it, the plan—just as Gilman devised it—has actually been put into practice in today's society—not for working women, however, but for the elderly. My aunt and uncle own a condominium in a retirement community that is very similar to the complex that Gilman devised. They have an almost kitchenless apartment. There are a small refrigerator and top-of-the-stove burners so that they can make light snacks. But all of the food for their meals is centrally and professionally prepared. They eat in a community dining room. Their apartment is professionally cleaned. There are service facilities within the complex, not for child care—since that is not a requirement of the elderly—but for on-site professional health service, which is a requirement of the elderly. They have a car and can come and go as they please. Not everyone might choose to own an apartment in this kind of complex, but the fact that this plan works indicates that Gilman's plan could be put into effect without much difficulty to provide living quarters for families and individuals—particularly working mothers of families—who wish to be free of the necessity of cooking, cleaning, and constant child care but also wish to have good food and reliable child-care facilities on the premises. The surprising thing is that it has not been done.

Gilman was not talking about utopian communal living; she did not like it, and she did not think that any system would work that depended upon cooperative living because there were too many problems deriving from differences in personality and the difficulty of people shirking responsibility. The driving force behind her plan was a problem that still has not been met today: how to free women of domestic responsibilities so that they can do meaningful and financially rewarding work outside the home without relying on makeshift, costly, or inefficient child care and without burdening themselves with overwhelming responsibilities by trying to do it all—housework, mothering, cooking, and working outside the home besides. Unlike Fern, who urged fathers to help with child rearing and domestic chores, Gilman does not address the issue of fathers sharing these responsibilities. But many women who work are single mothers, and in their case, there is no father to help out. Moreover, even in families in which fathers do share family responsibilities, unless the father is a househusband or the parents work on alternating schedules, there will be no one at home for some of the time. Gilman's plan addresses a problem that we are still struggling to solve.

Critics of Gilman's work have objected that her plan is primarily a white middle-class plan that would not benefit people of color or the working class. With respect to class differences, however, an important part of Gilman's thinking was the concern that society must be changed in order to eliminate class inequities. In *With Her in Our Land* (1910), the sequel to *Herland*, for example, she stated that democracy was not possible as long as class inequities were tolerated.[39] Moreover, in *What Diantha Did*, Diantha's plan for developing a food supply business frees working women from exploitative labor in individual homes and gives them professional careers with good wages and respectful treatment. Finally, in her utopian fiction Gilman attempted to eradicate class differences entirely. In *Herland*, for example, as the male visitors note, "our tutors seemed of rather finer quality than the guards, though all were on terms of easy friendliness" (32). In other words, the outsider notes a difference in "quality" (education, manner, etc.), but the Herlanders treat one another as equals in this apparently classless society.

More problematic among the criticisms of Gilman today is the accusation that Gilman was racist and/or anti-Semitic.[40] In *With Her in Our Land* Gilman comments that "only some of the races—or individuals in a given race—have reached the democratic stage" (121), and although she decries the exploitation of immigrants and asserts that children must be brought up without prejudice against Jews or blacks, her comments reveal the extent of her own ethnocentrism (119–120, 160–166). Although she envisioned a society in which class differences and ethnic, racial, or religious differences would be eradicated, she viewed the solution from the situatedness of her own background. This reminds us that however advanced her ideas were for her time, she was also a product of her time and place.

Gilman was much more adept at stepping outside her society's construction of gender. In her fiction she presents powerful arguments against essentialized femininity. In *Herland*, for example, the male narrator notes that the women there lack "femininity" and concludes that what he and other men regard as feminine traits are imposed on women by men: "This led me very promptly to the conviction that those 'feminine charms' we are so fond of are not feminine at all, but merely reflected masculinity—developed to please us because they had to please us" (73). The men note that specific faults that they had previously assumed were characteristic of all women are lacking in Herland: pettiness is replaced by social consciousness, vanity of dress is replaced by a simplicity of dress, jealousy is replaced by sisterly affection, and hysteria is replaced by calm (81). What the nineteenth-century regarded as inherently "feminine," Gilman insists, was socially constructed.

If Gilman did not accept compulsory femininity, she also questioned compulsory heterosexuality. Although assumed by most critics to be heterosexual, Gilman wrote many stories in which the relationships between women were stronger than those between men and women. Moreover, she herself had several intense relationships with women, including Martha Luther, Grace Channing, and Adeline Knapp. Most critics have treated these relationships as nonsexual female relationships, in the tradition of nineteenth-century "female love and ritual."[41] Yet the intensity of the relationships Gilman portrayed in her fiction and the importance of the relationships in her personal life suggest that more is involved. In addition, as Barbara White points out, Gilman confessed in a letter to her second husband that at least one of the relationships was sexual.[42] In 1900 Gilman wrote to Houghton Gilman of her two-year relationship with Adeline Knapp in 1891–1892: "I loved her that way," she said, and indicated that she was afraid that if the newspapers found out, they would write sensational stories about "Mrs. Stetson's Love Affair with a woman."[43] If, then, Gilman was herself lesbian or bisexual, why did she not write more explicitly of this aspect of difference? The answer may be, as Mary A. Hill suggests, that Gilman knew that radical statements about sexuality would have destroyed her credibility and prevented her from getting her message across: "The resulting scandal almost certainly would have discredited her life and work."[44] If Gilman did not explicitly advocate lesbian relationships, her awareness of an alternate sexuality enriched her ability to critique cultural definitions of female identity. Writing to her friend Grace Channing before Grace married Gilman's ex-husband, Walter Stetson, she indicated that it was Grace she would miss, not Walter, and articulated her awareness that her feelings did not conform to those prescribed for her as a woman: "Do you know I think I suffer more in giving you up than in Walter—for you were all joy to me. It is awful to be a man inside and not be able to marry the woman you love!"[45] A woman who feels like "a man inside" knows that cultural definitions of "woman" are suspect.

It was partly because of her ability to question gender identity that Gilman was able to envision a society in which women are economically independent. "Women," she said, "are not undeveloped men"; they are "undeveloped humans."[46] Moreover, because of her ability to see the present as part of a historical progression, Gilman could recognize that woman's cultural role was historically defined. In *Women and Economics* she points out that women have been "imprisoned" in historical time, and their traits are the result of their specific present: "The sexuo-economic relation has debarred [woman] from the social activities in which, and in which alone, are developed the social virtues. She has not been allowed to acquire the qualities needed in our racial advance;[47] and, in her position of arrested development, she has maintained the virtues and the vices of the period of human evolution at which she was imprisoned" (329–330).

Fern, Gilman, and Alcott all recognized the problem inherent in women's dependence and asserted the need for women's economic independence, but they differed principally in two respects. In one respect, Fern and Gilman were more radical than Alcott. Alcott, in her popular novels, was more cautious in her call for female power and independence than she was in her adult novels and in her pseudonymous fiction. And whereas Fern asserted the need for women's economic independence and Gilman was able to envision a workable plan for women's continual employment, Alcott had a difficult time reconciling the idea of marriage and motherhood with economic independence. However, in another respect Fern and Alcott might be said to have been more radical than Gilman. Whereas Gilman emphasized the need for professional women to work outside the home, Fern and Alcott were more concerned with the need to help working women and identified with the wage-earning woman rather than with the middle-class professional woman.

Fern, Alcott, and Gilman all recognized the vulnerability of the woman who was economically dependent, insisting that it was only after she acquired money of her own that a woman gained the power of self-determination. Radical spokespersons for an idea that was revolutionary in their time, they deconstructed the substantive appearance of gender, revealing that gender identity in their culture had been discursively produced. Refusing to reify cultural notions of identity, they fractured the concept of gender to assert the economics of independence for women. Fanny Fern wrote in the *New York Ledger* in 1869, "I want all women to render themselves independent of marriage as a mere means of support." Charlotte Perkins Gilman attempted to show us one way that it could be done.

INTO THE
TWENTY-FIRST
CENTURY

In their recognition of the necessity of economic independence for women, Fern, Alcott, and Gilman, along with African American writers like Harper and Jacobs, took a stand on an issue that was counter to the dominant discourse throughout the nineteenth century. Moreover, many of the women in the court cases in this study lived independently, coping with the legal and economic restraints of their culture while making money for themselves and, in most cases, for their families as well. At the same time, many women writers, even when they did not publicly advocate economic independence for women, supported themselves and their families and in their fiction portrayed the importance of money in women's lives. Women who could not write their names and women who lived in comfort, white women and women of color, urban women and farm wives, independent businesswomen and abused wives—women from all backgrounds were very much a part of the money economy. The nature of their involvement was as varied as their backgrounds and ranged from the flounderings of women who were defeated by ignorance or placidity to the successes of astute businesswomen, some of whom were as ruthless and callous as the most hardened businessmen.

Yet twentieth- and twenty-first-century scholars have had difficulty recognizing the complexity of women's economic roles in the nineteenth century. Earlier critics romanticized women as removed from the marketplace, victims of an unjust legal and economic system, while more recent scholars, seeking to give women agency, identified middle- and upper-class women as self-oriented consumers, complicitous in the maintenance of capitalism. What my findings show is that women were both and neither; the victim could also be agent, while the woman who seemed to have agency was herself powerless within the system. But most of all, what my research has shown is that, in spite of cultural prescriptions that constructed women as outside the economy except as exploited workers, many women were actively involved in money matters of their own. Moreover, evidence of this tendency was apparent in every class. Generalizations about women's involvement with money lose sight of these complexities because they do not allow room for the many and varied ways in which individual women resolved their economic situations. It is for this reason that I chose to examine a multiplicity of individual court cases and a multiplicity of writers and fictional works. It is their *particularity* that is significant, yet it is this very particularity that can be lost in too-easy generalizations. By combining a study of the court cases with a look at the lives and works of a broad selection of fiction writers, what I have attempted to do (to borrow a phrase from Harriet Jacobs) is to give the twenty-first-century reader "a realizing sense" of what nineteenth-century women's lives were like with respect to economics.[1] What emerges from this study, is, I think, a closer approximation of the lived situation than we have previously been able to obtain.

But this study is important not only as a corrective to prevailing views of nineteenth-century women but also as a backdrop to women's economic situation in the twentieth century and today. Although women writers were wrestling with the question of woman's economic independence throughout the nineteenth century—and the court cases reveal that many ordinary nineteenth-century women were living their lives independently in spite of law and custom—the concept of woman's financial independence remained flagged by a question mark in the greater culture throughout most of the twentieth century. Just how problematic this issue has been is suggested by the following passage from a letter written by a liberal former congressman from Wisconsin in the mid-twentieth century. On August 15, 1954, a hundred years after the publication of Fanny Fern's *Ruth Hall*, Tom Amlie wrote to his son Tom regarding Tom's wife, Polly, who apparently wanted to finish college and get a job. Amlie wrote: "This determination on Polly's part to be in control took the form of an attitude of *self indulgence*. Polly told me that she considered her own career to be as important as your career. There is no use in going into the *absurdity* of that statement" [my italics].[2]

The author of this letter was no timid conservative. He was a radical lawyer whose support of "production for use" as opposed to the profit motive in capitalism in the 1930s had prevented him from realizing a successful political career. He was too radical for either political party, but his radicalism obviously did not include looking at women as autonomous beings. A sad footnote to the 1954 letter is a letter from his own wife ten years earlier, begging him to let her have a regular allowance and not make her have to plead for money for household expenses. Sounding very much like the nineteenth-century woman who had to "beg, tease, or wheedle" for her money, Mrs. Amlie describes her own humiliation: "I have *no* feeling of independence. I must ask you every other day for a few dollars."[3]

At the time that Amlie was writing his letter to his son and Mrs. Amlie was describing a situation that Fern had argued against a hundred years before, women had obtained the vote, and a married woman's earnings were no longer the legal property of her husband. Yet apparently little had changed with respect to cultural attitudes toward the question of woman's economic independence. How much have they changed today? And even if they have changed in view of the economic necessity of two-paycheck families, what about practical concerns? Today most people in the United States would agree that women have the right to independent employment. Women—married and single, white women and women of color, lesbian women and heterosexual women, middle-class women and working-class women—are working today. Still, how much do cultural attitudes support women's economic independence?

Unfortunately, the "absurdity" that Tom Amlie associated with women's independence, and his assertion that his daughter-in-law's wish to be economically independent was an "attitude of self indulgence," are still with us today. Today, however, the condescension implicit in such attitudes more often takes the form of hostility. As more and more women have managed to make woman's economic independence a reality, the concept is no longer simply absurd; it is often perceived as threatening. In an interview in *Currency* magazine in 1998, for example, a white male financial writer asserted that men often do not find successful women attractive. A woman's self-sufficiency, he said, keeps men away. "How can he [a man] prove he is competent," he asked, "if she has the money?"[4] Or, as African American writer Michael Dyson put it in his 2003 defense of black women, among black men there is a lamentable prevalence of "black male resentment of black female achievement."[5] Comments such as these reflect the cultural attitude that women, if they are financially successful—particularly if they are more successful than the man—somehow pose a threat to a man's "manhood." A 2004 study among undergraduates at the University of Michigan's Institute for Social Research found that the young men in the study were wary of successful women; although they were not averse to one-night stands with such women, they indicated that they would prefer to marry "less accomplished women."[6] Not only have individual men expressed resentment toward successful women, but cultural attitudes in general reflect this hostility. Hillary Rodham Clinton was demonized by many for seeming too "independent" and not "domestic" enough as the wife of the president, even though she had given up her law practice, unlike Cherie Booth, who, as the wife of British Prime Minister Tony Blair, retained not only her maiden name but her judgeship. In fact, it was only after Hillary Clinton was perceived as a "victim" of her husband's infidelity that she gained more widespread approval—although she lost some of that when she aggressively ran for and was elected to the U.S. Senate. Similarly, the missteps of women entrepreneurs like Leona Helmsley (dubbed "The Queen of Mean") and Martha Stewart in recent years have caused them to be vilified by the press in far greater proportion than the corporate businessmen who have broken the law.

In spite of cultural attitudes that still do not regard financially independent women favorably, however, women themselves have increasingly indicated that economic concerns are one of their foremost priorities. In opinion polls, women have said that what upsets them the most is their lack of money, and 80 to 95 percent say they suffer from job discrimination and unequal pay.[7] An AFL-CIO study in 1997 showed that 94 percent of American women saw "equal pay for equal work" as their top priority.[8] In recent years also there has been a greater recognition of women's need and desire to function independently with money. Evidence of this growing interest in women and money is all around us: the American Association of University Women is developing a financial literacy curriculum for women; Web sites on the subject are proliferating;

entrepreneurial summer camps for girls are expanding; and private girls' schools (where the curriculum is not tied to state mandates as it is in public schools) are introducing courses in financial planning for girls.[9] Yet the majority of working women remain in the lowest-paying jobs. Of the top twenty occupations that women hold, all but three are female dominated, and among African American women, of the top ten jobs, all are female dominated.[10] In 2001, the number of working women earning more than $78,000 a year was just two and a half times greater than the number earning only $7,800 a year; among working men, however, the number earning more than $78,000 a year was fourteen times greater than the number earning only $7,800 a year.[11] For the most part, women are clustered near the bottom of the pay scale: five times as many men who work full-time earn a salary of more than $75,000 than do women who work full time.[12] The median earnings of women who work full-time is 72 percent of men's earnings.[13] Moreover, studies have shown that after divorce women's standard of living typically nose-dives while that of men rises. Lenore Weitzman, in her study of twenty-five hundred California court cases, discovered that within the first year after divorce, women's standard of living fell by more than 70 percent, whereas men's rose by more than 40 percent.[14]

Not only do cultural attitudes and salary inequities continue to stand in the way of women's financial independence, but the practical concern of child care remains a serious obstacle for many women. During World War II, the federal government set up a system of day-care facilities to enable women to work in the defense plants and heavy industry. With funding from the Lanham Act and the Works Progress Administration—the WPA—the government established more than 3,000 child-care centers nationwide, which served 130,000 children, in addition to an Extended School Services program, which served 320,000 school-age and preschool children. According to the U.S. Children's Bureau, at the peak of the war effort in July 1945 there were 1.6 million children in federally funded child-care facilities.[15] After the war was over, however, the facilities were disbanded, and the women were laid off and told to go back home. The fact is, though, that many of the women did not go home. They found other jobs—jobs that did not pay nearly as well as the "men's jobs" they had held during the war. Since then, the number of women working outside the home has steadily grown so that today two-thirds of all women over the age of sixteen are working.[16] Of those women who are working full-time outside the home, almost 40 percent have children under eighteen, and 59 percent of all women with infants under the age of one are in the labor force.[17]

What do women do with their children when they are at work? Some women have nannies or send their children to day care. But nannies and good day care are expensive. The average annual cost of one child in a day-care facility in almost half of the states is more than a year's tuition at a public college, and among low-income single mothers, child care "consumes nearly twenty percent of their income."[18] Most women's finances do not permit expensive child-care services, and they must rely on a hodgepodge of inadequate arrangements—babysitters, neighbors, relatives, and, when he is on the scene and not at work himself (and is willing), a husband or boyfriend. That cultural attitudes influence the failure of governmental institutions to provide child care as they did during World War II when it was necessary for the "war effort" is apparent in the "work-fare" legislation of 1996, which mandated that a woman must get a job after two years on welfare but did not make adequate provision for childcare for working mothers leaving welfare and did nothing at all for other low-income women.[19]

Child care is clearly a problem for working-class mothers, but most professional women have not solved the child-care problem either. Just how problematic it is is apparent from the difficulty that presidents have had in making cabinet appointments to women who are mothers. In 1993, then-President Clinton, who wanted to appoint a woman as attorney general, found that he could not appoint a woman who was a mother because too many professional women who were mothers had employed undocumented caregivers and had not paid them social security wages. His first two appointees (Zoe Baird and Kimba Wood) were rejected, and he solved the problem by appointing Janet Reno, an unmarried woman with no children. Similarly, President George W. Bush appointed Condoleezza Rice as national security advisor and then secretary of state, but she too is unmarried with no children. The shortage of women with young children in high-level jobs suggests that the question of how to reconcile outside employment with a family continues to be a problem for working women. Lisa Belkin, in an October 2003 *New York Times* article, "The Opt-Out Revolution," notes that "the talk of this new decade is less about the obstacles faced by women than it is about the obstacles faced by mothers."[20] As Joan C. Williams, director of the Program on WorkLife Law at American University, wrote in the *Harvard Women's Law Journal*, "[m]any women never get near" the glass ceiling; "they are stopped long before by the maternal wall"; or, as Sylvia Ann Hewlett pointed out in her book *Creating a Life* (2002), the more successful women are, the less likely they are to have children."[21]

For too long, women have been left on their own to solve child-care problems as best they can. Women have been told they can work, and many of them have to work. But little has been done to make the prospect easier. In 1899 Gilman wrote in *Women and Economics* of her plan for apartment buildings for working women: "If there should be built and opened in any of our large cities today a commodious apartment house [with professional cooking, cleaning, and child-care services] for women with families, it would be filled at once" (242). I suspect that this is even more true today. The principal opposition to such a plan for kitchenless apartments on a wide scale would probably come from the manufacturers of kitchen appliances. Gilman's plan might not work for everybody, but it provides one alternative to the present situation, in which more than three million children are regularly left to care for themselves, and mothers must make decisions that either put their children or their jobs at risk—particularly difficult decisions when the job is necessary to support the children.[22] In one respect, plans like Gilman's have not gained wide approval because of the hard-core strain of individualism running through American culture. Americans shy away from anything that smacks of communal living. Even Gilman herself was opposed to communal living; her plan was designed to provide quality support for individual families, not to force people into what she regarded as unworkable cooperative arrangements.

But it is not only the fear of communal living that has kept Americans from doing something that would help mothers to work outside the home. The federally funded child-care facilities during World War II did not require communal living; they were at the work site instead of the home. Some of the centers even provided other aspects of Gilman's plan: home-cooked meals for the mother to pick up when she picked up her child at the end of her shift, and professionally trained teachers and nutritionists who were very well paid.[23] The main reason why the wartime child-care facilities were closed down after the war was that the country as a whole did not want to encourage women to work outside the home. Not only did the government want to free-up jobs for the returning servicemen, but Americans generally did not like the idea of women working for money. A *Fortune* magazine poll after World War II indicated that most Americans did not approve of married women working for wages and stressed that mothers should stay home to care for their children.[24] The chairman of the Womanpower Committee of the War Manpower Commission reported in 1944 that there was "alarm" at the "new independence that has come to married women from their experience as wage earners," and a New York newspaper charged that the idea of day care was a "communist plot."[25] In fact, when the facilities were initially proposed, their advocates were careful to propound other reasons than the benefits to working mothers as the rationale for the centers. They stressed the "educational" benefits for the children and the need for women's labor for the defense of the nation.[26] After the war, there was an attempt by some to maintain the child-care system, but the emphasis on "motherhood" and "family" won out. Within a few years after the war, all but a few of the centers had been closed, leaving more than a million working mothers without adequate child-care services.[27]

The principal reason why Americans have not moved forward with child care as many other countries have done is that American cultural attitudes still highlight a woman's domesticity to such an extent that independent work is constructed as "self-indulgent" in women.[28] As Mary Frances Berry points out in *The Politics of Parenthood* (1993), if Americans were not so ambivalent about child care, they would have "found the money in the budget to pay the costs." What has retarded the process, she says, is the "deep ambivalence and well-entrenched attitudes about gender roles and the care of children."[29] Our culture has conditioned women to believe that they are nurturers, not money earners. In 2003 a nationwide study of forty-two hundred teenagers found that whereas 70 percent of the boys said that the most important factor in choosing a career was to make money, 73 percent of the girls said that the principal factor in their choice of career was the "desire to help others."[30] The altruism of the girls' response is noble, but as long as the same proportion of boys do not have the same response as the girls, we cannot assume that cultural conditioning is equally applied by gender.

Ultimately, the value of this study of nineteenth-century women's experience in relation to money lies in the example that these women provide—not only for women but for any group that has to struggle against a socially constructed identity which seeks to restrict people's achievement. In spite of the most egregious gender restrictions of law and custom, many nineteenth-century women lived independently, managing their lives and their money with courage and tenacity and fracturing constructed gender identities by their lived experience. They did what Fanny Fern advised in 1870: "*Take* your rights, my sisters; don't beg for them! Never mind what objectors say or think. Success will soon shut their mouths."[31] And if success does not "shut their mouths," said Fern in 1866, women who are successful do not have to worry about narrow-minded criticism: "They can stand the spiteful criticism with a good house over their independent heads, secured and paid for by their own honest industry . . . with greenbacks and Treasury notes stowed away against a rainy day."[32] Few nineteenth-century women were able to attain Fern's success, but like the self-sufficient Mary Trust in her fourteen-year-long pursuit of justice, many were able to support themselves and even to turn the law to their own advantage. Even when defeated by the law and an abusive husband, Kate Heermance, a factory worker whose 1864 court case is discussed in chapter 6, could bravely and proudly assert her independence: "When I worked at Stotts [factory] I worked for my board and that of my child. I can average from $25 to $30 per month. I can paint and sew. I can take care of myself and of these two children with all ease. All I wish is to be left alone." These words echo throughout women's work space today, from factories to boardrooms, underscoring the perseverance of women who, although still handicapped by cultural attitudes regarding gender, continue to, as Fanny Fern said, "take their rights."

Reading these nineteenth-century legal documents alongside the literary texts, then, helps to concretize the historical, economic, and legal context within which the literary texts were produced. The juxtaposition not only illuminates the legal inequities that underlay the economic structure but provides a rare glimpse into nineteenth-century gender identities while affording important insights into the cultural attitudes that still determine governmental policy today.

NOTES

Introduction | FRACTURING GENDER

1. Charlotte Perkins Gilman, "If I Were a Man," *The Charlotte Perkins Gilman Reader*, ed. Ann J. Lane (New York: Pantheon Books, 1980), 33–34.

2. Charlotte Perkins Gilman, *The Living of Charlotte Perkins Gilman* (1935; New York: Arno Press, 1972), 131.

3. The ubiquitousness of the nineteenth-century emphasis on domesticity for women across lines of class and race is discussed more fully in chapter 2. The construction of gendered spheres is, of course, not unique to American experience. One explanation for the origin of the differentiation between men's and women's roles is contained in the time-discipline studies of historian E. P. Thompson. In his influential essay "Time, Work-Discipline, and Industrial Capitalism," *Past & Present, A Journal of Historical Studies* 38 (December 1967): 56–97, Thompson noted that in the eighteenth century in England, and subsequently in other countries as they became (and are becoming) industrialized, the natural work rhythms of task-work were replaced by time-discipline. As men were integrated into a time-discipline system, however, says Thompson, women's work in the home remained task oriented (78–79). A late-nineteenth-century theory regarding the enforced economic dependency of women is that of Thorstein Veblen, who noted in his *Theory of the Leisure Class* that in capitalist societies the economic dependency of women, their enforced leisure, was perceived as a necessary gauge of men's prosperity and success. Thorstein Veblen, *The Theory of the Leisure Class* (1899; New York: Modern Library, 1934), e.g., 354–355. Critics in various disciplines have called attention to a causal relationship in Western society between capitalism and what psychologist Kaja Silverman identifies in *Male Subjectivity at the Margins* (New York: Routledge, 1992) as the "dominant fiction" of masculine privilege and feminine "lack" (16, 49).

4. In "The Discourse on Language," Michel Foucault designates as "systems of exclusion" the methods used by the dominant culture to silence counterdiscourse. See *The Archaeology of Knowledge*, trans. A. M. Sheridan Smith (New York: Pantheon Books, 1972), 215–220.

5. Lora Romero, *Home Fronts: Domesticity and Its Critics in the Antebellum United States* (Durham: Duke University Press, 1997), e.g., 11–12.

6. For significant analyses of the debate concerning the separate spheres binary in American literature and culture, see, e.g., the essays in *No More Separate Spheres!: A Next Wave American Studies Reader*, eds. Cathy N. Davidson and Jessamyn Hatcher (Durham: Duke University Press, 2002). Particularly effective for its clarity in stating the complexities of the debate is the editors' introduction (7–26). Their essay collection is expanded from a forum in *American Literature* 70 (September 1998). For a deconstruction of the concept of separate spheres in the antebellum period, see the forum in *Journal of the Early Republic* 21 (Spring 2001): 71–124. In addition, the *Journal of Women's History* 14 (Spring 2002) contains a retrospective on Barbara Welter's influential essay "The Cult of True Womanhood: 1820–1860," *American Quarterly* 18 (Summer 1966): 151–174. See also *Separate Spheres No More: Gender Convergence in American Literature, 1830–1930*, ed. Monika M. Elbert (Tuscaloosa: University of Alabama Press, 2000). Other critiques of the separate spheres model include the following: Michelle Rosaldo, "The Use and Abuse of Anthropology: Reflections on Feminism and Cross-Cultural Understanding," *Signs* 5 (Spring 1980): 389–417, which points out that such a paradigm "simply reflects the prevailing gender belief system" (399–400); Elizabeth Blackmar, *Manhattan for Rent, 1785–1850* (Ithaca: Cornell University Press, 1989), which stresses that the separate spheres model does not reflect the "social reality" (112, 126); Lora Romero, *Home Fronts*, cited above; and Amy Dru Stanley, "Home Life and Morality," *The Market Revolution in America: Social, Political, and Religious Expressions, 1800–1880*, eds. Melvyn Stokes and Stephen Conway (Charlottesville: University Press of Virginia, 1996), 78–81. Of particular importance is the essay by Linda K. Kerber, "Separate Spheres, Female Worlds, Woman's Place: The Rhetoric of Women's History," *Journal of American History* 75 (June 1988): 9–39, reprinted in *No More Separate Spheres!*, 29–65. Critiques of the separate spheres model by African American feminists include *All the Women Are White, All the Blacks Are Men, But Some of Us Are Brave*, eds. Gloria T. Hull, Patricia Bell Scott, and Barbara Smith (Old Westbury, NY: Feminist Press, 1982) and Hazel V. Carby, *Reconstructing Womanhood: The Emergence of the Afro-American Woman Novelist* (New York: Oxford University Press, 1987).

7. Numerous critics have noted women's participation in the public sphere as reformers, writers, suffragists, etc., for example, Mary Kelley, *Private Woman, Public Stage: Literary Domesticity in Nineteenth-Century America* (New York: Oxford University Press, 1984); Kathryn Kish Sklar, "Hull House in the 1890s: A Community of Women Reformers," *Signs* 10 (Summer 1985): 658–677; Mary Ryan, *Women in Public: Between Banners and Ballots, 1825–1880* (Baltimore: Johns Hopkins University Press, 1990); Dorothy Helly and Susan M. Reverby, "Introduction:

Converging on History," *Gendered Domains: Rethinking Public and Private in Women's History*, eds. Dorothy O. Helly and Susan M. Reverby (Ithaca: Cornell University Press, 1992), 1–27; Nina Baym, *American Women Writers and the Work of History, 1790–1860* (New Brunswick: Rutgers University Press, 1995); and Nicole Tonkovich, *Domesticity with a Difference: The Nonfiction of Catharine Beecher, Sarah J. Hale, Fanny Fern, and Margaret Fuller* (Jackson: University Press of Mississippi, 1997). For a discussion of the public role of working women, particularly labor organizers, see, e.g., Judith A. Ranta, " 'A true woman's courage and hopefulness,': Martha W. Tyler's *A Book without a Title: or, Thrilling Events in the Life of Mira Dana* (1855–56)," *Legacy* 21.1 (2004): 17–33, esp. 24–28; Christine Stansell, *City of Women: Sex and Class in New York, 1789–1860* (New York: Knopf, 1986), 130–137; and You-me Park and Gayle Wald, "Native Daughters in the Promised Land: Gender, Race, and the Question of Separate Spheres," *No More Separate Spheres!*, ed. Davidson, 263–287.

8. Gillian Brown, *Domestic Individualism: Imagining Self in Nineteenth-Century America* (Berkeley: University of California Press, 1990), 3. A similar argument has been made with respect to women's complicity in imperialism. Amy Kaplan, for example, in "Manifest Domesticity," *American Literature* 70 (September 1998): 582–606 (reprinted in *No More Separate Spheres!*, 183–207), argues that "domesticity relies on, abets, and reproduces the contradictions of nationalist expansion" (584). Particularly important with respect to the connection between domesticity and the market is Lori Merish, *Sentimental Materialism: Gender, Commodity Culture, and Nineteenth-Century American Literature* (Durham: Duke University Press, 2000). Examining the processes through which middle-class consumerism was "produced" in conjunction with domestic womanhood, Merish maintains that sentimental fictions "construct market capitalism and middle-class personal life as mutually determining spheres" (4).

9. One of the few writers who comments on the money-earning work of nineteenth-century middle-class women is Jeanne Boydston, *Home and Work: Housework, Wages, and the Ideology of Labor* (New York: Oxford University Press, 1990). However, the only cash work that she mentions is writing. Other writers discuss middle-class women other than writers who did earn money from their work. Amy Dru Stanley, in "Home Life and Morality," discusses the "commodity production" of farm women (78–79); Elizabeth Blackmar, in *Manhattan for Rent*, discusses women who took in boarders (63, 67); Lori Ginzberg, in *Women and the Work of Benevolence: Morality, Politics, and Class in the Nineteenth-Century United States* (New Haven: Yale University Press, 1990), discusses women's business activities in benevolence societies (esp. 42, 53, 59); and Glenna Matthews, in *The Rise of Public Woman: Woman's Power and Place in the United States 1630–1970* (New York: Oxford University Press, 1992), includes in her discussion of nineteenth-

century women's public activities their "gainful employment," not only as domestic servants and factory workers but also as preachers, teachers, typesetters, and lecturers (99–108).

10. For a comprehensive discussion of performance and the construction of identity, see Judith Butler, *Gender Trouble* (New York: Routledge, 1990), e.g., 24–25. See also Judith Butler, "Contingent Foundations: Feminism and the Question of 'Postmodernism,'" in *Feminists Theorize the Political*, eds. Joan Scott and Judith Butler (New York: Routledge, 1992), 3–21.

11. For a discussion of this "panic fiction," particularly the 1837 novels of Hannah Lee, see Mary Templin, "Panic Fiction: Women's Responses to Antebellum Economic Crisis," *Legacy* 21.1 (2004): 1–16.

12. Sarah M. Grimké, *Letters on the Equality of the Sexes and the Condition of Women* (Boston: Isaac Knapp, 1838), 75–78, 82.

13. Lydia Maria Child, *Letters From New-York* (New York: C. S. Francis, 1845), 250. See letter 34, January 1843.

14. Margaret Fuller, *Woman in the Nineteenth Century*, *The Essential Margaret Fuller*, ed. Jeffrey Steele (1845; New Brunswick: Rutgers University Press, 1992), 259. Subsequent references to this work will be cited parenthetically in the text.

15. Elizabeth Oakes Smith, *Woman and Her Needs* (New York: Fowlers and Wells, 1851), 44–45.

16. Fanny Fern, "A Practical Blue Stocking," *Olive Branch* (August 2, 1852), reprinted in *Ruth Hall and Other Writings*, ed. Joyce W. Warren (New Brunswick: Rutgers University Press, 1986), 232–235; Fern, "Pay for Women," *New York Ledger* (July 16, 1870).

17. Virginia Penny, *How Women Can Make Money, Married or Single, in All Branches of the Arts and Sciences, Professions, Trades, Agricultural and Mechanical* (1863; Philadelphia: Arno Press, Inc., 1971), v.

18. Penny, *How Women Can Make Money*, ix, xiii.

19. Leon Stein and Philip Taft, introduction to Penny, *How Women Can Make Money*, np.

20. Martha Louise Rayne, *What Can a Woman Do?, or Her Position in the Business and Literary World* (Petersburgh, NY: Eagle Publishing Co., 1893), 12.

21. Rayne, *What Can a Woman Do?*, 14.

22. Elizabeth Cady Stanton, Susan B. Anthony, and Matilda Joslyn Gage, eds., *History of Woman Suffrage*, 6 vols. (1881–1922; Rochester, NY: 1889; reprint, New York: Source Book Press, 1970), 1:98–100; Yuri Suhl, *Ernestine L. Rose and the Battle for Human Rights* (New York: Reynal, 1959), 57–65; and Peggy A. Rabkin, *Fathers to Daughters: The Legal Foundations of Female Emancipation* (Westport, CT: Greenwood Press, 1980), 106–107, 110–111.

23. Stanton, Anthony, and Gage, *History of Woman Suffrage*, 1:72.

24. Resolutions, First Worcester Convention, 1850, in Stanton, Anthony, and Gage, *History of Woman Suffrage*, 1:821.

25. Elizabeth Cady Stanton, "Address to the Legislature of the State of New York," 1854, in Stanton, Anthony, and Gage, *History of Woman Suffrage*, 1:605. The bill failed, but a similar one was passed in New York in 1860.

26. For information about the Lowell strikes, see, e.g., Harriet H. Robinson, *Loom and Spindle; or, Life among the Early Mill Girls*, revised edition, 1898 (Kailua, HI: Press Pacifica, 1976), 51–52; John B. Andrews and W. D. P. Bliss, *History of Women in Trade Unions* (1911; New York: Arno, 1974), 27–31; John R. Commons et al., *History of Labour in the United States*, 4 vols. (New York: Macmillan, 1918–1935), 1:423; Philip S. Foner, *Women and the American Labor Movement: From Colonial Times to the Eve of World War I* (New York: Free Press, 1979), 33–35; and Thomas Dublin, *Women at Work: The Transformation of Work and Community in Lowell, Massachusetts, 1826–1860* (New York: Columbia University Press, 1979), 89–103. Dublin includes a chart listing men's and women's comparative wages in one of the Lowell mills in 1836 (66).

27. Dublin, *Women at Work*, 92–93.

28. Quoted in Foner, *Women and the American Labor Movement*, 34, and in Dublin, *Women at Work*, 91.

29. "Union Is Power," *The Man* (February 22, 1834), quoted in Dublin, *Women at Work*, 93.

30. For information about women's strikes in other cities, including Baltimore, Paterson, Lynn, Dover, Springfield, Philadelphia, and New York in the 1830s, see Andrews and Bliss, *History*, 22–49, and Commons, *History of Labour*, 354–356, 422–423.

31. Christine Stansell, *City of Women*, 134–135.

32. See, e.g., James J. Kenneally, "Women in the United States and Trade Unionism," in *The World of Women's Trade Unionism: Comparative Historical Essays*, ed. Norbert C. Soldon (Westport, CT: Greenwood Press, 1985), 59, 63; see also Foner, *Women and the American Labor Movement*, 55–56, 181.

33. Meredith Tax, *The Rising of the Women: Feminist Solidarity and Class Conflict, 1880–1917* (New York: Monthly Review Press, 1980), 58.

34. See Jürgen Habermas, *The Structural Transformation of the Public Sphere: An Inquiry into a Category of Bourgeois Society*, trans. Thomas Burger with Frederick Lawrence (1962; Cambridge: MIT Press, 1989), e.g., 24, 37, 51. For a discussion of Fern as a representative of the counterpublic, using what in the public sphere is regarded as "inappropriate" or "improper" language and behavior to deflate repressive narratives, see my article, "Fanny Fern, Performative Incivilities, and Rap," *Studies in American Humor* 3 (1999): 17–36. For a cogent analysis of the Habermasian public sphere, see Nancy Fraser, *Justice Interruptus: Critical Reflections*

on the *'Postsocialist' Condition* (New York: Routledge, 1997), 69–98, and "Rethinking the Public Sphere: A Contribution to the Critique of Actually Existing Democracy," in *Habermas and the Public Sphere*, ed. Craig Calhoun (Cambridge: MIT Press, 1992), 108–141.

35. A woman's immediate relatives often destroyed potentially embarrassing material, and in later years disinterested heirs who found old papers in an attic were likely to preserve such papers as valuable only if they recognized a famous name attached to them. And even if an heir kept the papers, in most cases he/she would not have known what to do with them, i.e., donate them to a local history collection or to an academic library. In fact, it is only within the last few decades that libraries have been interested in preserving material by unknown women.

36. The collection is located in Special Collections, Hofstra University Library, and contains records of New York Supreme Court law cases from the 1840s to 1920. The Hofstra collection is uncatalogued but is arranged by date. Thus, instead of the usual law citations, I have been able to give only the dates of the cases as references. Since this collection has not previously been used for scholarly study, the stories contained in the cases are stories that have not been told since they were heard in the courts.

37. Although there is a certain amount of arbitrariness in any decision regarding the period of time to confine a study to, I have focused on the years 1845 to 1875 in the New York law cases because it was during the period between the 1840s and 1870s that the most significant legislation affecting women's property rights took place in New York and in the surrounding states. My study of the fiction extends through the turn of the century, however, because not all of the states passed legislation at the same time, and due to conservative interpretations of the laws in the courts in those states where laws were passed to protect women's economic status, the economic situation of women in the United States as a whole remained unresolved throughout the nineteenth century. By 1875, laws had been passed in all of the northeastern and mid-Atlantic states and in most of the southern and midwestern states giving married women ownership of property they had inherited or received as a bequest, but only sixty per cent of those states, including New York, had passed some type of Earnings Act, giving women control of their wages and other earnings—and the degree of control varied from state to state. For statistics on all of the states, see Joan Hoff, *Law, Gender, and Injustice: A Legal History of U.S. Women* (New York: New York University Press, 1991), 377–382.

38. Hendrik Hartog, in *Man and Wife in America, a History* (Cambridge: Harvard University Press, 2000), lists several reasons for New York's importance: New York was a publishing center; it exported many lawyers to other parts of the

country; and because of its complex court structure, it produced many legal opinions that could be cited as precedents in the other state courts (15).

39. The story was told to me by my mother about my grandmother Harriet Devey Hill, whom I never met.

40. Morton J. Horwitz, *The Transformation of American Law, 1780–1860* (Cambridge: Harvard University Press, 1977), xiv, 253. Christopher Tomlins, in *Law, Labor and Ideology in the Early American Republic* (New York: Cambridge University Press, 1993), does not believe that jurists deliberately benefited the rich but asserts that their acceptance of the ideology of "market liberalism" produced the same result (113, 190, 217). Economic developments were, of course, not the only cultural influences on the law. Peter Karsten, in *Heart versus Head: Judge-Made Law in Nineteenth-Century America* (Chapel Hill: University of North Carolina Press, 1997), maintains that, although economic considerations were a factor in legal decisions, other influences, particularly evangelical religion, brought jurists (most often those outside the northeastern states) to "alter certain common-law rules in order to produce 'justice.' " In doing so, he said, they "served the needs of relatively poor plaintiffs, not corporate defendants." Karsten called these innovations the "Jurisprudence of the Heart" (e.g., 4, 10, 300–301).

41. David M. Gold, *The Shaping of Nineteenth-Century Law: John Appleton and Responsible Individualism* (New York: Greenwood Press, 1990), 1, 168–169. As Christopher Tomlins writes in his introduction to *The Many Legalities of Early America*, eds. Tomlins and Bruce H. Mann (Chapel Hill: University of North Carolina Press, 2001), "Legalities are not produced in formal legal settings alone. They are social products, generated in the course of virtually any repetitive practice of wide acceptance within a specific locale" (2–3).

42. For a discussion of the gendered character of nineteenth-century individualism, see Joyce W. Warren, *The American Narcissus: Individualism and Women in Nineteenth-Century American Fiction* (New Brunswick: Rutgers University Press, 1984). Gillian Brown, in *Domestic Individualism*, equates woman's domesticity with individualism. However, in order to do so she must redefine the term *individualism* to mean interiority. For nineteenth-century Americans (and for Americans today), however, individualism connoted independent action and self-assertion, the Emersonian concept of self-reliant individualism that in the nineteenth century was gendered as male.

43. Hoff, *Law, Gender, and Injustice*, 117. See also Linda K. Kerber, " 'Ourselves and Our Daughters Forever': Women and the Constitution, 1787–1876," *This Constitution* 6 (Spring 1985): 29, and Carole Pateman, *The Sexual Contract* (Stanford: Stanford University Press, 1988). The idea that women are not mentioned in the Constitution is challenged by Jan Lewis in " 'Of Every Age Sex & Condi-

tion': The Representation of Women in the Constitution," in *What Did the Constitution Mean to Early Americans?*, ed. Edward Countryman (Boston: Bedford/St. Martin's, 1999), 115–140. (Lewis's article originally appeared in *Journal of the Early Republic* 15 [1995]: 359–357.) Lewis bases her challenge on the fact that the Constitution implies that women were to be included in the count to determine the number of representatives each state would have in the House of Representatives. However, although women were apparently included among the people to be counted—the Constitution states that the count should include "the whole number of free persons, including those bound to servitude for a term of years, and excluding Indians not taxed, three-fifths of all other persons [slaves]" (art. I, sec. 2)—only propertied men could vote or hold political office. The fact that women were to be counted does not detract from the essential point that women are not "mentioned" specifically (their rights are never referred to) in the document that was supposed to define the rights and liberties of the people in the new nation.

44. Hoff, *Law, Gender, and Injustice*, e.g., 23, 40–41, 121.

45. Debra A. Rosen, *Courts and Commerce: Gender, Law, and the Market Economy in Colonial New York* (Columbus: Ohio State University Press, 1997), esp. chapters 5 and 6. Some feminist historians have linked women's exclusion from the marketplace to the development of industrial capitalism, maintaining that as economic life moved out of the home in the eighteenth century, women, whose life was centered in the home, were increasingly perceived as outside the economy. One of the earliest discussions that helped to establish this position was Gerda Lerner's "The Lady and the Mill Girl: Changes in the Status of Women in the Age of Jackson," *Midcontinent American Studies Journal* 10 (1969): 5–15. Nancy F. Cott, in *The Bonds of Womanhood: "Woman's Sphere" in New England, 1780–1835* (New Haven: Yale University Press, 1977), chronicled the removal of women from economic productivity, maintaining that with the intensive social transformation that took place between 1780 and 1835, women were seen as increasingly "secondary to men in economic life" (20). Ann Douglas, in *The Feminization of American Culture* (New York: Alfred A. Knopf, 1978), attributed the rise of sentimentalism to the rise of aggressive capitalism creating a "cultural bifurcation" between 1820 and 1875 (6, 12). See also Mary P. Ryan, *Cradle of the Middle Class: The Family in Oneida County, New York, 1790–1865* (New York: Cambridge University Press, 1981), 191, and Carol Smith-Rosenberg, *Disorderly Conduct: Visions of Gender in Victorian America* (New York: Oxford University Press, 1985), 85–86. Amy Dru Stanley complicates the argument, arguing in "Home Life and Morality" that the ideology of separate spheres not only was used to resolve gender identities and moral problems inherent in the market but also was necessary as an answer to

proslavery proponents. She notes that the principal difference that abolitionists maintained existed between the slave and the free laborer was that the free man not only owned himself but also had a proprietary right to his wife and children (90). Writing within a Marxist framework, Julie Matthaei, in *An Economic History of Women in America: Women's Work, the Sexual Division of Labor, and the Development of Capitalism* (New York: Schocken Books, 1982), points to the separation of commodity production from the home in the eighteenth century, noting that, as economic life became more impersonal in the nineteenth century, women's work in the home was increasingly seen as a "distinct sphere," separate from men's (106). In a gendered revision of Marxist analysis, Jeanne Boydston, in *Home and Work*, changes the focus, highlighting the way that the ideology of separate spheres became a facilitator of capitalism. Boydston writes that the ideology "functioned to support the emergence of the wage system necessary to the development of industrial capitalism" (160).

46. Paul Gewirtz, "Narrative and Rhetoric in the Law," introduction to *Law's Stories: Narrative and Rhetoric in the Law*, eds. Peter Brooks and Paul Gewirtz (New Haven: Yale University Press, 1996), 4.

47. See Michel Foucault's pioneering discussion of the social construction of "truth" in "The Discourse on Language," e.g., 218. As Stephen Greenblatt wrote in the introduction to *The Power of Forms in the English Renaissance*, ed. Stephen Greenblatt (Norman: University of Oklahoma Press, 1982), the new historicism "tends to ask questions about its own methodological assumptions and those of others" (5). See also Clifford Geertz, *The Interpretation of Cultures: Selected Essays* (New York: Basic Books, 1973) and *Works and Lives: The Anthropologist as Author* (Stanford: Stanford University Press, 1988).

48. Michael Riffaterre, *Text Production*, trans. Terese Lyons (New York: Columbia University Press, 1983), 23.

49. Michael Riffaterre, *Fictional Truth* (1990; Baltimore: Johns Hopkins University Press, 1993), e.g., 130.

50. Robert A. Ferguson, "Story and Transcription in the Trial of John Brown," *Yale Journal of Law & the Humanities* 6 (Winter 1994): 37–73. For an excellent discussion of the narrative aspects of litigation in late-nineteenth-century adultery cases, see Laura Hanft Korobkin, *Criminal Conversations: Sentimentality and Nineteenth-Century Legal Stories of Adultery* (New York: Columbia University Press, 1998), 3–9. For a persuasive analysis of the significance of race and gender in legal narrative, see Mary Frances Berry, *The Pig Farmer's Daughter and Other Tales of American Justice: Episodes of Racism and Sexism in the Courts from 1865 to the Present* (1999; New York: Vintage Books, 2000). Noting that "stories provide a frame of reference that determines what each of us believes is true," Berry points out that

"whose story counts" depends on "who controls political and economic power" (4).

51. Gewirtz, "Narrative and Rhetoric in the Law," 3.

52. Wai Chee Dimock, *Residues of Justice: Literature, Law, Philosophy* (Berkeley: University of California Press, 1996), 5. Dimock says that her critique of justice was influenced by both political philosophy and feminist theory. Citing Michael Sandel's *Liberalism and the Limits of Justice* and Carol Gilligan's *In a Different Voice*, both published in 1982, Dimock indicates that she was struck by their exploration of the "unevenness" of justice, not only "across time" but within differing "cultural domains" (7–8).

53. Gewirtz, "Narrative and Rhetoric in the Law," 5. See also Richard Delgardo, "Storytelling for Oppositionists and Others: A Plea for Narrative," *Michigan Law Review* 87 (August 1989): 2411–2441. The August 1989 issue is a special issue on "Legal Storytelling."

54. Gewirtz, "Narrative and Rhetoric in the Law," 6.

Chapter One | MARRIAGE AND MONEY

1. The record of *Trust v. Trust* (1856–1870) is found in the legal archives of the New York Supreme Court housed in Special Collections, Hofstra University Library. As I indicated in the notes to the introduction, the records are uncatalogued and are arranged only by date.

2. According to English common law, which at that time was the law in most of the United States, a married woman's property belonged to her husband. See chapter 2 for details of the law with respect to married women.

3. See, for example, William A. Alcott, *The Young Wife; or, Duties of Woman in the Marriage Relation* (Boston: George W. Light, 1837).

4. The law with respect to divorce and child custody is discussed in chapter 2.

5. Congress enacted a law to impose an income tax in 1861 to pay Civil War expenses, but the tax was not collected that year because there was no administrative system. Congress passed a new law the following year. In 1862 the income tax applied to those whose annual income exceeded six hundred dollars; in 1867 the exemption was raised to one thousand dollars. The Civil War tax expired in 1871, and no income tax was imposed again until 1913. The 1040 form was introduced in 1913. See publication 1694 in *IRS Historical Fact Book: A Chronology, 1646–1992.* (Washington, DC: Department of the Treasury, Internal Revenue Service, 1992), 8, 31–50. See also the History section in the official site of the Internal Revenue Service, http://www.irs.gov.

Chapter Two | The Dominant Discourse

1. William Blackstone, *Commentaries on the Laws of England*, 4 vols. (Chicago: University of Chicago Press, 1979; reprint of 1765 edition), 1:430. In agreement, Tapping Reeve, the influential American justice who wrote the first treatise on domestic relations in the United States in 1816, *The Law of Baron and Femme* (New York: Source Book Press, 1970; reprint of 1862 edition), writes that "[t]he husband, by marriage, acquires an absolute title to all the personal property of the wife, which she had in possession at the time of marriage" (49). Reeve disagrees with Blackstone, however, regarding the question of whether or not the husband and wife are one person, pointing out that the law permits a wife to own real estate: "[A] deed or devise of land to a wife vests in her, and not in the husband. As to real property, then, they are two distinct persons" (171). For a discussion of coverture, see Lawrence Stone, *The Family, Sex and Marriage in England 1500–1800* (New York: Harper and Row, 1979), 136–142, and J. H. Baker, *An Introduction to English Legal History*, 3rd ed. (London: Butterworth, 1990), 550–557.

2. For a discussion of women's legal position in nineteenth-century United States, see, e.g., Elizabeth Bowles Warbasse, *The Changing Legal Rights of Married Women, 1800–1861* (New York: Garland Publishing, 1987; Ph.D. dissertation, Radcliffe College, 1960); and Linda E. Speth, "The Married Women's Property Acts, 1839–1865: Reform, Reaction, or Revolution?", *Women and the Law: A Social Historical Perspective*, ed. D. Kelly Weisberg, 2 vols. (Cambridge, MA: Schenkman Publishing Co., 1982), 2:69–91. In *Women and the Law of Property in Early America* (Chapel Hill: University of North Carolina Press, 1986), Marylynn Salmon responds to the belief of some feminist historians that colonial women had more rights than did nineteenth-century American women. Salmon points out that if one examines legal restrictions in colonial America, it is clear that women did not have any more freedom than they had in the nineteenth century (e.g., xii–xiii). In *Law, Gender, and Injustice: A Legal History of U.S. Women* (New York: New York University Press, 1991), Joan Hoff points out that the postrevolution draft of the Constitution, along with ensuing legal documents, undermined women's status and legitimized women's legal disabilities. For earlier twentieth-century discussions of women and law, see Leo Kanowitz, *Women and the Law: The Unfinished Revolution* (Albuquerque: University of New Mexico Press, 1969), e.g., 35–41, and Lawrence M. Friedman, *A History of American Law* (New York: Simon and Schuster, 1973), 202–210. Two books focus on New York: Peggy A. Rabkin, *Fathers to Daughters: The Legal Foundations of Female Emancipation* (Westport, CT: Greenwood Press, 1980), and Norma Basch, *In the Eyes of the Law: Women, Marriage and Property in Nineteenth-Century New York* (Ithaca: Cornell University Press, 1982).

3. Blackstone, *Commentaries*, 2:497–498. In the United States at the beginning of the nineteenth century, only Connecticut gave married women the right to write a will. A state law passed in 1809 stated that "married women shall have the power of disposing of their estates by last will and testament." See Warbasse, *Changing Legal Rights*, 15.

4. See Basch, *In the Eyes of the Law*, 81.

5. Warbasse, *Changing Legal Rights*, 7–11. This inequity was still in force in the late nineteenth century. In his 1884 book, *The Co-operative Commonwealth: An Exposition of Socialism* (1884; Boston: Lee and Shepard, 1896), Laurence Gronlund comments: "The enormity everywhere prevails that the wife as survivor of her husband has only a life interest in the third part of their common estate, though she may have—and if she has been a farmer's wife certainly has—contributed fully as much to its acquisition as he. The husband, if he be the survivor, on the other hand, takes all her property" (227).

6. Blackstone, *Commentaries*, 2:129–136.

7. Reeve, in *The Law of Baron and Femme*, writes: "We will now inquire what advantages the wife may gain, eventually by marriage, in point of property, during the coverture. She gains nothing during his life; but upon the death of her husband intestate, she is entitled to one-third part of his personal property, which remains after paying the debts due from the estate" (98).

8. Mary Ritter Beard, in *Women as Force in History: A Study in Tradition and Realities* (New York: Macmillan, 1946), maintains that the belief in women's subjection under common law was a myth because women had recourse to equity, by which they could protect their separate estates (97). However, Beard does not examine the shortcomings of equity, which was not universally available. For a discussion of this point, see Rabkin, *Fathers to Daughters*, 5, and Leo Kanowitz, *Women and the Law: The Unfinished Revolution* (Albuquerque: University of New Mexico Press, 1969), 39.

9. Jane Swisshelm, (Pittsburgh) *Daily Commercial Journal* (February 17, 1848).

10. James Kent, *Commentaries on American Law*, ed. O. W. Holmes, Jr., 4 vols. (Boston: Little Brown,1873), 2:127.

11. Blackstone, *Commentaries*, 1:432.

12. The 1871 laws in Alabama and Massachusetts used this language to describe what the law would no longer allow. See Terry Davidson, *Conjugal Crime: Understanding and Changing the Wifebeating Pattern* (New York: Hawthorn, 1978), 102.

13. Davidson, *Conjugal Crime*, 102–103.

14. For a discussion of the reasons behind the legislation, see Warbasse, *Changing Legal Rights*, 137–247.

15. For a contemporary description of the role of women's rights advocates in New York prior to the 1848 and 1860 laws, see Elizabeth Cady Stanton, Susan B.

Anthony, and Matilda Joslyn Gage, *History of Woman Suffrage*, 6 vols. (1881–1922; Rochester, NY: 1889; reprint, New York: Source Book Press, 1970), 1:63–67, 676–688.

16. For example, Stanton, Anthony, and Gage, in *History of Woman Suffrage*, state that New York "was the first state to emancipate wives from the slavery of the old common law of England, and to secure to them equal property rights. This occurred in 1848" (1:63). The mistaken belief that New York's 1848 law was the first married women's property law continued into the twentieth century. See, e.g., Carol Hymowitz and Michaele Weissman, *A History of Women in America* (New York: Bantam Books, 1978), 118. New York's law was highly publicized by women's rights advocates. For a comprehensive discussion of the events leading up to and the results of the 1848 Married Women's Property Act, see Norma Basch, *In the Eyes of the Law: Women, Marriage and Property in Nineteenth-Century New York* (Ithaca: Cornell University Press, 1982), 150–156 and Rabkin, *Fathers to Daughters*, 85–99.

17. Two other southern states passed married women's property laws. Alabama, in a series of laws passed in the 1840s, protected married women's property, although the husband retained control of it, and in 1838 and 1846 Kentucky passed laws to entitle a married woman to own stock in Kentucky institutions, free from her husband's debts. Both states allowed a woman to have control of her own earnings if she was abandoned by her husband. Bills in Georgia and Tennessee failed to pass, and in most southern states the common law prevailed. See Warbasse, *Changing Legal Rights*, 135–181. The states (in the order in which they passed their first laws) included Mississippi (1839, 1846), Texas (1840, 1846, 1848), Rhode Island (1841), Maryland (1843), Maine (1844), Michigan (1844), Massachusetts (1845), New Hampshire (1845), Connecticut (1845, 1849), Florida (1845), Alabama (1846), Arkansas (1846), Kentucky (1846), Vermont (1847), New York (1848), and Pennsylvania (1848). For a comprehensive discussion of the changing laws, see Warbasse, *Changing Legal Rights*, 135–236.

18. For the text of the 1848 New York law, see, e.g, Basch, *In the Eyes of the Law*, 233–234, and Linda K. Kerber and Jane Sherron de Hart, eds., *Women's America: Refocusing the Past* (New York: Oxford University Press, 1995), 570–571. For a comprehensive discussion of events leading up to the passage of the New York Law and the results, see, e.g., Basch, *In the Eyes of the Law*, 150–156, and Rabkin, *Fathers to Daughters*, 85–99.

19. (Pittsburgh) *Daily Commercial Journal* (October 4, 1847).

20. James Fenimore Cooper, *Complete Works*, Leatherstocking edition, 32 vols. (New York: Putnam, 1893?), 24:179–183, 364, 431, 436–438.

21. Warbasse, *Changing Legal Rights*, 237–247.

22. Warbasse, *Changing Legal Rights*, 243–244 .

23. Massachusetts, *Session Laws* (May 5, 1855), ch. 304, 710–711. For a discussion of the events leading up to this statute, see Warbasse, *Changing Legal Rights*, 267–270.

24. *Laws of New York*, 1860, ch. 90. For the text of this law, see, e.g., Stanton, Anthony, and Gage, *History of Woman Suffrage*, 1:686–687, and Basch, *In the Eyes of the Law*, 234–235. See also Kerber and de Hart, *Women's America*, 570–571, and Linda K. Kerber, "Ourselves and Our Daughters Forever," *One Woman, One Vote: Rediscovering the Woman Suffrage Movement*, ed. Marjorie Spruill Wheeler (Troutdale, OR: NewSage Press, 1995), 30–31.

25. Connecticut, *Session Laws* (June 22, 1850), 27, and (June 7, 1850), 28; Massachusetts, *Session Laws* (May 5, 1855), 711; Maine *Session Laws* (April 17, 1857), 49; New York, *Session Laws* (March 20, 1860), 157. See Warbasse, *Changing Legal Rights*, 263, 304.

26. Stanton, Anthony, and Gage, *History of Woman Suffrage*, 1:748. Anthony made the comment in a letter expressing her "astonishment" that the New York legislature in 1862 had repealed part of the 1860 law. See also Basch, *In the Eyes of the Law*, 207.

27. Amy Dru Stanley, "Conjugal Bonds and Wage Labor: Rights of Contract in the Age of Emancipation," *Women and the American Legal Order*, ed. Karen J. Maschke (New York: Garland, 1997), 161–163.

28. See Richard H. Chused, "Married Women's Property Law, 1800–1850," *Georgetown Law Journal* 71 (June 1983): 1424, and Stanley, "Conjugal Bonds," 160.

29. *Birkbeck v. Ackroyd*, 74 NY 356, 359 (1878). For a good discussion of the court decisions, see Stanley, "Conjugal Bonds," 172–175, and Basch, *In the Eyes of the Law*, 206–223. Other relevant court decisions include *Burke v. Cole*, 97 MA 113 (1867) and *Cunningham v. Hanney*, 12 ILL App. 437, 438 (1883). For a contemporary discussion of the law and relevant state decisions, see J. C. Wells, *A Treatise on the Separate Property of Married Women under the Recent Enabling Statutes* (Cincinnati: Robert Clarke & Co., 1878), 175–183.

30. *Congressional Globe*, 39 Cong., 1 sess., January 19, 1866, 1784. Amy Dru Stanley, in "Conjugal Bonds," discusses this debate in terms of the gendered interpretation of freedom of contract (157–159).

31. See, e.g., Kent, *Commentaries*, 2:193–196.

32. Massachusetts *Session Laws* (April 6, 1855), 579–580, sec. 7.

33. *Laws of New York*, 1862, ch. 172.

34. Jamil S. Zainaldin, "The Emergence of a Modern American Family Law: Child Custody, Adoption, and the Courts, 1796–1851," *Northwestern University Law Review* 73 (1979): 1039–1089. Zainaldin cites Judge Shaw's decision in *Commonwealth v. Briggs* (Massachusetts, 1834) and Judge Bronson's decision in *Mercein v. Barry* (New York, 1840), pointing out that in spite of decisions against the fa-

ther, "the paternal presumption of paternal right to custody was undisturbed" (1060, 1062, 1066).

35. Paul Sayre, "Awarding Custody of Children," in *Selected Essays on Family Law* (Brooklyn: Foundation Press, 1950), 588–620. Sayre cites a 1926 opinion that "the father will be preferred over the mother if all other things are equal" and points out that this rule was restated in a 1942 case (593). For a listing of the states' custody legislation by 1935, see Chester G. Vernier, *American Family Laws: A Comparative Study of the Family Law of the Forty-eight American States, Alaska, the District of Columbia, and Hawaii (to Jan. 1, 1931)*, 5 vols. (Stanford: University of California Press, 1931–1938), 4:18–19.

36. The principal exception, of course, was slave women before emancipation. However, even here there were traces of the middle-class ideal of conventional femininity, for example, in the hierarchy of house slaves and field hands—as recorded in Hannah Crafts, *The Bondwoman's Narrative*, ed. Henry Louis Gates, Jr. (New York: Warner Books, 2002)—and in the premium placed on female purity, as recorded by Harriet Jacobs in *Incidents in the Life of a Slave Girl*, ed. Jean Fagan Yellin (Cambridge: Harvard University Press, 1987).

37. Alice Kessler-Harris, *Women Have Always Worked* (Old Westbury, NY: Feminist Press, 1981), 17–18. See also Alice Kessler-Harris, *Out to Work: A History of Wage-Earning Women in the United States* (New York: Oxford University Press, 1982).

38. In the late 1960s, feminist scholars coined the terms "cult of domesticity" and "cult of true womanhood" to describe what they regarded as an ideology of domesticity that governed the lives of nineteenth-century white middle-class women. See, e.g., Barbara Welter, "The Cult of True Womanhood: 1820–1860," *American Quarterly* 18 (1966): 151–174, and Aileen S. Kraditor, Introduction, *Up from the Pedestal: Selected Writings in the History of American Feminism*, ed. Aileen S. Kraditor, (Chicago: Quadrangle Books, 1968), 3–24. Other discussions of the character of domesticity include Nancy F. Cott, *The Bonds of Womanhood: "Woman's Sphere" in New England, 1780–1835* (New Haven: Yale University Press, 1977); Carol Smith-Rosenberg, *Disorderly Conduct: Visions of Gender in Victorian America* (New York: Knopf, 1985); and Mary P. Ryan, *The Empire of the Mother: American Writing About Domesticity, 1830–1860* (New York: Harrington Park Press, 1985).

39. For a discussion of the debate about and recent challenges to the concept of "true womanhood," see the introduction and the notes to that chapter.

40. Samuel K. Jennings, *The Married Lady's Companion* (New York: Lorenzo Dow, 1808); William A. Alcott, *The Young Wife* (1837; reprint, Boston: George W. Light, 1839), 27–29.

41. *Albany Daily State Register* (March 7, 1854). Cited in Stanton, Anthony, and Gage, *History of Woman Suffrage*, 1:608.

42. Ralph Waldo Emerson, *Complete Works*, 12 vols., ed. Edward W. Emerson (Boston: Houghton Mifflin, 1903–1904), 11:403–426.

43. As Barbara Harris notes in *Beyond Her Sphere: Women and the Professions in American History* (Westport, CT: Greenwood Press, 1978), in both native-born and immigrant working-class families, "there was a conscious effort to imitate the bourgeois style of life, and wives tended to stay at home as soon as it was economically feasible" (61–62). See also Virginia Yans McLaughlin, "Patterns of Work and Family Organization: Buffalo's Italians," in *The Family in History*, eds. Theodore K. Rabb and Robert I. Rotberg (New York: Harper Torchbooks, 1971), 111–126, and Thomas Dublin, "Women, Work, and the Family: Female Operatives in the Lowell Mills, 1830–1860," *Feminist Studies* 3 (Fall 1975): 30–39. More recent critics have found evidence of greater assertiveness among working-class and minority women. See, e.g., Christine Stansell, *City of Women: Sex and Class in New York: 1789–1860* (New York: Alfred A. Knopf, 1986), 133–135, 144, and Nancy A. Hewitt, "Taking the True Woman Hostage," *Journal of Women's History* 14 (Spring 2002): 156–162.

44. Benita Eisler, ed., *The Lowell Offering: Writings by New England Mill Women (1840–1845)* (Philadelphia: J. B. Lippincott Company, 1977), 217.

45. Eisler, *Lowell Offering*, 19. Or as a former factory worker wrote sixty years later, the women had experienced great pleasure at feeling the "jingle of silver in their pockets" after payday, and they walked tall, "proudly" dropping their own money in the collection box on Sunday. Harriet Hanson Robinson, *Loom and Spindle, or Life Among the Early Mill Girls* (1898; Kailua, HI: Press Pacifica, 1976), 43.

46. Thomas Dublin, *Transforming Women's Work: New England Lives in the Industrial Revolution* (Ithaca: Cornell University Press, 1994), xv.

47. Martin R. Delany, *The Condition, Elevation, Emigration and Destiny of the Colored People of the United States* (Philadelphia: By the author, 1852), 43; quoted in Sharon Harley, "Northern Black Female Workers: Jacksonian Era," in *The Afro-American Woman: Struggles and Images*, eds. Sharon Harley and Rosalyn Terborg-Penn (New York: Kennikat Press, 1978), 5–16.

48. James Oliver Horton, "Freedom's Yoke: Gender Conventions among Antebellum Free Blacks," *Feminist Studies* 12 (Spring 1986): 51–76.

49. Carla L. Peterson, *"Doers of the Word": African-American Women Speakers and Writers in the North (1830–1880)* (New York: Oxford University Press, 1995), 12, 9, 15, 17, 112–118.

50. The Epistle of Paul to the Ephesians, 5:22

51. Stanton, Anthony, and Gage, *History of Woman Suffrage*, 1:532.

52. See, e.g., Nancy F. Cott, *Public Vows: A History of Marriage and the Nation* (Cambridge: Harvard University Press, 2000), esp. 6, 104, and Carol Weisbrod,

"Family, Church, and State: An Essay on Constitutionalism and Religious Authority," *Journal of Family Law* 26:4 (1987–88): 741–770.

53. Edward Deering Mansfield, *The Legal Rights, Disabilities and Duties of Women* (Salem, MA: J. P. Jewett & Co., 1845), 307.

54. *Bradwell v. Illinois*, 83 U.S. (16 Wall) 130 (1873). Cited in Hoff, *Law, Gender, and Injustice*, 165–166.

55. *Debates and Proceedings in the New-York State Convention, for the Revision of the Constitution*, eds. S. Croswell and R. Sutton (Albany: The Albany Argus, 1846), 907; reprinted in *The Convention of 1846*, ed. Milo M. Quaife (Madison, WI: State Historical Society, 1919), 631.

56. Stanton, Anthony, and Gage, *History of Woman Suffrage*, 1:81–82.

57. See Fanny Fern's response to Bushnell and Todd in the *New York Ledger* (November 6, 1869).

58. John W. Nevin, "Woman's Rights," *American Review* (October 1848): 367–381.

59. Reverend Jesse T. Peck, "The True Woman," *Ladies' Repository* (August 1853): 337.

60. Diane Lichtenstein, "The Tradition of American Jewish Women Writers," *The (Other) American Traditions: Nineteenth-Century Women Writers*, ed. Joyce W. Warren (New Brunswick: Rutgers University Press, 1993), 247.

61. Charlotte Baum, Paula Hyman, and Sonya Michel, *The Jewish Woman in America* (New York: New American Library, 1975), 53.

62. William P. Dewees, *A Treatise on the Diseases of Females* (Philadelphia: Lea & Blanchard, 1843), 14.

63. Ann Douglas Wood, " 'The Fashionable Diseases': Women's Complaints and Their Treatment in Nineteenth-Century America," *Journal of Interdisciplinary History* 4 (Summer 1973): 25–51; reprinted in *Clio's Consciousness: New Perspectives on the History of Women*, eds. Mary S. Hartman and Lois Banner (New York: Octagon Books, 1976), 1–22. See page 4 for quotation. Douglas Wood's insistence that male doctors' treatment of women was due to hostility and the need to punish women is corrected by Regina Morantz, who points out in "The Lady and Her Physician," *Clio's Consciousness: New Perspectives on the History of Women*, 37–53, that, although doctors may have been influenced by cultural attitudes toward women, the primitive character of medical practices was due primarily to ignorance and lack of training (45–47).

64. George Austin, *Perils of American Women: or, A Doctor's Talk with Maiden, Wife, and Mother* (Boston: Lee & Shepard, 1883); selections reprinted in *Root of Bitterness: Documents of the Social History of American Women*, ed. Nancy F. Cott (New York: Dutton, 1972), 293–298. Catharine Beecher, in *Letters to the People on*

Health and Happiness (New York: Harper & Brothers, 1855), strongly critiqued such medical practices with respect to women (136–138).

65. William F. Byford, *A Treatise on the Chronic Inflammation and Displacement of the Unimpregnated Uterus* (Philadelphia: Lindsay & Blackiston, 1864), 15.

66. Edward A. Clarke, *Sex in Education, or a Fair Chance for Girls* (1873; reprint, Boston: Houghton Mifflin, 1892), e.g., 31–60, 90, 98–109.

67. Clarke, *Sex in Education*, 127.

68. Thomas A. Emmet, *Principles and Practices of Gynaecology* (Philadelphia: Lea, 1879), 21.

69. S. Weir Mitchell, *Wear and Tear; Or, Hints for the Overworked* (1887; reprint, New York: Arno, 1973), 30, 46–47, 56–57.

70. This description of the S. Weir Mitchell method appeared in Joyce Proust and Gilbert Ballet, *The Treatment of Neurasthenia* (1902), 182–191, which is cited in Hermione Lee, *Virginia Woolf* (New York: Alfred A. Knopf, 1996), 780.

71. Sir George Savage, Woolf's principal doctor, was S. Weir Mitchell's disciple. Woolf was first placed under his care in 1904, and although she had various doctors during the years of her illness, as Woolf's biographer, Hermione Lee, notes in *Virginia Woolf*, "All her doctors recommended rest cures, milk and meat diets for weight gain, fresh air, avoidance of excitement, and early nights" (195, 179). Woolf's words in response to this treatment often sound as though they were uttered by the narrator of Gilman's "The Yellow Wallpaper." For example, in 1904 when she was confined to the country and not allowed to go to London, she wrote: "I have never spent such a wretched 8 months in my life . . . I wonder why Savage doesn't see this . . . really a doctor is worse than a husband!" And in 1910 she wrote to her sister, "I really dont [*sic*] think I can stand much more of this . . . you cant [*sic*] conceive how I want intelligent conversation." Then in 1928, after many years of rest cure treatment and sounding like Gilman's narrator near the end of the story, she wrote: "I can't spin a sentence, & sit mumbling & turning; & nothing flits by my brain which is as a blank window. So I . . . go to bed . . . And what leagues I travel in the time! Such 'sensations' spread over my spine & head directly I give them the chance; such an exaggerated tiredness; such anguishes & despairs" (180–182).

72. M. Carey Thomas, "Present Tendencies in Women's College and University Education," *Educational Review* 24 (1908): 68.

73. Cited in Rosalind Rosenberg, *Beyond Separate Spheres: Intellectual Roots of Modern Feminism* (New Haven: Yale University Press, 1982), 12. See Rosenberg's book for a comprehensive discussion of late-nineteenth-century ideas about biological restrictions on woman's nature (1–27).

74. Clarke, *Sex in Education*, 131–133.

75. Gillian Brown makes a similar point in *Domestic Individualism: Imagining*

Self in Nineteenth-Century America (Berkeley: University of California Press, 1990), 174.

76. See, e.g., Joan D. Hedrick, *Harriet Beecher Stowe: A Life* (New York: Oxford, 1994), 223-224.

77. Henry Clews, *Twenty-Eight Years in Wall Street* (New York: J. S. Ogilvie Publishing Company, 1887), 437-446.

78. Obituary of Hetty Green, *New York Times* (July 4, 1916).

79. See, e.g., Edith Wilds, "Madame Hirooka, the Invincible," *Everybody's Magazine* 40 (May 1919): 96-97; Arthur Lewis, *The Day They Shook the Plum Tree* (New York: Harcourt, Brace, 1963), 5; Boyden Sparkes, *Hetty Green: A Woman Who Loved Money* (Garden City: Doubleday, Moran, 1930), 182; and "The Burden of Money," *Outlook* 115 (28 February 1917): 300. For a balanced discussion of Green, see Charles Slack, *Hetty: The Genius and the Madness of America's First Female Tycoon* (New York: HarperCollins Publishers, 2004).

80. Fanny Fern, "A Bit of Injustice," *New York Ledger* (8 June 1861); reprinted in Fanny Fern, *Ruth Hall and Other Writings*, ed. Joyce W. Warren (New Brunswick: Rutgers University Press, 1986), 319.

81. For information on Walker, see A'Lelia Perry Bundles, *On Her Own Ground: The Life and Times of Madam C. J. Walker* (New York: Scribner's, 2001), and Beverly Lowry, *Her Dream of Dreams: The Rise and Triumph of Madam C. J. Walker* (New York: Alfred A. Knopf, 2003).

82. From the Walker Collection, A'Lelia Bundles. Cited in Joan Curl Elliott, "Madame C. J. Walker," in *Notable Black American Women*, ed. Jessie Carney Smith (Detroit: Gale Research, 1992), 1187.

83. A'Lelia Bundles, "Madame C. J. Walker: Cosmetics Tycoon," *Ms.* (July 1983): 91-94. For other information about Walker, in addition to the biographies cited above, see Bundles, "America's First Self-Made Woman Millionaire," *Radcliffe Quarterly* (December 1987): 11-12; Jill Nelson, "The Fortune That Madame Built," *Essence* (June 1983): 84-89; and Elliott, "Madame C. J. Walker," 1184-1188.

84. Eliza Potter, *A Hairdresser's Experience in High Life*, the Schomburg Library of Nineteenth-Century Black Women Writers, with an introduction by Sharon G. Dean (1859; New York: Oxford University Press, 1991), 11. Further references to this work will be noted in the text.

85. Cited in Stansell, *City of Women*, 138. See also John R. Commons, et al., *History of Labour in the United States*, 4 vols. (New York: Macmillan, 1918-1935), 1: 436-437, and John B. Andrews and W. D. P. Bliss, *History of Women in Trade Unions* (1911: New York, Arno, 1974), 45-49. In *Justice Interruptus: Critical Reflections of the "Postsocialist" Condition* (New York: Routledge, 1997), Nancy Fraser traces women's dependency to the rise of industrialism in the early nineteenth century and points out that as white workingmen gained independence from wage labor,

women were increasingly viewed as economically dependent. The organized workingmen in the United States endorsed women's dependency as the norm, she says, because this provided an argument for higher wages for men (129–130).

86. National Trades' Union Committee on Female Labor (1836); cited in Stansell, *City of Women*, 139.

87. See, e.g., Gladys Boone, *The Women's Trade Union Leagues in Great Britain and the United States of America* (1942; New York: AMS Press, 1968), 55–62; Stansell, *City of Women*, 133, 144, 150–153; Philip S. Foner, *Women and American Trade Unionism: From Colonial Times to the Eve of World War I* (New York: The Free Press, 1979), 49–51, 144–145; and Kessler-Harris, *Out to Work*, chapter 3.

88. Thomas Dublin, *Women at Work: The Transformation of Work and Community in Lowell, Massachusetts, 1826–1860* (New York: Columbia University Press, 1979), 200–201.

89. Stansell, *City of Women*, 152.

90. Philip S. Foner, *History of the Labor Movement in the United States*, vol. 2 (New York: International Publishers, 1955), 61–66.

91. The two unions that admitted women members were the Typographical Union and the Cigar-Makers' Union. The attitude of the latter is exemplified by a statement in its president's report in 1879: "We cannot drive the females out of the trade but we can restrict this daily quota of labor through factory laws." Boone, *Women's Trade Union Leagues*, 48–49. See also James J. Kenneally, "Women in the United States and Trade Unionism," in *The World of Women's Trade Unionism: Comparative Historical Essays*, ed. Norbert C. Soldon (Westport, CT: Greenwood Press, 1985), 63.

92. Foner, *History*, 2:367.

93. Foner, *History*, 2:364–366.

94. Kenneally, "Women in the United States and Trade Unionism," 65.

95. Foner, *Women and American Trade Unionism*, 205; Kenneally, "Women in the United States and Trade Unionism," 64.

96. Meredith Tax, *The Rising of the Women: Feminist Solidarity and Class Conflict, 1880–1917* (New York: Monthly Review Press, 1980), 20. Tax calls this alliance the "united front of women" and notes that it was particularly successful in the Illinois Woman's Alliance in Chicago in 1888 (21, 65–89). Some commentators have noted that the work of middle-class reformers was a mixed blessing. It took the initiative away from working-class women and introduced middle-class rhetoric. See Kenneally, "Women in the United States," 60; Dublin, *Women at Work*, 199–202; and Stansell, *City of Women*, 148–154.

97. Tax, *The Rising*, 60–61.

98. Tax, *The Rising*, 63.

99. Mari Jo Buhle, *Women and American Socialism, 1870–1920* (Urbana: University of Illinois Press, 1981), 9.

100. Karl Marx and Frederick Engels, *The Communist Manifesto* (1848; New York: Labor News, 1961), 40.

101. Buhle, *Women and American Socialism*, 3–12.

102. Buhle, *Women and American Socialism*, 9–11.

103. Friedrich Sorge, *Labor Movement in the United States: A History of the American Working Class from Colonial Times to 1890s*, eds. Philip S. Foner and Brewster Chamberlin (Westport, CT: Greenwood Press, 1977), 158–159. Section 12 was led by Victoria Woodhull.

104. Laurence Gronlund, *The Co-operative Commonwealth: An Exposition of Socialism* (Boston: Lee and Shepard, 1884), 219–234.

105. Edward Bellamy, *Looking Backward* (1888; New York: 1960), 176, 180. For a discussion of women's involvement in the Nationalist movement which derived from Bellamy's novel, see Mari Jo Buhle, *Women and American Socialism*, 75–82.

106. As Dolores Hayden points out in "Charlotte Perkins Gilman and the Kitchenless House," *Radical History Review* 21 (Fall 1979), Gilman objected to such communal efforts for two reasons: she felt that cooperative attempts would not work, and she objected to projects that included free-love principles (225–247). See also Hayden, *The Grand Domestic Revolution: A History of Feminist Designs for American Houses, Neighborhoods, and Cities* (Cambridge: MIT Press, 1981).

107. Robert Bonner, "Woman's True Sphere," *New York Ledger* (May 14, 1859).

108. Kate Chopin, "Development of the Literary West: A Review," *St. Louis Republic* (December 9, 1900), 1; reprinted in Emily Toth, *Kate Chopin* (New York: William Morrow & Co., 1990), 381–384. Although the story has long circulated that Chopin stopped writing because of negative reviews of *The Awakening*, this is not wholly true. The reviews were not all negative, and, as Alice Hall Petry points out in her introduction to *Critical Essays on Kate Chopin* (New York: G. K. Hall & Co., 1996), 1–33, Chopin continued to publish between April 1899, when the novel appeared, and her death in 1904 (11). However, since none of this later material challenges convention in the way that *The Awakening* did, one wonders if she might have written differently if the reaction to her novel had been different. According to Emily Toth, in her biography of Chopin, after the book appeared Chopin was "ostracized by some friends" and the book created a "minor scandal." For years afterward, says Toth, Kate Chopin "was talked about as something of a scandalous person" (369). Toth concludes that Chopin's response was to present herself as a "public puritan" (385).

109. For Child's career, see Carolyn Karcher, *The First Woman in the Republic: A*

Cultural Biography of Lydia Maria Child (Durham: University of North Carolina Press, 1994).

110. For a discussion of the relationship between Kirkland's self-suppression and her success in the marketplace, see, e.g., Sandra A. Zagarell's introduction to *A New Home, Who'll Follow?* (1839; New Brunswick: Rutgers University Press, 1990), xvii–xx.

111. Sarah Josepha Hale, "Editor's Table," *Godey's Lady's Book* (January 1848), 67; (February 1852), 88.

112. For information about Hale's attitudes, the most important sources are her articles and editorials in her fifty-year career as editor, first of the Boston *Ladies' Magazine* and then of *Godey's Lady's Book*. See also Hale's introduction to *Woman's Record: or Sketches of All Distinguished Women from "The Beginning" till A.D. 1850* and Patricia Okker, *Our Sister Editors: Sarah Josepha Hale and the Tradition of Nineteenth-Century American Women Editors* (Athens: University of Georgia Press, 1995).

Chapter Three | ECONOMICS AND THE AMERICAN RENAISSANCE WOMAN

1. F. O. Matthiessen, *The American Renaissance* (1941; New York: Oxford, 1964).

2. Matthiessen makes passing mention of Warner, Cummins, and Southworth in his introductory chapter, but only in reference to the vast sales of their books (as if this somehow disqualified them from consideration) and in conjunction with Hawthorne's disparaging comments about women writers. Fern he does not cite by name, referring to the sales of her first book, *Fern Leaves from Fanny's Portfolio* (1853), and identifying her only as the "sister of N. P. Willis" (x). He also mentions Fern's first book in a condescending footnote, saying with respect to Whitman's appropriation of it for *Leaves of Grass* that Whitman's use of such an "unlikely source" is indicative of his "generously undiscriminating" response to his culture (547n). Matthiessen's few references to Stowe include the explanation in his introduction that if a book were written on Fourierism, and if it was extended to "all the radical movements of the period," it would include *Uncle Tom's Cabin* (1852) (viii). But, he says, that is not the subject of his book; he is writing on five authors who share a "devotion to the possibilities of democracy"—although why this disqualifies Stowe's powerful condemnation of racial slavery, he does not explain (ix).

3. For discussions of the way in which twentieth-century criticism in American literature excluded serious consideration of nineteenth-century women writers, see, e.g., Nina Baym, "Melodramas of Beset Manhood: How Theories of American Fiction Exclude Women," *American Quarterly* 33 (Summer 1981): 123–

139, and Paul Lauter, *Canons and Contexts* (New York: Oxford University Press, 1991). See also Joyce W. Warren, *The American Narcissus: Individualism and Women in Nineteenth-Century American Fiction* (New Brunswick: Rutgers University Press, 1984), 1–19, and Warren, "Introduction: Canons and Canon Fodder," *The (Other) American Traditions: Nineteenth-Century Women Writers* (New Brunswick: Rutgers University Press, 1993), 25. In "The Other American Renaissance," chapter six in *Sensational Designs: The Cultural Work of American Fiction* (New York: Oxford University Press, 1985), 147–185, Jane Tompkins demonstrates the exclusionary character of Matthiessen's *American Renaissance*. For a comprehensive analysis of the origins and development of this exclusionary tradition, see Charlene Avallone, "What American Renaissance? The Gendered Genealogy of a Critical Discourse," *PMLA* 112 (October 1997): 1102–1120.

4. See, e.g., Carolyn Porter, *Seeing and Being: The Plight of the Participant Observer in Emerson, James, Adams, and Faulkner* (Middletown, CT: Wesleyan University Press, 1981). Porter maintains that Emerson's detachment from the world ("transparent eyeball") is a response to the development of capitalism (23–53, 57–118). Michael Gilmore, in *American Romanticism and the Marketplace* (Chicago: University of Chicago Press, 1985), says that the American Renaissance authors in his study were all affected by the economic changes occurring between the 1830s and 1860s, and they developed the use of symbolism as a reification of the exchange system inherent in commodity culture (e.g., 6–17, 152). Walter Benn Michaels, in his analysis of Hawthorne's *The House of the Seven Gables*, "Romance and Real Estate," *The American Renaissance Reconsidered*, eds. Walter Benn Michaels and Donald E. Pease (Baltimore: Johns Hopkins University Press, 1985), 156–182 — also printed in *The Gold Standard and the Logic of Naturalism: American Literature at the Turn of the Century* (Berkeley: University of California Press, 1987) — similarly points to the significance of the economic shifts at midcentury. Citing Holgrave's accession to the Pyncheon property and his refusal to take possession of Phoebe's soul through hypnosis (unlike his ancestor's appropriation of Alice Pyncheon's individuality), Michaels interprets Hawthorne's romance as an "attempt to imagine an escape from capitalism, defending the self against possession, property against appropriation" (168). What Michaels does not discuss is the fact that Holgrave's accession to the Pyncheon property through his marriage to Phoebe is possible only because law and custom at the time gave a man control of his wife's property, thus enabling what amounts to Holgrave's "appropriation" of Phoebe's inheritance. Holgrave does not "escape" from the conventions of the dominant culture; he profits from them.

5. Henry David Thoreau, *Walden*, ed. Larzer Ziff (New York: Holt, Rinehart, Winston, 1961), e.g., 22, 26, 55, 63–65, 72.

6. "Friend, client, child, sickness, fear, want, charity, all knock at once at thy closet door," but, says Emerson, "come not into their confusion"; "I cannot sell my liberty and my power, to save their sensibility." Ralph Waldo Emerson, "Self Reliance," *Complete Works*, Centenary Edition, ed. Edward W. Emerson, 12 vols. (Boston: Houghton Mifflin, 1903–1904), 2:72, 74.

7. Michael Riffaterre, *Fictional Truth* (1990; Baltimore: Johns Hopkins University Press, 1993), 3. Riffaterre adds that the narrative reflects "the wisdom and experience of the readership, or rather, the prevailing ideology or ideologies that may be mobilized in assessing a situation or individual behavior. These mental frames of reference . . . constitute potential ministries, ready to unfold when needed" (3–4).

8. Lauren Berlant, "The Female Woman: Fanny Fern and the Form of Sentiment," *The Culture of Sentiment: Race, Gender, and Sentimentality in Nineteenth-Century America*, ed. Shirley Samuels (New York: Oxford University Press, 1992), 269–270.

9. Tompkins, *Sensational Designs*, 134–136, 150–155.

10. Fanny Fern, for example, used religion not as an aid to submission but as a spur to female achievement. For a discussion of how Fern's religious views differed from those found in Tompkins's analysis, see Joyce W. Warren, *Fanny Fern: An Independent Woman* (New Brunswick: Rutgers University Press, 1992), e.g., 79–80, 237–238, 288, 302, 361n9. For an incisive analysis of the way in which Fern used religion to advance her progressive politics, see Jaime Harker, " 'Pious Cant' and Blasphemy: Fanny Fern's Radicalized Sentiment," *Legacy* 18 (2001): 52–64.

11. Nina Baym, *Woman's Fiction: A Guide to Novels by and about Women in America, 1820–1870* (Ithaca: Cornell University Press, 1978), 144.

12. Women reacted in various ways to the reality of gendered powerlessness. Lori Merish suggests that for privileged women it was instantiated in a "possessive domesticity": "The desire for control over, and psychic investment in, domestic possessions is an index of a psychic sense of futility in the larger social realm." Lori Merish, *Sentimental Materialism: Gender, Commodity Culture, and Nineteenth-Century American Literature* (Durham: Duke University Press, 2000), 5.

13. Wendy Brown, "Wounded Attachments: Late Modern Oppositional Political Formations," *The Identity in Question*, ed. John Rajchman (New York: Routledge, 1995), 199–227.

14. Works by late-nineteenth-century male realists include William Dean Howells, *The Rise of Silas Lapham* (1885) and *A Hazard of New Fortunes* (1890); Stephen Crane, *Maggie, A Girl of the Streets* (1893); Harold Frederic, *The Market-Place* (1886); and Theodore Dreiser, *Sister Carrie* (1900). Examples of labor conflicts that received national publicity include the Railroad Strike (1877); the

Haymarket Affair (1886) and the "red scare" that followed; the Steel Strike (1892); and the Pullman Strike (1894). For a discussion of the development of American literary realism with respect to women writers, see Joyce W. Warren, "Performativity and the Repositioning of American Literary Realism," in *Challenging Boundaries: Gender and Periodization*, eds. Joyce W. Warren and Margaret Dickie (Athens: University of Georgia Press, 2000), 3–25.

15. Ralph Waldo Emerson, *Journals and Miscellaneous Notes*, eds. William H. Gilman, *et al*., 16 vols. (Cambridge: Harvard University Press, 1960–1982), 7:200–201.

16. Thoreau lived with his parents all of his life, and, except for a six-month stint as a tutor on Staten Island, he did not work for a living. During the two years that he lived at Walden Pond, he went home every day, and every Saturday his mother and sisters brought him freshly baked doughnuts and pies. See, e.g., Leon Edel, *Henry David Thoreau* (Minneapolis: University of Minnesota Press, 1970), 23–26. See also Ellery Channing, *Thoreau: The Poet Naturalist*, ed. F. B. Sanborn (Boston: Charles F. Goodspeed, 1902), 24, and Walter Harding, *The Days of Henry Thoreau* (New York: Alfred A. Knopf, 1965), 184.

17. Walt Whitman, *Leaves of Grass and Selected Prose*, ed. John A. Kouwenhoven, Modern Library College Editions (New York: Modern Library, 1950), 24. For Whitman's reputation as a freeloader, see, e.g., the journal of Thomas Butler Gunn; Gunn wrote on July 29, 1860, "Walt Whitman is voted mean [at Pfaff's beer cellar] as he never stands drinks or pays for his own if it's possible to avoid it." The Thomas Butler Gunn Diaries, Missouri Historical Society, St. Louis. For Whitman's reputation as a loafer, see Ethel Parton's letter to William Sloane Kennedy, February 15, 1897. She reported that when her grandparents' lawyer called on Whitman to collect a debt, he "found him in bed, and his mother scrubbing the floor; and that he also encountered a brother who was a carpenter, and who told him that W. W. had always been lazy, and untrustful, and apt to lump down upon his relatives." Letter in the William Sloane Kennedy Papers, Rutgers University Library, cited in Warren, *Fanny Fern*, 171–172.

18. Whitman, "Song of Myself," section 15, *Leaves of Grass and Selected Prose*, 36. This line is left out of the first edition.

19. See Nina Baym, *Woman's Fiction*, 164.

20. Susan Warner, *The Wide, Wide World*, 2 vols. (New York: Putnam, 1852), 1:11. Future references to this edition will be made parenthetically in the text.

21. Harriet Beecher Stowe, *Uncle Tom's Cabin* (New York: Signet, 1981), 21. Future references to this volume will be cited parenthetically in the text.

22. Edward Halsey Foster, *Susan and Anna Warner* (Boston: Twayne Publishers, 1978), 35, 49.

23. Henry James, *The Nation* (September 4, 1865).

24. As Nina Baym says of *The Wide, Wide World* in *Woman's Fiction*, the focus in the novel is the "issue of power and how to live without it" (144).

25. Anna Warner (pseud. Amy Lothrop), *Dollars and Cents*, 2 vols. (New York: George P. Putnam, 1852), 2:272. According to Grace Overmeyer, the novel provides a description of the sheriff's sale of the Warners' possessions. See "Hudson River Bluestockings—The Warner Sisters of Constitution Island," *New York History* 4 (April 1959): 147.

26. Fanny Fern, "To Gentlemen: A Call to Be a Husband," *New York Ledger* (December 13, 1856). Subsequent references to the *Ledger* will be made in the text.

27. Merish, *Sentimental Materialism*, 18.

28. Tompkins, *Sensational Designs*, 168–178. Moreover, as Lori Merish points out in *Sentimental Materialism*, sentimental agency depends upon an "identification with subordination and dependency" (24). As Cathy Davidson and Jessamyn Hatcher write in *No More Separate Spheres!*, eds. Cathy Davidson and Jessamyn Hatcher (Durham: Duke University Press, 2002), "How can we even begin to assess a 'sentimental power' that both derives in compensatory fashion from political exclusion and, at the same time, is based on forms of privilege (of race and class, for example) that derive from exactly the same political system that excludes women (of all races) from voting?" (14).

29. Susan Warner, *The Wide, Wide World*, ed. Jane Tompkins (1852; New York: Feminist Press, 1997), 582. This final chapter was not printed in the original edition.

30. Genesis 3:16 tells the story of Hagar, who with her son Ishmael is cast out by Abraham and his wife, Sarah. They wander in the desert until they find the hidden spring, which represents God's word and brings salvation.

31. E. D. E. N. Southworth, *The Deserted Wife* (Philadelphia: T. B. Peterson and Brothers, 1855), 148. Subsequent references will be given parenthetically in the text.

32. Mary Frances Berry, *The Pig Farmer's Daughter and Other Tales of American Justice: Episodes of Racism and Sexism in the Courts from 1865 to the Present* (New York: Vintage Books, 2000), 4.

33. Susan K. Harris, in *19th-Century American Women's Novels: Interpretive Strategies* (New York: Cambridge University Press, 1990), interprets the houses in *The Deserted Wife* as "metaphors for women's capacities for independence," maintaining that Hagar's house, in contrast to the houses of the other more conventional women in the novel, reflects her independent selfhood (137, 150).

34. Ann M. Ingram, in "Melodrama and the Moral Economy of E. D. E. N. Southworth's *The Deserted Wife*," *The American Transcendental Quarterly* 4 (December 1999): 269–285, points out that Southworth "manipulates" the conventions of melodrama so that instead of the "victimized heroine" being rescued by a

"dashing hero," Hagar "saves herself and succeeds both emotionally and financially" (270).

35. As Joanne Dobson notes, the overarching theme of Southworth's many novels is the theme of woman's "power." Dobson, "Introduction to E. D. E. N. Southworth," *The Hidden Hand* (New Brunswick: Rutgers University Press, 1988), xxii.

36. E. D. E. N. Southworth, *India: The Pearl of Pearl River* (Philadelphia: T. B. Peterson, 1856), 22.

37. Dobson, introduction, *The Hidden Hand*, xx.

38. For an analysis of the importance of free-labor ideology in the antislavery Republican Party and as part of government policy during Reconstruction, see Eric Foner, *Free Soil, Free Labor, Free Men: The Ideology of the Republican Party before the Civil War* (New York: Oxford University Press, 1970) and *Politics and Ideology in the Age of the Civil War* (New York: Oxford University Press, 1980). Rachel Naomi Klein, in "Harriet Beecher Stowe and the Domestication of Free Labor Ideology," *Legacy* 18 (2001): 136–152, applies these theories to Stowe, pointing out that one of the problems with interpretations of Stowe as an anticapitalist is their dehistoricized conception of the market. In the mid-nineteenth century, notes Klein, many northerners who were opposed to slavery "identified freedom with contractual wage relationships" and assumed that "slavery and wage labor were fundamentally distinct and opposed systems" (137).

39. Elizabeth Ammons, in "Heroines in *Uncle Tom's Cabin*," focuses on Stowe's emphasis on feminine values, particularly motherhood, as an alternative to the "white masculine 'success' ethic" but points out that the novel concludes with three male models—George Harris, George Shelby, and Tom—to show that men can be "as beautiful morally" as women; see *Critical Essays on Harriet Beecher Stowe*, ed. Elizabeth Ammons (Boston: G. K. Hall & Co., 1980), 152–165; reprinted from *American Literature* 49 (1977): 161–179. Nina Baym, in *Woman's Fiction*, maintains that Stowe's novel is "permeated" with the ideology of "social revolution" where home values replace the greed and speculation of male society (49); Jane Tompkins, in *Sensational Designs*, argues that Stowe advocated a utopian society where "man-made institutions" would give way to a world where Christian women preside over cooperative human relationships (141–145); and Gillian Brown, in *Domestic Individualism*, asserts that "*Uncle Tom's Cabin* attacks not only the patriarchal institution but nineteenth-century patriarchy" (23).

40. The novel concludes with a sermonic warning to the United States: "Both North and South have been guilty before God; and the *Christian Church* has a heavy account to answer. Not by combining together, to protect injustice and cruelty, and making a common capital of sin, is this Union to be saved—but by repentance, justice, and mercy; for, not surer is the eternal law by which the mill-

stone sinks in the ocean, than that stronger law by which injustice and cruelty shall bring on nations the wrath of Almighty God!" (477). Ann Douglas, in *The Feminization of American Culture* (New York: Alfred A. Knopf, 1978), remarks that Stowe's novel is a "great book . . . because it is a great revival sermon" (245). For a comprehensive discussion centering on Stowe's use of religion in this novel, see Tompkins, *Sensational Designs*, 122–146.

41. Elizabeth Ammons, in "Heroines in *Uncle Tom's Cabin*," notes that Stowe had stated that Jesus Christ "had more of the pure feminine element than any other man" (154). Ammons provides an insightful defense of Stowe's portrayal of Tom, pointing out that if Stowe chose to give Tom feminine qualities, it was not because she could not imagine a black man any other way—Ammons cites Stowe's approval of George Harris's "manly defiance"—but because the "genius of her propaganda" was to gain her audience's support for Tom by deliberately associating him with her society's idolatry of feminine virtue (159). Twentieth- and twenty-first-century critiques of *Uncle Tom's Cabin* range from accusations of racism to queries about what some critics have identified as class- or gender-ridden protectionism. Perhaps the most well-known criticism is that of critics who, following James Baldwin, excoriated Stowe's racism for her portrayal of Uncle Tom as a black man, who, Baldwin said, is "divested of his sex." See Baldwin, "Everybody's Protest Novel," *Notes of a Native Son* (Boston: Beacon Press, 1955), 11–28. Such criticism, however, is indicative of a society that admires aggressive maleness, whether the male "hero" is a Western gunslinger, Cooper's Hawkeye, a filmic action hero, the Terminator, a gangsta rapper, or a president who dons cowboy boots and a flight suit. Other critics have contended that Stowe's use of white middle-class norms to promote sympathy for blacks was a form of colonization. See Karen Sanchez-Eppler, "Bodily Bonds: The Intersecting Rhetorics of Feminism and Abolition," *Representations* 24 (1988): 28–59. Lori Merish, in *Sentimental Materialism*, faults Stowe's reliance upon a "sentimental ideology of gender" and the "proprietary authority" that "asserts black dependency" (154). However, Merish correctly notes that Stowe's "sympathetic representations of black slaves constituted a powerful form of cultural and legal revisionism" (154). One might say that Stowe's use of sentimental rhetoric to accomplish her purpose was both a strategy and a limitation.

42. Herman Melville, *Moby-Dick*, ed. Tony Tanner (Oxford: Oxford University Press, 1988), 1.

43. After the passage of the Fugitive Slave Law, Stowe's sister-in-law wrote to her, "Hattie, if I could use a pen as you can, I would write something that would make this whole nation feel what an accursed thing slavery is." Cited in Joan D. Hedrick, *Harriet Beecher Stowe: A Life* (New York: Oxford University Press, 1994), 207.

44. Walter Benn Michaels tentatively posits a variation of this idea in "Romance and Real Estate," 156–182. He describes Stowe as "fearing slavery (if I am right) [his insertion] as an emblem of the market economy" (175).

45. See, e.g., Ammons, "Heroines in *Uncle Tom's Cabin*," 154.

46. Stowe is describing a situation that she had observed in other marriages and experienced in her own life—that the wife may have a better business sense than the husband. Calvin Stowe had handled the negotiations for a contract for *Uncle Tom's Cabin*, and Harriet believed that she had been cheated. He had allowed the publisher to talk him into accepting a royalty of 10 percent instead of the original 20 percent. Joan Hedrick, in her biography, writes that Calvin Stowe "had less practical sense than Harriet," and notes that Calvin characterized himself as a man with an "incapacity to manage money." See Hedrick, *Harriet Beecher Stowe*, 94, 223. In a letter to Harriet Stowe in 1868, Fanny Fern wrote of her own husband, James Parton, "he is no more fit to make a bargain than your dear Mr. Stowe is." Cited in Warren, *Fanny Fern*, 275.

47. Edith Wharton, *The House of Mirth* (1905; New York: Signet, 1980), 308.

48. George Orwell, "Charles Dickens," *The Collected Essays, Journalism, and Letters of George Orwell*, vol. 1, *An Age Like This, 1920–1940* (New York: Harcourt, Brace & World, 1968), 413–460; see, e.g., 416–417, 427.

49. Cited in Hedrick, *Harriet Beecher Stowe*, vii.

50. See, e.g., Hedrick, *Harriet Beecher Stowe*, 304.

51. Rebecca R. Saulsbury, "Maria Susanna Cummins," *Nineteenth-Century American Women Writers*, ed. Denise D. Knight (Westport, CT: Greenwood Press, 1997), 82. For information on the reception and sales of *The Lamplighter*, see, e.g., Frank Luther Mott, *Golden Multitudes: The Story of Best Sellers in the United States* (New York: Macmillan, 1947), and Susan S. Williams, " 'Promoting an Extensive Sale': The Production and Reception of *The Lamplighter*," *New England Quarterly* 69 (June 1996): 179–200.

52. Nathaniel Hawthorne, *The Letters of Hawthorne to William Ticknor, 1851–1869*, ed. C. E. Frazer Clark, Jr., 2 vols. (Newark, New Jersey: Carteret Book Club, 1972), 1:73–75.

53. Ibid., 1:78

54. E. D. E. N. Southworth, *The Hidden Hand*, ed. Joanne Dobson (New Brunswick: Rutgers University Press, 1988), 45.

55. Amy Schrager Lang, "Class and the Strategies of Sympathy," in *The Culture of Sentiment: Race, Gender, and Sentimentality in Nineteenth-Century America*, ed. Shirley Samuels (New York: Oxford University Press, 1992), 129–130.

56. Maria S. Cummins, *The Lamplighter* (Boston: Houghton Mifflin, 1902), 121. Subsequent references will be cited parenthetically in the text.

57. As Nina Baym notes in *Woman's Fiction*, although Gerty must submit to

God's will, Cummins "does not require such submission for Gerty in her human relations" (166).

58. Elizabeth Cady Stanton, Susan B. Anthony, and Matilda Joslyn Gage, eds., *History of Woman Suffrage*, 6 vols. (1881–1922; Rochester, NY: 1889; reprint, New York: Source Book Press, 1970), 1:73.

59. Fern wrote a favorable review of Whitman's *Leaves of Grass*, and she and Whitman were friends in the mid-1850s until Whitman borrowed money from Fern's husband under false pretenses and did not pay it back. For a discussion of Fern's relationship with Whitman, see Joyce W. Warren, "Subversion versus Celebration: The Aborted Friendship of Fanny Fern and Walt Whitman," in *Patrons and Protégées: Gender, Friendship, and Writing in Nineteenth-Century America*, ed. Shirley Marchalonis (New Brunswick: Rutgers University Press, 1988), 59–93, and Warren, *Fanny Fern*, 160–178.

60. For information on Fern's life, see Warren, *Fanny Fern*, which contains a discussion of critical and biographical sources (313–314) as well as a chapter on *Ruth Hall* (120–142).

61. Fanny Fern, "Servants," *New York Ledger* (Nov. 21, 1857) and Fanny Fern, *Folly as It Flies*, (New York: G. W. Carleton & Co., 1868), 112–114.

62. Fanny Fern, "Whose Fault Is It?", *New York Ledger* (August 9, 1862); see also Fern, *Folly*, 117.

63. Fanny Fern, "A Sedative in a Small Dose," *New York Ledger* (June 29, 1861). For other articles revealing Fern's cross-class perspective, see, e.g., "Soliloquy of a Housemaid," *True Flag* (September 11, 1852); "Sewing Machines," *True Flag* (January 29, 1853); "Whom Does It Concern?" *Saturday Evening Post* (January 7, 1854); and in the *New York Ledger*, "The Working-Girls of New York (January 26, 1867); "Tyrants of the Shop" (June 1, 1867); and "The Working Girls of Our City" (July 2, 1870). See also her novella, "Fanny Ford," serialized in the *Ledger* beginning June 9, 1855. Nicole Tonkovich addresses the issue of class in *Domesticity with a Difference: The Nonfiction of Catharine Beecher, Sarah J. Hale, Fanny Fern, and Margaret Fuller* (Jackson: University Press of Mississippi, 1997), and her book provides an interesting analysis of the interdependence of the public and private spheres for four nineteenth-century women writers. However, her claim that none of the writers she discusses had to maintain a "domestic establishment" nor did they have the care of children while they were writers is not applicable to Fern, who was the sole support and sole nursemaid for her children until she earned enough money to buy her way out of the working class. She had to take her daughter with her when she was peddling her articles because she had no one to leave her with, and she had to pass up opportunities to earn money sewing out-of-home because the sewing factories did not permit children on the premises. Also not applicable

to Fern is Tonkovich's claim that Fern and the other writers "sought to limit the class mobility" of working-class women (xiv–xv), an accusation that Tonkovich bases on an ahistorical and limited reading of Fern's work. On the basis of only two articles in an edited collection, she makes the claim because, for example, Fern criticizes a chambermaid for characterizing herself as "genteel" and a schoolgirl for wearing a dirty silk dress to school instead of a more appropriate de laine (a fine cotton or wool)—apparently unaware that Fern as a young woman wore de laine dresses herself, as does her heroine in *Ruth Hall* (see Fern, *Ruth Hall and Other Writings*, ed. Joyce W. Warren [New Brunswick: Rutgers University Press, 1986], 19). Clearly, Tonkovich misses the point of the article, which is to deplore the Victorians' pretentious use of the term "genteel"—"no matter where, or how, or to whom, or by whom it is applied"—and fails to note that in the same article (the title of which is "Gentility") Fern criticizes the "moneyed class" for the same affectations. The ubiquitousness of the pretentious "gentility" that Fern deplored is evidenced by the fact that Fern herself was a victim of it—even in this article in which she condemned it. The *Folly* editor, however, changed the word "slang" to "detestable expression-word," creating what he apparently regarded as a more "genteel" sentence but which is in fact a pompous affectation. See Fern, "Gentility," *New York Ledger* (April 25, 1863) and *Folly as It Flies* (New York: G. W. Carleton & Co., 1868), 109–111.

64. Fern, *Ruth Hall and Other Writings*, 175. Further references to *Ruth Hall* will be cited in the text.

65. Berlant, "The Female Woman," 278.

66. Fanny Fern to Harriet Beecher Stowe, February 14, 1868, Schlesinger Library, Radcliffe College. In *Ruth Hall* Fern uses two voices to accomplish her purpose, alternating the conventional sentimental voice with the cynical or independent voice of experience. For discussions of this strategy, see Warren, introduction to *Ruth Hall and Other Writings*, xxvii–xxviii, and Warren, *Fanny Fern*, 135–136. See also Harris, *19th-Century American Women's Novels*, 112–113. Ann Douglas Wood discusses Fern's use of the language of sentiment with respect to Fern's manipulation of contemporary rhetoric, but she attributes Fern's use of two voices to "confusion" rather than to deliberate strategy. See "The 'Scribbling Women' and Fanny Fern: Why Women Wrote," *American Quarterly* 23 (Spring 1971): 3–24.

Chapter Four | THE WOMAN PLAINTIFF

1. Unless otherwise indicated, the records for the court cases discussed in this chapter are from the New York Supreme Court cases housed in Special Collections in the Hofstra University Library. As noted in the introduction, these

records are uncatalogued, arranged only by date. Hence I have not been able to reference them by the usual law citations.

2. In researching this case and other cases for which such information was needed, I obtained addresses, occupations, and other relevant information from the *New York City Directory*, 1840–80.

3. For representative figures on incomes, see chapter 8, "The Economics of Divorce." See also Philip S. Foner, *Women and the American Labor Movement: From Colonial Times to the Eve of World War I* (New York: Free Press, 1979), 87, 91, and Thomas Dublin, *Women at Work* (New York: Columbia University Press, 1979), 188–192.

4. This was the 1865 case of *Nixon v. Witty*, in which Mary C. Ellingham, acting as executor for the estate of Caroline L. Nixon, sued Calvin Witty for ten thousand dollars. There is no indication of the relationship between the two women. Nixon had owned the Equestrian Circus, and Witty claimed that she had relinquished title to him before she died. Ellingham, however, had a witness who testified to the contrary. The case apparently was settled out of court.

5. A Retired Merchant, "My Wife and the Market Street Phantom," *Godey's Lady's Book* (September 1870): 339–342, and Fanny Fern, "A Bit of Injustice," *New York Ledger* (June 8, 1861), reprinted in Fern, *Ruth Hall and Other Writings*, 318–319.

6. Wai Chee Dimock, *Residues of Justice: Literature, Law, Philosophy* (Berkeley: University of California Press, 1996), 92.

7. The original case is in the New York Supreme Court records, not the records at Hofstra University (*Lemmon v. People*, 1857; no number in original). The case was appealed before the Court of Appeals of New York; see 20 NY 562 (1860). The New York legislation cited in the judges' 1860 decision includes *Laws of 1817*, chap. 137; *Revised Statutes of 1830*, 1 R.S., 656, chap. 20 part 1, tit. 7; and the *Repealing Act Laws 1841*, chap. 247. For a discussion of the Lemmon case and a partial text of the proceedings in the Appeals Court, see Paul Finkelman, *The Law of Freedom and Bondage: A Casebook* (New York: Oceana Publications, 1986), 83–94.

8. Frances Harper, "We Are All Bound Up Together," *A Brighter Coming Day*, ed. Frances Smith Foster (New York: Feminist Press, 1990), 218.

9. Franklin's wife had been abandoned by her first husband and had come home to her parents' house. Her parents were glad to marry her off to Franklin, who had been courting her earlier. *The Autobiography of Benjamin Franklin* (New York: Walter J. Black, 1941), 104–106.

10. Louisa May Alcott, "Behind a Mask, or A Woman's Power," *Behind a Mask: The Unknown Thrillers of Louisa May Alcott*, ed. Madeleine Stern (New York: Quill, 1984), 59.

11. See, e.g., Mary Frances Berry, *The Pig Farmer's Daughter and Other Tales of American Justice* (New York: Vintage Books, 1999), 237; William E. Nelson,

"Criminality and Sexual Morality in New York, 1920–1980," 5 *Yale Journal of Law and the Humanities* 265 (1993): 324–325; and Jason M. Price, "Constitutional Law— Sex, Lies and Rape Shield Statutes: The Constitutionality of Interpreting Rape Shield Statutes to Exclude Evidence Relating to the Victim's Motive to Fabricate," 18 *Western New England Law Review* 541 (1996): 459–552.

Chapter Five | THE ECONOMICS OF RACE

1. Barbara Christian, *Black Women Novelists: The Development of a Tradition, 1892–1976* (Westport, CT: Greenwood Press, 1980), notes that in *Iola Leroy* Harper sought to refute the image of black women that had been "created to keep a particular image about white women intact" (18); the "mammy," she says, was the "necessary correlate of the Southern lady" (12).

2. Hazel V. Carby, *Reconstructing Womanhood: The Emergence of the Afro-American Woman Novelist* (New York: Oxford University Press, 1987), 6.

3. Mary Helen Washington, *Invented Lives: Narratives of Black Women, 1860– 1960* (Garden City: Doubleday, 1987), 74. For a discussion of the insistence on separate spheres for black men and women during the early twentieth century, see Barbara Bair, "True Women, Real Men: Gender, Ideology, and Social Roles in the Garvey Movement," in *Gendered Spheres: Rethinking Public and Private in Women's History*, eds. Dorothy O. Helly and Susan M. Reverby (Ithaca: Cornell University Press, 1992), 154–180.

4. Frances Smith Foster, introduction to *A Brighter Coming Day: A Frances Ellen Watkins Harper Reader*, ed. Frances Smith Foster (New York: Feminist Press, 1990), 4. Subsequent references will be cited in the text.

5. Melba Joyce Boyd, *Discarded Legacy: Politics and Poetics in the Life of Frances E. W. Harper, 1825–1911* (Detroit: Wayne State University Press, 1994), 18–22. In the past two decades, scholars have rescued Harper's work from oblivion, and critics have reassessed her work.

6. Harper's father's race is unknown, but because of her light skin, critics have theorized that he may have been a white man. See, e.g., Foster, introduction to *A Brighter Coming Day*, 6.

7. One does not know whether or not the school curriculum included female students in the oratorical instruction, although they would have learned elocution.

8. William Still, *The Underground Rail Road* (1872; New York: Arno Press, 1968), 758. Subsequent references will be cited in the text.

9. Women had begun speaking in public only in the late 1830s, when the Grimké sisters spoke in churches, initially only to women, but gradually to

mixed audiences. In the 1840s and 1850s women reformers (e.g., Stowe and Willard) asked men to deliver their speeches. See Lillian O'Connor, *Pioneer Women Orators: Rhetoric in the Ante-Bellum Reform Movement* (New York: Columbia University Press, 1945), 32, 35.

10. Frances E. W. Harper, *Iola Leroy, or Shadows Uplifted*, ed. Frances Smith Foster (1892; New York: Oxford University Press, 1988), 271. Subsequent references will be cited in the text.

11. See *Minnie's Sacrifice, Sowing and Reaping, and Trial and Triumph: Three Rediscovered Novels by Frances E. W. Harper*, ed. Frances Smith Foster (Boston: Beacon Press, 1994), 91. Subsequent references will be cited in the text.

12. See, e.g., Benjamin Quarles, *Black Abolitionists* (New York: Oxford, 1969), 76.

13. See Carla L. Peterson, *"Doers of the Word": African-American Women Speakers and Writers in the North (1830–1880)* (New York: Oxford, 1995), 134–135.

14. See Robert Bone, *The Negro Novel in America* (New Haven: Yale University Press, 1958), 32. For a discussion of the political and feminist perspective of *Iola Leroy*, see, e. g., Carby, *Reconstructing Womanhood*, 92–94.

15. For a discussion of the attitudes of black male intellectuals at the turn of the century, see Washington, *Invented Lives*, 74–75.

16. Carby, in *Reconstructing Womanhood*, notes that most studies of late nineteenth-century black intellectuals focused on men (83–87).

17. Harper was not the only nineteenth-century African American leader who was of this opinion. Bernard W. Bell notes that Frank J. Webb's novel *The Garies and Their Friends* (1857) stresses the importance of economics: "Instead of Christian charity or black power, Webb's answer to racial discrimination is green power." The characters note that white society respects "the power of money and property more than democratic and Christian principles." See Bell, *The Afro-American Novel and Its Tradition* (Amherst: University of Massachusetts Press, 1987), 43.

18. Carby, *Reconstructing Womanhood*, 6.

19. Louisa May Alcott, *Work: A Story of Experience, The Alternative Alcott*, ed. Elaine Showalter (New Brunswick: Rutgers University Press, 1992), 239–349. Alcott's novel begins with young Christie Devon's "Declaration of Independence" to her aunt: "I'm going to take care of myself, and not be a burden any longer. . . . I'm old enough to take care of myself; and if I'd been a boy, I should have been told to do it long ago. I hate to be dependent. . . . There is plenty of work in the world, and I'm not afraid of it" (239–241).

20. Washington, *Invented Lives*, 77, 89.

21. For information about Wilson's life, see, e.g., the introduction to Harriet Wilson, *Our Nig; or, Sketches from the Life of a Free Black*, ed. Henry Louis Gates, Jr.

(New York: Vintage Books, 1983), xi–lv; Barbara White, " 'Our Nig' and the She Devil: New Information about Harriet Wilson and the 'Bellmont' Family," *American Literature* 65 (March 1993): 19–52; and Gabrielle Foreman and Reginald H. Pitts, introduction to Harriet E. Wilson, *Our Nig; or, Sketches from the Life of a Free Black* (New York: Penguin, 2005), vii–i. For a discussion of Wilson's health, see Cynthia J. Davis, "Speaking the Body's Pain: Harriet Wilson's *Our Nig*," *African American Review* 27 (Fall 1993): 391–404.

22. Little is known of Wilson's schooling, but since so much of her novel follows the outlines of her life, it seems likely that her schooling paralleled that of her protagonist in *Our Nig*, who had "three months of schooling, summer and winter" for three years (37). This indicates that she attended school for two three-month terms a year, one in the winter and one in the summer, for a period of three years. In farm communities in the nineteenth and early twentieth centuries, school either was not held or was sparsely attended during the spring and fall since many children were needed to help on the family farms during spring planting and fall harvest.

23. On the publishing history of *Our Nig*, see Eric Gardner, " 'This Attempt of Their Sister': Harriet Wilson's *Our Nig* from Printer to Readers," *The New England Quarterly* 66 (1993), 2: 226–246. Gates, in his introduction to *Our Nig*, notes that the book was "ignored or overlooked" by her contemporaries and by scholars. He says that a "systematic search of all extant copies of black and reform newspapers and magazines in circulation contemporaneously with the publication of *Our Nig* yielded not one notice or review" (xiii, xxix–xxx). However, although the book was not noticed by Wilson's contemporaries, it was, as Cynthia Davis points out, not unknown to readers and booksellers in the years since its publication; what was unknown was the gender and race of its author. See Cynthia J. Davis, "Harriet E. Wilson," *Nineteenth-Century American Women Writers: A Bio-Bibliographical Critical Sourcebook*, ed. Denise D. Knight (Westport, CT: Greenwood Press, 1997), 484. It was Gates who established the racial identity of the book's author. Earlier critics had assumed the author was white, but in his introduction to the 1983 edition, Gates cites as evidence of Wilson's race his discovery of the 1860 death certificate of her son, George (xiii).

24. John Ernest, *Resistance and Reformation in Nineteenth-Century African-American Literature: Brown, Wilson, Jacobs, Delany, Douglass, and Harper* (Jackson: University Press of Mississippi, 1995), 64. The chapter on Wilson is expanded from an earlier article, "Economies of Identity: Harriet E. Wilson's *Our Nig*," *PMLA* 109 (May 1994): 424–438.

25. Carla L. Peterson, in "Capitalism, Black (Under)development, and the Production of the African-American Novel in the 1850s," *American Literary History* 4 (1992): 559–583), maintains that Wilson rewrites the tragic mulatta story, strip-

ping it bare of all romance and exposing the "economic and sexual politics through which capitalism has systematically kept [African Americans] underdeveloped" (572).

26. Karla F. C. Holloway, "Economies of Space: Markets and Marketability in *Our Nig* and *Iola Leroy*," *The (Other) American Traditions: Nineteenth-Century Women Writers*, ed. Joyce W. Warren (New Brunswick: Rutgers University Press, 1993), 127–128, 131. See also Ernest, *Resistance and Reformation*, and Peterson, "Capitalism, Black (Under)development, and the Production of the African-American Novel in the 1850s." Although the emphases in these works differ, they all call attention to the importance of economics in Wilson's novel. As Ernest notes, Wilson conceives of her book as itself a "product" (70, 80). Peterson compares Wilson's need to earn money from her book to the motivation of other African American writers, all of whom sought to produce "literary commodities" (566).

27. Holloway, "Economies of Space," 138.

28. Wilson, *Our Nig*, n.p. Page references to the novel cited parenthetically in the text are to the 1983 Vintage edition edited by Henry Louis Gates, Jr.

29. As Gabrielle Foreman notes, Wilson "asserts her own agency by choosing to tell her story." See Foreman, "The Spoken and the Silenced in *Incidents in the Life of a Slave Girl* and *Our Nig*," *Callaloo* 13 (Spring 1990): 321. Or as Gates says in his introduction to *Our Nig*, Wilson transforms herself from object to subject (li).

30. In "'Our Nig' and the She Devil," Barbara White identifies the "Bellmonts" as the Haywards of Milford, New Hampshire. Pointing to a strong thread of materialism in the Hayward family, White calls attention to the economic themes of Wilson's book, noting that what is often thought of as "thrift and economy" can become "greed and rapaciousness" (33–34).

31. Barbara White describes the terms of the elder Hayward's will, in which he left a lifetime interest in the house to his widowed daughter Sally (Abby in the novel). The younger Mrs. Hayward ("Mrs. Bellmont") apparently was a difficult person to get along with; she and her husband moved out of the family home because she had trouble living in the house with others ("'Our Nig' and the She Devil," 32–33).

32. John Ernest, in *Resistance*, in discussing Mrs. Bellmont's treatment of people, says that the "great evil" of the book is the "will to dominate" (72). However, the evil is not so much one of domination as it is the lack of humanity. Like Stowe and Harper, Wilson is not out to change the economic system, but her portrayal of Mrs. Bellmont's profit-oriented behavior, along with other factors, suggests that she would agree with Stowe that what was needed was a moral shift from a society in which profit predominates to one in which it is tempered by humanity, or with Harper, who called for the development of "character."

33. See Davis, "Harriet E. Wilson," 487.

34. Beth Maclay Doriani, in "Black Womanhood in Nineteenth-Century America: Subversion and Self-Construction in Two Women's Autobiographies," *American Quarterly* 43 (June 1991), asserts that both Wilson and Jacobs show black women as "shapers of their own destinies" (202–203). It is important to note, however, that although Wilson succeeds in asserting her agency or defining herself as subject, her ability to change her destiny within the span of the novel is severely restricted.

35. Foreman and Pitts, introduction to *Our Nig*, xxx, xlviii.

36. *Banner of Light* (September 14, 1867), 5; cited in Foreman and Pitts, introduction to *Our Nig*, xl.

37. Foreman and Pitts, introduction to *Our Nig*, x–xi, xl–xliii.

38. Hannah Crafts, *The Bondwoman's Narrative*, ed. Henry Louis Gates, Jr. (New York: Warner Books, 2002). All references to Crafts's work will be cited parenthetically in the text.

39. In his introduction to Crafts, *The Bondwoman's Narrative*, Gates reports the conclusions of experts whose analysis of such criteria as paper, ink, and context date the manuscript as "circa 1853–1861" (xxviii–xxx). He also cites his own and other scholars' evidence for concluding that the novel is probably the work of a black woman. For example, Crafts makes blackness the default; she doesn't "signal blackness," as do white authors, but looks at black characters "as people first of all" (xvii–xxi, xxv). Possible gender indicators include handwriting and the use of a thimble as a seal (xxxi). Appended to the novel is the complete "Authentication Report" of Joe Nickell, who is an investigator and historical-document examiner. See appendix A, 285–315.

40. Gates, introduction to Crafts, *Bondwoman's*, xiii–xvi. For corroborating information about the Wheelers, including entries from John Hill Wheeler's diary, see Gates, notes to Crafts, *Bondwoman's*, 257, 260–277. Especially pertinent in relation to Crafts's mention of Mrs. Wheeler's former maid, "Jane," whose recent escape necessitated the purchase of Hannah as a replacement, is Gates's identification of the slave "Jane" as Jane Johnson, who with her two children escaped from Wheeler in Philadelphia in July 1855. See Gates, introduction and notes to Crafts, *Bondwoman's*, xlvi–lvi, 317–332.

41. Gates, introduction to Crafts, *Bondwoman's*, xii, xxii.

42. Crafts's unusual frankness with respect to the sexual use of slave women may be due, in part, to the fact that, like the poems of Emily Dickinson, her narrative has come to us apparently without the mediation of nineteenth-century editors and publishers, who backed away from mentioning in print anything that conflicted with nineteenth-century notions of propriety. Although Crafts's narrative's heavy borrowings from literature indicate a comprehensive awareness of the "mind of the age," her writing was not guided or censored by even a well-in-

tentioned editor as it would have been if it had been published when it was written. For an indication of her borrowings, see Gates, notes to Crafts, *Bondwoman's*, 331–332, and Gates, "Essay; Borrowing Privileges," *New York Times Book Review* (June 2, 2002), 18.

43. See Jean Fagan Yellin, *Harriet Jacobs: A Life* (New York: Basic Civitas Books, 2004). See also introduction and notes to Harriet Jacobs, *Incidents in the Life of a Slave Girl*, ed. Jean Fagan Yellin (Cambridge: Harvard University Press, 1987), xiii–xxxiv, 253–292, and Yellin, "*Written by Herself*: Harriet Jacobs's Slave Narrative," *American Literature* 53 (November 1981): 479–486.

44. Jacobs, *Incidents*, 5. Subsequent references will be cited parenthetically in the text.

45. Houston A. Baker, Jr., *Blues, Ideology, and Afro-American Literature: A Vernacular Theory* (Chicago: University of Chicago Press, 1984), suggests that Linda deliberately "commodifies" herself and her children in order to free them from the slave market (51–54).

46. Critics who have contrasted Jacobs's work with the male slave narrative include Frances Smith Foster, " 'In Respect to Females': Differences in the Portrayals of Women by Male and Female Slave Narrators," *Black American Literature* 15 (Summer 1981): 66–70; Nellie McKay, "Reflections on Black Women Writers: Revising the Literary Canon," in *Feminisms*, eds. Robyn R. Warhol and Diane Price Herndl (New Brunswick: Rutgers University Press, 1991), 249–261; Joanne M. Braxton, "Harriet Jacobs' *Incidents in the Life of a Slave Girl*: The Re-definition of the Slave Narrative Genre," *Massachusetts Review* 27 (Summer 1986), 380–381; Valerie Smith, *Self-Discovery and Authority in Afro-American Narrative* (Cambridge: Harvard University Press, 1987); Washington, *Invented Lives*; Mason Lowaree, Jr., "The Slave Narrative in American Literature," in *African American Writers*, ed. Valerie Smith (New York: Scribner's, 1991), 395–412; Doriani, "Black Womanhood in Nineteenth-Century America"; William L. Andrews, "The Changing Moral Discourse of Nineteenth-Century African American Women's Autobiography: Harriet Jacobs and Elizabeth Keckley," in *De/Colonizing the Subject*, eds. Sidonie Smith and Julia Watson (Minneapolis: University of Minnesota Press, 1992), 225–241; and Yellin, introduction to *Incidents*, xxvi.

47. Critics who have compared aspects of Jacobs's *Incidents* to sentimental fiction include Thomas Doherty, "Harriet Jacobs' Narrative Strategies: *Incidents in the Life of a Slave Girl*," *Southern Literary Journal* 19 (Fall 1986): 79–91; John F. Bayliss, ed., *Black Slave Narratives* (New York: Macmillan, 1970), 108; Frances Smith Foster, *Witnessing Slavery: The Development of the Ante-Bellum Slave Narratives* (Westport, CT: Greenwood Press, 1979), 58–59; Jean Fagan Yellin, "Text and Contexts in Harriet Jacobs' *Incidents in the Life of a Slave Girl: Written by Herself*," in *The Slave's Narrative*, eds. Charles T. Davis and Henry Louis Gates, Jr. (New

York: Oxford, 1985); Elizabeth Fox-Genovese, "To Write My Self: The Autobiographies of Afro-American Women," in *Feminist Issues in Literary Scholarship*, eds. Shari Benstock and Catharine Stimpson (Bloomington: Indiana University Press, 1987), 169–171; Doriani, "Black Womanhood," 204; Harryette Mullen, "Runaway Tongue: Resistant Orality in *Uncle Tom's Cabin, Our Nig, Incidents in the Life of a Slave Girl*, and *Beloved*," in *The Culture of Sentiment*, ed. Shirley Samuels (New York: Oxford, 1992), 244–245.

48. Jacobs's original manuscript ended with material on John Brown. It was Lydia Maria Child who suggested she omit the Brown sections and end with her grandmother's death. See Bruce Mills, "Lydia Maria Child and the Endings to Harriet Jacobs's *Incidents in the Life of a Slave Girl*," *American Literature* 64 (June 1992): 255–272.

Chapter Six | THE WOMAN DEFENDANT

1. Unless otherwise indicated, the records for the court cases discussed in this chapter are from the New York Supreme Court cases housed in Special Collections in the Hofstra University Library. As noted in the introduction, these records are uncatalogued but arranged by date. Hence I have not been able to refer to them by the usual legal citations.

2. For a discussion of the 1850 banking law in New York State, see, e.g., Norma Basch, *In the Eyes of the Law: Women, Marriage, and Property in Nineteenth-Century New York* (Ithaca: Cornell University Press, 1982), 160.

3. The story of Charles Eldredge's lawsuit and the consequences for Fern are discussed in chapter 7. See also Joyce W. Warren, *Fanny Fern: An Independent Woman* (New Brunswick: Rutgers University Press, 1992), 66–70, 76.

4. Frances Harper, *A Brighter Coming Day*, ed. Frances Smith Foster (New York: The Feminist Press, 1990), 217.

5. In response to a male-authored assertion that women do not have the intelligence or patience to understand complex ideas, Fern wrote that, in fact, women are quick to arrive at solutions while men are "still groping at the threshold." Women, she said, often do the work for which men get the credit: "If there's any mental Gordian knot you *can't* untwist, we'll lend you a feminine hand, and then *let you have the credit of it!*" See Fern, *Olive Branch* (February 2, 1853).

6. Fanny Fern, *A New Story Book for Children* (New York: Mason Brothers, 1864), 17–18. I discuss this question in more detail in chapter 7.

7. For the British common law requiring a judge to meet privately with the wife to be sure she was not being coerced when she signed a real estate document, see William Blackstone, *Commentaries on the Laws of England*, 4 vols. (1765; reprint, Chicago: University of Chicago Press, 1979), 2:129–136.

8. For a discussion of Fern's purchase of her first house in 1856 and her prenuptial agreement, see Warren, *Fanny Fern*, 153–154, 158.

9. An interesting footnote to this case is the fact that Thomas Emmet apparently had a reputation for overcharging. In 1851 he had been hired to do surveys and calculations for a group of men in upstate New York, but the men who hired him complained that they had been grossly overcharged and refused to pay what he demanded. He sued to compel payment, but they brought in witnesses—civil engineers—who testified that a "full and fair compensation" ought not to exceed five hundred dollars, whereas he had charged three times that amount. (The engineers also said that his work was "grossly inaccurate.")

10. Harriet Wilson, *Our Nig; or, Sketches from the Life of a Free Black*, ed. Henry Louis Gates, Jr. (New York: Vintage Books, 1983), 45. As indicated in chapter 5, this provision reflected the reality of the family on which Wilson based the Bellmonts.

11. For a copy of the New York State Married Women's Property Act of 1860 see, e.g., Elizabeth Cady Stanton, Susan B. Anthony, and Matilda Joslyn Gage, eds., *History of Woman Suffrage*, 6 vols. (1881–1922; Rochester, NY: 1889; reprint, New York: Source Book Press, 1970), 1:686–687.

Chapter Seven | Economics and
the Law in Fiction

1. Fanny Fern, *Ruth Hall and Other Writings*, ed. Joyce W. Warren (New Brunswick: Rutgers University Press, 1986), 76–77. Further references to this work will be cited in the text.

2. See Elizabeth Cady Stanton, Susan B. Anthony, and Joslyn Gage, eds., *History of Woman Suffrage*, 6 vols. (1881–1922; Rochester, NY: 1899; reprint, New York: Source Book Press, 1970), 1:469. For a discussion of the ease with which nineteenth-century women were institutionalized under the existing laws, see chapter 8.

3. Child custody laws are discussed in chapter 2 and chapter 8.

4. Fanny Fern, *A New Story Book for Children* (New York: Mason Brothers, 1864), 17–18.

5. For a discussion of Eldredge's legal and financial difficulties, see Joyce W. Warren, *Fanny Fern: An Independent Woman* (New Brunswick: Rutgers University Press, 1992), 67–70. The documents with Fern's signature are in the Middlesex County Register of Deeds, Cambridge, Massachusetts.

6. The letters and a copy of the divorce decree dated September 7, 1853, are in the Sophia Smith Collection at Smith College. See Warren, *Fanny Fern*, 118.

7. Fanny Fern, *Rose Clark* (New York: Mason Brothers, 1856), 345–346.

8. The prenuptial agreement is in the James Parton Papers, Houghton Library, Harvard University. The document is reprinted in Warren, *Fanny Fern*, 153.

9. Martha W. Tyler, *A Book without a Title: or, Thrilling Events in the Life of Mira Dana* (1855; Boston: Printed for the author, 1856). References to the 1856 novel will be cited parenthetically in the text. The 1856 edition of the novel was revised from the first edition to give it a truer ending. Whereas the 1855 edition ends happily, with Mira in a cozy cottage surrounded by her children, the 1856 edition ends the way that Tyler's own marriage ended—with Tyler bereft of her children and working to support herself. For biographical information, see Vicki Lynn Hill, "Martha W. Tyler," *American Women Writers*, ed. Lina Mainiero (NY: Frederick Ungar, 1982), 277–278, and Judith A. Ranta, "'A true woman's courage and hopefulness': Martha W. Tyler's *A Book without a Title: or, Thrilling Events in the Life of Mira Dana*," *Legacy* 21 (2004), 1:17–33. See also Abijah P. Marvin, *History of the Town of Lancaster, Massachusetts* (Lancaster: Town, 1879), 630, 785, and the court cases chronicling her divorce: *Tyler v. Tyler*, MA, Worcester County Supreme Judicial Court, Record Book, vol. 14 (1852–1854): 391, and vol. 18 (1859–1861): 105–106, 306, cited in Ranta, "'true woman's courage,'" 18, 22.

10. It is possible that Tyler was encouraged to write her revenge novel, particularly the 1856 version, after reading *Ruth Hall*, which, as Ranta points out, "strongly anticipates" the story Tyler narrates of Mira Dana (18).

11. See Martha W. Tyler, *Life Scenes in Our Village: Comprising Sketches from Real Life* (Boston: Published for the author, 1857).

12. Elizabeth Oakes Smith, *Bertha and Lily; or, The Parsonage of Beech Glen* (New York: J. C. Derby, 1854), 83. Further references to this work will be cited parenthetically in the text.

13. Elizabeth Oakes Smith, *Woman and Her Needs* (New York: Fowlers and Wells, 1851), 33–34. Further references to this work will be cited parenthetically in the text.

14. Elizabeth Stuart Phelps, *Hedged In* (Boston: Fields, Osgood, and Co., 1870), 256.

15. Caroline Chesebro', *Isa; A Pilgrimage* (Clinton Hall, NY: Redfield, 1852), 3–4, 320. In *Woman's Fiction: A Guide to Novels by and about Women in America, 1820–1870* (Ithaca: Cornell University Press, 1978), Nina Baym suggests that the condemnation of Isa at the end of the novel is "equivocal" and says that it "cannot counteract the overwhelming consistency of the rest of the presentation" (211). Although it is true that the story of Isa's apostasy "overwhelms" the condemnation at the end, it is not accurate to say that the condemnation appears only at the end of the novel. In fact, it appears at the beginning and the end and thus frames Isa's aberrant behavior. Also, the fact that Isa's child dies and she (Isa) is unhappy and living in misery at the end of the novel adds weight to the verbal condemnation.

16. Elizabeth Stuart Phelps, *The Story of Avis* (New Brunswick: Rutgers University Press, 1985), 160–161. Further references will be cited parenthetically in the text.

17. Elizabeth Stoddard, *The Morgesons and Other Writings, Published and Unpublished*, eds. Lawrence Buell and Sandra A. Zagarell (Philadelphia: University of Pennsylvania Press, 1984), 34–35. Future references to this work will be cited parenthetically in the text.

18. Susan Harris, *19th-Century American Women's Novels: Interpretive Strategies* (Cambridge: Cambridge University Press, 1990), maintains that by the end of the novel Cassandra is "freed from sexual and economic domination" (165).

19. James Fenimore Cooper, *The Ways of the Hour, Complete Works*, 32 vols. (New York: Putnam, 1893?), 24:311, 365–366, 378, 422–426.

20. Stoddard, *The Morgesons and Other Writings*, 267. Future references to this work will be cited parenthetically in the text.

21. See my discussion of this phenomenon in chapter 2.

22. For an excellent discussion of these two stories and the reasons for the differences in their appeal, see Carolyn L. Karcher, "Rape, Murder, and Revenge in 'Slavery's Pleasant Homes': Lydia Maria Child's Antislavery Fiction and the Limits of Genre," *The Culture of Sentiment: Race, Gender, and Sentimentality in Nineteenth-Century America*, ed. Shirley Samuels (New York: Oxford University Press, 1992), 58–72. Karcher points out that in "The Quadroons," Child introduced the figure of the "tragic mulatto," which soon became a popular figure in fiction and "made it possible to dramatize the sexual plight of the slave woman in terms that appealed to a genteel audience" (72). As Karcher goes on to say, however, the use of a near-white heroine "reinforced the very prejudices antislavery fiction sought to counteract" (72).

23. See Lydia Maria Child, "The Quadroons," *Rediscoveries: American Short Stories by Women, 1832–1916*, ed. Barbara H. Solomon (New York: Mentor, 1994), 88–98.

24. Rebecca Harding Davis, *Life in the Iron Mills and Other Stories*, ed. Tillie Olsen (1972; New York: Feminist Press, 1985), 50–51.

25. Rebecca Harding Davis, *Margret Howth—A Story of To-Day* (Boston: Ticknor and Fields, 1862), was originally serialized in the *Atlantic Monthly*, October 1861–March 1862. Sharon Harris, *Rebecca Harding Davis and American Realism* (Philadelphia: University of Pennsylvania Press, 1991), maintains that the passage regarding the "promise of the dawn" in "Life in the Iron-Mills" must be taken ironically (56). However, whether the conclusion is serious or ironic does not change the fact that Davis does not proffer legal remedies for the problems that she poses.

26. Elizabeth Stuart Phelps, *The Silent Partner* (Boston: James R. Osgood and Co., 1871), 111. Phelps also does not question the age of ten as a satisfactory age at

which to begin working in the mills. Further references to this work will be cited parenthetically in the text.

27. Elizabeth Stuart Phelps, "The Tenth of January," in Phelps, *Men, Women, and Ghosts* (Boston: Fields, Osgood, and Co., 1869), 43–89; originally published in the *Atlantic Monthly* in 1868.

28. Certainly Perley Kelso's speech to the workers who are threatening to strike at the end of *The Silent Partner* puts Perley squarely on the side of the capitalist class. After having gained their trust, Perley uses her influence to persuade the workers to accept the bosses' wage cuts. Judith Fetterley contends in "'Checkmate': Elizabeth Stuart Phelps's *The Silent Partner*," *Legacy* 3 (Fall 1986): 17–29, that by giving Perley such a speech to augment her feminine voice, Phelps reveals the class bias that enables Perley, after all she has learned of the workers' plight, to "become an agent of the voice of oppression" (27). In her discussion of male- and female-authored nineteenth-century fiction about working women, including these works by Phelps and Davis, Laura Hapke, in *Labor's Text: The Worker in American Fiction* (New Brunswick: Rutgers University Press, 2001), concludes that "white imaginers" of workers portrayed the woman worker "as she wasn't," erasing women's labor organizations and stressing middle-class values like domesticity (65–89).

29. María Amparo Ruiz de Burton, *The Squatter and the Don*, eds. Rosaura Sánchez and Beatrice Pita (Houston: Arte Público Press, 1992), 66. Further references to this work will be cited parenthetically in the text.

30. See Amelia María de la Luz Montes, "Ruiz de Burton Negotiates Literary Politics and Culture," *Challenging Boundaries: Gender and Periodization*, eds. Joyce W. Warren and Margaret Dickie (Athens: University of Georgia Press, 2000), 208.

31. Ibid., 202–225.

32. Rosaura Sánchez and Beatrice Pita, introduction to Ruiz de Burton, *The Squatter and the Don*, 20.

33. Sánchez and Pita make this point in the introduction to *The Squatter and the Don*, 32.

34. Sarah Winnemucca Hopkins, *Life Among the Piutes: Their Wrongs and Claims*, eds. Mary Mann and Catherine S. Fowler (1883; Reno: University of Nevada Press, 1994), 247.

35. It is interesting to note, however, that Winnemucca Hopkins's book is as anti-Mexican as Ruiz de Burton's is anti-Indian. Her grandfather had fought with the Americans against the Mexicans in the Mexican War (28).

36. S. Alice Callahan, *Wynema: A Child of the Forest*, ed. A. LaVonne Brown Ruoff (1891; Lincoln: University of Nebraska Press, 1997), 92–93.

37. Fern, *Rose Clark*, 345.

Chapter Eight | The Economics of Divorce

1. Divorce laws differed in the various states. English law did not permit absolute divorce until 1857, and many of the American states, particularly in the South, followed the English model. Divorce was unknown in South Carolina, for example, throughout the nineteenth century. The New England states had the most liberal divorce laws, with Connecticut being the most liberal: from colonial times Connecticut granted an absolute divorce (*a vinculo*) on grounds of adultery, desertion, or abuse. The Massachusetts divorce law of 1786 granted an absolute divorce on grounds of adultery, impotence, or criminal conviction, and in 1838 the law was extended to allow an absolute divorce after a desertion of five years. New York's divorce law of 1787 permitted an absolute divorce only on the ground of adultery. Pennsylvania's 1785 law permitted an absolute divorce for adultery, desertion, bigamy, or knowledge of sexual incapacity before marriage. See, e.g., Lawrence M. Friedman, *A History of American Law* (New York: Simon & Schuster, 1985), 204–207; Marylynn Salmon, *Women and the Law of Property in Early America* (Chapel Hill: University of North Carolina, 1986), 58–66; and Michael S. Hindus and Lynne E. Withey, "The Law of Husband and Wife in Nineteenth-Century America: Changing Views of Divorce," *Women and the Law: A Social Historical Perspective*, ed. D. Kelly Weisberg, 2 vols. (Cambridge, MA: Schenkman Publishing Company, 1982), 2:133–153.

2. In *A History of American Law*, Friedman theorizes that collusive divorce was common in New York since adultery was the only grounds for an absolute divorce (207–208). However, he does not consider the fact that the guilty party could not remarry.

3. James Kent, *Commentaries on American Law*, ed. Oliver Wendell Holmes, 4 vols. (Boston: Little, Brown, 1873), 2:147–148.

4. *Report of the Woman's Rights Convention Held at Seneca Falls, New York, July 19 and 20, 1848* (1848; reprint New York, 1969), 6.

5. See, e.g., Elizabeth Cady Stanton, Susan B. Anthony, and Matilda Joslyn Gage, eds., *History of Woman Suffrage*, 6 vols. (1881–1922; Rochester, NY: 1889, reprint, New York: Source Book Press, 1970), 1: 716–722, 738–742, 860–861.

6. For an excellent discussion of the differences between Stanton and her contemporaries, see Elizabeth B. Clark, "Matrimonial Bonds: Slavery and Divorce in Nineteenth-Century America," *Law and History Review* 8 (Spring 1990): 44–54.

7. See the *Lily*, January 1853–March 1854, and Clark, "Matrimonial Bonds," 26–27.

8. *Woman's Journal* (June 4, 1870), 173, and (September 12, 1874), 194.

9. *Harvey v. Harvey*, New York Supreme Court, legal archives, Special Collections, Hofstra University Library. As in the previous chapters, all court cases

cited are from this uncatalogued collection unless otherwise indicated. The collection is organized by date.

10. See, e.g., Karen Winner, *Divorced from Justice* (New York: HarperCollins, 1996), 13–14.

11. See U.S. Department of Labor, Bureau of Labor Statistics, May 2002, report 960. "In 2001, median weekly earnings for women who were full-time wage and salary workers were $511, or 76 percent of the $672 median for their male counterparts" (1). Women have always earned less than men in American history. It was not until the 1980s that the figure rose above 60 percent. The earning differential is greater among middle-aged and older women. In 2001, among workers ages 45 to 54 years old, women earned 73.6 percent of men, whereas 16- to 24-year-old women earned 90.2 percent of men (1). These figures suggest that although women begin at entry-level salaries equal to men's, they do not obtain promotions and salary increases at the same rate. They also interrupt their careers to follow their husbands to a new location and/or to have children.

12. As I indicated earlier, the first income tax law was passed in 1861 to help pay for the expenses of the Civil War. See Shelley Davis, *IRS Historical Fact Book: A Chronology, 1646–1992* (Washington: Department of the Treasury, U.S. Government Printing Office, 1992), 30–38. The law was to take effect in 1862, but no taxes were collected that year because "there was no administrative system established for this purpose" (32). In 1862 a new law was passed creating the office of the Commissioner of Internal Revenue"; it established a withholding tax to take effect in 1863 but only on the incomes of "civil, military, and naval" personnel (33). The bulk of the income taxes for 1863 were not collected until 1864 or 1865. See *Report of the Commissioner of Internal Revenue* for the year ending June 30, 1865 (Washington: U.S. Government Printing Office, 1865), 4. The office of Statistical Information Services can find no income tax forms before 1868, and the information contained in the publications suggests that an official form was not used until that time. I base this conclusion on the form itself, the publication accompanying it, and information contained in private letters from IRS researchers Sandra Byberg, June 13, 2002, and Cynthia Belmonte, July 17, 2002, Statistical Information Services, Internal Revenue Service. The income tax form was to be used in accordance with the act passed on March 2, 1867, requiring each person with an annual income of one thousand dollars or more to file a return. It is a simple one-page form. (See forms and publication, "Annual Taxes, 1869," the United States Internal Revenue Service, 1869.)

13. This precedent was established early in American law. For example, in a 1796 case, *Nickols v. Giles*, in which the child lived with the mother and maternal grandfather and was well provided for, the judge ruled that the child should stay with the mother because it was "well taken care of, and not likely to be so by the

father." The father had "very little property" and "no house" (Giles 2 root 461, CT 1796). In another early decision, custody was awarded to the mother who was living with her parents because the grandfather was "very affluent" and could not only "educate and maintain" but could leave a substantial inheritance to the child (*In re. Waldron*, 13 Johns. 418, 419, NY 1816). For a discussion of these cases, see Jamil S. Zainaldin, "The Emergence of a Modern American Family Law: Child Custody, Adoption, and the Courts, 1796–1851," *Northwestern University Law Review* 73 (1979): 1052–1057.

14. For a discussion of Thoreau's psychosomatic lockjaw, see, e.g., Joyce W. Warren, *The American Narcissus: Individualism and Women in Nineteenth-Century American Fiction* (New Brunswick: Rutgers University Press, 1984), 64–65.

15. E. P. W. Packard, *Modern Persecution, or Insane Asylums Unveiled, as Demonstrated by the Report of the Investigating Committee of the Legislature of Illinois*, 2 vols. (Hartford, CT: Case, Lockwood and Brainard, 1873).

16. Ellen Dwyer, "The Weaker Vessel: Legal Versus Social Reality in Mental Commitments in Nineteenth-Century New York," *Women and the Law*, ed. D. Kelly Weisberg, 2 vols. (Cambridge, MA: Schenkman Publishing Co., 1982), 1: 85–102. See also Phyllis Chesler, *Women and Madness* (New York: Avon Books, 1972), 54–67, and Peter Tyor, "Denied the Power to Choose the Good: Sexuality and Mental Defect in American Medical Practice, 1850–1920," in *The Medicine Show*, ed. Patricia Branca (New York: Science History Publications, 1977), 165–182.

Chapter Nine | WOMAN'S
ECONOMIC INDEPENDENCE

1. The only review I can find that recognized Fern's call for woman's economic independence was by Elizabeth Cady Stanton, who praised the novel as a female success story in her review of *Ruth Hall* in the suffragist journal *The Una* (February 1855): 29–30. For a discussion of the critics' reaction to *Ruth Hall*, see Joyce W. Warren, *Fanny Fern: An Independent Woman* (New Brunswick: Rutgers University Press, 1992), 124–128.

2. For a discussion of the criticism of Alcott's 1867 publication of *Moods*, see, e.g., Sarah Elbert, introduction to *Moods* (New Brunswick: Rutgers University Press, 1991), xxxvii. As Elbert points out, Henry James saw the novel as a triangle and could not imagine that there was anything more to it than that (cited in Elbert, xxxvii).

3. Elaine R. Hedges discusses the reception of Gilman's story in her afterword to *The Yellow Wallpaper* (Old Westbury, NY: Feminist Press, 1973), 39. Gilman describes the reaction to her story in *The Living of Charlotte Perkins Gilman: An Au-*

tobiography (New York: Appleton-Century, 1935), 118–121. Although Gilman hyphenated the word "wall-paper" in the title of her manuscript, she at other times wrote "wallpaper" and "wall paper." In this text I will use the most common spelling, "wallpaper," in this text except when citing a secondary source that uses a different spelling.

4. Fanny Fern, *Ruth Hall and Other Writings*, ed. Joyce W. Warren (New Brunswick: Rutgers University Press, 1986), 115. Subsequent references to this volume will be cited in the text. Articles not reprinted in *Ruth Hall and Other Writings* (thereafter RHOW) will be referenced by date and source.

5. For information about Fern's treatment by the critics and in her personal life, see Warren, *Fanny Fern*, e.g., 124–130, 179–194.

6. I discuss Fern's experience in detail in my biography, *Fanny Fern*. For information about Fern's experience after the death of her first husband, Charles Eldredge, see 76–82; about her second marriage, 83–89; and regarding Hezekiah Eldredge's will, 106–107.

7. Quoted in Florence Adams, *Fanny Fern, A Pair of Flaming Shoes* (West Trenton, NJ: Hermitage Press, 1966), 23.

8. The prenuptial agreement is in the papers of James Parton, Houghton Library, Harvard University. The text is reprinted in Warren, *Fanny Fern*, 153.

9. The slander spread by Fern's second husband, Samuel Farrington, and his brother Thomas is discussed in Warren, *Fanny Fern*, 85–87. In January 1851 Thomas Farrington apologized to Fern, admitting that the stories were false. His letter, which is in her papers in the Sophia Smith Collection at Smith College, is reprinted in Warren, *Fanny Fern*, 86. I discuss Fern's nothing-to-lose mindset and its effect on her writing in "Uncommon Discourse: Fanny Fern and the *New York Ledger*," in *Periodical Literature in Nineteenth-Century America*, ed. Kenneth Price and Susan Belasco Smith (Charlottesville: University Press of Virginia, 1995), 51–68.

10. Louisa May Alcott, *Moods*, ed. Sarah Elbert (1867; reprint, New Brunswick: Rutgers University Press, 1991), 135. Subsequent references to this work will be cited in the text.

11. This statement appears in chapter 8 of the 1882 edition of *Moods*. The chapter is not in the original version but is printed in the appendix to the Rutgers edition, where Warwick's statement regarding work appears on page 254.

12. Louisa May Alcott, cited in Martha Saxton, *Louisa May Alcott: A Modern Biography* (New York: Farrar, Straus, and Giroux, 1977), 353.

13. Louisa May Alcott, *Rose in Bloom* (Boston: Roberts Brothers, 1880), 11.

14. Louisa May Alcott, *An Old-Fashioned Girl* (Boston: Little, Brown and Co., 1922), 257–263. Further references to this work will be cited parenthetically in the text.

15. Louisa May Alcott, "The Mysterious Key," *Behind a Mask: The Unknown Thrillers of Louisa May Alcott*, ed. Madeleine B. Stern (New York: Quill, 1975), 206.

16. Louisa May Alcott, "A Pair of Eyes," *A Double Life: Newly Discovered Thrillers of Louisa May Alcott*, ed. Madeleine B. Stern (Boston: Little, Brown and Co., 1988), 68.

17. Alcott, "Taming a Tartar," *A Double Life*, 241.

18. Ibid., 244.

19. Louisa May Alcott, *A Long Fatal Love Chase* (New York: Random House, 1995), 3. Subsequent references to this volume will be cited parenthetically in the text.

20. Louisa May Alcott, *Her Life, Letters, and Journals*, ed. Ednah D. Cheney (Boston: Roberts Brothers, 1891), 88.

21. Louisa May Alcott, *Little Women* (Garden City, NY: Literary Guild, 1950), 201.

22. Alcott, *Her Life, Letters, and Journals*, 193.

23. Alcott, *Her life, Letters and Journals*, e.g., 80, 107.

24. A. Bronson Alcott, *The Letters of A. Bronson Alcott*, ed. Richard L. Herrnstadt (Ames: Iowa State University, 1969), 397.

25. Ibid., 89.

26. Louisa May Alcott, *Work: A Story of Experience*, ed. Sarah Elbert (New York: Schocken Books, 1977), 1–2. Further references to this work will be cited in the text.

27. Louisa May Alcott, "Happy Women," *New York Ledger* (April 11, 1868); reprinted in *Alternative Alcott*, ed. Elaine Showalter (New Brunswick: Rutgers University Press, 1992), 203–204. Further references will be cited parenthetically in the text.

28. Louisa May Alcott, cited in "Louisa Alcott's 'Natural Ambition' for the 'Lurid Style,'" *Critical Essays on Louisa May Alcott*, ed. Madeleine B. Stern (Boston: G. K. Hall, 1984), 42.

29. The two thriller stories that were originally published under Alcott's name were "The Mysterious Key and What It Opened" (1867), reprinted in *Behind a Mask: The Unknown Thrillers of Louisa May Alcott*, and "The Skeleton in the Closet" (1867), reprinted in *Plots and Counterplots: More Unknown Thrillers of Louisa May Alcott*, ed. Madeleine Stern (New York: William Morrow and Company, 1976). Not only are the heroines of these stories *not* power seekers, but they are wholly selfless.

30. In 1892 William Randolph Hearst began printing sensational stories about Gilman's personal life in his papers. For a discussion of Hearst's actions and Gilman's response to them, see Denise D. Knight, "Charlotte Perkins Gilman,

Randolph Hearst, and the Practice of Ethical Journalism," *American Journalism* 11 (Fall 1994): 336–347.

31. Charlotte Perkins Gilman, *Women and Economics: A Study of the Economic Relation Between Men and Women as a Factor in Social Evolution*, eds. Michael Kimmel and Amy Aronson (1898; Berkeley: University of California Press, 1998), 2–3. Further references to this work will be noted parenthetically in the text.

32. Edward Bellamy proposes a similar arrangement in *Looking Backward* (1888). Gilman was much influenced by the ideas of political justice and gender equality in Bellamy's work, and in the 1890s she became actively involved with the Nationalist movement that grew out of the publication of his novel. See, e.g., Denise D. Knight, *Charlotte Perkins Gilman: A Study of the Short Fiction* (New York: Twayne, 1997), 5, 78.

33. Gilman's stories were never collected in book form during her lifetime. They appeared in many periodicals, including the magazine that she edited, *The Forerunner*, vols. 1–7 (1909–1916). Many of Gilman's short stories have been reprinted in recent years. See *Charlotte Perkins Gilman Reader*, ed. Ann J. Lane (New York: Pantheon, 1980); *"Herland" and Selected Stories by Charlotte Perkins Gilman*, ed. Barbara H. Solomon (New York: Signet, 1992); *"The Yellow Wallpaper" and Other Writings by Charlotte Perkins Gilman*, ed. Lynne Sharon Schwartz (New York: Bantam Books, 1989); and *"The Yellow Wall-Paper" and Selected Stories of Charlotte Perkins Gilman*, ed. Denise D. Knight (Newark, DE: University of Delaware Press, 1994).

34. Charlotte Perkins Gilman, *Benigna Machiavelli* (Santa Barbara: Bandanna Books, 1993), 156.

35. Charlotte Perkins Gilman, *What Diantha Did* (New York: Charlton Company, 1910), 249.

36. Charlotte Perkins Gilman, *Moving the Mountain* (New York: Charlton Company, 1911), 289. Subsequent references will be noted parenthetically in the text.

37. Charlotte Perkins Gilman, *Herland*, ed. Ann J. Lane (New York: Pantheon, 1979). Subsequent references will be cited parenthetically in the text.

38. Gilman, *The Living of Charlotte Perkins Gilman* (1935), 121.

39. Charlotte Perkins Gilman, *With Her in Our Land*, (Westport, CT: Praeger, 1997), 123. Subsequent references will be cited parenthetically in the text.

40. See, e.g., Ann J. Lane, introduction to *Herland* (1979), xvii–xviii. As Lane says, Gilman's comments can be "unsettling." See Denise Knight, "Charlotte Perkins Gilman and the Shadow of Racism," *American Literary Realism* 32 (Winter 2000): 159–169.

41. See, e.g., Ann J. Lane, *To Herland and Beyond: The Life and Times of Charlotte*

Perkins Gilman (New York: Pantheon, 1990), 78, 166, 349, and Thomas L. Erskine and Connie L. Richards, introduction to *"The Yellow Wallpaper": Charlotte Perkins Gilman* (New Brunswick, NJ: Rutgers University Press, 1993), 4. For a discussion of romantic friendships between women, see Carroll Smith-Rosenberg, "The Female World of Love and Ritual: Relations between Women in Nineteenth-Century America," *Signs* 1.1 (1975): 1–29.

42. See Barbara White's untitled essay in Knight, *Charlotte Perkins Gilman*, 198.

43. Charlotte Perkins Gilman, *A Journey from Within: The Love Letters of Charlotte Perkins Glman, 1897–1900*, ed. Mary A. Hill (Lewisburg, PA: Bucknell University Press, 1995), 246.

44. Mary A. Hill, introduction to *A Journey from Within*, 233. In a relevant reading of "The Yellow Wallpaper," Carla Kaplan suggests that the story can be read as a critique of compulsory heterosexuality. See "Reading Feminist Readings: Recuperative Reading and the Silent Heroine of Feminist Criticism," *Listening to Silence: New Essays in Feminist Criticism*, eds. Elaine Hedges and Shelley Fisher Fishkin (New York: Oxford University Press, 1994), 168–194.

45. Gilman, *Love Letters*, 404.

46. Gilman, cited in Ann J. Lane, introduction to *Herland*, xi.

47. Here, as elsewhere, Gilman uses the word "racial" to refer to the human race or species.

Epilogue

1. See Harriet Jacobs, *Incidents in the Life of a Slave Girl*, ed. Jean Fagan Yellin (Cambridge: Harvard University Press, 1987), 1. Jacobs writes in her preface that, by telling her story, she hopes to give the women of the North "a realizing sense" of black women's experience under slavery.

2. Thomas Amlie Papers, Wisconsin Historical Society.

3. Thomas Amlie Papers, Wisconsin Historical Society.

4. "Mars and Venus," interview with John Gray, *Currency* (April 1998), 56. Cited in Sandra F. VanBurkleo, *"Belonging to the World": Women's Rights and American Constitutional Culture* (New York: Oxford University Press, 2001), 305–306.

5. Michael Eric Dyson, *Why I Love Black Women* (New York: Basic Civitas Books, 2003), 207, 221–222.

6. John Schwartz, "Glass Ceilings at Altar as Well as Boardroom," *New York Times* (December 14, 2004), F7.

7. Virginia Slims opinion poll, 1990; Gallop Organization polls, 1986; and *New York Times* poll, 1989. Cited in Susan Faludi, *Backlash* (1991; New York: Doubleday, 1992), xv–xvi.

8. "Equal Pay for Equal Work Is No. 1 Goal of Women," *New York Times* (September 5, 1997), A13.

9. Jane Gross, "At Girls' Schools, Teaching Finances as Sum of Equality," *New York Times* (March 17, 2003), A1, B6.

10. 9 to 5, National Association of Working Women, *Women in the Workforce: Highlights of the 9to5 Profile of Working Women*, 2, www.9to5.org/mediaresources.

11. U.S. Department of Labor, Bureau of Labor Statistics, May 2002, *Highlights of Women's Earnings in 2001*, report 960, 19, www.bls.gov/cps/cpswom2001.

12. U.S. Census Bureau, *Women in the United States*, March 2000, table 13, www.census.gov/population/socdemo/gender/ppl-121/tab13.

13. U.S. Census Bureau, *Profile of Nation's Women*, March 15, 2001, 2, www.census.gov/Press-Release/www/2000/cb01-49. About six out of ten employed women work in administrative support, including clerical, secretarial, and service work.

14. VanBurkleo, *"Belonging to the World,"* 281. See Susan Muller Okin, *Justice, Gender, and the Family* (New York: Basic Books, 1989), 161, and Lenore J. Weitzman, *The Divorce Revolution: The Unexpected Social and Economic Consequences for Women and Children in America* (New York: Free Press, 1985), 323.

15. See Sonya Michel, *Children's Interests/Mothers' Rights: The Shaping of America's Child Care Policy* (New Haven: Yale University Press, 1999), 142, and Geraldine Youcha, *Minding the Children: Child Care in America from Colonial Times to the Present* (New York: Scribner, 1995), 312.

16. U.S. Census Bureau, *Women in the United States*, March 2000, table 9, "Labor Force Status of the Civilian Population 16 Years and Over," March 15, 2000, www.census.gov/population/www/socdemo/ppl-121/tab9. The figure for civilian, noninstitutionalized women over sixteen in the labor force is 60.7 percent.

17. U.S. Department of Labor, Bureau of Labor Statistics, May 2002, *Highlights of Women's Earnings in 2001*, report 960, 20, and U.S. Census Bureau, *Census Bureau Facts for Features*, March 15, 2001, 2, www.bls.gov/cps/cpswom2001.

18. 9 to 5, National Association of Working Women, *Women in the Workforce*, 2, www.9to5.org/mediaresources.

19. For information about the Personal Responsibility and Work Opportunity Reconciliation Act of 1996, see, e.g., the *Fact Sheet: Administration for Children and Families* put out by the U.S. Department of Health and Human Services in September 1996 at www.acf.dhs.gov/news/welfare/wr. See also Michel, *Children's Interests*, 281. With respect to the failure of the legislation to help low-income families not receiving welfare, see, e.g., Sara Rimer, "Children of Working Poor Are Day Care's Forgotten," *New York Times* (November 25, 1997), 1, 13.

20. Lisa Belkin, "The Opt-Out Revolution," *New York Times*, section 6 (October 26, 2003), 42–47, 58, 85–86. Quotation on p. 44.

21. Cited in Belkin, "The Opt-Out Revolution," 44, 58.

22. Nina Bernstein, "Daily Choice Turned Deadly: Children Left on Their Own," *New York Times* (October 19, 2003), A1, 40. Bernstein's article chronicles the case of a Brooklyn woman who, when her babysitter failed to come, made the hard decision to leave her nine-year-old and one-year-old children to care for themselves while she went to work as manager of a McDonald's, a position to which she had recently been appointed and which she feared she would lose if she did not show up for work. The apartment caught fire while she was at work, and both children died. She was charged with recklessly endangering her children and, at the time the article was written, faced sixteen years in prison. Bernstein points out that this situation is not only a problem for poor working women; the Child Trends researchers' data indicate that, in fact, higher-income children ages six to nine were "more likely than poor children to be left unsupervised" (40). Richard Wexler, director of the National Coalition for Child Protection Reform, notes that his data showed that many parents take such risks daily, but we hear about them only "if something goes wrong" (40).

23. The federally supported Child Care Service Centers at the Kaiser shipyards in Portland, Oregon—called the "jewels of the system"—provided home-cooked meals for a modest price and paid their well-trained staff the same wages as the highly paid Kaiser factory workers, wages that were proportionally much higher than those received by the staff at most day-care centers today. See Michel, *Children's Interests*, 143; see also Youcha, *Minding the Children*, 329.

24. Cited in William H. Chafe, *The American Woman: Her Changing Social, Economic and Political Roles, 1920–1970* (New York: Oxford University Press, 1972), 178.

25. Cited in Youcha, *Minding the Children*, 330–331.

26. Michel, *Children's Interests*, 126–128.

27. Michel, *Children's Interests*, 151.

28. For a discussion of the child care provided by many other countries—including France, Sweden, Japan, Canada, and Australia, all of which have done much more to help working mothers than has been done in the United States—see Michel, *Children's Interests*, 281–296.

29. Mary Frances Berry, *The Politics of Parenthood: Child Care, Women's Rights, and the Myth of the Good Mother* (New York: Viking Penguin, 1993), 218.

30. Gross, "At Girls' Schools," B6.

31. Fanny Fern, "Pay for Women," *New York Ledger* (July 16, 1870).

32. Fanny Fern, "Female Lecturers," *New York Ledger* (December 8, 1866).

INDEX